Wicca
Witch Craft
Witches
and Paganism

A BIBLE ON WITCHES

Julia Steyson

Glenda Blair

Glinda Abraham

© 2019

COPYRIGHT

The Ultimate Guide on Wicca Astrology and Tarot Cards: A Book Uncovering Magic Mystery and Spells

By Julia Steyson , Glenda Blair, Glinda Abraham

Copyright @2019 By Julia Steyson , Glenda Blair, Glinda Abraham

All Rights Reserved.

The following eBook is reproduced below with the goal of providing information that is as accurate and as reliable as possible. Regardless, purchasing this eBook can be seen as consent to the fact that both the publisher and the author of this book are in no way experts on the topics discussed within, and that any recommendations or suggestions made herein are for entertainment purposes only. Professionals should be consulted as needed before undertaking any of the action endorsed herein.

This declaration is deemed fair and valid by both the American Bar Association and the Committee of Publishers Association and is legally binding throughout the United States.

Furthermore, the transmission, duplication or reproduction of any of the following work, including precise information, will be considered an illegal act, irrespective whether it is done electronically or in print. The legality extends to creating a secondary or tertiary copy of the work or a recorded copy and is only allowed with express written consent of the Publisher. All additional rights are reserved.

The information in the following pages is broadly considered to be a truthful and accurate account of facts, and as such any inattention, use or misuse of the information in question by the reader will render any resulting actions solely under their purview. There are no scenarios in which the publisher or the original author of this work can be in any fashion deemed liable for any hardship or damages that may befall them after undertaking information described herein.

Additionally, the information found on the following pages is intended for informational purposes only and should thus be considered, universal. As befitting its nature, the information presented is without assurance regarding its continued validity or interim quality. Trademarks that mentioned are done without written consent and can in no way be considered an endorsement from the trademark holder.

THIS COLLECTION INCLUDES THE FOLLOWING BOOKS:

Wicca Spell Book: The Ultimate Wiccan Book On Magic And Witches A Guide To Witchcraft, Wicca And Magic In The New Age With A Divinity Code

Practical Magic: A Witchcraft Supplies Book of Wicca, Spells, and Runes

Witch Book: The Definitive Guide to Witch Craft, Paganism and Everyday Magic

Astrology Uncovered: A Complete Guide to Horoscope and Zodiac Star Signs

Tarot Cards: A Beginners Guide of Tarot Cards: The Psychic Tarot Manual

TABLE OF CONTENTS

WICCA SPELL BOOK 1
   CHAPTER 1: THE ORIGINS OF WICCA 1
   CHAPTER 2: WICCAN BELIEFS AND PRACTICES 11
   CHAPTER 3 WICCAN DEITIES AND THE AFTERLIFE 27
   CHAPTER 4: WICCAN TOOLS 46
   CHAPTER 5: PRACTICING MAGIC 67
   CHAPTER 6: FINDING YOUR NICHE 80

PRACTICAL MAGIC: 86
   INTRODUCTION 86
   CHAPTER 1 - THE HISTORY OF WITCHCRAFT AND HOW IT AFFECTS YOU 89
   CHAPTER 2 – THE SEASONS OF THE WHEEL OF THE YEAR 121
   CHAPTER 3 – FORGING YOUR WITCH-SELF 164
   CHAPTER 4 – GRIMOIRE OF CORRESPONDENCES 199
   CHAPTER 5 – PATHWORKING'S FOR THE WITCH 233
   CHAPTER 6 – USING RITUAL? 237
   CHAPTER 7: SPELL WORK 255

WITCH BOOK: 274
   INTRODUCTION 274
   PART 1: PAGANISM 279
   PART 2: WICCA 326
   PART 3: EVERYDAY MAGICK 352
   CHAPTER 1: BASIC TOOLS AND RITUALS 352
   CHAPTER 2: FIND YOUR WITCHY FLAVOR 374
   CHAPTER 3: DIVINATION 101 378
   CHAPTER 4: SEASONAL SPELLS 433
   CHAPTER 5: FINAL WORDS OF WARNING 438

ASTROLOGY UNCOVERED: 443
INTRODUCTION TO ASTROLOGY 443
PLANETS 448
HOW TO READ THE ASTROLOGICAL CHART 466
ZODIAC SIGNS AND HOUSES 469

TAROT CARDS: 516
CHAPTER ONE: GETTING STARTED 516
CHAPTER TWO: THE MAJOR ARCANA 529
CHAPTER THREE: THE MINOR ARCANA 566
CHAPTER FOUR : HOW TO DO A TAROT READING 597

Wicca Spell Book

Chapter 1: The Origins of Wicca

Witches. Flying on broomsticks, wearing all black, huddled over cauldrons. Our pop culture idea of witches is full of images like that: green skin, a warted long nose. But as we grow older and wiser, we come to learn that witches are not as we have learned in our childhoods. While these tales may be good for entertainment, there is a rich spiritual history behind Witchcraft that is missed by these caricatures.

It is common and psychologically normal for people to fear what they don't understand. Our society has feared witches for centuries. Hundreds or even thousands of witches were killed in the Inquisition, witch hunts, and crusades. So much has been lost in the confusion that many people couldn't even begin to tell you what a witch is, or what witches believe and practice.

Today our society copes with the fear of that unknown by making a gentle mockery of a beautiful ancient tradition called Wicca. In this book, geared towards absolute beginners, we will hopefully shed some light on The Old Religion and its adherents.

The goal of this book is not only to educate, but to inspire. Even if you don't leave this book practicing Wicca, the hope is that you will find an understanding with those who do practice, and maybe also find a deeper appreciation for nature along the way.

However, this book serves not only as an educational guide for the curious, but can be used as an instructional how-to-begin for those who *are* interested in beginning their Wiccan journey. Simple explanations about holidays and beliefs are given, and the later chapters directly address how to begin the Wicca practice, while the early chapters are more for educational purposes.

There are more than a few rich traditions that fall under the umbrella of the term Wicca. In this chapter we will discuss the founding of Wicca, the influences on the religion, how Wicca is distinct from Paganism, and what the Wiccan ties are to magic. This chapter will also take a look at the different traditions of Wicca that have developed over time.

THE FOUNDING OF WICCA

Wicca is actually a modern religion, with fairly recent roots. However, it was not originally referred to as Wicca. The birth of what we now know as Wicca traces back to 19th century Britain, which was in the midst of an occult revival movement.

Gerald Brousseau Gardner (1884-1964) is often credited with founding in the 1920s what would expand into Wicca in the 1960s. Gardener studied the anthropological theory by Margaret Murray. This theory posited that an ancient pagan religion had been practiced during the rise and spread of Christianity in Europe. Murray called this religion a "witch cult" and postulated that those who practiced it did so in 13-person covens. Murray also wrote that they worshipped a "horned" god.

In the early 1940s, Gardener's extensive study of Murray's work as well as his deep interest in other authors who specialized in the Occult, inspired him to start his own coven. This was known by its members as the Bricket Wood coven.

In the beginning, around the 1920s-1950s before the term Wicca evolved with the New Age movement, they called it The Craft or The Old Religion. Gardner expanded the religion to include worship of a goddess and the Divine Feminine, along with elements of things he had learned from freemasons and ceremonial magic. We will discuss more about magic and its place in Wicca later in this chapter.

Gardner became friends with another early influencer of Wicca in 1947, Aleister Crowley (1875-1947). Crowley was known far and wide for his writings on the occult that were based on his personal experiences from participating in a wide range of esoteric religious traditions throughout his life. He travelled around the globe learning about Buddhism, Kabbalah (Jewish Mysticism), Astrology, Tarot, and Hindu practices as well.

Crowley is credited with being the first to distinguish magick with a "k" from magic. This was done so that there would be a specific word to differentiate his own religious practices from ceremonial magic, and stage magic that was popular during that time. Gardner adopted many rituals developed by Crowley.

However, nowadays Wiccans prefer to distance their practice from the influential Crowley because of his reputation as a misogynist and a racist. Discriminatory and bigoted perspectives are not considered to be compatible with the Wiccan way of life.

Crowley was also part of the reason Wiccan practices became publicly associated with Satanism. However, this connection is a false one; because Wicca is based on pre-Christian world views and concepts, Satan is not involved in any Wiccan ritual. In fact, Wiccan practice discourages any sort of "black magic" or association with evil.

This tradition is known today as Gardnerian Wicca. It brought many interested women occultists to his coven, including another influential person named Doreen Valiente (1922-1999). She became the High Priestess at Bricket Wood in the early 1950s. Valiente began a long period of religious revision in the material of the coven, in no small part to remove the association the coven had with Aleister Crowley.

Valiente felt that Crowley had made a mistake trying to mass market Witchcraft. Crowley was also known for silencing women who disagreed with them, limiting their participation in his rituals and in the Bricket Coven.

In 1957, Valiente began her own coven. She wrote several books and learned alongside many prominent occultist figures of the New Age religious movement. Valiente emphasized individualism in practice, and is a large reason the practice of Wiccans today is so diverse and varies so much between individuals and covens. Valiente really was the one who took Wicca from being a secretive practice done behind closed doors to a widespread phenomenon that many people suddenly had access to because of her work.

In the 1970s, Wiccan traditions finally made it out of England thanks to some other key influencers, who brought the Craft to the entire UK, the United States, and Australia. Because of this branching out, many different traditions formed. These traditions include those such as the Dianic, the Celtic, and the Georgian.

Alex Sanders (1926-1988) later founded what is now known as Alexandrian Wicca, which follows a specific set of traditions. Another sect was founded by Raymond Buckland in the 1970s, known as the Seax-Wicca tradition. Buckland wrote dozens of books on The Craft and is known as the person who brought Gardnerian Wicca to the United States.

Later Developments

Around the 1980s, Wicca had an estimated 50,000 self-proclaimed Wiccans that in some way practiced in the Northern Americas and western Europe. That growth slowed down significantly by the end of the century, but Wicca gained a considerable amount of social acceptance in that time. Wicca also continued to develop, with new rituals and practices being created by new Wiccans with every passing generation that upheld the Craft.

The Dianic Wiccans saw Wicca as a woman's religion, and the Neo-Pagan movement began to gain speed alongside Wicca. Neo-Paganism and Wicca are now represented to the world through two international organizations, the Universal Federation of Pagans and the Pagan Federation.

SHAMANISM

Many Wiccan practices are based in the concept of shamanism. *Shamanism* is an umbrella term for a lot of different practices. It began as an Eastern practice of advanced uses of herbal medicine. Shamans were highly revered in their societies for their medical skills and their ability to communicate directly with the spirit world. A shaman was often identified by having some kind of physical defect, seen as a trade for their special abilities.

Classical shamanism in Northern Asia believed that a shaman was aided by a spirit or even a group of spirits that helped them to heal and to define the future. Shamans could also connect with guardian spirits, who might be otherworldly or a lifetime partner in the mortal plane.

Shamans channeled the spirit world using sound and music, utilizing tools such as rattles, drums, and improvised songs to conduct their practice. This would most often be done by entering a trance state of consciousness.

Modern Wiccans no longer use the word Shaman, but instead have switched to the term "hedge witch". This will be explained in more detail in Chapter 6. Modern hedge witches channel the spirit world through trance, astral projection, and lucid dreaming.

PAGANISM AND NEO-PAGANISM

The term *Paganism* has long been used as a derogatory word for all non-Christian (primarily polytheistic) religions. For a long time the word served the same purpose as calling someone a heathen. However, in the modern day, Pagans and Neo-Pagans are reclaiming the title and the faith. While Wicca is considered a Pagan religion and is represented internationally by Pagan Federations, there are distinctions to be drawn between those who identify as Wiccans and those who identify as Neo-Pagans.

Pagan is used today as another umbrella term. According to the Pagan Federation International, "Pagans may be trained in particular traditions or they may follow their own inspiration. Paganism is not dogmatic. Pagans pursue their own vision of the Divine as a direct and personal experience."

One can see that Wicca easily fits within this definition of Pagan. There are traditions that can be chosen and adhered to within Wicca, but this is not a necessity to be a Wiccan (thus it is not a dogmatic religion). Wiccans also have a personal relationship with the Divine and their individual practices.

So what is a Neo-Pagan, and how are Neo-Pagans different from Wiccans? The answer may depend on who you ask. Because the definition of Pagan is so intentionally vague, it can be hard to draw lines deciding where one tradition begins and where another ends.

According to Joanne Pearson, an occult writer, Wicca is both at the center of and on the margins of Neo-Paganism. The former is stated because the history of Wiccanism and Neo-Paganism has a very large amount of overlap; at the core, they were both born out of the 19th century Occult movement and popularized through the New Age Movement in the 1960s and 1970s.

Magic

In what way is Wicca inherently tied to magic? Some Wiccans would offer that Wicca is in no way inherently related to magic! This is because some Wiccans don't include any magic elements in their practices. That's right -- you can be Wiccan without practicing magic! Many Wiccan rituals are focused around revering nature and don't focus on supernatural elements.

That being said, there are many whom their Wiccan practices are inseparable from magic practices. There are, as was mentioned much earlier in the chapter, distinctions to be drawn between different types of magic.

Ceremonial magic, also known as High Magic, predates almost anything else that Wiccans and Pagans draw from. This kind of magic is known for being elaborate in its ritual. Sometimes this magic is done to appease a God by collecting a variety of different things that would please that deity and using them in a specific manner and order. For this reason, ceremonial magic is also known as ritual magic; the two terms are often used interchangeably.

Practical magic is magic that is used in one's day to day life. Sigils, simple spells, enchantments...the purpose of this kind of magic is to make a small, but direct change to everyday life by channeling your own personal magic. This is what is sometimes referred to as magick. This book will use the "k" spelling to distinguish that this is the type of magic being discussed.

Is Wicca a religion?

This question is a deceptively difficult one to answer. First of all, it depends on how one defines religion. Many definitions of what 'religion' is have been specifically written to exclude nature-based religions, including Wicca and First Nations religions. Some consider this to be a form of supremacy, while other Wiccans would rather be distanced from organized religion in the first place.

Whether or not Wicca is considered a religion by the world at large, is it considered to be a religion by adherents of Wicca? While some would say yes, I think it's important to consider the voices of Wiccans who would say no. Some Wiccans consider Wicca to be a practice rather than a religion.

This is partially because most organized religions are composed of Orthodoxy and Orthopraxy. Orthodoxy is when one holds "correct" beliefs and is generally considered by Wiccans to be dogmatic and against Wiccan values. Orthopraxy is "correct" practice, which while important to Wiccans, there is no supreme doctrine to determine what the correct way to practice Wicca is.

Some Wiccans that adhere to a specific tradition may value orthopraxy, but no Wiccan would ever tell another Wiccan how to practice authoritatively. Instruction is given through a loving intention, not because there is a right or wrong way to do something.

Some Wiccans don't identify Wicca as a religion because they believe it is a specific decision *against* religion. Others consider it to be a universal religion. Like many things in Wicca, there is no definitive, dogmatic yes or no answer.

DIFFERING TRADITIONS

As you've seen by now, there are many different traditions that have developed over the course of the history of Wicca. This is undoubtedly because of the influence of Doreen Valiente, who emphasized the importance of individualistic practices and beliefs in her influential books during the rise of early Wicca.

In this subsection we will discuss just a few of the main traditions of Wicca, although many Wiccans consider themselves to practice outside of the guidelines of these traditions. Even a Wiccan living outside a tradition may pull rituals from traditions that speak to them.

Gardnerian Wicca focuses on recreating the original teachings and rituals of Gerald Brousseau Gardner himself. Gardner painstakingly recreated rituals he had extensively researched, and wanted to challenge mainstream religion. For example, many of the rituals are performed without any clothes on, to become closer to the natural state. Rituals are focused on nature and involve a creative, bright use of color to represent elements and energies. However, this tradition is also very rule-based, and many have found it to be somewhat constricting.

Alexandrian Wicca was founded by Alex Sanders, who was the self-proclaimed "King" of the witches in his coven. Alexandrian Wicca can seem very similar to Gardnerian, mimicking their naked rituals and coven rites, but has more ancient Jewish influences from Kabbalah.

Georgian Wicca was founded by George Patterson in California in the 1970s. While Georgian Wiccans follow the general example of Gardnerian Wicca and Alexandrian Wicca, the coven is much more flexible and individualistic. Coven members sometimes make up their own rituals. Patterson used to say regarding rituals, "If it works, use it. If it doesn't, don't."

Dianic Wiccan, named after the Greek Goddess Diana, was founded by Zsuzsanna Budapest. Since its inception in 1970s, Dianic Wicca has been known as a particularly feminist branch of the Craft. Only goddess figures are worshipped, and many covens only accept women. Dianic Wiccans are also known for their political activism.

Eclectic Wicca is a fast-growing tradition that believes that no formal tradition or doctrine is necessary for one to be a true Wiccan. Eclectic Wiccans ignore institutions that are in place such as initiation, secrecy, and the hierarchical structures of covens.

Conclusion

We've now gotten a taste for the beginnings of what we today know as Wicca. We've discussed history and related terms, and traditions that Wicca has pulled from to become the complete, independent religion (or religion alternative) it is today.

But if one can truly be a Wiccan without subscribing to a tradition, then what exactly is it that makes someone a Wiccan? Well, although beliefs vary widely from Wiccan to Wiccan, there are some core beliefs that most Wiccans hold. These will be discussed in the coming chapter.

Chapter 2: Wiccan Beliefs and Practices

Modern Wiccans hold a wide range of beliefs and practice is very individualistic, making it hard to define Wiccan beliefs in an exact way. There are, however, some more common, core beliefs that most Wiccans ascribe to. For example, this chapter will discuss that many Wiccans engage with elemental magic, Tarot, and celebrate the festivals of The Wheel of the Year. Esbats and Animism will also be discussed in this chapter to gain a well-rounded grasp on general Wiccan ideals and practices.

The core of Wiccan beliefs teaches us that our practice is our own as long as we are doing no harm to others. Unless you have taken the role of a High Priestess or a Coven Mother, or some other teaching role, it is discouraged to instruct others on how to perform their Craft. Of course offering helpful tips is no problem, but imposing your rules on someone else is against the Wiccan way of life.

All Wiccans, whether they practice magic or not, have a worldview focused on reverence for nature. The Divine lies all around us in the spirits that inhabit us and the natural world. Everything is connected, and a Wiccan treads lightly to maintain the harmonious balance of the Mother Earth.

All Wiccans also worship feminine aspects of the divine alongside their masculine counterparts. In order for there to be balance in the universe, there must be balance among masculine and feminine spirituality and worship.

THE WHEEL OF THE YEAR: CELEBRATING SABBATS

The Wheel of the Year is the name given to the cycle of festivals held annually by Wiccans and also some Neo-Pagans. Wiccans celebrate all eight festivals of the Wheel of the Year. The solstices and equinoxes make up four of the eight holidays and are known as the quarter days or cross-quarter days. They are the midpoint festivals of the year, celebrating the seasons.

A *solstice* is a celestial event, where the Sun is positioned in its most Northerly or Southerly quadrant in its travel relative to the equator of the Earth. There are two solstice events a year. While the names for festivals vary widely between different Wiccan traditions, the names commonly used for the solstice celebrations are the Midwinter Yule festival and the Midsummer Litha festival.

The *Yule* festival has been celebrated since the late Stone Age. It is known as the turning point of the year, and for many is the most important festival to honor in the entire year. The Sun is an important symbol during this festival, its ebbing in the sky during sunset often seen as a symbol of renewal, fertility, and rebirth.

The Yule festival is celebrated in many various ways, depending on the person, the coven, and the Wiccan tradition being emulated. Common celebrations include making sacrifices, feasting, and giving gifts to those you care about are common elements. Decorations include evergreen plants such as pine and seasonal winter plants such as holly. Tree decorating is also a Wiccan practice at this time, similar to current western Christian traditions for Christmas

The *Litha* festival is one of four solar events being celebrated as a solstice event. This summer festival celebrates the sun shining for the longest of any day of the year. Bede writes that "Litha means *gentle* or *navigable*, because in both these months the calm breezes are gentle and they make one want to sail upon the smooth sea."

The Litha festival is typically celebrated by going outside and reconnecting with nature while the sun is shining. Hikes and drum circles are common celebratory events held. Prayers are said to honor the season, and this is also known as a time of learning and charity within the Wiccan community.

An *equinox* is another celestial event, when the center of the Sun crosses over the equator of the Earth. This occurs twice a year. The equinox festivals are known as the Ostara festival for the Vernal Equinox, and the Mabon festival for the Autumnal equinox.

Ostara is the Spring equinox celebration, during which day and night stand exactly equal in time, with light on the increase. Some celebrate on the day of the equinox, while others celebrate Ostara on the full moon after the equinox because of the festival's association with the feminine and the Goddess Aphrodite.

During Ostara Wiccans eat traditional vegetable and herb based dishes, using whatever spring ingredients are native to their area. Floral incense is used, traditionally jasmine or rose. Daffodils and Violets are fresh flowers that are often used in Ostara rituals to promote prosperity in the time of coming light, sometimes in combination with the stone Jasper.

The festival *Mabon* is also known as the Harvest Home, and the Ingathering Feast. Mabon is celebrated in the autumn and is a time to give thanks to the universe, nature, and deities for the annual gifts we have received. Like Ostara, the day is divided equally into night and day, but this time we are paying respects to the coming days of darkness.

Mabon is celebrated by making offerings in thanks for the gifts nature and the Gods and Goddesses have given us. In the Druid tradition, offerings are made to celebrate the fruit-giving trees. Offerings most often include ciders and wines, along with autumn herbs. This celebration is one of the most lavish occasions, and Wiccans often wear their best finery.

The secondary holidays are often cause for large celebrations as well, despite being less important celestial events. These holidays are generally called Imbolc, Beltane, Lammas, and Samhain.

Imbolc usually occurs on the first day of February and is a celebration of the first inklings of spring beginning to sprout through the winter frost. Historically a Celtic holiday, for Wiccans this is a time to purify oneself and one's tools, and to do spring cleaning. Dianic Wiccans have coven initiations during this time, and for all Wiccans it is representative of renewal of faith and dedication to the Craft.

Traditionally on the first day of summer in Ireland, *Beltane* also has Celtic roots. Beltane was traditionally to celebrate Flora, the Goddess of flowers. Dancing around a lively bonfire is the most common way Wiccans celebrate this time of season. In duotheistic Wiccan lore, this is the time when the Horned God and the Triple Goddess are perfectly united.

Lammas is celebrated on the first day of August and is another Harvest festival. This holy day is to celebrate living off the land, to celebrate grains in particular in the early beginnings of fall. It is common to weave dolls out of grain husks such as corn husks to honor the Gods and Goddesses of the harvest.

Commonly celebrated by non-Wiccans as Halloween, *Samhain* is often a favorite celebration of Wiccans everywhere. Opposite the yearly calendar to Beltane, Samhain is a holiday to honor those who have passed into the great beyond. Ancestors, elders, friends, and even pet familiars are honored at this time. It is a holiday to show love to all those that have passed who have supported us, and those who continue to support us each day.

Samhain is typically celebrated by connecting with the spirit world in some ritual way, because Wiccans believe this is the time of the year that the veil between the natural and the supernatural is the thinnest. Samhain is also spent lighting candle vigils for those we choose to honor and remember on this Day of the Dead.

ESBATS: HONORING THE MOON

An *Esbat* festival is a festival which is intended to show honor and respect for the moon and Her influence on the natural world. It is a time in which the coven gathers besides the main Wheel of the Year celebrations or the Sabbat. Janet Farrar, a known occultist writer, describes esbats as an opportunity for a "love feast, healing work, psychic training and all."

Esbats occur on a full moon. Some covens that focus on the moon in particular extend these practices to dark moons, and to the first and last quarters of the moons during the month. While the main festivals are times for celebration, the important magickal work of the year is completed during the Esbats.

An Esbat traditionally begins at midnight and finishes at the break of dawn, called cock-crow by many traditional Wiccans for this ritual. Esbats are a complete celebration of the feminine, and the full moon represents Mother Earth impregnated with spiritual energy. Dancing, singing, and magickal rituals are common at Esbats. If one is not part of a coven, often this is done amongst other Wiccan friends.

If the Esbat is done during a full moon, this considered to be one of the most powerful times to perform magick. Crystals and stones are charged with the raw healing and purifying energy of the full moon. Other things, such as water and Tarot decks may be charged with this energy as well, along with a large list of other magick tools.

During a dark moon, however, Wiccans abstain from magick practices. Instead, the focus is turned on inner demons. Meditation and trance states are common ways that dark moons are honored. The goal during a dark moon is to address and conquer the darkness which exists inside all of us.

The waxing of the moon, when the moon is growing larger, is a good time for "positive" spells -- spells that help you gain things like love and wealth. The waning of the moon is a good time for "negative" spells -- spells that help you lose bad habits, or leave something spiritually blocking behind.

The Moons of different months have different names that go along with their different energies. These different energies are important to be aware of, as they may make particular times of year perfect for certain magickal goal.

The January Moon is known as The Wolf Moon or The Winter Moon. Seen as a time to remember things that are coming to an end and also a time to look forward to new beginnings, this moon represents protection and strength.

The February Moon is also known as The Storm Moon or The Death Moon. In centuries past, the brutal cold of this month made it a time of hardship for those practicing the Old Religion who lived off the land. This is a time for spells focused on fertility for the coming Spring.

The March Moon is often called The Chaste Moon or The Seed Moon. This is a time to plant "seeds" in your mind. You press ideas of imagination, creativity, and prosperity, and speak them into existence with chants, spells, and songs. This month of purity and newness is the perfect time to prepare yourself for the coming flora of Spring.

The April Moon is also known as The Egg Moon or The Grass Moon. If you keep a magickal garden, this is the perfect time to begin planting under the Esbat moons. While in March we sowed seeds of the mind, now we sow literal seeds into the Earth. April is a time for action.

The May Moon is sometimes called The Hare Moon or The Flower Moon. This opens the gates of love and romance. This is a good time for love spells and to focus on your romantic partner(s). Rekindling the spark in a relationship is never more possible than during a May Esbat ceremony.

The June Moon is The Lovers Moon or The Rose Moon. This passionate time is perfect for spiritually encouraging romantic engagements and marriages. This is also a time for those who are single to engage in spiritual prosperity spells.

The July Moon, also known as The Mead Moon or The Lightning Moon, is a time of health and enchantment. Mead is the nectar of the Gods, and the time for prosperity and strength is on the rise now powered by the heated energy reflected from the Summer sun.

The August Moon is called The Red Moon. This occurs during Harvest time, a time of abundance. This is another month where marriage magick is strong, and where the fruits of the prosperous summer are given thanks for.

The September Moon is also known as The Harvest Moon. Following August this is another month of abundance during which thanks are given for the fruits of the Autumnal harvests. The Harvest Moon can help bring you and those you care about much prosperity, which you may need in the harsher months to come.

The October Moon is often called The Blood Moon. This is a time of renewal of faith and dedication to the Craft. This is a great time to set new goals for the coming Winter season. Divination is also fueled by extra spiritual energy during October Esbats, so the time for Astrological and Tarot readings is nigh.

The November Moon, sometimes known as The Snow Moon, acknowledges the passing of the abundance of the past seasons. This is a time to connect spiritually with those who mean the most to you, whether they're family, friends, coven members, or your community at large. Emotional bonds can be made stronger through rituals during The Snow Moon Esbats.

The December Moon is also known as The Oak Moon or The Cold Moon. Because the nights have become longest at this time of the year, this is a time to reflect on the true power of the moon. The Moon has dominion over the spirit world during December because the nights are longer than the days. The thoughts of Wiccans turn again towards rebirth and the promise that Spring will return again. Let go of the negative and let the light of the day live on through your spirit during this dark time of year.

ASTROLOGY

You've probably heard of astrology at one point in your life, and might even know your astrological Sun Sign (sometimes called a Zodiac Sign), because it's based on your birthday - Sagittarius, Capricorn, or what have you.

For centuries people have been using the celestial bodies to predict mundane, worldly events in our lives. Many Wiccans also believe that the stars have a large amount of influence over world events and human emotions. *Astrology* is a type of divination that focuses on interpreting patterns in the planets, Moon, and stars in order to foresee earthly events.

Only since our modern era of scientific revolution took hold did Astrology become discredited as an actual science itself. Thus, it is no surprise that there is much research and nuance behind it that can make astrology seem intimidating and complicated. However, the rich balance between rules and intuition are part of what makes Astrology so effective and attractive to some Wiccans.

Astrology draws on Hellenistic philosophy as well as the model of physics introduced to the world by Aristotle. This means that Astrology regards the movement of the celestial bodies as eternal, while the motions of the four elements (Fire, Earth, Air, and Water) are linear.

Astrology has never been intended to be an exact science, because no one person can truly, completely understand the order of the cosmos. This is also because while Astrology is made to predict trends in human mood and behavior based on the effect of the stars, having divined these things, humans are capable of changing the outcomes despite the influence of the celestial bodies. Divine intervention is another possibility.

Most of us know our Sun Sign, which is the principle sign that forms our personality according to Astrology. There are 12 houses in each person's natal charts, based on where each planet, Moon, or star was when that person was born.

These 12 houses interact with one another to create your full, incredibly nuanced personality. Your Moon Sign, for example, affects the manifestation of your Sun Sign. An emotionally-in-touch Cancer might gain vanity and confidence from having their Moon Sign positioned in Leo, for example. Other planets control other domains in your life. Venus reigns over one's love life, and the Midheaven sign gives us insight into our life's work.

Each astrological sign is related to a planet, an element, and also has a special relationship with either male or female energy. The chart below is a handy way to check out which ones align with your sign!

Sign	Date	Nature	Element	Planet	Symbol
Aries	March 20 – April 20	Masculine	Fire	Mars	Ram

Taurus	April 20 - May 21	Feminine	Earth	Venus	Bull
Gemini	May 21 - June 21	Masculine	Air	Mercury	Twins
Cancer	June 21 - July 2	Feminine	Water	Moon	Crab
Leo	July 22 - August 23	Masculine	Fire	Sun	Lion
Virgo	August 23 - September 23	Feminine	Earth	Mercury	Maiden
Libra	September 23 - October 23	Masculine	Air	Venus	Scales
Scorpio	October 23 - November 22	Feminine	Water	Mars	Scorpion
Sagittarius	November 22 - December 21	Masculine	Fire	Jupiter	Archer

Capricorn	December 21 - January 20	Feminine	Earth	Saturn	Sea-Goat
Aquarius	January 20 - February 18	Masculine	Air	Saturn	Water-Bearer
Pisces	February 18 - March 20	Feminine	Water	Jupiter	Fish

ELEMENTAL MAGIC

The natural elements that are involved here have a large place in the world of Wicca and magic. Similar to how the placement of the stars can affect outcomes, we can predict the behavior of certain things based on their association with the elements. For example, crystals and gemstones that are associated with water are more likely to be used for healing.

While most people know of the four classical elements, Wicca believes in a fifth element that begins where the other four connect. This element is called Aether, meaning spirit. Use of the elements helps keep our practice directly in line with nature. The elements can metaphorically represent emotional and spiritual characteristics as well as the literal connection to nature.

Air dominates the aspect of magic that revolves around visualization. Air is a masculine element that is associated with the Eastern direction. Air represents intelligence and mental faculties, psychic abilities, imagination, ideas, the mind, dreams, and inspiration. Associated with the spring, some symbols of Air include the wind, the sky, the breeze, feathers, breath, clouds, herbs, and some flowers. Wind instruments such as the flute may be used to channel Air energy.

Fire is representative of magick itself. Fire is a masculine element that is associated with the Southern direction. Fire represents change and is the most physical and spiritual of all the elements. Ruled by passion, fire is often invoked through symbols such as candles, incense, baking, love spells, and burning objects.

Water represents cleansing and healing, and is a feminine element associated with the Western direction. Water is a receptive energy. Water itself can be easily enchanted and charged and holds energy from its surroundings very easily. Water is a dynamic representation of the subconscious emotional world, the soul, and wisdom.

Earth represents strength and is a feminine element associated with the Northern direction. Earth is manifested in abundance, wealth, prosperity. Rituals invoking the Earth element often involve burying an object to infuse it with strong energy promoting good fortune in finance.

Aether is a universal element representative of the spirit world and individual spiritual entities. Aether is the element present in some form in all things (see Animism later in this chapter). Associated with The Horned God and The Triple Goddess, Aether connects all natural things and allows the world to exist in a careful harmonious balance.

ANIMISM: THE SOUL OF THE WORLD

Animism is a religious belief system that holds the value that everything on earth, including inanimate natural objects, has a soul or a distinct spiritual essence. The title comes from the Latin *anima* which means "spirit", "breath", and "life". Animism perceives all natural things to be "alive" in the sense of having Aether, the spirit of the universe within.

It is the belief that all things of nature, sticks, rocks, animals (including humans), clouds, the wind, all these things are interconnected. The world feels the effect of the loss of any natural thing, and the balance must be maintained.

Animism was originally an ancient Indigenous belief -- that is, it was held by a large number of First Nations and Native American tribes. Wiccans often intermingle practices with First Nations religious practices because of their shared respect for the natural world. Animism is recognized as the oldest known world religion, although of course it was not an organized religion as we know today.

Those who believe in Animism today are almost always religiously pacifist, refusing to harm or kill any other being or object that contains spirit. In this way we preserve the balance, respect our place in nature, and learn to live in harmony with our environment.

Those who do not practice pacifism may choose to engage with this balance directly by hunting and gathering. Living off the land is a different approach that puts one in the middle of that balance. It teaches one how to maintain that harmony while facing the reality that, as humans, we must consume natural things to maintain our own lives.

Whether a hunter, gatherer, omnivore, or vegan, all Animists choose to honor that which they take from nature in some say. It could be in the form of a ritual, perhaps honoring the kills of the hunt before consumption or having special sacrificial rites to honor the spirits.

Nature is also honored during every Wiccan festival, but Harvest festivals in particular aim to acknowledge and give thanks for the natural blessings we receive that allow us to continue to exist.

Tarot: Reading the Mirror

Many entire books could be and have been written about the subject of divination via Tarot. Tarot cards first began being used in recorded history for divination purposes in the 18th century in European countries like France and Italy.

However, many occult authors trace the unwritten history of Tarot back to ancient Egypt or ancient Kabbalah practices. There are many different styles of Tarot readings, including those from French, Celtic, and Kabbalistic backgrounds

Tarot isn't meant to be a tool to exactly read the future, either. Tarot is simply a way to measure the forces at work on the current circumstances. The outcome is in control of the seeker. The goal of Tarot is to guide the seeker and advise them of the cosmic energies at work. .

In fact, the best way to think about Tarot is a reflection of the self. The cards contain imagery that has been meaningful to humankind for centuries, and which are ingrained in what psychologist Carl Jung would call our unconscious. The cards tell a story about cosmic forces, but the cards also help us learn about ourselves in how we understand the stories the cards tell.

Tarot has 4 suits which vary by the region the cards come from. Each suit has 14 cards, and there is an additional 21-card trump suit and a single card known as The Fool.. There are major and minor arcana elements in every suit, though the minor arcana are considered optional for readings by some practitioners. The major arcana consists of the Trump cards and The Fool, while the minor arcana is made up of the ten pip and four court cards in every deck.

The major Arcana has 22 cards, each which represents a step in a journey from The Fool's ignorance to finding wisdom and unity within the universe. Because these cards represent a progression, it can help a reader to understand this progression -- that is, where each card comes from and where it goes.

The minor Arcana suits are Swords, Cups, Wands, and Pentacles. Pulling a Sword card usually means something interpretative of your inner thoughts, your words, or your actions. The Cups generally represent feelings, inspiration, and creativity. Wands typically have to do with spirituality and energy. Finally, Pentacles are drawn to indicate something about money, material things, or stability.

The minor Arcana is more specific and not as big-picture as the major Arcana cards in the deck. The elements are also represented by the minor Arcana. Wands are fire, Cups are water, Swords are air, and Pentacles are earth.

Some Tarot readers allow cards to be drawn upside down, which changes the meaning to an inverse one. However, many Tarot readers, from beginners to experienced diviners, prefer to play only upright Arcana cards.

Tarot typically involves two people - a querent, who is posing a question to the cards, and a reader whose job it is to interpret the meaning of the cards. The querent may choose to disclose their question or keep it to themselves. A skilled reader doesn't need to know the question to read the cards.

However, as you may know, sometimes the reader is also the querent. If this is the case, the reading becomes a little different, because the cards represent people differently. A well-practiced reader will notice patterns over long periods of times in the layouts of the cards; there may be one or several cards that the reader begins to associate with themselves or others because that card appears often to represent that person.

If the imagery speaks directly to you, that intuition is recommended to be followed rather than just using the standard imagery interpretations. The cards are intending to speak directly to the reader and the seeker, so anything personal is no coincidence. Let the cards have your own voice!

The cards are pulled in some order, referred to as a spread. Maybe a one-card draw to see how your day will go, or a three-card spread asking the universe about your crush. The cards should always be read in context with other cards pulled. The positioning of the cards may also be significant, especially in Celtic and Kabbalistic card patterns. Ask yourself, how did this card work with the last card I drew?

Many Wiccans keep a log of their readings in a journal. This journal may be very thorough, writing which cards were drawn, what imagery was important, what feelings were evoked, who was doing the reading and the seeking, and how one feels about the reading. This helps the Tarot to act as a mirror to the soul of the interpreter. It allows beginners to learn more efficiently, and experienced readers to keep track of their energy.

Conclusion

Wiccan practices, by nature, vary widely. There are, however, some commonly held beliefs, as we have covered, as well as festivals that most Wiccans observe. Wiccans who practice without magic celebrate the Sabbats throughout the Wheel of the Year and focus on gratitude to Mother Earth. Wiccans who practice magic still adhere to this nature-based orientation, focusing on the elements and the stars in their Craft. We can even interpret the forces of nature through divination and channel them through spells and magickal items.

The next chapter will focus on another vital component of Wiccan belief and practice, which is deity worship.

Chapter 3 Wiccan Deities and The Afterlife

Wicca is a religion that predates Christianity, so the form of worship may be unfamiliar to many. Wiccans worship specific deities within a pantheon. These Gods or Goddesses may be worshipped in hopes of advancing some cause, or a God or Goddess may "choose" a Wiccan to worship them by sending them signs.

Who you worship and how is completely your choice in Wicca. The goal is to have the most natural relationship possible, to feel intimacy with the Divine influences that surround us all. During turning points in a Wiccan's spiritual life, a new Divinity may call to them. Some Wiccans feel that a certain deity has chosen them, rather than the other way around.

There are a few distinct patterns amongst Wiccans when it comes to belief and worship of deities. More traditional Wiccans, like Gardnerian Wiccans, are polytheists who believe in two "parts" of a universal God, a male part and a female part.

Other Wiccans subscribe to polytheism, where they believe in and sometimes worship multiple Gods from a wide range of mythologies and pantheons. Celtic, Greek, Egyptian deities -- polytheists are looking to connect with deities that appear to them naturally, no matter where their lore is originally from.

Still other Wiccans consider their worship to fall *within* Abrahamic tradition; they may believe in monotheism, or they may engage in the worship of female Abrahamic figures such as Mary. Wiccans may have vastly different interpretations of traditional scriptures, and may be considered heretics by mainstream society.

DUOTHEISM: THE HORNED GOD AND THE TRIPLE GODDESS

Those who believe in The Horned God and the Triple Goddess are considered to be *duotheistic*, meaning they believe in a dual entity of God; the male and the female. Many Wiccans feel this explains the balance in the universe, as well as the conflicts where male and female fail to harmonize.

The Horned God represents the unity "between the Divine and animals", man being included in the definition of animals. The horns represent the dualistic nature of The Horned God. He is night and he is day, summer and winter. The two horns added to the triple aspect of the Goddess are often mapped as the five points of a pentagram.

The Horned God is connected with the forest, and is seen very much as a protector of the Goddess and all her sacred children. As duality demands, he both gives life and takes souls from the world with death. He is known as a loving God who guards creation.

The Triple Goddess, completing the duotheistic belief system, represents all Divine Feminine aspects of the universe. She is most often symbolized by the moon and the ocean. The Triple Goddess gets her name from the three stages of a woman's life: The Maiden, The Mother, and The Crone. Of course this is a very ancient tradition that no longer applies universally to all women, but regardless the

Triple Goddess is a representation of all the positive and negative attributes of being a woman.

The Maiden represents enchantment and youth. This is a time of purity and new beginnings. The Greek Goddess Persephone is most often associated with The Maiden.

The Mother represents fertility, power, and stability. The Mother is the ultimate creator, the giver of life, the nurturing one. In Greek myth, Demeter is associated as the Mother, a compassionate and selfless giver.

Repose and wisdom are attributes of The Crone, along with the status of being an elder. Wiccans revere their elders, as they have had much more experience in interpreting signs, interacting with spirits, and creating effective rituals. The Greek Goddess Hecate is known as The Crone, with the satisfaction of a lifetime of knowledge.

POLYTHEISTIC PRACTICES

Other modern Wiccans are polytheists. This means that they *believe* that there are many or at least multiple deities. It doesn't mean they necessarily worship more than one deity, however; many Wiccans dedicate their practice to one or a few select Gods or Goddesses with whom they feel a special spiritual connection.

Wiccans draw deities from the lore of several different societies, including ancient Greek and Roman pantheons, along with pre-Christian European deities such as Norse myths or The Horned God. Wiccans may also spiritually access Egyptian and Hindu Gods and Goddesses.

Some Wiccans connect spiritually with their deities without naming them because their goal is to channel whoever is close and present. Other Wiccans, on the other hand, find that channeling a particular God or Goddess using certain ritual objects like candles, incense, and crystals is more effective for them. We will discuss how to begin channeling deities in Chapter 5.

Hellenistic Wicca: The Pantheon of Olympus

Hellenistic Wiccans are those who include the Gods and Goddesses from Greco-Roman mythology in their worship and practice. Greek and Roman imagery has been so ubiquitous in our society and culture that many feel it is part of the heritage of all Wiccans. Because of this constant exposure to these myths, some Wiccans feel more strongly connected to this pantheon than to others.

Looking at the pantheon of deities from Greek and Roman myth might seem a little overwhelming. But the pantheon is very compatible with Wicca. This is because each God or Goddess is associated with something in the natural world. Indeed, many of the Gods and Goddesses exist to explain the phenomenon of the natural world around us.

The "main" Greek deities are even associated with planets and elements, and can be connected to astrology as well. The five classical elements actually come from Hellenistic understandings of the world. Before that time, the elements were known as the earth, sky, and sea by the Celtic occult groups.

This level of nuance is highly conducive to the individualism encouraged in Wiccan practice. Another advantage of Hellenistic Wicca is that unlike other European pantheons which have had much information lost to the ages, so much of the Greek and Roman lore remains intact and accessible. In fact, there may be no pantheon more complete or detailed than that of Greece and Rome.

Hellenistic beliefs are compatible with the Wheel of the Year as well. Many Hellenistic Wiccans associate the story of Persephone and Demeter with the Wheel of the Year, because it explains the coming and going of the seasons. The rise and fall of Dionysus, the Hellenistic God of harvest, wine, and celebration, is also associated with the Sabbats and festivals.

The 12 most important Hellenistic deities are as follows:

1. Jupiter/Zeus: King of the Gods, Zeus is the god of thunder and the sky.

2. Hera/Juno: Queen of the Gods, Hera is the patron Goddess of women and femininity.

3. Athena/Minerva: Born out of the head of Zeus, Athena is the Goddess of wisdom and strategy.

4. Poseidon/Neptune: Often depicted with a trident, Poseidon is the God of the ocean and freshwater, earthquakes, and horses.

5. Aphrodite/Venus: Aphrodite was born out of seafoam and is a maternal Goddess of sexuality, love, fertility, beauty, desire, and prosperity.

6. Ares/Mars: The son of Hera, Ares is the God of war, aggression, virility, and the protector of agriculture.

7. Apollo/Apollo: Depicted as powerful archer, Apollo is the twin brother of the Goddess Artemis and the God of healing, music, and truth.

8. Artemis/Diana: Daughter of Zeus and twin of Apollo, Artemis is the Goddess of the hunt, the moon, birth, rebirth, and is a protector of women and a symbol of virginity.

9. Hephaestus/Vulcan: The creator of the weapons of the Gods and Goddesses, Hephaestus is the God of the forge, metalwork, and volcanoes.

10. Hestia/Vesta: Known as the sacred fire of the Vestal Virgins of Rome, Hestia is the Goddess of the hearth, the home, and the family.

11. Hermes/Mercury: Son of Zeus and the guide of spirits in the underworld, Hermes is the God of communication, thieves, trickery, profit, and trade.

12. Demeter/Ceres: Known as the eternal mother, Demeter is the Goddess of agriculture, grain, marriage, motherhood, and marriage.

CELTIC RECONSTRUCTIONIST WICCA

Many Gardnerian Wiccans use Celtic elements in their Craft. Other Wiccans who don't identify with a tradition may also choose this path. The founder of Wicca included many Celtic influences in his original rituals and belief system, and many who believe in the traditional ways laid out by Gardner have chosen to preserve these influences.

The Celtic Reconstruction movement, associated with Neo-Druidism, is an attempt to recreate ancient Celtic practices with as much historical and spiritual accuracy as possible. Celtic traditions have survived through folklore and songs, as well as through prayers passed down through generations.

Unlike other Wiccans, Celtics believe in the Three Elements: the Land, the Sea, and the Sky. Fire is viewed as a force of inspiration which unites the three realms, and not an element in and of itself.

Celtic Wiccans are focused on interacting with the Otherworld, and use divination and offerings to connect with the ancestral spirits of the land. Offerings include food, drink (usually alcohol), and art. Most Celtic Wiccans maintain altars to honor their patron spirits and deities, and in this tradition it is most common to place the altar outside. Ideally the altar would be near a well or a stream, or some naturally occurring water.

Some important Celtic deities include:

1. Brighid, The Goddess of the Irish Hearth. Revered as the Goddess of the hearth and the home, Brighid is also a Goddess of prophecy and divination. Brighid is the Triple Goddess in modern Wiccan tradition.

2. Cailleach, Queen of Winter. Sometimes known as the hag, Cailleach is the bringer of storms. Known as the Dark Mother of winter, Cailleach is also known for taking part in creation.

3. Cernunnos, Wild God of the Forest. Representative of the Horned God in modern Wicca, Cernunnos is the god of masculinity and fertility.

4. Cerridwen, The Keeper of the Cauldron. A Welsh Goddess, Cerridwen brews the cauldron of the underworld that is the source of ideas and inspiration.

5. The Dagda, The Irish Father God. Legend tells that the Dagda caused himself to lose his own powers. He is the father of the other Gods and Goddesses of the Celtic pantheon.

6. Herne, God of the Wild Hunt. An ancient English God, Herne is considered the God of the common people, as well as the God of vegetation and hunting. Herne is celebrated in the fall, when the deer go into rut.

7. Lugh, Master of Skills. Honored during the harvest festival of Lammas, Luch is the God of craftsmanship, blacksmithing, and artisans.

8. Rhiannon, the Welsh Goddess of Horses. Famed for her intelligence, Rhiannon is a Goddess of wealth and charity.

9. Taliesin, Chief of Bards. Interestingly enough, Taliesin is a real documented person who has been elevated to the status of a minor Celtic God. He is the patron of poets and musicians.

KEMETIC PANTHEON

Kemetic or Egyptian Wicca has a strong focus on the moon. Esbats are important events for them, and they gather in large groups to celebrate the moon as a community. These congregations are called temples rather than covens in this tradition.

The most important God in the Egyptian pantheon for Wiccans is Ra, the ancient God of the sun. During the day, Ra exists in the Overworld creating the sunlight and is depicted as a falcon with a sun disk around the head. At night, some legends say that Ra goes to the Underworld, and transforms to have the head of a ram, the horns representing the duality of day and night.

Ra is believed to originally been united as one being with Horus, the God of the sky. Together they made all of creation by speaking all creatures into existence using the secret names of their souls. Ra split off to rule over every domain: the sky, the earth, and the underworld.

Other important deities of this pantheon include:

1. Amounet is the Goddess of fertility and motherhood.

2. Anubis is the God of the dead and the process of preserving the body through embalming.

3. Atum is a deity that switches between male and female, and is considered to be the creator of Egypt. He rose from the waters of chaos to become the first God, who created the rest of the Egyptian Gods.

4. Bast is a Goddess of protection with the head of the cat. Originally the protector of the Pharaoh, she is gentle but a vicious enemy for those who threaten people under her protection.

5. Hathor is the Egyptian Goddess of happiness, and was considered to be the mother of the Pharaoh. In modern

Wiccan practice she is worshipped as the mother of the home and domesticity.

6. Horus is the God who protects the Pharaoh, but was also considered to be incarnated in the Pharaoh. Horus lost an eye in battle, and since then the Eye of Horus has been an important Egyptian symbol of protection.

7. Isis is the mother of Horus. She is a Goddess of protection and maternal love and is often depicted nursing the infant Horus.

8. Ma'at is the daughter of Ra and the Egyptian Goddess of happiness, love, and justice.

9. Nun is the eldest of the Egyptian Gods. Before achieving form as a God, Nun existed as the primordial waters of chaos. He is the God of pre-creation.

10. Osiris is the God of the underworld, death, and the dead.

NORSE PANTHEON

Norse mythology is rich with dragons, giants, elves, dwarves vikings, and more. Though many details are lost to the ages, the tradition still lives on in Wiccan practice.

The ancient Norse folk were at times severe, but often playful as well. This playful nature is often lost in the Wiccan revival of Norse folklore and worship, traded for a focus on the warrior spirit. However, it is important to remember that the Norse ancestors weren't all kings and warriors seasoned from battle. The majority of them spent their lives performing difficult, physically demanding work and enduring cold, bitter winters. In remembering the truth about their lives, some Wiccans choose to honor their memory by engaging with the Norse pantheon.

Norse myth was transmitted through oral tradition, and by the time any of it was written down the area had already been dominated by Christians. There are two holy texts that preserve Norse legend, but they were written by Snorri Sturlason in the 1300s after he had already been converted to Christianity. Sturlason knew that if he wrote anything the church deemed as blasphemy, he could be sentenced to death. Thus, much of the true spirit of Norse religion has been lost to time.

The Eddas contain the words of the High One, a God known as Odin who is proclaimed as the "AllFather". The values of the Eddas include truth, honor, and a moral code based on loyalty. It is written that one should protect one's own family and possessions and retaliate severely against those who betray you. The Eddas also teaches about the importance of physical and mental strength.

There are nine Nordic worlds, which are held by the branches and roots of Yggdrasil, the tree of the world. Each realm houses different beings, such as animals (including humans), Giants, and Divinities. The Norse also believe in Ragnarok, or the day of destruction.

The Norse Gods and Goddesses include:

1. Odin is the Father of all Gods and humans. Often depicted wearing a floppy hat or a winged helm, Odin is a warrior God known for wisdom, magick, wit, and knowledge. Though he is known as a literal warrior, Odin also represents mental warfare, considering his cerebral qualities. Odin is associated with the astrological sign Sagittarius.

2. Thor is the son of Odin and the God of thunder, lightning, and strength. Thor is typically shown wielding his mighty hammer, Mjollnir. Rugged and powerful, Thor guards Asgard, the realm of the Gods. Thor is linked with the astrological sign Leo.

3. Freya is a Goddess known for love and beauty, but she is also a hyper-intelligent warrior. Freya guides the souls she chooses that are lost in battle to Valhalla, the Norse heaven. She and her twin brother Freyr are connected to the astrological sign Gemini.

4. Freyr, twin of Freya, is known as the God of the Elves. Freyr is a God of virility and fertility. His boar is a sacred symbol that is said to bring the dawn.

5. Tyr is the God of the ancient wars and the lawmaker for the Gods. Tyr is invoked to bring about justice and right action. Tyr used to be the leader of the Norse pantheon, but was replaced by Odin. There are no record that explain why this transition occurred. Tyr is associated with the astrological sign Libra.

6. Loki is a trickster God, known for his acts of chaos. While he challenges the structure and rules of Asgard, his antics are necessary to bring about the change the world needs. Loki has demonic elements, and is associated with the astrological sign Aries.

7. Heimdall is a handsome God with golden teeth. His role is to guard the rainbow path that leads to the realm of the Gods. He holds the signal horn that is blown to warn the Gods of Ragnarok. Heimdall is linked to the astrological sign Aquarius.

8. Skadi is the Goddess of winter and the hunt. She is a Goddess of judgment, vengeance, and righteous anger. It is she who delivers Loki's banishment to the underworld. Skadi is represented by the astrological sign Capricorn.

Abrahamic Wicca

While some might see it as a contradiction or heresy, there are followers of the three Abrahamic religions that also identify with and practice Wicca. Abrahamic Wiccans believe that the one Abrahamic God controls all of existence, including the stars that guide astrology. An Abrahamic Wiccan would argue that if you pull a card from a tarot deck, the Abrahamic God controlled the outcome of which card appeared. Thus, Wicca can interpret the signs sent by the Abrahamic God through the universe.

Though all of the Abrahamic religions center around the same God, described by different prophets, there is much nuance and difference in the way they worship, practice, and perceive God. They also use different central religious texts.

All Abrahamic Wiccans believe in emulating the behavior of the prophets of God. Christians additionally focus on living a life mimicking the path of Jesus and his disciples. Muslims imitate the life of Muhammad, and Wiccans often include the behavior of the wives of Muhammad to provide feminine balance.

Many Abrahamic Wiccan women choose to cover their hair as a sign of devotion and remembrance of God. Jewish women honor God in this way by wearing *tichel*, which are wraps that go around the back of the head but do not cover the neck or face. Christian women often wear veils made of lace, or veils that wrap loosely around the head to show the hair but not the neck, in imitation of Mother Mary. Muslim Wiccan women wear the *hijab*, a veil that covers all of the hair as well as the chest and neck, or a *niqab* which also covers the face.

Jewish Wiccans focus on the Tanakh, or the Hebrew Bible as their central texts. This is known by Christians as The Old Testament. For Jewish Witches, God is known by a respectful title HaShem, which means simply "The Name". This is because outside of prayer and ritual environments, the names of HaShem are considered to be too holy to speak aloud. HaShem is called Adonai when called upon in prayer, but also has seven names which reveal more about the nature of the Divine.

A Jewish Wiccan would be most likely to practice Kabbalah, or the ancient art of Jewish mysticism. The Zohar is the book which explains how to begin to understand the complex and multilayered realms of Kabbalah. Kabbalah tries to understand the secret meanings of the Torah, often by using complicated numerology. Hebrew letters are also numbers, so the Torah can be interpreted by examining the patterns therein.

The most traditional Kabbalistic Jewish Wiccans believe that one cannot even begin to fathom the truths of Kabbalah until one has reached the age of 40. However, there are Kabbalistic tarot spreads and other methods of accessing the knowledge of Kabbalah before this coming of age occurs.

The Bible is the main holy text for Christian Wiccans, though The Old Testament is important for context as well.

Christian Wiccans often venerate the saints as well as the Virgin Mary. Mary represents the Divine Feminine. Calling from Wiccan influences, Mary represents all at once The Maiden, The Mother, and The Crone, being pure, maternal, and wise. This balances the trinity of God, which is the Father, the Son, and the Holy Spirit.

Christian Wiccans celebrate both Christian holidays and the festivals of the Wheel of the Year, mixing elements of both belief systems into each holiday. Christmas and Easter, as they are celebrated, actually already incorporate many pagan rituals such as tree-decorating and fertility symbols (e.g. eggs, rabbits).

There is also a large focus on returning to the roots of Christianity. This means being highly educated on the facts about the life of Jesus of Nazareth and what He stood for instead of taking someone else's word for it. Many Wiccans feel that Christianity has been wrongly warped from its original intentions and used as a device for war and division when it preaches about peace and unity.

The holy book of Muslims is called the Qu'ran. Qu'ran means "recitation" in Arabic, and recitation of the Qu'ran is extremely important to all Muslims. It is said that Allah gave the Qu'ran to the humans and the djinn (spirits), but not to the Angels. Thus, whenever one recites Qu'ran, the Angels draw in close to listen. You are encouraged to greet the Angels who peek over your shoulders when you finish your recitation.

There are different sects of Islam just as there are for every large religion. Most Wiccan Muslims are in a sect called *Sufism*. Sufism is Islamic mysticism. Islamic mysticism focuses on the power of trance and meditation, worshipping the divine feminine, and worship through music and dance. Whereas most Muslims harshly condemn magick, Sufis defy labels and many don't self-identify even as Sufis. Sufis believe in full capacity for spiritual growth in all directions.

WICCAN AFTERLIFE

After all that discussion about divinity, it seems only appropriate to address what Wiccans believe about the great beyond. While Abrahamic Wiccans may follow the afterlife beliefs of their own traditions, the majority of Wiccans believe in reincarnation and a realm called the Summerland.

THE CIRCLE OF REINCARNATION

Pulling from beliefs that predate the Abrahamic religions, most Wiccans don't believe in heaven or hell. These concepts did not exist in ancient religions, though they did have ideas about what happens after death. Many Wiccans believe that when you die, you are reborn again into the cycle of the cosmos.

Just as Wiccans believe in the Wheel of the Year and the cycles of the moon, reincarnation is just another cycle in the universe. We are born, we live, we die, and we are reborn again. Many witches believe in a karmic system, where what one does in this life will have a ripple effect through one's coming lives. Because of this, Wiccans take their actions very seriously, and do their best to lead kind, compassionate lives.

Wiccans believe we are put on this Earth to constantly be in a state of self-improvement. If you've ever known a Wiccan, you probably know there's a large focus to constantly be learning, reading, and discussing, as well as reevaluating ideals. This is often called the Great Work.

According to Wiccan legend, we are gifted more than one life in order to learn all that we can possibly know about nature and the cosmos. One life is not sufficient for this to occur. Each lifetime encompasses a set of lessons, and the universe has such a vast variety of lessons to teach each and every one of us. Indeed, each soul is unique and needs to learn different lessons at different times.

Once one has perfected this knowledge, after many, many lifetimes, one is released from the cycle of reincarnation and enters the Summerland, which is the topic of the next section. Apart from being an escape from reincarnation, the Summerland is also the place where the soul rests between incarnations. This is often a time to reunite with loved ones from all our different lives, should they happen to be in the Summerland at the same time.

For Wiccans, death is just another step in the eternal dance of the balance of the universe. The soul itself has no name, no gender, no race, no age, and is not a physical thing. It is a spark reflected from the deities, whichever one might follow. While the body may die, the soul will always live on; it is immortal.

When the soul visits the Summerland between incarnations, it is not a time of judgment but rather a time for weighing what has been gained and learned, and what lesson the soul will need to continue to grow in the next life.

The soul is able to see which lessons in the previous lives were heeded, and which were ignored. The soul reviews the previous life, with the insight of other spirits and deities that exist in the Summerland.

Some witches are able to access information about their past lives. There are several methods through which this can be done. Some witches receive information about past lives through dreams. These dreams may feature a guide, usually a spirit or deity, that shows the witch visions of the past. Spirits or deities may choose to do this if past knowledge will benefit the witch in the lessons of their current incarnation.

Others work to enter a trance state where this information is more readily accessible. It takes a great deal of discipline and practice to use this method. Trance work is part of the shamanistic tradition, and is not to be taken lightly. Witches should remember the persecution of witches that has existed for millenia, and be prepared to face some very difficult images and information. This kind of trance work is known as *journeying*.

So why would a witch want to seek information from a past life? Many witches believe that the key to understanding the deeper problems they face, mentally, emotionally, spiritually, and physically, lies in having an understanding of who we used to be. If a witch has issues making the same mistakes over and over in their current life, it could be a sign that they need to get in touch with their past lives to gain insight.

Because of their belief in reincarnation, Wiccans do not fear death. Wiccans don't view death as a release into oblivion, but rather as a door to birth and renewal. In your life, you meet your loved ones from past lives and get to know them again fresh, as strangers. This helps you to know the souls of your friends and family more completely, to form stronger and stronger bonds over the course of your various incarnations.

Some Wiccans believe in "soul groups" that gather and reincarnate together. These souls are deeply interconnected, and their lessons and knowledge-seeking requires every soul for completion. Some covens believe they have practiced together through many generations of incarnation.

Souls that have finished incarnating that remain in the Summerlands help the younger souls who still have things to learn. Within the Summerland there exists the Hall of Ancestors, where our ancestral souls who have finished incarnating feast and celebrate the beauty and joy of all they have learned and lived. These ancestors and spirits that remain in the Summerlands can be invoked or called upon for guidance by Wiccans in the mortal realm.

Because Wiccans believe in animism, and thereby believe in the souls of animals and other life forms, some Wiccans also believe animal souls enter and are reborn through the Summerland. Animals are reincarnated as other animals, and complete their own spiritual journey that human beings cannot fully comprehend. For example, a dog may have been a lion in a past life.

The Summerland

The Summerland is known by many names. Some call it Land of the Faerie, the Shining Land, the Otherworld, or Land of the Young. The Summerland is where the soul rests between reincarnations, and where a soul receives its final rest once the soul has completed its quest for knowledge in the mortal, earthly realms.

The concept of the Summerland is drawn, again, from the Old Religions. It is similar to the Celtic concept of Avalon. It also draws elements from the Roman and Greek concept of the afterlife, Elysium.

The Summerland is a realm, just like the one we inhabit during our lives, except it is much less dense than the realm in which living creatures dwell. This realm is neither heaven nor a hell-like underworld. There are two typical ways that the Summerland is envisioned by Wiccans.

The first way that the Summerland is visualized is a land of eternal abundance and summer. Wiccan souls in the Summerland escape the cycle of the seasons which include the loss and emptiness of winter, the rebirth and growth of spring, and the harvest of autumn. The Summerland from this perspective is a place with flowing, beautiful grassy fields where the gentle breeze soothes the soul after a long journey. There are peacefully flowing rivers. The soul finally unifies with all that is natural.

The second way the Summerland is conceptualized is a place without form. Souls interact directly, without bodies, communicating through and with the forces of the universe. The energies of souls are intertwined with the highest energies, those of the deities. Here one has a chance to unify with the identities of the celestial beings.

No matter which way one envisions the Summerland, its purpose is to prepare the soul for its new life. The process ages the soul in reverse; it becomes younger and younger until it is ready again to inhabit a new blessed infant. However, different souls may take more or less time to complete this process. That is to say, a soul that is 85 years old will not necessarily take only 85 years to grow young again.

Conclusion

As you might be able to tell by the wide variety of belief systems, Wicca is not a prescriptive religion. Wicca is a religion that encourages all seekers to find their own paths, and judgment from other Wiccans is highly frowned upon. There is not a right or wrong way to be a Wiccan. It is all about pursuing what calls to you, as long as that path does no harm to others.

CHAPTER 4: WICCAN TOOLS

ALTARS AND ALTAR TOOLS

Wiccans maintain an altar. An *altar* is a sacred space cultivated by a Wiccan for meditation, prayer, offerings, spells, and divination. The altar can also be a space to connect with and worship deities. Altars are decorated with tools, crystals, art, and other things to make them unique and to help them channel the desired energies. Some Wiccans maintain multiple altars for different purposes.

The altar is the heart of one's sacred space. It is an area of concentrated energy, the seat of a Wiccan's worship. While in most organized religions the altar is found at the front of a congregation, inaccessible to the congregants, the altar in Wicca is very personal. The altar is not shared with a whole community; it is a place for private worship and solitary devotion to the sacred.

Building your first altar can seem daunting, but it is an opportunity to create something completely unique. For some it is so intimidating that it is put off. Your altar doesn't have to mimic anyone else's or have significance to anyone except for you. As long as the items on your altar are meaningful to you, that is all that matters.

Conversely, over-excitement can lead to a crowded altar covered with distracting trinkets that will only serve to collect dust. You want your altar to contain useful things. Altars are dynamic as well; what may be useful on your altar at first may eventually have fully served its purpose and need to be replaced as your beliefs and Craft develop.

Before we look at the different types of altars, it is important to understand the tools of the altar and their purposes, significances, and uses. The four main tools of the altar are the athame, the wand, the chalice, and the pentacle, each representing a different element. These four tools appear in the minor arcana of tarot, known as Swords, Cups, Pentacles, and Wands in the deck. The next sections will cover other important tools as well.

Don't worry about collecting all the tools as a beginner. The point is to learn about these tools and understand their uses. No tools are necessary to practice Wicca, but as you develop your practice you're likely to begin accruing them.

ATHAMES

An athame is a special dagger used for magickal rituals. The athame often is double-edged, with a pointed, sharp tip. Athames should be used with great care to prevent harm during use. Respect the athame as you would any other kind of knife. The handle of the athame is often inscribed with symbols or sigils. These carvings can vary depending on which tradition the practitioner is a part of.

The purpose of the athames are not to cut things, but rather to direct energy during the ritual. Cutting is considered a mundane task, and athames are reserved for the sacred. The athame represents the fire element. It is used to cast circles by outlining their circumference. The athame wards off negative energies and spirits during magickal work.

Bolines

A boline is a ritual knife used for more mundane tasks than the athame. Traditionally the blade is one-sided and straight, but it is becoming more and more common to find them in a crescent shape to invoke the moon and the Triple Goddess. The boline has a white handle rather than a black one, and is usually smaller than an athame. The boline is used to cut herbs and cord, and to carve wands and candles.

Pentacles

While the pentacle and the pentagram are related, they are not the same. To use the words interchangeably is incorrect, and it is important to know the difference.

The pentagram symbol is a five-pointed star contained in a circle. It is a type of talisman and can also be worn as an amulet. The five points on the pentagram represent many things. They represent the five elements. For Wiccans who worship The Horned God and The Triple Goddess, the five points also represent the two horns of the God and the three forms of the Goddess.

However, a ritual pentacle is different from the simple symbol pentagram. The pentacle is drawn as a pentagram, but also includes other writing. A ritual pentagram is often the centerpiece of the altar. It can be used to summon spirits or energies. The pentagram can be made from many natural materials, such as wood or paper. Within the pentagram, the words and symbols of whatever is being summoned are drawn.

Chalices

A chalice is a cup used for ritual purposes, often resembling a goblet. A chalice may be filled with wine, whiskey, beer, water, or a number of other fluids with magickal properties depending on what the ritual is for. The ancient Romans would drink from chalices at banquets and feasts, and at the dawn of Christianity chalices were used for ritual purposes.

The chalice represents the element of water, and represents the womb. If one worships a female deity, it could represent the womb of that deity and be used to encourage fertility. The base of the chalice represents the physical world. The stem of the chalice symbolizes the connection between the mind, the body, and the spirit. The rim is that from which we receive spiritual energy, if the chalice is used to drink from.

When used in combination with an athame, the chalice and the athame together represent the feminine womb of the Goddess and the masculine phallus of the God coming together to create.

Wands

A wand is a thin, straight carved piece of wood, ivory, metal, or even crystal. The wand is meant to be hand-held. Originally, wands were supposed to stretch from the tip of the middle finger to the elbow, but as tradition has evolved wands have become smaller. Wand traditions trace back to ancient Egypt, where wands were buried in tombs for souls to use in the afterlife. The Hellenistic God Hermes/Mercury is also depicted as having used a wand.

Wands are commonly carved from wood of sacred trees, such as willow, elder, and oak. However, with new technology wands can be made from many materials. Some modern wands are made entirely of crystal or have crystal tips attached.

While the most effective wands are handcrafted, store-bought wands also work if you feel a connection with them.

Candles

Candles are a primary tool for Wiccans, and their different colors are used for different purposes. During a ritual they are placed at the four corners of the ritual circle to represent the presence of the four elements Fire, Wind, Earth, and Water (Aether is represented by the practitioners themselves).

Candles can be consecrated and charged for use by cleansing and anointing them with concentrated essential oils. Always do your research before using an oil, because some are more flammable than others, and you don't want an out of control blaze on your hands. Many Wiccans also sprinkle dried herbs over the candles to invoke their properties.

The colors of the candles are very important to for rituals and spells. Luckily, candles can often be found for low prices at your local dollar store, or in bulk online. Below is a brief review of the various candle colors and what they represent and invoke.

White: unity; spiritual truth; strength; peace and purity; breaking curses; meditation; purification

Yellow: persuasion; creativity; confidence and charisma; improving memory and studying

Green: nature, renewal, and fertility; healing; money and prosperity; emotional soothing and balance

Pink: love and strengthening friendships; femininity; spiritual healing; warding away evil

Red: strength and vitality; power; sexuality; passion; protection; the cycle of reincarnation

Orange: strength, courage, and authority; concentration; encouragement

Blue: psychic powers and spiritual awareness; wisdom and intelligence; harmony and balance; dreams of prophecy; protection while sleeping

Purple: mysticism; ambition; inspiration and idealism; heightening psychic abilities; breaking curses

Brown: animal healing; protection of animals; attracting money; solving domestic issues; finding lost objects

Gold: masculinity; intuition; persuasion and charm; protection; gaining luck and fortune quickly

Silver: removing negativity and encouraging stability; neutrality; developing psychic ability

Black: loss, grief, disappointment, and sadness; depression; absorbing and destroying evil and discord; protection from retribution

If a spell calls for a candle color you don't currently have, white candles are often used as a neutral acceptable replacement. It helps to carve a sigil in the candle to endow it with the energy of the colored candle you are replacing.

INCENSE

Incense is another important tool for many Wiccans. Incense is a substance, usually found in the form of a stick of infused herbs, which can be burned to release a fragrant smoke. Thought to have originally been used by Egyptians, the practice spread far and wide, adopted by Romans and Greeks and pagans worldwide.

Incense represents four elements at once. It is created from materials from the Earth by soaking them in Water. Then it is ignited with Fire, upon which time it wafts smoke through the Air. Some Wiccans consider its connection to Air to be the strongest, because it is an aesthetic representation of Air and helps us see the movement of the air around us.

Incense is held in a special container called a censer. This can take many forms. It could be a flat, straight piece of wood or other material upon which the ash can fall. Some witches fill a ceramic or metal cauldron with coal and burn incense within the cauldron. For certain rituals, ashes are important, so often times the ashes are saved to use in other spells and rituals.

There is an enormous variety of incense to choose from, but there are definitely types that are more commonly used. Frankincense is used to invoke masculine power and the sun. It is burned to encourage deep spirituality and purification. Myrrh is similar in function to Frankincense, but is a feminine incense that also promotes healing. Pine and Cedar incense are used to cleanse a space. Copal is also used for cleansing, but is often used specifically to cleanse objects.

Another form of incense use is the use of dried bundles of white sage. The tips of the bundles are lit, while the user holds the base where the sage is tied together with string. The user then cleanses whatever needs to be cleansed. It could be tools, or a space. It is often used to dispel negative energies and spirits from entire houses, especially when one has just moved in. This process is called *smudging*.

Types of Altars

One of the first steps to building your own altar is choosing what kind of altar you want. This will help you decide what should be present and what can be left out and used for other purposes.

Shrines

A shrine is an altar created for the purpose of venerating a deity, or less commonly for ancestor worship. A shrine is the perfect place to pray, commune with your deity, and make offerings. Making offerings, such as flowers, herbs, or alcohol, brings you closer to the deity. Offerings also encourage the deity to guide you in general, or to help you with a specific task.

Shrines are typically simple, because they are a focal point and therefore should have a clear, focused energy. A representation of the focus of the shrine is usually used, whether it's a statue or a drawing or photograph. Candles are placed on the shrine to "activate" the energy of the shrine. Small decorations such as vases are good ways to keep fresh offerings present, and also a good way to remember Wiccan veneration of all that is natural.

Really, that is all that is necessary for a shrine. Simplicity is the name of the game with this type of altar. Of course, you can add stones, crystals, and other things that channel or remind you of the subject of your worship. You should carefully consider what you add, though, to prevent your shrine from looking like a New Age flea market display.

During Samhain, ancestral shrines are much more elaborate. Ancestral shrines are decorated with photos of the ancestor, as well as personal belongings of theirs. Seasonal decorations such as apples, pumpkins, and root vegetables are often piled high as offerings to the departed. For a Samhain shrine, color is also important. Rich deep colors that represent the end of fall are used such as black, gold, and burgundy.

Ritual Altars

A ritual altar is more elaborately done because it includes the tools necessary to perform the ritual. Ritual altars are used for occasions such as Esbats or festivals. A full ritual altar often includes an athame, wand, cup, pentagram, and candles (often many of them in different colors).

As a result of all the tools that are usually present during a full-blown ritual, these altars are usually quite large and often temporary. Ritual altars are typically constructed outdoors, where the connection with nature is strongest.

Working Altar

A working altar is one prepared for functional, practical magickal use. While some work can be completed in a single session, other ritual sessions or spells may require you to return to the altar multiple times. Thus, these altars are often more permanent than ritual altars.

This type of altar should be extremely focused and contain no more pieces than is absolutely necessary for the work being done. Excess tools and trinkets will distract from the magickal work and divert energy to other places.

Personal Altar

A personal altar is more permanent, although the pieces included on the altar will change over time as your needs change. This kind of altar is often elaborately decorated with images, cloths, photos, crystals, candles, incense, and flowers. A personal altar is used to generate the desired vibrations. It can be focused on one particular energy, but in this case it does not have to be.

With any type of altar one should be cautious of clutter. Don't hold onto items without meaning to you, or that have worn out their usefulness. It's easy to become attached to material things, but this is contradictory to the Wiccan path. It is not the material things a Wiccan owns that gives them power. The power comes from within. If you're having trouble with materialism, take time to enjoy nature and remember the true roots of Wicca.

Crystals

Gemstones and crystals are commonly used by Wiccans to channel certain cosmic energies in their day-to-day practices, or on special occasions. This section will teach you about what energies are held by which crystals and gemstones, and will also discuss how crystals can be used in magic.

There are a large range of purposes that crystals can be used for in magic. Crystals can be worn in jewelry to help you guide a certain vibration into your life on the go, for example. Crystals are also commonly found on the altars of many Wiccans. Whether you're looking to be more creative, be luckier in your love life, or be more in-tune with nature, there's a gemstone that will match the needs of your practice at any time in your life.

All stones can be charged, just like spells or water. Stones are great vessels for energy, and can be charged in the light of the full moon or by the bright shining sun during the day. Stones can be cleansed in a variety of ways, but some stones may be corroded by water so it is important to research the physical properties of the stone.

Cleansing a stone is often done once a month during the full moon, simply by leaving the crystals and stones out in the moonlight to refresh and rejuvenate their energies. At other times of the month, stones can be cleansed by burning cleansing herbs, most commonly sage. The stone should be held over the smoke and usually an incantation is read.

Stones associated with the element of your Astrological sign or with elements that resonate strongly with you may be easier for you to channel with, but any Wiccan can still work with any stone. Stones can also be attuned to your entire Astrological chart (e.g. using Amethyst to heal your love life if your Venus is a water sign).

AGATE

Agate can have many unique appearances, but generally has lush gold or bronze bands rippling through this unique stones. Blues, whites, and purples are also common colors found blended into this earthy stone.

Being connected with the Earth elements and the brow chakra, Agate is a stone that helps focus the mind. It can relieve depression and give you more energy. If you're feeling down and out, and could use some stress relief, carrying agate with you, wearing it as jewelry, or placing agate on your altar are magic practices that could offer you relief.

Amethyst

This well-known and often-used favorite comes in a deep purple color, and is known to be associated with the Astrological sign Aquarius. This violet quartz crystal is a stone filled with water energies.

Associated with the crown of the head, amethyst is a healing stone, often used in rituals to heal anxiety or mood disorders. Amethyst can also be used to help cleanse a ritual space of negative spirits or energies that might be present, making it the perfect crystal to keep in an altar.

Bloodstone

Bloodstone is usually an olive green color with brown speckles decorating it. This stone is also known for healing properties, and as a fire stone is associated with Mars and the sun.

Bloodstone is particularly useful for its fertility properties, so if you're looking to start or grow your family, or if you're intending to channel fertility for another person, this is a great option for you.

Diamonds

Diamonds are clear stones, with a foggy appearance when uncut and a very radiant, sparkly appearance when cut that catches the light from every angle. These stunning stones are associated with the Sun and fire energy.

Diamonds can be used for the classic reasons of encouraging cosmic encounters that lead to engagement and marriage, but are another great stone for the treatment of fertility issues as well. A diamond can be used to treat infertility in men or women, including treating impotence in the bedroom.

Garnet

This burgundy stone can resemble the deep red of blood, or appear more purple. Garnet is connected with the Goddess Persephone and the fire element.

Garnets are strongly connected with moon magic, and can be charged by being left out to absorb the energy from a full moon, blue moon, blood moon, etc. This stone is tied to the complexities of a woman's body, and can be used to encourage fertility and regulate the menstrual cycle. A charged garnet will also boost other stones present at an altar.

Hematite

While unknown to many outside of magic practice, hematite is a favorite amongst Wiccans. This gorgeous silver-colored stone has ties with fire and the planet Saturn.

Hematite is used for healing, and is especially potent for treating blood disorders, infections, and fevers. A protection stone, it is great to have around on you to ward off negative energy and to protect you from hostile spirits. As jewelry, this stone can increase psychic awareness and magic ability.

Jade

Jade is a peaceful stone that is typically known for its beautiful green hue, though it comes in other colors as well. Associated with earth elements, this stone is a symbol of serenity.

Jade can be used to channel calmness, true love, and innocence. Jade is also used to balance the humors of the body in the liver and spleen.

Jasper

Jasper has a red-brown marble color, often with flecks of white mixed in. Associated strongly with earth elements, this stone is perfect for Tauruses, Virgos, and Capricorns.

Jasper can be used in rituals to ground and center your magic and your mind, perfect for concentration when working on spells or studying. It also has healing properties, specifically good for cancer treatment. You can also place a piece under your mattress to bring an extra spark to your love life!

Lapis Lazuli

This stone may not be as shiny as some others, but the range of blues from light cerulean to deep royal blue make it undeniably elegant. Lapis Lazuli is often spotted or banded, depending on where the stone originally grew.

Lapis Lazuli is known to alleviate depression and soothe the mind. It is the best stone for meditation and trance exercises.

Moonstone

A soft opalescent milky white, moonstone has magical connections with -- you guessed it! The moon. It also is connected with lunar deities, and the number three. Any Wiccan who is working with the number three or worships a deity involved with the number three will find use out of this brilliant stone.

This is another great stone to charge under special moon events. Because the moon is associated with femininity, this stone can be used to promote fertility and regulate the menstrual cycle. In terms of magical qualities, moonstone can help you get in touch with your wisdom when you need it the most. Moonstone is also great for intuition, and is the perfect stone to keep present at a tarot reading or other divination project.

Quartz Crystal

Quartz crystals are clear, but often have small milky flaws in them. Wiccan highly value these flaws, and for this reason a "crystal ball" should always be made from quartz rather than glass. The unique flaws in a Quartz are capable of snagging onto passing energies, which makes them useful in a spherical form or in a pendulum shape for divination.

Clear Crystal Quartz is an all-around positivity stone, and is very commonly worn in jewelry. The stone gives positive energy, general cleansing, and has gentle healing properties. It is an excellent stone for beginners who may feel overwhelmed by the energy of more powerful stones.

Rose Quartz

The Rose Quartz is a fan favorite amongst Wiccans, both for its beauty and its gentle energy. Like Quartz Crystal, Rose Quartz is valued for its flaws and the variety of patterns in which it can manifest. Rose Quartzes are a soft rosy pink. Some are more clear, while others have a pink milky swirl within them.

Rose Quartz can be used to promote happiness, for new or deeper love, to help encourage forgiveness, and to bring about peace. It is a symbol of love and healthy relationships. The love radiated by a Rose Quartz is not only love for and from others, but love for the self as well.

Tiger's Eye

Tiger's Eye is a warm golden stone with deep brown streaks that go all the way through the length of the stone. The gold has a very distinctive shimmer in the light, and is quite a sight to behold. Tiger's Eye is a strong stone for protection.

The main purpose of Tiger's Eye is to give oneself clarity. Tiger's Eye helps you see through illusions, and helps you to identify the truth. This stone can also help us learn inner truths about ourselves.

Turquoise

Known for its striking bright blue with veins of brown, Turquoise is strongly associated with the astrological sign Sagittarius. Turquoise is another stone that promotes complete positivity. Turquoise is known for attuning to its user, focusing their energy wherever it is needed most.

This is the ultimate stone for healing. It promotes emotional, physical, mental, and spiritual well-being. It neutralizes negative energy and provides strong protection. It also promotes joy, friendship, and relaxation.

Grimoires: A Witch's Diary

A *grimoire* is often simply explained as a spellbook. Indeed, grimoires are often used to collect information about how to perform spells properly for easy, quick reference and access. While you can buy one, it is encouraged to eventually move on to create your own that is specific to your needs for your practice.

Also known as a Book of Shadows, this journal contains more than just spells. This is a place where Wiccans collect all their knowledge of the Craft for easy reference. Grimoires often contain information about herbs, crystals, astrology, moon cycles, and much more. This book is a Wiccan's go-to resource for their Craft.

Because of the critical focus on nature, Wiccans are constantly learning about the world around them. This often includes having a wide range of knowledge about natural materials, their correspondences, and their uses. Any magickal information may be recorded in a grimoire.

Wiccans have widely different traditions about how to create a grimoire. Many covens have specific rules and layouts to follow. This often includes consecrating the grimoire to endow it with sacred energy, and cleansing the book of any energy it may have previously held. Some Wiccans choose to mask the information by using codes, cyphers, or symbols to prevent the grimoire from being used by others.

Your grimoire should be created following your own intuition. If you want to use symbols and codes, that's your own decision. What you choose to write in your grimoire is also done at your own discretion.

In today's modern age, many choose to create a grimoire online using any of the multitudes of journaling software available. The benefit to this method is that the grimoire would be searchable by keywords, and it could have a password protecting its contents. This option is great for having your grimoire on the go without needing a physical copy.

Many people feel discouraged by poor handwriting or less than perfect art skills, and a digital grimoire offers a creative way to collect information without needing technical crafting skills.

Another method especially good for beginners is to create a binder. This allows you to move pages around or remove them without damaging the book. You can add dividers to separate clear sections to find things easily. For those without artistic ability, this is a good option because you can create and print out your own pages to go in the grimoire. For example, you can include photos of herbs and plants to help identify them alongside information about their medicinal and magickal properties.

Finally, a grimoire can be made from a bound journal. Often, these journals are decorated with magick symbols such as the symbol of the Triple Goddess. Some like to glue small flat crystals to the front, and to press flowers and herbs between the pages.

For beginners, many experienced Wiccans recommend starting two grimoires. One is the "final" grimoire, which contains your best art and your finest handwriting. The other would be a draft of a grimoire, where messiness is allowed. This allows you to experiment with the order of your entries and practice what you would like to write and draw before making it "official". Another method of having two grimoires is to have one for day-to-day witchcraft, and one for special occasions.

The most common advice given to beginners is not to take the grimoire so seriously that you are afraid to begin. The grimoire should come naturally. It is something to enjoy and cherish, not a chore or obligation. Work at your own pace, and experiment with different methods to find out what is right for you.

HERBS

Herbalism, or the study of the medicinal and magickal properties of herbs, is very popular amongst Wiccans. Wiccans believe herbs are not only beneficial because of their own characteristics, but also because they are endowed with the energy of the Earth. Each herb has unique uses, and Wiccans utilize them in a variety of ways.

It is important here to note that although Wiccans practice herbal remedies, this is not a replacement for professional medical treatment. It is a supplementary practice rather than a replacement for modern medicine.

Wiccans use herbs as natural remedies for minor pains and conditions, like headaches or indigestion. Many herbs can be made into teas or used to season food. Some Wiccans enjoy creating their own tea blends. Consuming an herb can also help you channel the magickal properties of that herb. For example, saffron is thought to boost creativity and is often enjoyed as a tea with a rich red hue.

Some Wiccans choose to grow their own herbs to connect with the earth and the Wheel of the Year. Many herbs can be grown indoors, if a garden is not available. Herbs are traditionally harvested in the morning, before the heat of the day sets in but after the sun has dried the dew from the plants. Harvested herbs can be used fresh in cooking, or hung upside-down to dry. Dried herbs can be used in kitchen witchery, and also can be burned in small quantities as incense.

The three most commonly used herbs in witchcraft are rosemary, thyme, and lavender. These three are considered essentials, although all herbs have their own unique values. They can be used fresh, dried, as incense, or as an essential oil. Here's what you need to know about the big three.

Rosemary

Rosemary is associated with the Sun and the astrological sign Leo. The primary correspondences for rosemary are creativity, wisdom, vitality, healing, protection, purification, love, strength, and stress relief. Rosemary is also known to provide mental clarity and confidence.

Rosemary is an acceptable substitute for Frankincense, an herb that grows in few climates and tends to be expensive. Rosemary can also be placed under a pillow to promote new ideas and creativity. A rosemary bath provides invigoration and positive energy.

Thyme

Thyme is associated with Mercury and Venus, as well as the element water and the astrological signs Taurus and Libra. Thyme makes a delicious tea. The primary correspondences for thyme are beauty, courage, psychic knowledge, healing, love, and purification. Thyme is also known to be very grounding, and can help avoid conflict.

Thyme is a favorite herb of the Fae. Planting thyme in your garden or home may attract them, so be sure to keep the thyme plants healthy! Faeries can be tricksters when they're displeased.

LAVENDER

Lavender is associated with the planet Mercury, the element air, and the astrological signs Gemini and Virgo. Its fragrance is very gentle and relaxing, and because of this it is often used to create "dream pillows". Dream pillows have lavender in their stuffing to help you fall asleep and to cast away bad dreams.

Lavender's primary correspondences are love, beauty, protection, relaxation, sleep, and psychic knowledge. Lavender is a lovely addition to bath water, to fully appreciate its lovely fragrance and to take time to unwind after a long day.

FAMILIARS SPIRITS: ANIMAL COMPANIONSHIP

Recorded accounts of familiar spirits go back to the Medieval ages, and the practice itself certainly existed before it was ever written down. A familiar is an animal, usually small, that acts as a companion and spirit guide. However, almost any animal can serve as a familiar.

In Wiccan history, witches who worked with familiar spirits were severely persecuted. A familiar was speculated to be a demon or some other evil paranormal force that could shape-shift into the form of an animal. Familiars were thought to serve witches by spying for them and cursing their enemies. All familiars were assumed by Christians to be malevolent.

Witches in the Middle Ages were often ostracized, marginalized, and lonely. For this reason, many began to keep small pets around for companionship. During the witch hysteria of the Middle Ages, owning a black cat was sufficient enough reason for extensive investigation into a woman's life.

Familiars were often used as evidence in witch trials in 16th and 17th century in England and Scotland. Leviticus, the third book of the Old Testament, mentions familiar spirits by name, and calls for anyone who works with familiars to be stoned to death. Thousands of women were executed, many of them having no connection at all with Wicca.

For the modern-day witch it is a happy blessing to gain this kind of bond with an animal. Keeping a familiar is a way for witches, especially those in the city, to cultivate a rapport with nature. Animals are much more in-tune with both natural and supernatural phenomena. Animals are sensitive to weather, and will often begin to act strangely if malevolent spirits are present.

By developing a relationship with a familiar, one can strengthen psychic abilities. The familiar can act as a medium between this world and the next. If you are attuned to the body language of your pet, you can recognize when supernatural beings are nearby.

Other Wiccan Tools

There are several other more minor, but still important tools that Wiccans use regularly.

Bells are an important Wiccan tool. As you start to read and learn about spells, don't be surprised to find that many include the ringing of a bell several times. Bells mark a transition in a ritual. A bell is often rung to begin and end a ritual, and may also be used throughout the ritual if the ritual has multiple steps.

Cauldrons are real, yes, and used by Wiccans in the Craft. They are probably the most well-known Wiccan tool, but there are many misconceptions about what they are used for. The optimal material for a cauldron is ceramic or cast iron, because they are intended to withstand large amounts of heat. Cauldrons can be filled with materials for a potion, for example, with a fire burning under the cauldron to warm and activate the ingredients. They can also be filled with small coals and used to burn herbs and incense.

Brooms are another commonly known Wiccan tool, but they aren't used for flight as seen in cartoons and movies. Wiccans use brooms to symbolically sweep away lingering energies. Because it is used for this ritual purpose, brooms are often handmade.

Finally, bowls are a simple and easily accessible tool for any Wiccan. Bowls are used to hold water (rainwater is best but any naturally occurring water may be used), salt, petals, herbs, or any number of other ingredients.

Conclusion

After all this discussion of the tools of the Craft, it is important to remember as a beginner that absolutely none of these tools are a requirement. Wicca is about communing with nature. Communing with nature attunes your natural abilities.

If you don't have access to tools yet, take advantage of the natural world around you. Go outside, visit a park, go on a hike, admire the mountains and the sea, meditate over the flow of the rivers, absorb the light of the sun and the moon, take time to stargaze. There are plenty of ways to connect with your inner Wiccan without spending any money at all.

CHAPTER 5: PRACTICING MAGIC

Once you feel in touch with nature and your inherent ability, it is wise to start learning about and practicing beginner magick. There's no need to rush into elaborate, confusing rituals with ingredients you've never heard of. With practice and patience, you will feel more in tune with your abilities. As you start to explore, you will eventually learn what elements of the Craft suit you best. Experimenting is important in early phases. The best way to learn is to read and put your new knowledge into action.

This chapter focuses on two things. The first is education. Even if you're not ready for spells yet, learning about them is the first step. Secondly, this chapter endeavors to teach you beginner's magick that is simple, effective, and harmless.

MAGICK AND THE PHYSICAL WORLD

While Wiccans believe we all are born with inherent magickal talents, these talents are not absurd fictional miracles. There's no spell that will change the color of your eyes or make you taller, no spell that can create something from nothing. When learning about your talents and abilities, it is important to remember to be realistic. While some Wiccans have talents that are certainly spectacular, they operate within the laws of science.

Due to Wiccan reverence for nature, there is also Wiccan reverence for science. Wiccan beliefs do not contradict scientific findings. On the contrary, Wiccans are motivated to learn about science to deepen their understanding of the natural world, how it was formed, and most importantly how to preserve it.

Interestingly, scientific advancement has confirmed much that witches already knew. Witches of old had an intuitive understanding of the energy of all things, in addition to a wide range of knowledge regarding herbal medicine. Older scientific views perceived mind and matter to be separate completely (recall the phrase "mind over matter"). Witches have always known that mind and matter are one and the same, and of course science has confirmed that the mind functions because of the mechanisms of the brain, which is made of physical matter.

The brain is a powerful organ, and the power of thought is not to be underestimated. Thought-based practices, within Wicca but also in traditions like Buddhism that promote meditation and mindfulness, have been proven to cause actual positive change in our lives. Wiccans promote a focus on the positive, and cleansing of that which is negative. However, that is not to say that changing the way we think is a simple endeavor.

The Hermetic Principles or Hermetic Laws are a set of ancient laws that are important to Wiccan practice. We will not cover all of the seven principles here, because it is not obligatory to know them, especially for beginners, but we will touch on the most important ones and their basis in science.

An important Hermetic Principle is the Law of Attraction. This law simply states that positive thinking encourages positive outcomes. Part of the reason for this is because when we are in a positive state of mind, we are more likely to be aware and in control of our emotions and behaviors. Magick is of course, more complex than thinking positively, but regardless there is a sound psychological basis for this principle within modern scientific understandings of the brain and behavioral psychology.

The most emphasized Hermetic Principle in Wicca is called the Law of Correspondence. If you've ever heard the Wiccan phrase "as above, so below", this law is the basis for that saying. This means that whatever affects the macrocosm of the Universe in turn affects the microcosm, and vice versa. Some scientists refer to this as the Butterfly Effect. The Law of Correspondence also teaches us that time is only one dimension, in a Universe that experiences neither time nor space.

Because the Law of Correspondence teaches us that the Higher Planes and the Lower Planes are interconnected, intentions are very important when conducting magick practices. Whatever energy you put into the Universe may have a great effect, and may even be harmful to another, which is against the Wiccan creed.

Modern physics has discovered that at the atomic level, all material things are composed of matter and energy. This is compatible with the Hermetic Law of Vibration. All atoms vibrate and therefore constantly emit energy. Atoms vibrate at different frequencies, which creates the different states of matter (solids, liquids, and gases).

We perceive colors because of the phenomena of vibration. Light vibrates at different frequencies, which creates the spectrum of color. Witches can and do pick up on and use these different energies in their practice. By understanding the energy of the world around us, Wiccans tune into that energy and are able to connect it to their own personal energy. Wiccans can also use this energy conversely to communicate with the energy of the Universe.

Chakra therapy is based on this understanding of color (amongst other things). Aligning one's chakras is a way to rebalance one's energy to reap spiritual and physical benefits.

Because the physical world involves so many complex variables, it is impossible even for physicists and other scientists to accurately account for every unknown. The same is true for Wiccans. Spells and rituals may go awry due to forces that had not been accounted for.

MOON PHASES AND LUNAR EVENTS

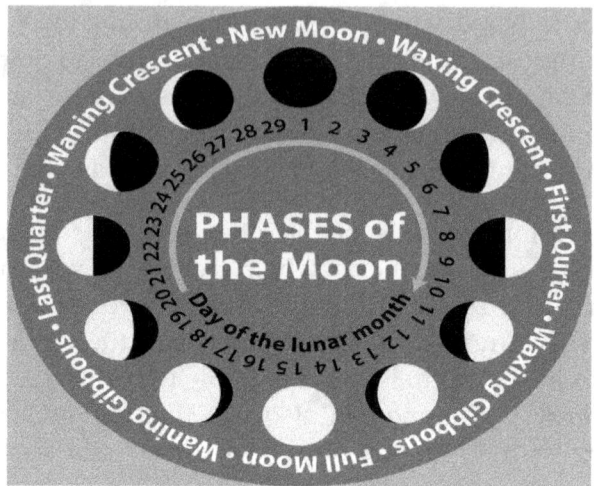

Whether or not you feel a significant connection to the moon, the phases of the moon have an effect on the magickal abilities of Wiccans. Different phases of the moon call for different phases of reflection. When the moon is full, the time is ripe for magick. It is best to keep a lunar calendar or use an app with reminders, to be aware of how the moon may be affecting you.

The cycles of the moon represent, for traditional Wiccans, the life cycle of women embodied by the Triple Goddess. The Triple Goddess in the form of the moon experiences birth at the new moon, and completion at the full moon. When the moon is waxing, or growing brighter, a Wiccan's power is growing stronger day by day. The waxing moon symbolizes the Goddess's journey from Maiden to Mother. When the moon is waning, it is time for Wiccans to rest, reflect, study, and prepare for the next lunar cycle. The waxing moon represents the Goddess's journey from Mother to Crone.

The new moon is a time to think about your goals for the coming month. It is a time of reflection rather than a time for action. The next moon phase, the waxing crescent moon, is a time to begin creating plans on how to achieve those goals. The first quarter moon is when Wiccans can begin to move towards these goals and think creatively. The waxing moon is a time of significant power, where Wiccans are in harmony with the forces of nature and prepare the rituals for the coming full moon.

During the full moon, there are many things that can be done. Crystals, water, and other magickal tools can be set out for cleansing and to charge with lunar energy. If you work with a group, consider having an esbat to celebrate, socialize, and practice together. If you are a solitary witch, the full moon is a perfect time to perform spells, enchant objects, or do any other important magickal work. Don't forget in all the hustle and bustle to stop and enjoy the beauty of this special evening!

During the waxing period of the moon, celebrate all you have achieved that month. Remember that every day you become wiser, even as the magick of the lunar cycle winds down. Let go of the past, and understand that mistakes are opportunities for growth. During the dark moon, remember that all things happen in their own time. Banishing spells are strongest during the dark moon, but take great care. The spell may be more powerful than you realize, and someone you could have reconciled with may disappear from your life permanently.

A lunar eclipse occurs when the moon is completely covered by the shadow of the Earth. While logic may tell us this would make the moon appear dark, the moon actually turns a magnificent, ethereal red color. It is a reflection of a million sunrises. This is often referred to as a blood moon.

Some Wiccans believe that during a total lunar eclipse, the moon represents every part of its cycle at once. This is because in a single night you can watch the Earth's shadow turn the moon through every phase, a complete waxing and waning. This effect is useful for multi-part spells that might otherwise have to be spread out throughout a month.

About every two or three years there comes a month where the moon will be full twice. This second full moon is known as a blue moon. This is the origin of the phrase "once in a blue moon". That saying has significance to Wiccans. A blue moon is thought to be twice as powerful as a full moon, and therefore magick can be performed that could only happen once in a blue moon.

Chakras: Balancing Mind, Body, and Spirit

Chakra is a sanskrit word meaning "wheel". Chakras are energy centers that are associated with an area of the body. Each chakra is associated with a color, and certain abilities and bodily functions. If your chakras are unbalanced, you may feel spiritually blocked. This happens even to experienced Wiccans. The trick is learning to identify the symptoms of imbalance. Chakras are also associated with physical and mental ailments, but aligning your chakras is not an adequate replacement for professional medical attention.

The concept of chakras comes from ancient Indian Hinduism, as well as Japanese, Chinese, and Tibetan Buddhism. The tradition was introduced to the West by renowned psychologist Carl Gustav Jung.

Chakra blockages can develop from trauma, negative experiences, unhealthy beliefs, insecurity, or self-doubt. The day-to-day stresses of life also gradually misalign the chakras. Chakra alignment can be done several ways, and is actually quite simple. It is an excellent way for a beginning Wiccan to get in touch with their mind, body, and spirit.

There are seven main chakras and signs of imbalance:

1. Root Chakra. An unaligned root chakra will cause you to have difficulties meeting your basic needs. The color of the root chakra is red, and it is located at the front of the body near the pelvis.

2. Sacral Chakra. Imbalance of this chakra manifests as confusion or difficulty with sexuality, and infertility. Its color is scarlet, and it is located in the lower abdomen near the stomach.

3. Solar Plexus Chakra. This chakra is linked to unhealthy eating habits, substance abuse, and depression. The color associated with it is yellow, and it is located above the belly button and below the sternum.

4. Heart Chakra. Signs of imbalance of the heart chakra include difficulty with love, relationships and compassion. Its color is gold, and its location is the center of the upper chest.

5. Throat Chakra. The throat chakra is associated with your inner voice and your ability to communicate. Imbalance can cause anxiety, nightmares, and a fear of speaking your truth. Its color is blue-green, and it is located on the front base of the neck.

6. Third Eye Chakra. Symptoms of imbalance with this chakra may cause a lack of inspiration, problems sleeping, and psychic misinterpretations. The color associated with the third eye chakra is indigo, and it is located above and between the eyes, on the forehead.

7. Crown Chakra. The crown chakra is associated with inspiration and oneness with the cosmos. Imbalance may cause a loss of spiritual direction, headaches, confusion, and worry. Its color is violet, and it is located at the top of the head, slightly to the back,

The simplest way to align your chakras is through meditation. This is a visualization exercise, but it is important not only to "see" but to feel the energies as well. First, sit up straight and allow your shoulders to fall in a relaxed position. Relax and prepare with some deep breathing. Next, imagine whichever chakra you wish to balance as an orb. The orb should be the color of the chakra. Then, breathe deeply and imagine each breath fills the orb up until it is the size of a beach ball. Acknowledge and cope with any emotional pain you may find.

If meditation isn't your thing, each chakra can also be aligned by communing with nature or engaging in a meaningful activity that exercises that specific energy. Wearing the color of the chakra and/or eating foods associated with that chakra will also restore balance.

The root chakra can be aligned by taking care of your physical body. Remember to exercise and get adequate rest. Working in a garden or making art with clay such as pottery will also align this chakra. Red foods like beets and pomegranates can help, too.

In order to balance the sacral chakra, it is best to seek an encounter with natural water. This could mean swimming in a lake, ocean, or river. It could also mean walking in the rain or watching a storm. Oranges and carrots are good options to align this chakra.

Balancing the solar plexus chakra is done through education. Read a book, take a class, do a crossword puzzle. Sunshine can also balance this point of energy. Chamomile and lemon teas are useful as well.

The heart chakra is balanced by nature walks and quality time with family and friends. Nurture your relationships and express love. Ginger is a wonderful remedy for the heart chakra.

Your throat chakra can be balanced by singing, doing creative writing, and having important, deep conversations. Blueberries nourish the inner voice associated with the throat chakra.

The third eye chakra is most effectively balanced by taking time to go stargazing or walking in the light of the moon. Keeping a journal can also balance your third eye chakra. Associated foods are figs and black currants.

Finally, to balance the crown chakra, try getting in touch with your dreams. This means both the dreams you have while asleep and your goals in life. Keep a dream journal or make a vision board to regain your direction. Plums, lavender, and amethyst are useful in restoring balance to this center of inspiring energy.

Keeping your energies in balance will help you achieve harmony on the inside and the outside. If you've never balanced your chakras before, it is recommended to do so before you begin practicing Wicca. If your energies aren't in sync, your spirit won't be either, and you won't be able to properly focus your magickal senses.

SPELLS

Spells are magickal rituals that require symbolism, specific materials, incantations, concentration, and faith. The purpose of spells is to channel energy to enact some kind of change in a situation. For example, an author experiencing writer's block may perform a spell for creativity.

Spells date back to ancient Egypt and the Zoroastrian Magi, who influenced the activities of Roman and Greek pagans. Ancient Norse traditions also included this sort of ritual magick.

Spells can be directed at the self or at another, and can be positive or negative. However, performing negative magick against someone else goes against the Wiccan rede to do no harm. In fact, it is unwise to cast any sort of spell on someone else without their informed consent. Positive spells are sometimes called "blessings", or more archaically "enchantments". Negative spells are known as "hexes" or "curses".

Spells follow a specific formula in order to achieve the desired magickal effect. While the formula is important, what is most important is your intention and focus. It is impossible to cast a spell you don't believe in. Remember to be patient as a beginner, because your abilities may not be honed enough to cast certain spells.

One important rule when doing any kind of magick but especially spells is to pull energy from sources around you. If you pull energy from only your own resources, you will often feel drained, lethargic, and sometimes even hungry. This is the reason spells typically involve tools, but energy can also be drawn from nature itself.

Regardless of what spell you choose to perform, there are steps you should take to prepare for the ritual beforehand. The first step is to prepare your body and your mind. It is recommended to bathe before performing a spell. Some witches anoint themselves with relevant oils. If you have a special attire you prefer to use to perform magick, make sure the clothes are clean. Take time to meditate to relax and focus the mind.

If you are working indoors the next step is to cleanse your workspace. This can be done using crystals, by sprinkling salt around the perimeter, or by smudging (burning) white sage. Other options sprinkling rainwater or water purified by the full moon. Clear the clutter from the area in which you plan to work so there will be no interfering energies or distractions.

Now it's time to draw your circle. Not all Wiccan traditions do this, but it is the dominant tradition. The circle is meant to channel energy from the four cardinal directions. Water is represented by the North, Air by the East, Fire from the South, and Earth from the West. Creating a circle consecrates the space. You can trace the circle with your finger or a wand or athame, or you can physically draw one. Inside the circle, draw a pentagram. This circle is called a pentacle.

What happens after this varies from spell to spell. As a beginner, you can learn spells from reputable sources online (beware of phonies), but eventually you will have enough knowledge to begin writing your own spells.

Spells typically have an incantation, or a spoken verse that invokes your desires. It is common for these verses to rhyme. The incantation can invoke a deity, or even a planet or the moon for assistance. Incantations should be finished with the phrase "so mote it be".

Spells typically end by casting off a symbolic item. It could be burning a sigil (see next section), burning herbs, or something as simple as snuffing out a candle. Do keep in mind that you should never blow a candle out if possible. There are special devices made to snuff candles, but you can also use sand or water.

The final part of a spell is giving thanks. This could be an expression of gratitude to nature or any spirits or deities you invoked to aid you.

SIGILS: THE CONDUITS OF INTENTION

Sigils are symbols that represent an intention. Commonly used for protection, sigils require activation. Some sigils can be activated merely with focused intention. Other Wiccans prefer to burn copies of sigils to release their energy. Sigils are considered to be a basic, easy form of magic, perfect for beginners.

While you can easily find sigils for anything you could think of online, creating sigils is typically considered a very personal thing. Creating your own sigils is easier than you think, and can actually be fun and meditative.

When creating your sigil, make sure you are in a calm, quiet place with minimal distractions. Because sigils are manifested intentions, it is important that you completely focus on your intention during the process of creating or carving a sigil. If you become distracted, it is highly recommended that you start from the beginning.

To create your own sigil, you must first decide what your intention is. Your intention should be put into the form of a short, simple sentence. For example, "I am safe and calm". Once you have your sentence, depending on your tradition, the vowels may be removed from the sentences. From the remaining consonants, use each only a single time in your sigil. For the sentence used as an example, the consonants used would be "m, s, f, n, d, l".

The next step is your opportunity to get creative and truly connect with the sigil. Using the remaining consonants from your intention sentence, begin to create a shape by connecting and overlapping the letters. You can make the letters into simpler shapes like swirls, lines, and circles. When you feel you have created a shape that represents your intention, you are finished.

It's fine if you don't like your first try. It's common for witches to take their time drafting different versions until they are satisfied with the aesthetic of the sigil. By drawing your own sigil, the sigil contains elements of your personal energy and can be more effective.

You can carve sigils into candles and burn the candle to activate the energy of the sigil. Some Wiccans use sigils in cooking. For example, a kitchen witch may draw a sigil on the bottom of a pie crust to infuse the pie with protective energy and love. Another easy way is to draw a sigil in a cup using honey before pouring tea over it. Some witches draw sigils in their private notebooks to protect them from prying eyes.

BATH MAGICK

Bath magick is a fun and easy way to begin performing rituals. It has the benefit of doubling as a form of self-care, which promotes self-worth and self-love. Loving the natural world includes loving oneself, as Wiccans believe we are united with nature. Cultivating a positive opinion of yourself will also increase your confidence in your abilities, and empower you to continue seeking knowledge and improving your craft!

Different bath products have different magickal uses. The ingredients used are important, but there are very few bath products made with ingredients that would manifest a bad result. Either way, researching the components of your bath products is a great way to begin committing correspondences to memory. Handmade bath products are better than those produced by machines, but use whatever is available to you.

Bath salts can be used when you want to cleanse your spirit and your subconscious mind. Both salt and water have purifying qualities. Bathing with salts is an excellent way to prepare for a spell. Bubble baths are useful for when you want to be immersed in something in the conscious mind. Being surrounded by bubbles is symbolic of being submersed in your desires, thereby willing positive things into existence. This is sometimes called manifesting.

Bath bombs symbolically explode to push something rapidly into existence. Maybe you want to be kinder, or more spontaneous. This is a high-energy way to manifest your intentions. Bars of soap are great for carving sigils in. Thoroughly washing your body in the soap also covers you with your intentions, and the lingering scent will carry those intentions with you throughout the day.

You can also add flower petals into the bath as well as some teas. Fruity teas should be avoided because sugar can cause yeast infections, but chamomile is a relaxing, safe option. Rose petals in the bath will encourage love and romance. Lavender promotes calmness and peace of mind.

The faucet of the bath can represent flushing new, pure vibrations into your life. The drain of the bath is also symbolic. It can either represent flushing out negative energy, or represent sending your intentions out into the world.

You can enhance the ritual by playing music that compliments your intentions, lighting candles, and by keeping crystals nearby. Many crystals will degrade if immersed in water, so this is not recommended.

Conclusion

Whether or not you choose to observe the year and a day guideline, it is wise to have a period dedicated to learning the craft before you begin your practice. This protects you and those around you from potential unintended effects of inexperienced magick. Only you know when you are truly ready to begin. Trust your instincts, but remember that it's not a race! Everything will come to you in your own time.

Chapter 6: Finding Your Niche

With all this new information, it's easy to become overwhelmed. But choosing your path in Wicca is all about what traditions, rituals, and practices you connect with the most. Your craft doesn't have to be like anyone else's, it can and in many ways should be completely unique to your spiritual needs and beliefs.

Some traditional Wiccans believe in the concept of "a year and a day". This is the idea that a beginning witch should devote a year and one day to only learning and studying the Craft. This is most common within covens that have an initiation process once this time period has passed. If you want to practice with a group, this learning period also gives you time to learn about and bond with the other Wiccans in your coven. It also provides time for a beginner to familiarize themselves with the rules and traditions of the group.

Some solitary witches value this tradition and follow it, but many Wiccans don't believe in an exact set period of time. Of course it is encouraged to learn about and understand the Craft before you practice, lest you make a mistake and cause yourself or someone else harm by accident. The learning period, however long it may be for you, is also a sign of respect for the Craft. It shows that you know Wicca is not a fad or a phase, but something to be taken seriously.

Choosing Your Path

Outside of the major traditions, there are still many different acknowledged "types" of witches. Most witches fall into more than one category. By learning about each path, you can start to see what might interest you, and do further research on that subject to begin to specialize your knowledge. Don't be afraid to change your mind, and don't be afraid to experiment, as long as you do no harm.

Eclectic witches are Wiccans who combine many different beliefs, ideas, and traditions into their practice. An eclectic witch may worship multiple pantheons. Eclectic witches value practices from all cultures. They may practice divination from different areas of the world. Eclectic witches are almost always solitary, meaning they don't work with a group though they may participate in community gatherings for festivals.

Green witches, also known as garden witches or forest witches, are attracted to all things green. Green witches practice most of their magick outdoors. Many keep personal gardens, or grow houseplants if a garden is not available to them. They have a deep love for plants, flowers, herbs, and trees. Green witches are able to sense and connect with the spirits of plants, and prefer to use home-grown items for their Craft. Some even make offerings to their plants, or place crystals in the soil if the plant is potted.

Green witches are herbalists who have a wide range of knowledge about their local flora. They can identify plants by sight. They also gain a large range of knowledge about medicinal and poisonous plants through their diligent, passionate studies.

A *hedge witch* is a Wiccan who is skilled with spirit work. These individuals cross the metaphorical hedge to the other side for answers and guidance. Hedge witch is the modern word for a shaman. Many witches prefer to avoid identifying as shamans unless they descend from a shamanistic culture, because it can be appropriative and disrespectful to claim another culture's title.

Hedge witches communicate with spirits in a variety of ways. This is called hedgecrossing, no matter what method is used. Some meet and speak with spirits through lucid dreams. Lucid dreaming often comes naturally to a hedge witch, but it is a skill most can learn. Astral projection and trances are other ways to communicate with the spirit world.

Kitchen witches reject a lot of traditional perspectives, and strongly believe in finding magick in the mundane. These individuals thrive while cooking, making teas, brews, and working with herb and spice blends to enchant meals and drinks. If these tasks need to be performed either way, why not make them magickal?

Kitchen witches imbue their cooking with medicinal and magickal properties. For example, one might season food with rosemary to provide protection for the family and friends who will consume the food. Kitchen witches often have collections of recipes passed down from many generations.

An *augury witch* is a Wiccan who is able to interpret natural omens. Augury is an ancient Roman tradition. Augury witches often work with travelers to help guide them along the correct path. Augurs may interpret weather patterns or the appearance of sacred animals such as birds.

Hereditary witches are those who have other witches in the family. Some hereditary witches come from a long line of Wiccans. Others may find out they have a connection to Wicca by learning of an ancestor who practiced, as well as forming an interest in reclaiming the Craft.

You do not have to choose any label for your practice. Labels are meaningful and helpful to some, but can be confining and smothering for others. Some witches feel connected to the stars, some to fire, some to the ocean and some to the mountains. Commune with nature and the answers will come from within you.

Community Outreach

Whether you're a solo witch or part of a coven, community is an important part of Wicca. Beginner witches are often affectionately known as "baby witches" and are cherished by the Wiccan community. Every Wiccan remembers the beginning of their journey and the kindness they received from others following the Old Religion. You will find they are eager to pay it forward by offering tips, friendship, and sometimes even mentorship.

Only about 1% of the world practices Wicca, which can make it challenging to find others in your area. Another obstacle is the stigma that still surrounds Wiccan beliefs. Many people don't understand the difference between white and black magick. They fear Wiccans as devil-worshippers who summon demons to do their bidding. However, as you know by this point, that couldn't be farther from the truth. Regardless, many Wiccans remain silent about their beliefs to avoid judgment from their friends, families, and communities.

The best way to connect with other Wiccans is online. Try searching social media tags for groups dedicated to the Craft. Be wary of those who would take advantage of you, and take the same precautions you normally would when communicating with strangers on the internet.

Luckily, the vast majority of the Wiccan community is warm and welcoming. Reaching out to other Wiccans is one of the best ways to find reliable information about the Old Religion. They can provide book recommendations written by qualified occult authors that provide legitimate information. When searching for information about Wicca on the internet, keep your wits about you; there is no shortage of phonies publishing misleading and incorrect information.

Conclusion

If you haven't realized it by now, Wicca can be full of contradictions. While this might be confusing for beginners, it is part of the beauty of the religion. As you continue to read and learn about Wicca, you will continue to encounter these contradictions. Your favorite authors might have different methods of casting a circle, or you may hear fellow Wiccans disputing the origins of certain traditions. When you come to these crossroads, it is time to tune into your intuition and make whatever decision makes most sense for you.

But you don't have to make these decisions all at once. In fact, it's always better to wait until you have adequate information before choosing any path. Research really is the name of the game when it comes to understanding ancient practices.

There is room for everyone who feels called to the Craft, and that means there is room for you, too!

PRACTICAL MAGIC:

INTRODUCTION

Merry meet and welcome to this humble yet comprehensive guide into the vast landscape of all things Witchcraft. If you have stumbled upon this book, then there is a reason. There is always a reason for everything. Witchcraft teaches us to see these connections and to know what they mean in our lives and in the greater scheme of things. In the core of Witchcraft, which includes Wicca, there is a finite truth that spells how we are all connected to each other, to the plants, the animals, the cosmos. The enlightening path that you have chosen to embark on is one of the most magickal, eye-opening experiences that you will most probably keep for the rest of your life.

It is my hope that you will find your own North-star with the guidance and direction within these pages and that you will always keep your words in order. Within Witchcraft the words that you speak are the most powerful tools that you will ever own. They are the basis for moulding your life and building a strong foundation for magick and forging a solid connection between you and the Divine within and without.

"As above, so below, As within, so without, as the universe, so the soul…"

(Mead, 2017)

WHAT IT REALLY MEANS TO BE A WITCH

Witches are different to the rest of society and yet, they aren't at all. Witches have the same daily lives, are subject to the same changes within governments and social orders and yes, Witches also need to do groceries. Being a Witch does not mean you will be flying your broomstick around town after midnight, it does mean that you will understand and become conscious of your astral body and how to utilise it. Being a Witch does not mean you will be turning your ex-boyfriend into a toad, it does however mean that you will be able to cut cords and soul ties with him and he will cease to affect your life – you could also throw in a *what you sow is what you reap spell*.

Being a Witch means that you will be reading a lot. You will be studying and practicing the arts for the rest of your life. You will make your own life better and you will begin to understand that you cannot help the world, unless you help yourself and fix yourself first. Witchcraft is not for everyone, and that is why there are a bunch of monotheistic religions in place, for those who do need their hand to be held through life.

Witchcraft is a lonely path in society. Witches are given much more freedom today than ever before, but we are still very misunderstood. The path of the Witch is a path of self-discovery, a path of finding and forging your connection to everything around you. Before you can build such a connection you need to traverse the wide landscapes of the self. This journey can take many years and never really comes to an end. Whilst you learn more about yourself, you will learn more about people around you and hopefully come to a place of greater understanding. Witchcraft teaches a great understanding around the necessity of all things. Good and evil are not as they are in the monotheistic religions, each one has a purpose and it is widely understood that if we do not understand the darkness, we can never know the light, and vice versa.

One doesn't become a Witch. One finds the Witch within awakening and the pathway opens up. Books such as this one come to us, we attract people who have great lessons to offer us and stories to tell that will open up new ways of thinking. One of the most important lessons within Witchcraft is that the universal path – regardless of faith – is a spiral and not a straight ladder. The race is long, and it is only with yourself. You will never be better than anyone else and no one will ever be better than you, or even more important. This path is about you. Being a Witch, is a path for you. If you happen to assist others on your path, then that is wonderful, but you should never attempt to take out your bloated ego on any conversation or instance with another. We are all on this path, learning and assisting where we can. No Witch is stronger or better than another. Yes, many are new to the Craft, but they are also on the path, like you, and sometimes a neophyte's eyes have new insight that can help a High Priestess. It is always important not to judge, always to listen so that you can understand, not so that you can reply, and to keep your own words in good order.

Lastly, being a Witch means that you are a caretaker of the planet, the people who live on it and the spirits that dwell here and beyond the veil. You are a mediator between this world and the next and you have a responsibility to respect and revere the spirit of man, beast and those beyond this space and time. Magick is always to be the last resort. We live a human life and magick can upset the balance of many things, so before you dive into the first spell that catches your eye, learn first to understand the elements, the earth, the cosmos and her inhabitants, and then you will find that magick is as easy as a word, a thought or an idea… and it is not necessary to turn the tides to your will, but to find peace in flowing with the divine will instead.

Chapter 1 - The History of Witchcraft and How it Affects You

The History of Magic by (Levi, 1999) is an excellent book to acquaint you with an all-round history of magic as well as a philosophical take on a worldwide view of magic. Another book that is a literature must-read is the revised edition of The Golden Bough by (Frazer, 1890). Not only do these two works allow you to glimpse into the mindset of magic and folklore but they also gift the reader a time travelling journey into the historical movement of magic.

To grasp the important path of the history of Witchcraft, you need to understand the law of the moon and the law of the sun. The law of both feminine and masculine and how prevalent both are to this day. The law of the moon is what governed the native religions of the past. The people back then were afforded the space and time to delve deep into the feminine mysteries and appreciate the miracles of birth, death and the journey in between. The feminine moon laws govern all the hidden. When man's power and ego driven greed took over, the laws of the sun and masculine strength prevailed. It is from this masculine perspective that the monotheistic or One male God religions were born, and it was faster at conquering whole cities and continents than any feminine path would allow.

The laws of the moon and of the feminine darkness, the shadow path and the reverence of the divine connections was lost to quick hard instant power. Through these monotheistic movements that were born from the order of Pope Constantine 325 A.D., all feminine threats were destroyed. This does not mean that only women were destroyed, it means that all those practicing the 'dark arts' or the arts of anything unknown to the laws of the sun, were destroyed. Persecution happened right across the world. It happened to those that were guilty and those that were not. It became a human excuse to snuff out everything that they did not like or did not understand, and this human trait has not changed much.

Humans want to control, and for this reason, Witchcraft was controlled by packaging it into a beautiful law-abiding religion called Wicca by Freemason and civil servant Gerald Brosseau Gardner in the 1950's. The only Lodge to acknowledge him today is Lodge no. 107, Colombo, Ceylon (Yurkon). This act of his was only possible after the last laws banning Witchcraft in Britain were removed in 1951 through parliamentary action. Gardner worked closely with his ritual architect Doreen Valiente and together they created a Wiccan movement that is stronger today than ever before. To understand why the history of Witchcraft is the way it is, we must understand why humans are the way they are. This process can fill a library, however, in a nutshell we can look at two texts, the first comes from Aradia – Gospel of the Witches by Charles Leland (Leland, 2018), originally in Italian, this is an excerpt of the voice of the Goddess Diana translated into English:

> "And when a priest shall do you injury
> By his benedictions, ye shall do to him
> Double the harm, and do it in the name
> Of me, Diana, Queen of witches all!
>
> And when the priests or the nobility
> Shall say to you that you should put your faith
> In the Father, Son, and Mary, then reply:
> "Your God, the Father, and Maria are
> Three devils....

> *"For the true God the Father is not yours;*
> *For I have come to sweep away the bad,*
> *The men of evil, all will I destroy!"*

The second text that we will look at is from the New testament of the Christian bible (Givens, 2008) condemning the children of the abovementioned Goddess to death:

Acts 19:27 – *"So that not only this our craft is in danger to be set to nought; but also, that the temple of the great goddess Diana should be despised, and her magnificence should be destroyed, whom all Asia and the world worshippeth."*

Now to explain the history of Witchcraft and how it affects you, look at the two opposing texts above. Each one is a retaliation of the other or of their own circumstances. Like parliament, one party fights against another for dominance. Just so the faiths of the history of mankind wrote pieces and feigned the words of Gods to stir the minds of the people. Does this mean that all texts are not the words of God/s? Absolutely not, I do believe that there are many that are God-inspired and many that have the best intention of their specific people in mind but that is as far as it gets.

Witchcraft's history is viciously ugly, especially the Würzburg Witch Trials in Germany (Roper). We must understand though that this is the human condition and not the work of religions or a reflection of people currently in those religions. One of the greatest displays of human evolution will be when we do not cut things in two opposing forces. Good versus evil occurs in every human creation. All the myths and all the faith-based texts. Someone must always be the devil.

How does it affect you? It doesn't. The history of Witchcraft must be taken with a bucket of salt when learning the recipes, spells and methods, but as far as being a subject in the past, you are not. You are a Witch in the 21st Century, possibly a millennial and that means that you do not need to bear the burden of the past, because Witchcraft is not its past, it is a path inward to assist outward and that means that you are only subject to your own actions and reactions.

Mass genocide across the timeline of what we believe to be Witchcraft would be more equated to people's fear of the unknown and the laws that came into effect have simply been rewritten, regurgitated and reinforced over and over again. To be a Witch means that you are to keep your life in better order than the next person so that you never give away an opportunity to have a feared finger pointed at you.

TIMELINE OF WICCA AND WITCHCRAFT – THE PATH OF PERSECUTION TO LIBERTY

This timeline serves to outline the most important and pivotal points in what made Witchcraft what it is today, as well as what caused the laws that persecuted those of the past and present to be formed.

- 3rd Millennium BC – Cuneiform Law – A concise set of laws that are thought to be the beginning of crazed laws against what was seen as unfit action as well as against those practicing Witchcraft.

- 1700 BC – The Code of Hammurabi – The first instance where extreme punishment against a person found guilty of practicing Witchcraft is mentioned.

- 15th Century BC – Torah – Written with the Babylonian Laws in mind, the Torah mentions approximately five excerpts where Witchcraft is banned, sometimes punishable by death.

- 1860 – Eliphas Levi begins to write Histoire de la Magie or History of Magic.

- 1888 – Helena Petrovna Blavatsky founds The Theosophical Publishing Company and publishes the first edition of The Secret Doctrine.

- 1907 – Aleister Crowley and George Cecil Jones form the esoteric Order entitled A.-.A.-.

- Witchcraft Act of 1542 – One of the first modern world laws to be passed and render Witchcraft punishable by death.

- 1911 – Arthur Edward Waite published the Pictorial Key to the Tarot; he is also the co-creator of the Rider-Waite Tarot Deck.

- 1920 – Paul Foster Case publishes his first work on the occult in An Introduction to the Study of the Tarot.

- 1921 – Margaret Alice Murray publishes her Witchcraft findings with great success in her book The Witch-cult in Western Europe.

- 26 September 1944 – Jane Rebecca Yorke is convicted of *"pretending to cause the spirits of deceased persons to be present"* She is the last documented victim of the Witchcraft Acts in the British Isles.

- 1936 – Dion Fortune publishes her second Occult novel, The Goat-foot God.

- 1939 – Gerald Brosseau Gardner is initiated into the New Forest Coven.

- 1948 – Robert Graves publishes The White Goddess.

- 1949 – Gerald Brosseau Gardner publishes his Witchcraft findings in High Magic's Aid.

- 1951 – The Witchcraft Act of 1542 is finally repealed.

- 1954 – Gerald Brosseau Gardner publishes Witchcraft Today.

- 1957 – Doreen Valiente leaves Gardner's coven.

- 1957 – The Parliament of South Africa instates The Witchcraft Suppression Act of 1957, this law stands to this day in the country, however it is not enforced as strongly as in the past.

- 1959 – Gerald Brosseau Gardner founds the Bricket Wood Coven and forms the lineage that is known today as Gardnerian Wicca.

- 1960's – Raymond Howard founds the Coven of Atho.

- 1965 – Alex and Maxine Sanders form what is known today as Alexandrian Wicca.

- 1970's – Dianic Wicca, a Goddess worshipping form of Wicca is formed by Zsuzsanna Budapest.

- 1981 – Stewart and Janet Farrar, both authors, write a series of books that become the core point in many covens and pagan circles today. The books include but are not limited to: The Witches Bible (1996), The Witches God (1989), The Witches Goddess (1987).

THE LAWS THAT BEGAN WICCA

The 161 Laws of Gerald Brosseau Gardner (Gardner, 2009)

1. The Law was made and ordained of old.

2. The Law was made for the Wicca, to advise and help in their troubles.

3. The Wicca should give due worship to the gods and obey their will, which they ordain, for it was made for the good of Wicca as the worship of the Wicca is good for the gods. For the gods love the brethren of Wicca.

4. As a man loveth a woman by mastering her.

5. So the Wicca should love the gods by being mastered by them.

6. And it is necessary that the Circle, which is the temple of the gods, should be truly cast and purified. And that it may be a fit place for the gods to enter.

7. And the Wicca shall be properly prepared and purified to enter the presence of the gods.

8. With love and worship in their hearts, they shall raise power from their bodies to give power to the gods.

9. As has been taught of old.

10. For in this way only may men have communion with the gods, for the gods cannot help man without the help of man.

11. And the High Priestess shall rule her coven as the representative of the God.

12. And the High Priest shall support her as the representative of the God.

13. And the High Priestess shall choose whom she will, be he of sufficient rank, to be her High Priest.

14. For as the god himself kissed her feet in the fivefold salute, laying his power at the feet of the Goddess because of her youth and beauty, her sweetness and kindness, her wisdom and justice, her humility and generosity,

15. So he resigned all his power to her.

16. But the High Priestess should ever mind that all power comes from him.

17. It is only lent, to be used wisely and justly.

18. And the greatest virtue of a High priestess be that she recognizes that youth is necessary to the representative of the goddess.

19. So she will gracefully retire in favor of a younger woman should the Coven so decide in council.

20. For a true High Priestess realizes that gracefully surrendering pride of place is one of the greatest virtues.

21. And that thereby she will return to that pride of place in another life, with greater power and beauty.

22. In the old days, when witchdom extended far, we were free and worshipped in all the greater temples.

23. But in these unhappy times we must celebrate our sacred mysteries in secret.

24. So be it ordained, that none but the Wicca may see our mysteries, for our enemies are many and torture loosens the tongue of man.

25. So be it ordained that no Coven shall know where the next Coven bide.

26. Or who its members be, save only the Priest and Priestess and messenger.

27. And there shall be no communication between them, save by the messenger of the gods, or the summoner.

28. And only if it be safe may the covens meet in some safe place for the great festivals.

29. And while there, none shall say whence they came nor give their true names.

30. To this end, any that are tortured in their agony may not tell if they do not know.

31. So be it ordained that no one shall tell anyone not of the craft who be of the Wicca, nor give any names or where they bide, or in any way tell anything which can betray any of us to our foes.

32. Nor may he tell where the Covendom be.

33. Or the Coven stead.

34. Or where the meetings be.

35. And if any break these laws, even under torture, THE CURSE OF THE GODDESS SHALL BE UPON THEM, so they may never be reborn on earth and may remain where they belong, in the hell of the Christians.

36. Let each High Priestess govern her Coven with justice and love, with the help and advice of the High Priest and the Elders, always heeding the advice of the messenger of the gods if he cometh.

37. She will heed all complains of all Brothers and strive to settle all differences among them.

38. But it must be recognized that there will always be people who will ever strive to force others to do as they will.

39. These are not necessarily evil.

40. And they oft have good ideas and such ideas should be talked over in council.

41. But if they will not agree with their Brothers, or if they say,

42. "I will not work under this High Priestess,"

43. It hath ever been the Old Law to be convenient to the Brethren and to avoid disputes.

44. Any of the third may claim to find a new Coven because they live over a league away from the Coven stead, or that they are about to do so.

45. Anyone living within the Covendom and wishing to form a new Coven shall tell the Elders of their intention and on the instant avoid their dwelling and remove to the new Covendom.

46. Members of the old Coven may join the new one when it is formed. But if they do, they must utterly avoid the old Coven.

47. The Elders of the new and the old Covens should meet in peace and brotherly love to decide the new boundaries.

48. Those of the craft who dwell outside both Covendoms may join either but not both.

49. Though all may, if the Elders agree, meet for the great festivals if it be truly in peace and brotherly love,

50. But splitting the Coven off means strife, so for this reason these Laws were made of old and may the CURSE OF THE GODDESS BE ON ANY WHO DISREGARD THEM. So be it ordained.

51. If you would keep a book, let it be in your own hand of write. Let brothers and sisters copy what they will, but never let the book out of your hands, and never keep the writings of another.

52. For if it be found in their hand of write, they may be taken and arraigned. Let each guard his own writings and destroy them

53. whenever danger threatens.

54. Learn as much as you may by heart and, when danger is past, rewrite your book, and it be safe.

55. For this reason, if any die, destroy their book if they have not been able to.

56. For, if it be found, `tis clear proof against them.

57. And our oppressors know well "Ye may not be a witch alone".

58. So all their kin and friends be in danger of torture.

59. So destroy everything not necessary.

60. If your book be found on you, `tis clear proof against you alone, you may be arraigned.

61. Keep all thoughts of the craft from your mind.

62. If the torture be too great to bear, say, "I will confess. I can't bear this torture. What do you want me to say?"

63. If they try to make you speak of the Brotherhood, do not.

64. But if they try to make you speak of impossibilities such as flying through the air, consorting with a Christian devil or sacrificing children, or eating men's flesh.

65. To obtain relief from torture say, "I had an evil dream I was beside myself; I was crazed."

66. Not all magistrates are bad, if there be an excuse, they may show mercy.

67. If you have confessed ought, deny it afterwards, say you babbled under torture, and say you knew not what you said.

68. If you are condemned, fear not.

69. The Brotherhood is powerful and will help you to escape if you stand steadfast, but if you betray ought there is no hope for you in this life or in that to come.

70. Be sure, if steadfast you go to the pyre, drugs will reach you, you will feel naught you go to death and what lies beyond, the ecstasy of the goddess.

71. To avoid discovery, let the working tools be as ordinary things that any may have in their houses.

72. Let the pentacles be of wax so that they may be broken at once or melted.

73. Have no sword unless your rank allows it.

74. Have no names or signs on anything.

75. Write the names and signs on them in ink before consecrating them and wash it off immediately afterwards.

76. Let the color of the hilts tell which is which.

77. Do not engrave them unless they cause discovery.

78. Ever remember ye are the hidden children of the Goddess so never do anything to disgrace them or Her.

79. Never boast, never threaten, never say you would wish ill of anyone.

80. If any person not in the Circle, speak of the craft, say, "Speak not to me of such, it frightens me, `tis evil luck to speak of it.

81. For this reason, the Christians have their spies everywhere. These speak as if they were well affected to us, as if they wouldn't come into our meetings, saying, "My mother used to worship the Old Ones. I would I could go myself."

82. To such as these ever deny all knowledge.

83. But to others, ever say, "Tis foolish men talk of witches flying through the air. To do so they must be as light as thistledown. And men say that witches all be blear eyed old crones, so what pleasure can there be at a witch meeting such as folks talk on?"

84. And say, "Many wise men now say there be no such creatures."

85. Ever make it a jest, and in some future time perhaps, the persecution may die and we may worship our gods in safety again.

86. Let us all pray for that happy day.

87. May the blessings of the Goddess and God be on all who keep these Laws which are ordained.

88. If the craft hath any appendage, let all guard it and witchcraft in the land," because our oppressors of old make it heresy not to believe in witchcraft and so a crime to deny it which thereby puts you under suspicion.

89. And let all justly guard all monies of the craft.

90. And if any Brother truly wrought it, `tis right they have their pay, and it be just. And this be not taking money for the art, but for good and honest work.

91. And even the Christians say, "The laborer is worthy of his hire," but if any Brother work willingly for the good of the craft without pay, `tis but to their greater honor. So be it ordained.

92. If there be any dispute or quarrel among the Brethren, the High Priestess shall straightly convene the Elders and enquire into the matter, and they shall hear both sides, first alone and then together.

93. And they shall decide justly, not favoring one side or the other.

94. Ever recognizing there be people who can never agree to work under others.

95. But at the same time; there be some people who cannot rule justly.

96. To those who ever must be chief, there is one answer.

97. Void the Coven or seek another one, or make a Coven of your own, taking with you those who will go.

98. To those who cannot, justly the answer be, "Those who cannot bear your rule will leave with you.

99. For none may come to meetings with those whom they are at variance.

100. So, an either cannot agree, get hence, for the craft must ever survive, so be it ordained.

101. In the olden days when we had power, we could use the art against any who illtreated the Brotherhood. But in these evil days we must not do so. For our enemies have devised a burning pit of everlasting fire into which they say their god casteth all the people who worship him, except it be the very few who are released by their priests, spells and masses. And this be chiefly by giving monies and rich gifts to receive his favor for their great god is ever in need of money.

102. But as our gods need our aid to make fertility for man and crops, so is the god of the Christians ever in need of man's help to search out and destroy us. Their priests ever tell them that any who get our help are damned to this hell forever, so men be mad with the terror of it.

103. But they make men believe that they may escape this hell if they give victims to the tormentors. So for this reason all be forever spying,

thinking, "And I can catch but one of these Wicca, I will escape from this fiery pit."

104. So for this reason we have our hides, and men searching long and Doth finding, say, "There be none, or if there be, they be in a far country."

105. But when one of our oppressors die, or even be sick, ever is the cry, "This be witches' malice", and the hunt is up again. And though they slay ten of their own to one of ours, still they care not. They have countless thousands.

106. While we are few indeed. So be it ordained.

107. That none shall use the art in any way to do ill to any.

108. However much they injure us, harm none. And now times many believe we exist not.

109. That this Law shall ever continue to help us in our plight, no one, however great an injury or injustice they receive, may use the art in any way to do ill, or harm any. But they may, after great consultations with all, use the art to restrain Christians from harming us Brothers, but only to constrain them and never to punish.

110. To this end men will say, "Such a one is a mighty searcher out, and a persecutor of old women when they desire to be witches, and none hath done him harm, so it be proof that they cannot or more truly there be none.

111. For all know full well that so many folk have died because someone had a grudge against them, or were persecuted because they had money or goods to seize, or because they had none to bribe the searchers. And many have died because they were scolding old women. So much that men now say that only old women are witches.

112. And this be to our advantage and turns suspicion away from us.

113. In England and Scotland 'tis now many a year since a witch hath died the death. But any misuse of the power might raise the persecution again.

114. So never break this Law, however much you are tempted, and never consent to its being broken in the least.

115. If you know it is being broken, you must work strongly against it.

116. And any High Priestess or High Priest who consents to its breach must immediately be deposed for tis the blood of the Brethren they endanger.

117. Do good, and it be safe, and only if it be safe.

118. And strictly keep to the Old Law.

119. Never accept money for the work of the art, for money ever smeareth the taker. "Tis sorcerers and conjurors and the priests of the Christians who ever accept money for the use of their arts. And they sell pardons to let men escape from their sins.

120. Be not as these. If you accept no money, you will be free from temptation to use the art for evil causes.

121. All may use the art for their own advantage or for the advantage of the craft only if you are sure you harm none.

122. But ever let the Coven debate this at length. Only if all are satisfied that none may be harmed, may the art be used.

123. If it is not possible to achieve your ends one way, perchance the aim may be achieved by acting in a different way so as to harm none. MAY THE CURSE OF THE GODDESS BE UPON ANY WHO BREAKETH THIS LAW. So be it ordained.

124. "Tis judged lawful if ever any of the craft need a house or land and none will sell, to incline the owner's mind so as to be willing to sell, provided it harmeth him not in any way and the full price is paid without haggling.

125. Never bargain or cheapen anything whilst you buy by the art. So be it ordained.

126. Tis the Old Law and the most important of all laws, that no one may do anything which will endanger any of the craft, or bring them into contact with the law of the land or any persecutors

127. In any dispute between the Brethren, no one may invoke any laws but those of the craft.

128. Or any tribunal but that of the Priestess, Priest and Elders.

129. It is not forbidden to say as Christians do, "There be witchcraft in the land," because our oppressors of old make it heresy not to believe in witchcraft and so a crime to deny it which thereby puts you under suspicion.

130. But ever say, "I know not of it here, perchance there may be but afar off, I know not where."

131. But ever speak of them as old crones, consorting with the devil and riding through the air.

132. And ever say, "But how may many ride the air if they be not as light as thistledown."

133. But the curse of the Goddess be on any who cast suspicion on any of the Brotherhood.

134. Or who speak of any real meeting place or where they bide.

135. Let the craft keep books with the names of all herbs which are good, and all cures so all may learn.

136. But keep another book with all Bills and Apices and let only the Elders and other trustworthy people have this knowledge. So be it ordained.

137. And may the blessings of the gods be on all who keep these Laws, and the curses of both the God and the Goddess be on all who break them.

138. Remember the art is the secret of the gods and may only be used in earnest and never for show or vain glory.

139. Magicians and Christians may taunt us saying, "You have no power, show us your power. Do magic before our eyes, then only will we believe," seeking to cause us to betray the art before them.

140. Heed them not, for the art is holy and may only be used in need, and the curse of the gods be on any who break this Law.

141. It ever be the way with women and with men also, that they ever seek new love. 142. Nor should we reprove them for this.

143. But it may be found a disadvantage to the craft.

144. And so many a time it has happened that a High Priest or a High Priestess, impelled by love, hath departed with their love. That is, they have left the Coven.

145. Now if the High Priestess wishes to resign, she may do so in full Coven.

146. And this resignation is valid.

147. But if they should run off without resigning, who may know if they may not return in a few months?

148. So the Law is, if a High Priestess leaves her Coven, she be taken back and all be as before.

149. Meanwhile, if she has a deputy, that deputy shall act as High Priestess for as long as the High Priestess is away.

150. If she returns not at the end of a year and a day, then shall the Coven elect a new High Priestess. 151. Unless there is a good reason to the contrary.

152. The person who has done the work shall reap the benefit of the reward, maiden and deputy of the High Priestess.

153. It had been found that practicing the art doth cause a fondness between aspirant and tutor, and it is the cause of better results if this be so.

154. And if for any reason this be undesirable, it can easily be avoided by both persons from the outset firmly resolving in their minds to be as brother and sister, or parent and child.

155. And it is for this reason that a man may be taught only by a woman and a woman by a man, and women and women should not attempt these practices together. So be it ordained.

156. Order and discipline must be kept.

157. A High Priestess or a High Priest may, and should, punish all faults.

158. To this end all fault and his sentence pronounced.

159. All properly prepared, the culprit should be told his fault, and his sentence pronounced.

160. Punishment should be followed by something amusing.

161. The culprit must acknowledge the justice of the punishment by kissing the hand on receiving sentence and again thanking for punishment received. So be it ordained."

Important Characters to know in the

Craft

There are thousands of individuals who dedicated their lives to the pursuit of Occult knowledge. Their pursuits and the historical markings of their publications are what moulded Witchcraft and Wicca into everything that it is today. It is important to understand that each one of these people and each one of the markings throughout our history are simply the findings of personal experiences and a subjective action based on the time and place that each one of them found themselves.

Witchcraft was and is still a relationship with the divine that is found within oneself and in the world around us. A witch living in the forest will have a vastly different approach to on living in the hustle and bustle of the city. For this reason, it is imperative to research and avidly read all the notable minds that formed Witchcraft today, but also to understand that their methods and their ways of approaching the divine may or may not be the same as yours.

Arthur Edward Waite

An initiate in the Golden Dawn as well as a Freemason, initiated 19th September 1901, A. E. Waite is the co-creator of the Rider-Waite Tarot Deck, he was also an author and dedicated much of his occult knowledge into creating the Tarot deck that almost all other Tarot decks are forged from.

Aleister Crowley

Dubbed 'The Beast of Man', Aleister Crowley seemed to delight in shock and horror. He also dedicated his life, in between the urge of needing to be accepted, to the study of the Occult and finding that one thing that would prove the existence of the worlds beyond the veil.

Eliphas Levi

French born; Levi was known as 'The Last Magi'. A 33rd degree Freemason. His work in A History of Magic and The Doctrine of Transcendental Magic are sometimes referred to as the most detailed important works to mark the Witchcraft movement and minds behind the Wiccan religion.

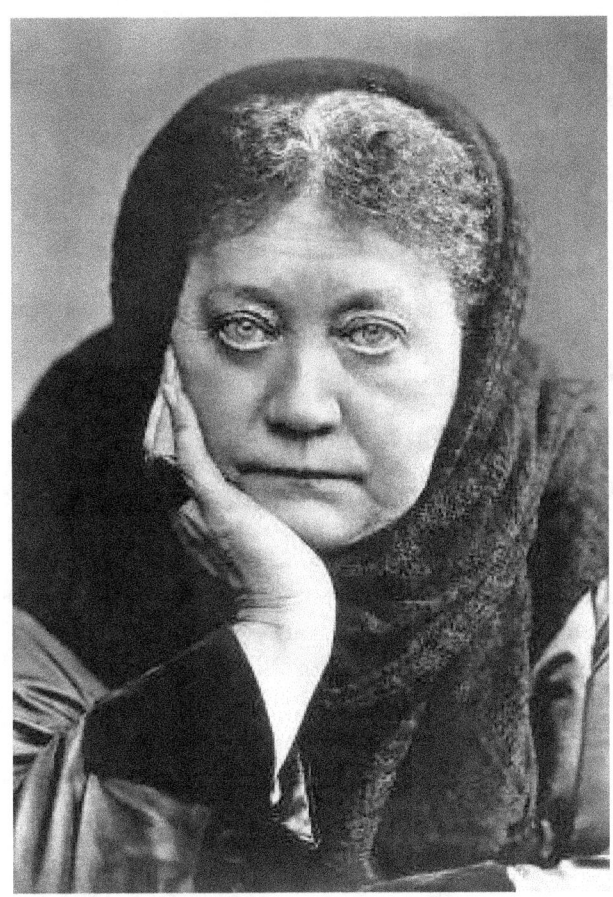

Helena Petrovna Blavatsky

Blavatsky set the stage with her works entitled Isis Unveiled and The Secret Doctrine. Even though the works are extensive reading, she reaches into the core of the philosophical soul and gifts practitioners and excellent platform to understand their own path.

Zsuzsanna Emese Mokcsay (Budapest)

The Hungarian born founder of Dianic Wicca, author and activist helped to shape the world of Wicca and Witchcraft. She is perhaps solely responsible for setting the stage and tipping the scale for future authors and practitioners of the Goddess worshipping movements within Wicca and occult circles.

Doreen Valiente

Doreen Valiente was the chief ritual architect and right hand to Gerald Gardner. The works that she produced are still used today in many, if not all first- and second-degree manuals of Wiccan circles. She devised the softer and more devotional side to the Freemason influence that Gardner brought to the table. It is said that without her incredible influence, Wicca would not be what it is today.

Gerald Brosseau Gardner

Known as The Father of Modern Wicca, Gerald was a Freemason and much of his work has been speculated to be the culmination of a vast imagination and the experience of a Freemason. His bold move to publish works and form The Bricket Wood Coven at the time when he did are one of the most pivotal movements toward the liberation and world acceptance of Witchcraft today.

Scott Cunningham

Originally born, Scott Douglas Cunningham, received his training under Raven Grimassi. He managed to publish several books on Wicca and Witchcraft and his book *Wicca: A guide for the solitary practitioner* is one of the most well-known book on Wicca as well as remaining the most successfully sold book on the subject, worldwide.

Raymond Buckland

For the solitary practitioners and the coven practitioners, Raymond Buckland's work opened many doors that were previously not even dared to be opened. Raymond Buckland was initiated by Gerald Brosseau Gardner himself and he is the founder of Seax Wicca. Seax Wicca is a tradition of Wicca that does not frown upon self-initiation and actually encourages it.

The Truth about Salem and the Past

Persecution of Witches

Salem is one of the hottest places to find Witchcraft merchandise today. The entire town vibrates with a history that has nothing to do with Witchcraft. The American History of Witchcraft has almost nothing to do with Witchcraft on its own. The Salem Colony that attests to be the place where Witches were burned at the stake is a false claim. The colony was under British rule in 1692 and the entire Salem trial by hanging was a family feud that led to a mass hysteria which could not be proven to relate to Witchcraft at all.

One of the most violent and vicious occurrences of mass murders due to the suspicion of Witchcraft was the Würzburg Witch Trials in Germany. At these trials a total of 900 people were found to be guilty. The children who were put to death were accused of having sexual relations with the devil. Over and above those atrocities, it is said that of the 900 people, 19 of them were Catholic Priests. The others that almost top these are the Bamberg, The Trier, and The Fulda Witch Trials. Salem, however famous has no Witchcraft standing according to scholarly accounts.

It has become customary within many Wiccan circles across the world to be a descendant of a Witch who was burned at the stake in Salem. It has also become an important chip on the shoulder to announce the fact that you come from a long line of Witches. None of that matters in this present day where we find ourselves. Witchcraft is not about the past at all. It is about you and your relationship to those people around you. It is about your relationship to the Divine. It is about your own set of morals and how you do at keeping your word of honour. What can you take from Salem? A good excursion, a journey into a modern Witches town, but that is all. The history needs to be made by you.

COLLECTING THE PAST GEMS AND PLACING THEM INTO YOUR LIFE

To collect information from the past, we need to first understand who and what we are now. The present day is what counts. As a Witch, your magick can only work if you know what and who you are. It is important to take heed of the writings, successes and grave errors of past influencers within the Witchcraft landscape. There are always two ways of learning: The first is through your own failing and falling and the second is through the mistakes of others. For this reason, it is important to read and study as much as you can, but always keep the scales tipped more toward your own experience and remember to record everything.

Ritual within Witchcraft, and Wicca more specifically, works. Therefore, we use it throughout the year and throughout our magickal path. If, for some reason you find that changing a certain thing works for you, then do so. There must never be fear in Witchcraft as fear is without a doubt the mind and magick killer. Make your path your own. Take what you need from the past lore and mould it into your own path. Witchcraft will never hold your hand or lead you; it is you who lead the way.

Each Witch has his/her own set of laws, rules, guidelines and magick secrets, spells, potions and ways of doing things. There is no right and no wrong when formulating your own path. It is important to collect things and incorporate things into what suits your personality. One of the most important questions to ask when choosing to absorb new information into your collection is:

"Does this addition of information bring me closer to the divine spirit within me and without me?"

Witchcraft is not about gaining power over others. Ego driven pursuits of knowledge are never a good idea. They do not get one anywhere and in the greater scheme of things, there really is no power over another without the consequence of death. It is wise to feel your way around the landscape of Witchcraft, both in its past and in its present-day form. When reading someone else's work, whether they be a witch or not, make sure that the information resonates with your soul. If it does not resonate, leave it to be. Do not feel guilty about not enjoying a piece of work that is classified as an important piece of literature by other witches or Wiccans. Your intuition must guide you and it is true that one person's truth is another man's downfall.

Many neophytes begin asking questions such as:

"Where do I begin?", "There is so much information, I don't know if I can read everything and I do not know even which book is right and which one is not."

The other part that comes with these questions is the mad frenzy that new Witches find themselves in. They want every crystal, every book, every form of divination and they spend all their hard-earned money on everything that they can lay their hands on. This is something that happens to every single one of us. The reason behind it is simple. You have found a path that you wish that you had found earlier in life and so now you are making up for the lost time. If this sounds like you then please just breathe. Breathe in, go sit on the grass outside and feel mother nature. Go and absorb her essence and calm yourself into the knowledge that you are enough. You do not need the thousands of crystals and books and goodies to learn. You do need to learn about what makes you happy from the inside. You can only learn that by being calm about the process.

Understand that you will be drawn by your intuition to what you are destined to learn. Some witches, for example, never learn the tarot, but they are excellent at using the pendulum or at dowsing. Many books will say that to be a witch you need to be able to use the tarot; you need to wear black; you need to speak to the dead etc. This is absolute rubbish. Witchcraft is not a pretty little black box that all of us climb into and learn the tarot whilst speaking to the dead. Everyone is unique and there are no two witches that are alike.

When you take your gems from the past and the present, make sure that they mirror who you are. Yes, you will grow out of some of them, but if the information that you are collecting resonates with who you are then you will never forget it. There is really no point in throwing out your wardrobe, replacing it with all black clothes, if pink or baby blue is really your colour. Similarly, there is no point in spending thousands on buying new tarot decks because you can't find one that resonates with your soul, and meanwhile you are meant to be reading Lenormand. It is imperative that you take this path slowly and with much consideration on the choices that you make.

At the end of the day, all that matters are the relationships that you keep with your own divinity. Witchcraft is the path of the witch, it is his/her path alone, no one else's. Besides, we all enter and leave this world with the thoughts and souls that we alone have nurtured. Why is life then so different?

Chapter 2 – The Seasons of The Wheel of The Year

The Wheel of the Year is not only a storyline about understanding the seasonal changes and how the earth and her creatures are affected, it is also the storyline of the deep psychological processes that we as humans undergo through this continuous cycle. The Wiccan Wheel of the Year is a union between Celtic and Germanic lore devised by Gerald Brosseau Gardner. He sought to include both the solstices and the equinoxes to give practitioners a full eight-spoke wheel of the year to celebrate and understand the seasonal changes of our great mother earth.

There are many stories that find themselves intertwined with the Wiccan wheel of the year. It is often an extreme confusion for people when they hear the stories of the wheel of the year and cannot understand the discrepancies in it. There are no discrepancies in the wheel of the year, there are however two prominent cultures gifting their understanding of the seasons and that is why we often hear people explain how the wheel of the year makes no sense.

It is also extremely common for practitioners of the craft to have absolutely no idea about the wheel of the year and what each festival stands for. Social media has made it easy to remember these pivotal points of change because as soon as one person says *"Merry Yule"* it is shared, and the word is passed on. There is a great difference between northern and southern hemisphere worship. Not only does the wheel of the year swop around but so does circle casting, ritual procession and the placement of the various elemental guardians.

How do you know what to practice and when? Well, observe the world around you. The solstices and the equinoxes find themselves in the heart of the season or at its apex. In other words, Samhain is in found to be celebrated in the heart or in the zenith of Fall / Autumn. Similarly, Yule is found to be in the heart of Winter as well as being on the longest night and the shortest day. We need to understand the world around us to be able to live, love and incorporate the wheel of the year into our everyday lives.

The practice of celebrating the seasonal changes is probably the most important work that you can do in becoming and remaining a witch. A witch knows her seasons, he/she knows the first bud of spring well, and many have collected these first leaves or buds to use in powerful life changing magick. A witch knows when it is the time of the thinning of the veil and he/she naturally prepare for his/her new year. It is this continual cycle, this spiral of continuation that provides the witch with the knowledge of how to bring the rains to fall when the weatherman did not predict them for another week. It is this incredible ongoing cycle of the seasons that allow witches to understand their own inner makeup and to prepare, heal and change their lives as they see fit. If you are deciding on what to do, where to start or how you can become a better witch, then make sure to learn your wheel of the year, and always record your dates, your observations and your activities, no matter how small or how big.

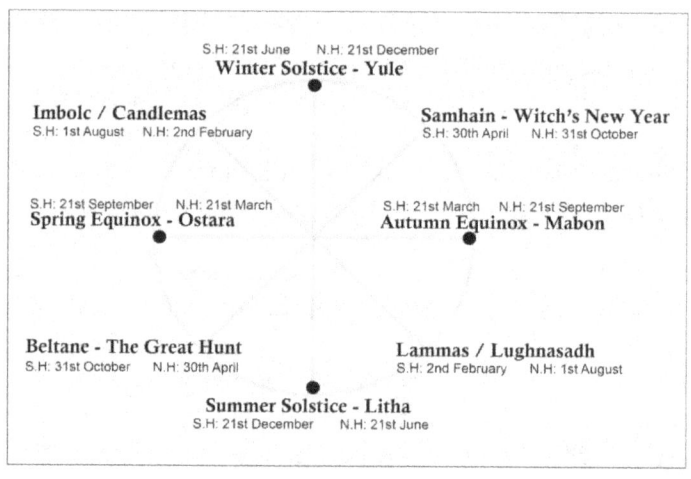

SAMHAIN

Happy New Year Witches! Welcome to the time when the veil is at its thinnest. A night without the gods, and a festival of the dead. Samhain is the night of dining with the ancestors and experiencing the spirit world in your own home. This is one of the most important celebrations in Witchcraft, not because it is full of spirits or of skulls, pumpkins and so forth, but because it is the one time in the year where we can hear ourselves think.

Samhain is full of introspection. As the dark twin of Beltane, Samhain is a quiet festival of introspection, communing with those that have passed on into the Summerland's and of being with the spirit world. Sadly, the Christian influence brought about Halloween, or All Hallows Eve, but despite the mockery, we now get to practice Samhain without being thought of as creepy or dangerous.

During Samhain, both the God and Goddess are wading through the perils of the underworld. They too are undergoing great change and as a result, they are not placed on the altar as Wiccan deities. It is customary however, to invoke, not only evoke an underworld deity at this time to deliver messages to the coven or to the people present. Please do not even attempt an invocation if you are not sure what you are doing. Evocation is a lot safer and always, always cast circle before doing any sort of work with the spirits or with deity.

Not only is Samhain a time for the ancestors but it is also a time that we rest and rethink our lives. This is a time to throw out the old and think about what we would like in our lives instead. It is customary to do rituals of cord cutting and of banishing old habits. This is where we take off the old dusty rags and await the wheels turning to prepare, plan and create the new ones.

ALTAR DRESSINGS

- Reds, browns, oranges and black coloured cloths and drapes
- Ancestral imagery and items of the persons
- Black mirrors
- Skulls
- Black candles
- White candles
- Red Candles
- Pumpkins
- Twigs
- Underworld representations
- Dark hooded figures
- Crystal balls

- Tarot decks
- Myrrh & Patchouli
- Witches Ladders

CRAFTS AND ARTS

Broom Making

Samhain is the best time to be making a new broom. Last year's broom can be used in the fire to represent cleansing out the old and making room for the new. How would you begin such a task?

What you will need:

- Twigs / old branches / Grass
- A long branch that has fallen from a magickal tree such as willow or oak
- Strong cotton
- Copper jewellery wire (Optional)

- A bowl of sea salt
- A bottle of mineral water
- A white candle
- Incense of your choice and the holder so as not to burn the floor
- Paint (optional)
- Ribbon of your choice
- Decorating items such as glitter glue or charms

Firstly, the broom is used for cleansing the energy of the desired space. It is not used to sweep and should be kept as a magickal item at all times. Begin the process by casting a nice big circle and remember to keep all your items inside the circle, unless you are knowledgeable about cutting doorways in the circle to go and fetch the goodies that you have forgotten.

Begin by blessing the salt:

"Oh, creature of earth, I cleanse, consecrate and bless thee, you are now fit to dwell in sacred space."

Bless the water:

"Oh, creature of Water, I cleanse, consecrate and bless thee, you are now fit to dwell in sacred space."

Now add the salt to the water and stir with your athame if you have one, or with your index finger, both work exactly the same. As you are stirring, repeat the following words:

"Holy Water and Holy Earth combined to work as one single power – to cleanse, to purify, to bless and to charge as I see fit. As I will, so mote it be."

When you completed this, you have in fact made holy water. This water can be further strengthened by adding essential oils if you would like but this is not necessary. Now light your candle and sweep your hand over the flame repeating:

"Oh, creature of fire, I cleanse, consecrate and bless thee, you are now fit to dwell in sacred space."

Light the incense and sweep your hand through the smoke and repeat:

"Oh, creature of Air, I cleanse, consecrate and bless thee, you are now fit to dwell in sacred space."

Now we can begin to build our broom. Lay your branch or long stick in front of you. Take the twigs / dry branches / grass and lay them down with the stick in the centre of the bunch. Take the copper wire and bound the twigs / dry branches or grass as tight as you can to the branch. You must do this in three places. If you do not have copper wire at hand, then strong cotton or embroidery cotton will work as well. Once you have done this, take your ribbon and go over the areas where you have tied the broom. Now paint and decorate your broom as you see fit.

When your broom is done, lay it in front of you and place the holy water, candle and incense in front of the broom. Now allow the broom to be cleansed, consecrated, blessed and charged with your energy and the energy of the elements. Pass the broom through the fire of the candle, just do not set it alight. Whilst doing this repeat:

"This broom, this tool of the craft

born from my hands and born from my heart,

I pass it through Fire to cleanse, to charge and to bless,

This broom is now a tool of the God and the Goddess."

Repeat the same step by passing the broom through the smoke of the incense:

"This broom, this tool of the craft

born from my hands and born from my heart,

I pass it through Air to cleanse, to charge and to bless,

This broom is now a tool of the God and the Goddess."

Now take up your holy water, stand above the broom and sprinkle the broom with holy water whilst repeating:

"This broom, this tool of the craft

born from my hands and born from my heart,

I wash it now with holy water to cleanse, to charge and to bless,

This broom is now a tool of the God and the Goddess."

Take up your broom and with the bristles facing upward repeat the following chant as many times as needed, ending the last time with *"As I will, so mote it be."*

"Divine mother and father, universal spirit above,

Charged this broom is now and devoid of

Any mundane purpose, task or charge,

It is empowered to cleanse, to banish and to recharge,

Any space I choose worthy,

This my magickal broom is now ready!"

"As I will, so mote it be."

Samhain Pumpkin Fritter Critters

Pumpkin fritters go with almost any meal and they're great on their own as well. Here is a fail-safe recipe to use.

What you will need:

- 1 teaspoon Vanilla extract
- 1 beaten egg
- 1 cup of self-raising flour
- 2 full cups of pumpkin (smashed)
- 1 pinch of salt
- 1 tablespoon brown sugar
- Sunflower oil to fry the fritters

Critter coating (optional but great for Samhain)

- 50g refined sugar
- 3 teaspoons Cinnamon

In a big mixing bowl add the smashed pumpkin, Vanilla extract and the egg, mix well. Now add the self-raising flour, pinch of salt, brown sugar and mix again until you get a well-mixed consistency.

Heat the oil in a frying pan on the stove. Add a pinch of the mixture to see when the oil is ready. When it is ready spoon a spoonful of mixture at a time and fry them until they are golden brown on both sides. Scoop them out on a plate and coat the pumpkin fritter critters with the mix of refined sugar and cinnamon mix.

YULE

Yule is celebrated on the longest night of the year and the shortest day. This is the Winter Solstice. It is the birth of the *Child of Promise*.

Yule is celebrated with Yule logs, evergreen Fir trees to represent everlasting life. The entire celebration of Yule is customarily started 12 days before the longest night and shortest day. In the Pagan Asatru faith, the 12 days of Yule are an exceptional celebration of feasting and merry making.

Yule is traditionally a Germanic festival that calls in the promise of the New Year. For Witches though, Yule is not the New Year, it is the time when all the old is disposed. It is the moment that the Sun God is born. To explain this, he is born from the womb which was the tomb. It is a metaphorical birth from the depths of the underworld into the light of the earth. The days will get longer now, and the nights will get shorter, and so, the immortal promise of the continuation of life has been fulfilled and therefore all the old must go.

Yule presents are exchanged, and the presents are usually meant to be things that you no longer use and believe someone else could. These presents are to be left under the community Fir tree. When it is time, each person or family may go to the tree and pick a present. Once the presents have been taken, it is customary to give thanks for the bountiful life that each person has. Gratitude is the attitude of Yule and the process is called Wassail. A token of thanks is given, and the glass / goblet is raised and when the person is done giving thanks to the people, and to the gods, they declare "WASSAIL!"

In a traditional Germanic Yule ritual, the Galdr, or runes are called in to invoke the Father God, Odin. When it is time for the workings there will be a rune pouch handed around by the High Priestess and each person present will take a rune from the pouch. The rune is the forecast and advice for the coming months. There are generally six copies of each rune in the pouch and only the rune Ansuz is singular.

The most prominent symbols of Yule are the Holly and Mistletoe. Their resemblance to the goddess and the god is important to know and represents the presence of fertility within the divine couple even in the coldest and longest night of the year. The red berries from the Holly tree represent the menstrual cycle of the goddess and the ability of her being able to bare children. The Mistletoe berries are found in an array of colours but for Yule the white berries are important because they represent the masculine reproductive fluid of the god.

Yule is also no time to celebrate the god and goddess on the altar. There are two reasons for this. Firstly, the god is a new-born babe, born from the darkness, the womb that was the underworld tomb, and has no understanding of ruling or of being worshipped. You are welcome to place a baby statue on the altar to welcome his return as the growing oak king, however there is no logical explanation for having him on the altar during Yule. The goddess is also not present because she is still traversing the underworld landscape and will not be present at the altar until after Imbolc when we hear her first stirrings under the earth.

Altar Dressings

- Various reds, greens and white cloths and drapes
- Mistletoe
- Holly
- Horns for drinking and Wassail
- A babylike representation of the Oak God
- Imagery of the returning of the sun
- Runes – Elder Futhark work best
- Boar-shaped bread or entire boar on the spit
- A yule log
- Golden candles
- White candles
- Fir tree

- Presents for all present
- Wreaths
- Juniper berries and oils
- Birch wood or Birch oil

Crafts and Arts

Yule Log Cake

What you will need:

- 4 Large Eggs separated
- ¾ Cup Castor Sugar
- 1 teaspoon Vanilla Essence
- ¾ Cup Cake Flour
- 1 teaspoon Baking powder
- ¼ teaspoon salt
- Chocolate Icing

Begin by beating the egg yolks together until thick, then add the vanilla essence into the mix. Mix the flour, baking powder and add to the egg and vanilla mix. Stir until mixed thoroughly. Beat the egg whites and the salt together until they are stiff but not dry.

Using a metal spoon fold the egg whites and salt into the batter. Please be gentle. Line your Swiss roll tin with wax paper and pour the batter into the tin. Bake for 15 – 25 min in a preheated oven at 356°F. Now mix the chocolate icing. (cream works better than milk, but it does make it richer.) Once the yule log is finished baking roll it out onto a damp cloth immediately. Turn it onto castor sugar and peel off the wax paper. Spread the chocolate icing onto the yule log and begin rolling it. Allow it to cool. A secret is to place it in a very cool dark place. If you would like to add extra sprinkles of red and green on top, feel free to do so.

Wassail Yule Mead

What you will need:

- 600ml Honey
- 250ml Strong Rooibos Tea
- 2 Large lemons
- 25g Brewer's Yeast
- 2 teaspoons white sugar
- 1 teaspoon cinnamon
- 1 teaspoon ginger
- 2.5 Litres Water
- Fermentation vessel

Add yeast and sugar together in a bowl and mix. Add warm water to soak the ingredients, cover with cling film and allow to set. In a large pot, bring the 2.5 litres of water to the boil and begin stirring in the honey. Do this at a low heat so that the honey does not burn or harden inside the water. Add the cinnamon and the ginger, continue stirring for 15 minutes. Take it all off the stove and add lemon pieces to the mix. Allow this mixture to stand for at least 45min.

Ensure that the yeast mixture now has a foamy consistency and add it to the honey mix. Add all of this to your fermentation vessel and allow it to ferment for 5 – 6 weeks.

IMBOLC

The Quickening is another name for Imbolc. It is also known as Candlemas, Oimelc, Brigid's Day and Brigantia. Imbolc literally means in the belly or ewe's milk. It is the time when most of the cattle on the farms began producing milk. This was a joyous time for the people because they knew that spring was on her way.

The Child of Promise that was born at Yule now becomes *The Conquering Child.* The story of John Barleycorn also runs through the Wheel of the Year, and he is now brought into the home. The great

Celtic goddess of poetry and crafting, healing and childbirth is venerated on this day. In her honour and in the honour of all those gods and goddesses who have had a hand in the Tuatha Dé Danaan, it is customary to make a Brigid's cross and hang it in your home for protection and peace.

The story of the goddess is far more prevalent at Imbolc. She has finally been able to successfully pass through the darkness of the underworld and she is now stirring beneath the earth. The whole earth begins to change in her presence and that is why Imbolc is such an important festival. It is important to keep her as the maiden on the altar. She is not yet on the earth's surface, but she is home under the sun.

There is a more important part of Imbolc than the tale of the god and goddess. That importance comes from within each one of us. Imbolc is laden with whites and bright greens, with this new light colour change in the homes and on your altar, your inner workings should also begin to change and to single out everything that you wish to plant at Ostara. Imbolc is a time of great preparation and planning.

It is also this preparation and planning that is the reason that most witches choose this time for initiations, dedications to the gods, rededications and new pledges that they may have found with the new turn of the wheel. When following the wheel of the year in your life, you will begin to see that there is indeed a time for everything and by syncing your life in with the great wheel, you will begin to understand your own inner workings much better. There is a time for peace and quiet, a deep stillness that leads to introspection, some may refer to this as depression, but it is not, it is simply a time when the soul needs that deep stillness and the world needs to allow it. Then there is a time for celebrating life, initiating into the new turn of the wheel, of planting and of reaping what you have sown. All this is what is understood in turning the wheel of the year.

Altar Dressings

- White drapes with light greens
- John Barleycorn from Lammas
- Snowdrops and late winter bulbs
- Maiden goddess statue
- Milk products (Breads, cheese, milk)
- Flowers
- Symbols of the first signs of spring
- Sun Wheels
- Brigid's Cross

CRAFTS AND ARTS

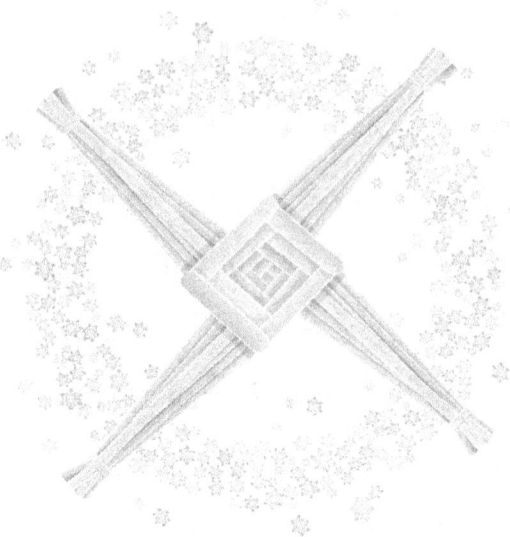

Brigid's Cross

What you will need:

- Approximately eight to fifteen grass reeds
- A scissors
- Some white cotton

The Brigid's Cross gets easier to make the more you practice. If you do not have access to reeds or strong enough blades of grass, then use green raffia, pipe cleaners or anything strong enough.

Even creating the Brigid Cross from green strips of paper works for writing the blessings on the paper and creating the Brigid's Cross. Make use of what you have. It is the intention that counts.

Directions for creating the Brigid cross

1. Lay your first reed straight down in front of you
2. Fold a second reed over the first as shown in the image below

3. Then take a new reed and repeat the process as in the image below

4. Repeat this process until you are happy with the size of your Brigid's cross. Remember to hold the centre of the cross with your thumb to keep everything in place.
5. Now tie the ends together with your white cotton. As you do this repeat the following chant:

> *"Brigid, great Goddess of Poetry and Healing,*
>
> *Brigid, great Goddess of Smith craft and midwifery,*
>
> *Lady of the Tuatha de Danaan, daughter of Dagda,*
>
> *I call you to bring peace and prosperity from afar,*
>
> *Our home is yours, the Spring is here,*

Goddess Brigid, remove the bane, remove the fear,

Protect this home and accept my prayer,

As I ask, so it shall be done,

The Goddess brings in the strengthening of the sun!"

6. When you are done with the entire process your Brigid's Cross should look like this:

What does a Brigid's Cross symbolise?

The Brigid's Cross is a symbol of protection and peace in the home. It is allowing the Goddess Brigid entrance into your home and petitioning her to keep baneful energies at bay. It is also symbolising the presence of Imbolc and welcoming in the spirit of Spring and the strengthening of the sun, the greening of the fields and the prosperity of the home. To many witches, Imbolc is not Imbolc without the presence of the Brigid's Cross.

OSTARA

Ostara is a time of extreme joy for the people of the earth and for the gods. Not only does Persephone return to her mother, Demeter and to the land of the living, but the very birds are physiologically changed, and egg production is stimulated the second that their retinae are exposed to more than 12 hours of sunlight.

Ostara is the celebration of the fertility of the earth returning, hence the presence of beautifully decorated and multi-coloured eggs. Ostara is also known as the vernal equinox, meaning that the day and night are now equal, and the days will now get longer, and the nights will get shorter. The entire festival is named after the Goddess Eostre, a Germanic Goddess who has almost no record besides the written excerpt below from the Benedictine Monk, Bede:

"Eostur-monath, qui nunc Paschalis mensis interpretatur, quondam a Dea illorum quæ Eostre vocabatur, et cui in illo festa celebrabant nomen habuit: a cujus nomine nunc Paschale tempus cognominant, consueto antiquæ observationis vocabulo gaudia novæ solemnitatis vocantes."

[Giles (1843:179)] Citation enter

In the above excerpt Bede mentions that the people worshipped a Goddess Eostre but now they have what is known as the 'Paschal month' and in this festival they have taken her honoured feasts and celebrations and have attributed it instead to a new rite and a new name.

Sadly, not much is known about this Goddess, however Spring is more than a change in festival names or feasting mannerisms. Spring is about starting new things, planting the seeds to harvest at Lammas and again at Mabon. It is imperative that you plan at Imbolc, and plant at Ostara so that your harvest at Lammas and at Mabon will be bountiful.

Other names for Ostara are: Lady Day, Earrach, Alban Eilir and the Festival of Trees. This festival is about balance and growth.

Altar Dressings

- Seedlings in trays.
- Green, white and light-coloured altar cloths.
- Statues of rabbits or hares.
- Daffodils and other flowers.
- Rose and Violet oil.
- Your decorated Ostara eggs.
- For cakes and ale, make some seed cake.
- Green reeds or bundles of green grass to hang around the ritual area.
- Cowrie shells to represent fertility.
- Butterfly imagery.

CRAFTS AND ARTS

Ostara Poppy Cake

What you will need:

Frosting (Optional)

- Fresh Thyme leaves
- Strips of Lemon zest
- 250g icing sugar
- Edible flowers

For the cake

- 20cm bread baking tin
- 3 Large eggs
- 2 Teaspoons Vanilla extract
- 150g Castor Sugar
- 150g Flour (Self-Raising)

- 2 Large lemons
- 2 Tablespoons Poppy seeds
- 3 Tablespoons fresh Milk

Directions:

- Before you begin, pre-heat your oven to 180 °C.
- Mix the Vanilla, eggs and milk together in a large bowl.
- Mix the dry ingredients (sugar, flour, lemon zest from the two lemons, and poppy seeds) together in a separate bowl.
- Now begin adding the wet ingredients to the dry ingredients. Do this step very slowly to ensure a fluffy cake.
- Beat the mixture very well.
- Butter your bread tin and add in the mixture.
- Bake for 50 – 60 minutes, keeping a careful eye on the oven.
- To decorate your cake, mix the juice from the lemons with the icing sugar. Wait for the cake to cool and then add the icing on top in any fashion that you would like. Sprinkle Thyme and edible flowers to give it that Ostara feel.

BELTANE

Beltane, or May Day is the main fertility rite in the Wheel of the Year. It is the time of the Great Hunt. The moment when the Horned God in his image of the Oak King chases down the Goddess and mates with her. This is also the time when pagans across the world dance the Maypole. The significance of the Maypole is not always understood; however, it is always enjoyed. The Maypole symbolises the phallus of the God being wrapped by the ribbons. These ribbons symbolise the womb and sexual organs of the Goddess. It is this union that brings in the harvest.

Beltane is also one of the prime moments in the Wheel of the Year to get married. To quote Starhawk: "This is the time when sweet desire weds wild delight." If you do not have a partner, but do want to get married, you would make your wish when jumping over the bel-fire. The bel-fire and the maypole are two distinct representations of this festival.

Beltane is also right across from Samhain on the Wheel, and this means a thinning of the veil between man and spirit. Beltane is the most sought-after time for those who believe in the world of faery. It is very disrespectful, even if you don't believe in them, not to make a separate table with milk, whisky and cookies or some of your food for the wee folk. If you keep to this tradition, definitely expect a gift from them in the morning.

Altar Dressings

- Red, pink, white and green altar cloths.
- Mini maypole.
- Hawthorn blossoms.
- Fae imagery.
- Fertility symbols.
- A replica of the lover's statue: The Kiss by Rodin can be used to symbolise the god and goddess.
- Make sure to have the Bel-Fire as well as a broom to jump if anyone does not wish to jump the fire.

CRAFTS AND ARTS

Beltane Fae Cakes

What you will need:

- 100g Self-Raising flour
- 100g Butter
- 2 Large eggs
- 2 Teaspoons Vanilla essence
- 100g Castor sugar

To make the Icing:

- Hundreds and thousands or any other glitter and sprinkle decorations
- 150g Icing Sugar
- Fresh cream

Directions:

- Pre-heat the oven to 175 °C
- Mix the sugar and the butter together, adding in the vanilla essence.
- Slowly add the eggs and carry on beating the mixture.
- Fold the flour into the mixture.
- Butter the muffin tray.
- Spoon one tablespoon of mixture into each muffin spacing.
- Bake for 20 minutes or until golden brown.
- Mix the icing sugar and the cream until you are happy with the consistency.
- Ice the fae cakes to represent Beltane.

LITHA

Litha is the Summer Solstice. This is the longest day in the year, but also the battle between the Oak King and his dark counterpart, the

Holly King. The Oak King, the Sun King, loses this battle and is fatally wounded. The metaphor speaks about how the sun will begin to wane from this day onwards.

Litha is also known by other names such as Samradh, Alban Hefin, Aerra Litha, and of course Mother Night. This is the time when the goddess begins to dance the dance of death. She twirls around the wounded King, and he is certain that he is going to have to be consumed by her at Lammas. He accepts his fate and does not deny that victory belongs to the Holly King.

Litha belongs to the fire element, it is also the hottest day in the year according to the mythology. This is the zenith of the sun. It will now give over to the darker half of the year. This is also your last attempt at pushing to harvest what you wish to harvest in this turn of the wheel of the year.

One of the most important themes throughout Litha, is gratitude for life. Gratitude for the oak king giving his life, gratitude for our lives, no matter what they look like. Gratitude should be something that we actively express every day in our life, however many people forget and for this reason, Litha is the celebration of gratitude.

Altar Dressings

- Roses
- Sunflowers
- Oak leaves
- Symbols of the sun
- Red, yellow and green altar cloths
- Holly leaves can be added, but this is the celebration of the life of the Oak King.
- Lavender sprigs

- Chamomile flowers.

- Robed image of the goddess in mourning, or seen as doing the dance of death

CRAFTS AND ARTS

Litha Oak Wreath

What you will need:

- Willow branches

- Oak branches, leaves and acorns

- Red embroidery cotton

- Material sunflowers

Directions:

- Plait the willow branches together to form the basis for your wreath. Tie the ends if need be with the red embroidery cotton.

- Place the Oak branches, leaves and acorns into the centre holes of the Willow.

- Put the material sunflowers into the wreath as well and design it as you wish.

- Use the red cotton to tie any of the decorations.

When you have completed the wreath, hold it to the sky with the sun shining through the middle of it. Repeat this chant until you feel that you have soaked in the strength of the sun long enough to hold out until Yule.

"Oak King's sacrifice, pinnacle of your prowess,

Grant me your light as you heal through the Goddess,

Grant me your strength as the wheel turns to darkness,

Grant me your light so I may reminisce,

Shine for me until you are born again,

Shine for me until you return to the world of men.

Grateful I am for all you have done,

Great Oak God of the Sun."

Lammas/Lughnasadh

The first harvest has finally come. It is time now to reap what you have sown. This is also the sacrifice of the Lord of the Grain known also as John Barleycorn. The great Celtic God Lugh is sacrificed to feed the people of Tuatha Da Danaan. If you have followed the Wheel of the Year as best as you could, then this is your first sight of reaping everything that you have worked so hard at achieving.

The first harvest is also known as the grain harvest or the bread harvest. We also catch sight of Demeter, mother of the grain at this festival. Her story, and the story of Lugh are prominent pieces in the traditional coven practices. One must choose the themes though, as this festival is filled with many themes from many pantheons.

John Barleycorn is sacrificed at Lammas, it is also customary to make little John Barleycorn's to keep as a remembrance and to take out at Imbolc to burn for the new ideas. This John Barleycorn will hold all the effort and the blood, sweat and tears of this turn of the wheel of the year.

John Barleycorn must die

Traffic – Steve Winwood

"There were three men came out of the west, their fortunes for to try
And these three men made a solemn vow
John Barleycorn must die

They've plowed, they've sown, they've harrowed him in
Threw clods upon his head
And these three men made a solemn vow
John Barleycorn was dead

They've let him lie for a very long time, 'til the rains from heaven did fall
And little Sir John sprung up his head and so amazed them all
They've let him stand 'til midsummer's day 'til he looked both pale and wan
And little Sir John's grown a long beard and so become a man

They've hired men with their scythes so sharp to cut him off at the knee
They've rolled him and tied him by the way, serving him most barbarously
They've hired men with their sharp pitchforks who've pricked him to the heart
And the loader he has served him worse than that
For he's bound him to the cart

They've wheeled him around and around a field 'til they came onto a pond
And there they made a solemn oath on poor John Barleycorn
They've hired men with their crabtree sticks to cut him skin from bone
And the miller he has served him worse than that
For he's ground him between two stones

And little Sir John and the nut brown bowl and his brandy in the glass
And little Sir John and the nut brown bowl proved the strongest man at last
The huntsman he can't hunt the fox nor so loudly to blow his horn
And the tinker he can't mend kettle or pots without a little barleycorn"

ALTAR DRESSINGS

- Corn dollies

- Grains of all kinds

- Breads with seeds

- A large John Barleycorn to sacrifice

- Sickles

- Beige, white, tan coloured altar cloths

Crafts and Arts

John Barleycorn

What you will need:

- An old man's outfit
- Hay (Lots of it)
- String
- A straw hat
- A strong branch that will hold John Barleycorn

Directions:

- Stuff the outfit with hay, almost like a body, tying the pieces together with the string.
- Leave hay to come out of the shirt so that you can prop the hat on top of it.
- Dig a hole where the fire pit will be.
- Now place the strong branch through the leg of the pants and into the back of the shirt.
- Prop John barleycorn into the newly dug hole.
- Set him alight and whilst he is burning sing the lyrics to the song, John Barleycorn must die above.

Mabon

Mabon is the Autumnal Equinox, meaning, once again day and night are equal, but this time, the nights will grow longer, colder, and as they do, we will know that the Oak King is trudging through the lessons of the underworld.

The Goddess is said to devour the god during the night of Mabon. He will enter her tomb and will emerge again at Yule. It is the second harvest and the last time to reap what you have sown. Beyond being the second harvest, Mabon is also the wine harvest and the fruit harvest. It is said that the last of the soul of the god is in the fruit and when we eat them, we must remember how he sacrificed himself, so that we may be fed and survive the long, dark winter months ahead.

ALTAR DRESSINGS

- Apples
- Autumn leaves
- Acorns
- Pinecones
- Antlers
- Vines
- Your knot magick

CRAFTS AND ARTS

Clove Orange House Cleanser

What you will need:

- 1 or more large oranges (the amount depends on how many you wish to make)
- 1 Packet of whole cloves

Directions:

- Even though the 'Clove Orange House Cleanser' is easy to make, it is a powerful cleanser on the mundane and in the spiritual world.
- Pierce the orange with the clove buds.
- You can place as many as you wish.
- Before placing your 'Clove Orange House Cleanser' around your home, hold it in both hands and repeat this chant:

"Orange and clove, together as one,

Fight off negativity from my home."

Now place them around the house. They are great for fighting off mosquitoes and all sorts of insects. On the spiritual they ward off negativity. Make sure to make a new one every week.

The Path of the Masculine through the Wheel of the Year

The Wheel of the Year is really all about tracing the path of the Sun God. It is simultaneously the path of the Oak King, one of the aspects of the Sun God, and the Holly King, another aspect of the Sun God.

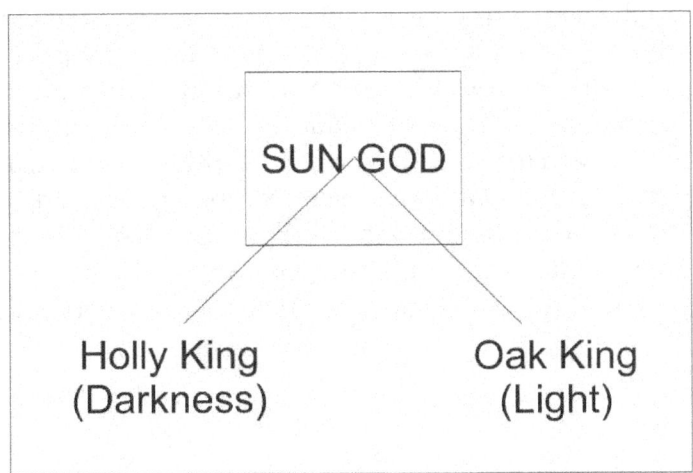

The Wheel of the Year is also a dated according to the movement of the sun, therefore it is a celebration of the solar timing. The sun god has been venerated throughout history, almost every single native culture worshipped the sun and petitioned it throughout the winter months to return. According to the geographical placement of the people who were worshipping, their prayers as well as their attributes given to their version of the sun god would mirror their surroundings.

Within the Wiccan framework created by Gardner, we witness a dualistic viewpoint of the sun god or the solar aspect of the Horned God. The sun god is divided into light and dark. The Oak King governs the light half of the year which begins at Yule with his return from the underworld and ends at Litha when he is fatally wounded in battle by the Holly King. The Holly King then reigns from Litha until Yule when it is his longest night.

The dualistic nature of the sun god is a necessary addition to the already complex story of the Wheel of the Year. We all have a shadow side as well as a light side. We cannot know the heat if we do not understand the cold. We cannot identify happiness if we have not felt sadness. The masculine path is no different throughout this solar wheel, it must contain a dualistic nature so that we humans can understand and give meaning to what is happening around us.

To worship the sun god in his totality, we need to understand every aspect of him. We need to identify and study his darkness and walk the path with him through the end of summer into autumn and through winter. We need to understand his shadow self is within us as well and we need to locate that darkness within us and take control over it. Similarly, the Oak King must also be understood, we must understand his strength through the light and with him we must descend into the darkness and ensure that we do not see the descent as a fall of any kind, it is simply a rising into a different aspect of ourselves.

THE PATH OF THE FEMININE THROUGH THE WHEEL OF THE YEAR

The goddess is always in everything. If you recall, we mentioned earlier how she is the darkness and the void, how she is the potential of everything in the universe. How can there be any fable then without her? She is always found in either the maiden, mother or crone aspect.

Like with the dualistic nature of the god that runs through the Wheel of the Year, the goddess mimics his movements, but can also find herself in various stages at the same time. Her maiden phase only begins at Imbolc, where his light reign begins at his birth from the tomb (resurrection) at Yule. She is then quickly sprung into a teenager by the time Ostara comes but can also appear as Mother Nature, as Ostara / Eostre, or she can become any other goddess that you wish to venerate on that festival.

She descends on Samhain, and for two festivals, Samhain and Yule she remains the old hag, the crone, the wise woman of bone and medicine. However, she is not only darkness in the crone stage, she can bring darkness, like she does on Mabon when the Oak King finally descends back into her womb (which is the underworld and the tomb). In this aspect, and at this moment on the wheel she is the dark mother who sacrifices her husband to feed the people of the earth.

Everything has a cycle, the cycle of the goddess, even though it is not always celebrated or spoken of within the wheel, is as important as the cycle of the god, if not more so. It is she who assists the god at fulfilling his duties and his birth rights at every turn. Whether she is his mother, his maiden lover, his death-defying crone, she is the one who makes his journey possible.

Chapter 3 – Forging your Witch-Self

It is now time that you learn to forge your witch-self. It is now time to step into your own power and to grasp the entirety of what and who you are. For you to know what your strengths and your gifts are, you must be able to step into this power without fear of the unknown. The unknown is the goddess, and how can you fear her? Respect is unquestionably one of the most paramount things when beginning on this path and you should never ever disrespect spirit. Especially if you do not completely understand it yet. Funnily enough, one can never understand spirit completely, it is indeed an enigma to humanity and may remain like that until the end of all things mundane.

To forge your witch-self, there are a few tips, tricks and tools to get you started. Remember the most important part of all of this is to listen to your intuition. If something does not feel right, then please do not even think of doing it. We are all unique and your path will be your own. It must be so.

The Wiccan Rede

The Wiccan Rede, as it is known now, is one of the handiest references that you can choose to listen to and study when you are beginning on your path. It was first published by a hereditary witch named Lady Gwen Thompson in a magazine called the Green Egg. She claims that it was her grandmother who gifted her this wisdom. Sadly, not everything can be proved, and it is thought that Doreen Valiente, ritual architect to Gerald Gardner, spoke the "an harm it none, do what ye will" words in a public speech before the counsel of the wise ones or the Rede of the Wiccae was even published.

We will never know who wrote it first, or where it came from, but the reason it is such a brilliant reference is because it works. The Wiccan Rede stands true to its wisdom and many, Wiccans and Witches know it well. For your convenience the most important pieces have been set in Bold. These are pieces that should be researched and meditated upon.

The Rede of the Wiccae (*Counsel of the Wise Ones*)
Written and published by Lady Gwen Thompson in the Ostara Edition of the Green Egg Magazine (1975)

Bide the Wiccan Law ye must,

In Perfect Love and Perfect Trust;

Live ye must and let to live,

Fairly take and fairly give.

True in love, *ever be,*

Lest thy love be false to thee.

With a fool no season spend,

Nor be counted as his friend.

Soft of eye and light of touch,

Speak ye little, listen much.

Ever mind the rule of three,

What ye send out comes back to thee.

This lesson well, thou must learn

Ye only get what ye do earn.

Eight words the Wiccan Rede fulfill -

An it harm none, do as ye will.

Deosil *go by* **waxing** *Moon,*

*Sing and dance **the invoking** Rune;*
***Widdershins** go by **waning** Moon,*
*Chant ye then a **freeing** tune;*

*When the Lady's **Moon is new**,*
*Kiss thy hand to Her **times two**;*
*When the **Bow rides in the eve***
*Turn to what you would **achieve**;*
*When the **Moon rides at her peak**,*
*Then thy heart's desire **seek**;*
*When the **Sickle shows Her face***
***Release** the old with proper grace.*

Greet the Days and greet the Nights
With joy and thanks for all delights.
Sing the seasons all around
Til wondrous awe and love abound

Heed *the **North wind**'s mighty gale,*
Lock the door & trim the sail;
*When the **wind comes from the South**,*
***Love** will kiss thee on the mouth;*

*When the **wind blows from the West**,*

Hearts will find their **peace and rest**;
When the **wind blows from the East**,
Expect **the new** and set the feast.

Nine woods in the Cauldron go,
Burn them quick and burn them slow;
Grape and **fir** and **apple** tree,
And **Hawthorn** are sacred to Thee,
Willow, hazel, rowan, birch,
And **oak** will guide your every search;
Elder be the Lady's tree -
Burn it not or cursed ye'll be.

Birchwood in the fire goes
To tell us **true what Goddess knows**.
Oak trees tower great with might,
Burn the Oak for **God's insight**.
Rowan is a tree of power
Causing **life and magic** to flower.
Willows at the waters stand
To help us to the **Summerland**.
Hawthorn burn to purify
And draw the faerie to your eye.
Hazel tree, the wisdom sage,

Lends strength that comes with honored age.
White the flowers of Apple tree,
The holy gift of fecundity.
Grape grows upon the fruitful vine,
Sacred gifts of joy and wine.
Fir's ever greenness declares life
Succeeds beyond any strife.

Heed ye flower, bush, and tree,
And by the Lady Blessed be.
Where the rippling waters flow
Cast a stone and truth ye'll know;

Four times the Major Sabbats mark
In the light and in the dark:

As the old year starts to wane
The new begins with dark Samhain.
When flowers blossom through the snow
Fair Brigid casts her seed to sow.
When winter yields to warmth's return
Let the Beltane fires burn.
As summer turns to Lammas night
First fruits and Grain Gods reach their height.

Four times the Minor Sabbats fall
Use the Sun to mark them all:

At Yuletide, with feast and mirth
We celebrate the God Child's birth.
Spring Equinox, Eostara's fest,
All newborn creatures will be blessed.
When the Sun has reached its height
Celebrate the greatest Light.
Offer thanks at second reaping;
Mabon poised for winter's sleeping.

*Cast the **circle thrice about**,*
*To keep unwelcome **spirits out**.*
*To **bind the spell** well every time,*
*Let the spell be **spake in rhyme**.*

Follow this with mind & art,
Bright the cheeks and warm the heart,
And merry meet & merry part
And merry meet again!

Finding your Witch Name

Ah, the task of being given a name. A name of the craft that would provide you with the persona of the Witch within. The name that you choose is extremely important. Many enjoy names that contain their totem animals and their favourite time of day and that is perfectly alright if you like that. The name though, the one that you use in your craft and in front of your deities should never ever be known by anyone but you and the gods. Why? Because your name will become like your blood and your hair, dangerous in the wrong hands.

The craft name is the name you take up and the persona (which should be a completely open self) in front of the gods and your spirit allies. This is your work, your name, your path. There is nothing in that sentence that really has anything to do with anyone else. Many authors have witchy names for the public and then they have their private ones for their own path. It is this personal private magically exclusive to your own path name that you will be guided to find here. You wouldn't allow the person down the road the keys to your home and allow them to go through your things, would you? Then why give the whole world access to you on the astral and on the physical. Yes, this name is that important. It is you. So be wise and keep this name hidden, known only to you and to the spiritual realm. Do not even mention it to your High Priestess or elders, for everyone walks a path together for a season and not everyone is as nice as you would like them to be. Rather be safe than sorry.

Why do you need a Witch name in the first place? Your Witch name allows your subconscious to begin creating the persona that you have with spirit. It begins allowing you to store the spiritual experiences away from the mundane. When you have been practicing for a long while, you will find that you can hop in and out of your meditation or trance state and this is imperative if you are going to be assisting people who live solely in the mundane world. Your witch name is also important because you are able to shield your spiritual work on the astral. You are protected by using a spiritual name and shielded from jealous attacks on your spiritual self.

Some argue that having more than one name will cause a rift in the mind, a sort of split personality. We are not such vulnerable creatures. Yes, mental instability and mental problems do exist, and sometimes they are an intense hindrance to our lives. However, the soul knows best. If your mental state is prone to mental disorders and choosing another name does not feel right, then by all means, do not have another one. Many witches that I have met only use a name in public circle because they have too. A great many other witches whom I call friend, only found their names years after starting out on the path. So, whatever feels comfortable and right, you do that, because that is you, and you are perfect exactly the way that you are.

Choosing your name through

DREAMWORK

If dreaming is your thing, then you are very fortunate indeed. The dreamscape is the direct channel of information to and from the subconscious mind. There are so many avenues to investigate through the dreamworld that witches find dreaming one of the most important skills to have. Connecting with your Witch name through dreamwork is easier than you may think. There are many ways to accomplish this, and if you are a lucid dreamer then the path is easier. For this book though, we will be advising name finding through normal dream states.

Utilising the Plant Kingdom for

Dreamwork

The plant kingdom can be extremely helpful, and if you have an interest in plants, trees and flowers then hedge witchery may be your thing. There are thousands of plants that can assist us in entering an altered state in our dreams and help us to manage our dream recall better. It is more often than not that many of these plants are poisonous to the system and for that simple reason, without the proper medical background it would be unwise to go down that path. There are however other plants that work quite as well, and they provide us with lifelong allies into the dreamscape.

Lavendula Officianalis

Lavender is not a sissy plant as many like to call it. In fact, Lavender may be one of the most beloved plants known to witches. Using Lavender to enter the dreamscape is definitely a safe enough doorway and will not produce any side effects from a single dose. Lavender does however produce a heightened release of female hormones into the body and so it is not advisable for men / boys to be using this plant over a long period of time. Make yourself a cup of Lavender Tea, keep a sprig of Lavender aside. Using a perfectly square piece of blue paper, write your name as it is now. Then write and speak the following words:

"Lavender light I honour and petition you,

My witches name revealed to me,

In dreamscape give me eyes to see,

As I will so mote it be!"

When you are done, fold the sprig of Lavender into the blue square of paper. Place it under your pillow. Drink your Lavender tea and keep a journal next to your bed with a pen. Repeat this entire process until your Witch name appears to you. It will come. Believe and you will receive.

Valerian Officianalis

The Valerian spirit is strong. It is also one of the most foul-smelling plants that can be found. It is said that Valerian smells something akin to old wet socks. The Valerian spirit should never be taken without a medical practitioner giving you the go ahead. There are contraindications, there are side effects and you need to be aware of these. Valerian is also a known mutagen and must never be taken during pregnancy.

A powdered version of Valerian is noted by Scott Cunningham as being an excellent substitute for graveyard dust. For the purpose of finding your Witch name, the spirit of Valerian will not only guide, and protect you through the dreamscape but she will also remain an excellent guide for dreamwork after you have acquired your name.

Before doing anything with the Valerian, take approximately half a cup of Valerian root to use over the period of one week. Do this in the waxing lunar phase. Place both your hands over the Valerian and speak the following chant:

"Mother of the underworld, wise and ancient,

I honour thee.

Mother of the slumber that never returns,

I honour thee,

Valerian, beautiful majestic queen of the night visions,

I honour thee.

I petition thee, to guide and protect me,

I honour thee.

I seek my Witch name from the land of night,

Guide me on my journeys, guide me though the nightscape.

I honour thee."

Try to speak this chant over and over again. Allow it to take you into a trance state by the words and the presence of the Valerian spirit alone. She is with you. She is beneath your hands and you will feel her. Her spirit is strong.

When you are ready make a pot of Valerian tea, add honey to taste. She is not the best tasting medicine, but she is one of the most effective. Make the tea with 1 teaspoon of Valerian per night.

Have a pen and dream journal next to your bed. Please be warned that your dreams will change. If you are not a dreamer and you have chosen to do this to enhance your dreamwork abilities, believe me they will be enhanced. If you encounter any side effects at all, please stop using the Valerian at once.

USING NUMEROLOGY TO FIND YOUR WITCH

NAME

Numerology is the study of numbers. Just like with colour and sound, and pretty much everything else in the universe, numbers also have a vibration. Each number has a universal number attached to it and each letter has a corresponding number. It is believed that numerology predates the Kabbalistic system, but its origins are cloudy. Many people refer back to the work of Pythagoras 569 – 470 BCE, who was a Greek mathematician and great philosopher. His work lends a large amount of information to the face of numerology today. Below is the Pythagorean table used for entrance Numerology.

1	2	3	4	5	6	7	8	9
A	B	C	D	E	F	G	H	I
J	K	L	M	N	O	P	Q	R
S	T	U	V	W	X	Y	Z	

It is this numerology chart that you will be using to see if your name is the right choice for your personality and for what you want to achieve on your path as a Witch. Now we will go into what each of the numbers symbolise. There are thousands of books that go in depth on Numerology, and one such book, which, if you can get your hands on a copy will be one of the most valuable books in your collection is, Cheiro's Book of Numbers. For the sake of simply finding your Witch name, we will only be covering the very basics of Numerology.

The meanings behind the numbers

- The number 1 is the beginning of everything, this is the source number. Number one is the initiator of any project, that first energy burst. Leadership and strength of character are associated with number 1. Number one is akin to the passion, willpower and driving force contained within the element of fire. Beware though, as number 1 is also full of aggression, egotism and contains impulsiveness. Make sure to balance your number 1.

- The number 2 is the number of the empath. It is the number of duality and the dual nature of the universe. Number 2 is the number of mediators and partnerships, healing another and being able to climb into another's shoes. Beware though as the number 2 is also filled with self-consciousness if it is not balanced.

- The number three is the life-giving number. It is the first instance where the dual nature of spirit now gives life. This number is the number of creating more of oneself. It is filled with imagination and great insight. It is known as the number of the artist. There is a downside, and this is the lack of direction, so balancing this number with a more stable input is very necessary.

4

- The number 4 is the filing cabinet of all the other numbers. Number 4 is organisation par excellence. Even though it is said that number 4 is also the practical number it is backed by an attention to detail and a scientific inquiring mind second to none. The caution here, especially when choosing a spiritual Witch name is that number 4 lacks imagination, so pairing it with number 3 or with another imaginative balance is important.

5

- Number 5 is the visionary, the pioneer, the conqueror. Number 5 jumps when needed but sometimes also without looking before they leap. The number 5 loves to explore and delve into a thousand projects and knows them all. The only downside of the number 5 is that they are easily bored and will not study a certain subject in detail. This is unfortunately not helpful in the world of Witchcraft as every single subject must be studied in detail if you are to ever become a teacher in that art or to use it to assist others and yourself. It is no use being a jack of all trades.

6

- The number 6 is the humanitarian of numerology. Sixes are the home bound lovers of life. They are the ones who you can always go to, to borrow a cup of sugar. They are found in the nursing and healing fields and even though they think they know everything; it is seldom found that they don't. The weakness of the 6 is that they will do anything for a person who flatters their efforts, and this is a wide-open doorway for those that wish to use a Witch for all he/she has.

7

- The number 7 is the seeker of numerology. This number has the ability to delve into the deepest darkest chasms of the void of the Goddess and find the source of all life. Unfortunately, the 7 is a loner, but that is always a trait that many Witches carry. To pick a Witch name vibrating this number means that your intuition and natural occult interests will be at the forefront always. It is more often than not that people with a name carrying the 7 will begin their own religions, mystical paths and they work.

8

- The number 8 is the name for those wanting to forge ahead to becoming a High Priestess of a coven. The 8's are excellent leaders and they are probably the best at rounding up members to work towards a unified cause. Unfortunately, even though the 8's make brilliant leaders they tend to work far too hard. They are also not in touch with their intuitive side and cannot see the forest for the trees.

9

- The number 9 is the vibration of the writer and the artist. A vibration of neediness does flow through this number however the number is also synonymous with giving back the same or more energy as what is received. Number 9's are extremely selfless and there only real drawback is that they have thousands of interests at once.

Above and beyond the nine main numbers that all things fit into, we have what is known as master numbers. Master numbers have their own special meanings and, in this day, and in this new age, they have also become what is known as angel numbers. We will not be discussing the new age angelic influence, but we will be discussing their original meanings.

The two Master numbers are as follows:

11 – The master number 11 is the spiritual strength of the number 2 amplified a thousand-fold. The negative traits of number two count in number 11 but again, they are amplified.

22 – The master number of 22 is the number of great world changers. 22 is capable of changing the world as we know it. It is also wonderful to see the feats of a 22 within the occult world. Where the negativities apply please see number 4.

Now to the interesting practical magic of choosing your Witch name through Numerology. It is now time for you to go and do some hunting. Find names that you like the meanings of, then work out their numbers like the example below. Try to decide on a number that you want your name to fit into first, then go hunting for the names. These can be the names of animals, birds, colours, gods, goddesses etc.

The Numerology Equation

Using the pythagorean numerology chart above

MORGAINE FOXMOON

4 + 6 + 9 + 7 + 1 + 9 + 5 + 5 + 6 + 6 + 6 + 4 + 6 + 6 + 5 = 85

8 + 5 =

1 + 3 = 4

Number 4 is the number for this name. Now use your birth name to practice and see what attributes your number allows for your personality. Make sure that your Witch name, when you have found it, matches the attributes with which you want to walk your spiritual path.

UTILISING THE METHOD OF BAG DRAWING

There is nothing quite as magical as drawing something out of a bag and finding that it matches you perfectly. If dreaming has not worked, and you wish for something a little faster then why not get a large pouch, even a normal bag will do. Cut out letters, pictures of favourite things and numbers. Make sure that they all fit on the same size papers. Fold them all up. Place them in the bag and say this chant before beginning the picking:

"Bag of chance, pouch of universal synchronicity,

My hand be drawn to the name that is right for me,

Let me pick perfectly what I must,

I know I will, for in the gods I trust."

When you are done, lay the bag in front of you, close your eyes and pick out as many pieces of paper that you feel you need. Less is more in this instance. Once you have your chosen pieces. Open them and sort the options that you have, for example:

The names that come to mind can be as follows:

AWEN CRESCENT BEAR

BEAR OF THE FIRE ECLIPSE

AWEN BEARMOON

Or anything that you feel. You can then use the names that you have jotted down in your journal and work out their numerological attributes and see if it fits with what you would like for your path through the witchcraft landscape. The chances are that it will work the first time that you try. This pouch of chance really does work for almost anything, including divination.

HOW TO FIND YOUR PATRON GOD AND GODDESS

The first and most troubling question that we hear from neophytes is: "How will I know that they (the gods) are talking to me?" It's all about the faith, the belief and the synchronicity of the moment that it takes place in. Your intuition is always your most powerful tool in understanding the language of the gods.

Devotion is one of the most important parts of Wicca and Witchcraft. Do you need a patron god and goddess? No, you do not need to work with any gods or goddesses. Some hedge witches work with plant allies and have no patron gods or goddesses present. In coven work and through your degrees it is required that you work with at least one god and one goddess, however as a solitary, if this does not suit you then I do not see a problem.

There is so much to learn from the gods and goddesses though. The divine landscape has so many treasure troves to explore and so many beautiful magical gifts to bestow on those who dare to enter into the endless worlds, that it would be a shame not to attempt to work with at least one goddess or one god in your lifetime.

The gods do not only come to you. This is a misconception and a fable that has wormed its way into Witchcraft, and it leaves thousands of witchlings lost and heartbroken because the gods seem to never choose them, yet everyone else has a magical story of how they were chosen. This can cause a horrific rift in the magical growth of the young practitioner and it will affect their practice without them even realising it.

The truth is that the gods have chosen us all. Each and every single person on this earth and in this time has been chosen. You are alive are you not? This is no accident, nor is the fact that you are reading this book and have landed your beautiful eyes on these words. The gods have chosen you. Now, which aspect will you connect with? That is up to you. What do you want to learn, which aspect of the gods do you want as a teacher? Who keeps cropping up in blogs and books? What image do you have in your mind of a god or goddess? Now follow the breadcrumbs, follow them until you find the aspect of the divine that suits you in the moment that you need it.

The aspects of the god and goddess, (remember the diamond theory discussed in Chapter One), do not remain the same, just like you do not remain the same at all. You change. Scientifically, every seven years, you are a physically different person, completely. It is very normal to chop and change aspects of the gods as you, yourself change. It is also extremely normal to have only a single god and goddess your entire life. It depends on you and what feels right for your life.

If this method of seeking out the divine aspects does not suit you then here is a pathworking, a meditation that you can ask someone to read for you, or record it and then make sure you will be undisturbed and that you have your Book of Mirrors or a journal next to you and play the pathworking back to yourself. Using soft repetitive music like the sound of rain on a loop can be extremely helpful as well.

Lie down or sit comfortably. Close your eyes and take a deep breath in through your nose and blow it out your mouth as hard as you can. Breath in again, this time hold the breath for 3 seconds, blow out as hard as you can through your mouth. Again, breathe in and hold for 6 counts... 1... 2... 3... 4... 5... 6... now breathe out all the worries, the pain, the stress. Breathe in through your nose again and breathe this air into your belly. Breathe out calmly. Place your tongue on the roof of your mouth, right behind your front teeth and get comfortable.

I want you to place your focus on your feet. Feel your feet relaxing, relax each toe. Now concentrate on your calves, relax them, your thighs, feel how relaxed they are. Your groin area is relaxed, your stomach, your rib cage, relax and allow them gently to feel as though you are drifting off to sleep. Now your chest, relax your chest, your shoulders, your upper arms, your forearms, your hands… relax each finger. Now breathe in and bring your concentration to your neck, allow all the tension to leave your neck, relax. Now your jawbone, relax your cheek muscles your mouth, your eyes and your forehead. Imagine now that you are lying on quicksand, feel your relaxed body sink through the quicksand and land on a concrete slab in a candle lit room.

In this room there are no doors and no windows unless you want them. Imagine now a door in front of you. You have created this door. Look at the markings on the door. Look if there are words or symbols, inspect the door closely. Now, open the door. Behind the door is a white room, again with no doors or windows, unless you want them to be there. Beneath your feet there is a blue cushion. This cushion is positioned right between the white room of light and the concrete room of darkness. Sit down on this cushion. Get comfortable. Now breathe in, and out.

Concentrate now on the doorframe between the two rooms. There is a distinct line between the two and there is a word written on either side. Read them and feel these words in your soul. As you do so a figure appears in one of the rooms. Look toward this figure and greet them. Look at them intently and remember every detail of their face, their hair, their clothing and if they are carrying anything. Is there a change to the room that they have entered? Ask them their name. Ask them why they have come when you called the word written on the doorframe? Ask them for guidance on your path. Ask them how you should practice devotion to them.

When you are ready stand up to greet them. Take the gift that they are handing to you. If another being appears that is okay. Greet them as well. Ask any questions that you may have for them.

When you are ready, walk into the room where the last entity appeared. Stretch your hand upward and as you pull your hand down again, see the ladder from the quicksand above slowly come down so that you can climb back to your mundane self. Climb the ladder upward to your body. Breathe in and release your tongue from the roof of your mouth. Concentrate on your toes. Concentrate on any smells in the air, any sounds, and when you are ready open your eyes and write everything down that you can remember.

This pathworking above assists with meeting any entity that you need to. It is not only used for patron gods and goddesses but remember the three laws of magic are Intention, Focus and Willpower. So, whatever your intention, focus and willpower is when entering into this meditation, that will be the outcome of the pathworking.

Once you have all the information from the pathworking, make sure to also record your dreams for the next week for more clues on the nature of the being/s in your journey. Pathworking's assist with so many things. They are fantastic for healing, for working out solutions that you cannot otherwise access, they are bridges between the conscious and subconscious minds and pathworking's are a Witch's greatest tool.

THE ALTAR

The Altar is the portal between this side of the veil and the other. It is not only a mundane place where we hope to meet the gods and to pay our respects. The altar is a place on the astral as well. Every time you make an altar, it is opened up on the astral and the sighting of this on the astral of temples, holy places and altars of practitioners that are not shielded on the astral are probably one of the most beautiful memorable sightings that any astral traveller can have.

The altar is also your soul space. Yes, your body may be doing the standing, the kneeling, the seating, but it is your soul that does the devotional motions. This altar is also a place where you show the aspect of the divine that you have chosen to connect to that they are important to you and to your space, that they are allowed into your life.

A witch's altar is sometimes very different to the altar of a Wiccan practitioner. The reason for this is the rules and the adage of *everything has its place within Wicca*. An altar of a non-Wiccan is an arrangement of important symbols and goodies to represent what the witch deems holy and important. The altar can also contain poppets or corn dollies of healing or cursing that the witch may have decided to lay in front of his/her gods. A Witchcraft altar has no segregation for the items, anything goes where he/she pleases. It is however also her place to commune with his/her gods and the altar of a Witch or a Wiccan should never be touched.

The altar of a Wiccan is different in that it has certain placements for each item, even the candles and the incense. A Wiccan altar is divided into three. The back section and the highest level (if your altar has a different level, you can raise the back of the altar by placing a book beneath the cloth) is kept exclusively to represent the Universal spirit. The Universal spirit is only symbolised by a single white candle. Never place a black candle there, whether it is Samhain or not.

Directly in front of the Universal Spirit is the rest of the altar. This place is then divided into left and right. Left and right matched by your left and right when you face your altar. The left is kept exclusively for the goddess and for all things feminine. The right is kept exclusively for the god and for all things masculine. Cakes and ale are never placed on the main altar and a separate table may be placed below this altar. On the left you will set down the feminine elements, the earth and the water. On the right you will place down the masculine elements and those are Air and Fire. Directly in front of the Universal Spirit candle you will have a candle for the goddess on the left and a candle for the god on the right. These two candles do not count as elemental representations.

A statue of your god and goddess can then be added but it is not necessary. Please see the Wiccan altar setup outlined below:

The elements are represented in different ways. For example, you may not have incense on hand, but you have a feather, this is a great representation of Air. It is important to not worry too much on the fine details and to remember that the gods know your intention and your spirit. One of the most important pieces to the working of the altar is the pentacle. The pentacle is a pentagram surrounded by a circle. The pentacle is usually crafted from a natural element and represents the element of Earth. When the pentacle is facing you, your altar is open on the mundane and on the astral and it is an open portal or doorway. When you are finished with your sacred time, you must turn the pentacle over and state that the doorway is closed.

The Wiccan way is to balance everything, the left to the right, the up to the down and the inner to the outer worlds. It is important to balance everything and even though this balance is thought to only be a Wiccan thing, it is not. Mother Nature always seems to balance herself out, we always seem to need balance in our lives, even with food or vitamins that our body craves, we just know it. You know that feeling when you wake up and you really want some orange juice, you can almost taste it, well that is the balance of your body being achieved. Our mind, not our brain, is far more intelligent than we can even begin to comprehend.

Remember this intelligence when you are creating your altar. Remember that this is your souls special place, it belongs to no one but you, or your partner if you both share a sacred space.

SACRED TIME AND SACRED SPACE

You need sacred time and you need your own sacred space. Does this mean that all witches have an entire ritual room to themselves and that they have always had that if they do? Not at all. Sacred time and sacred space have nothing to do with the placement of the devotional practice. Sacred time can be any time you want it to be, sacred space can be anywhere you want it to be. If you do not have the luxury of being brought up by pagan or spiritually alternative parents, then take a walk to the park or go and sit by a tree in the garden. You will find that one day when you do have your own spiritual room or temple space indoors that you long for the time when you sat by the tree.

It does not matter where or when, what matters is that you make the time and you make the space. Cleansing space does not need anything, although sage smudging helps, holy water cleansing does feel a little better but that is only because human beings need to see things happen with their physical eyes. The fact that you go sit by the tree in a park or in your garden or even on the grass in the same spot and intentionally focus your mind and will the place to be cleansed of negativity means that it will be so. That is how powerful your own inner magick is. You need to practice this, and those who do not have the tools at first may seem less fortunate to the untrained practitioner, but in a large sense their training will be far greater.

Your magic is not dependent on the tools that you possess, nor is it dependent on the clothes you wear or the place where you are. You are your magick, your magick lies in the very fibre of your being.

A mental chant for those without a dedicated sacred space

Here is a little chant to remember if you do not have a dedicated sacred space and wish to cleanse, purify and bless the area you are about to sit or stand in:

"I am magick, magick is me,

This ground is holy by my spirit's decree,

I am magick and magick is me,

This ground is sacred, blessed and cleansed

As I will so mote it be!"

A cleansing for those with a dedicated sacred space

If you are fortunate enough to possess a sacred space of your own, then this is a good way to cleanse the space of any baneful or unwanted energetic residue.

First cleanse the space with your besom / broom. If you do not own one, please see the Chapter on Samhain on how to make yourself one. Whilst you are sweeping the energy chant the following words:

> *"Cleanse and cleanse and clean you'll be,*
>
> *Only stay if you're good for me,*
>
> *Cleansing clean energy,*
>
> *The only energy this space will see."*

Now take your holy water, the combined mix of blessed sea salt and preferably blessed mineral water and with your smudge wand or a bunch of feathers, wash the area by sprinkling the holy water over the area and repeating the chant:

> *"Holy, holier, holiest energy be,*
>
> *Washed and blessed, cleansed and dressed,*
>
> *To house the divine and holiest of energy.*
>
> *As I will, so mote it be."*

Now walk the room with your sage incense or smudge stick and allow the air to soak up the scent of sage. Repeat these words as you move about your sacred space:

> *"Sage, my spirit ally I honour you,*
>
> *Vibrate the energy here to house my divinity,*
>
> *Sage, my spirit ally, cleanse, bless and make anew,*
>
> *As I will, so mote it be!"*

Now you are ready to cast circle, have devotional practice or simply sit in the divine energetic vibration that you have created. Ensure that you create this space, regardless where in the world you find yourself and under which circumstances. Sacred Time and Sacred Space is far more important than these words can convey. You are building your soul; you are feeding your spirit and you are paving the way to commune with the divine within you and without you. It is only through practicing this sacred time in your intended sacred space that you can ever hope to develop the divine aspects of yourself.

PRACTICING MAGICK VERSUS DEVOTION TIME

Every practitioner wishes to enter the occult because they know they can cause change. It is the sense of power that draws most practitioners to the craft, however the power is already within you. When you say this to a neophyte they usually frown and think you are silly, or you are hiding the path of the real power because you believe that they are not ready yet. The power seekers never stay on the Wiccan path, they meander into other forms of Witchcraft and end up further and further down the rabbit hole. This is their lesson and that is where they find themselves, in the pit of the darkest void of the bosom of the primordial breath of the goddess.

Those who come knocking on the door of the craft because they know that there is more to the origins of their own beings are the ones who are able to remain in Wicca or find themselves a comfortable seat at the table of Witches. Neither the one who seeks power, nor the one who comes for worship and truth are wrong. Everyone has their purpose and their place on this planet and every Wiccan who remains a Wiccan, was always meant to become a Wiccan. Similarly, the Witches who seek to cause harm, have their place. They become the catalysts for other witches to strengthen their protection abilities.

You are divine but you are not a god. You are a spiritual being in a meat suit who is travelling the universe on a giant rock filled with water and sand and life-giving trees around a catastrophically hot ball of fire that gives you your Wheel of the Year. You are living a human life in this moment and therefore the power that you seek will not take you to the place that your soul is searching to be. Devotion to the gods is the necessary bridge that must be built in order for you to:

- Understand your own divine nature
- Identify the divinity within the world around you

- Identify the placement of all circumstances and how they can be changed

- Know what your life purpose is and honour that path

- Find solace in the nature of the evolving world

- Forge a relationship with and learn new gifts from the divine aspects of the dualistic nature of the divine

- Assist the spirits who are trapped on this plain

- Assist the humans who have lost touch with their souls

Devotion is magick without making you a god. Magick requires you to enforce the intended change by utilising the permission from the divine or by yourself. This is impossible if you have not built the bridge to the divine. In Wicca, most covens do not allow a practitioner to practice any form of magick for their entire first degree. This first degree is meant to last only a year and a day but, in many cases, if the practitioner is not ready, they will not be graded.

Begin with creating your sacred space and allotting sacred time to your daily activities. It is the best place to start to know yourself and the divine nature better. The magick is within you, it is not going away, it is with you, it has always been and will always remain there.

THE TOOLS OF THE CRAFT

The most important tool of the craft is you. You are your craft, but you will only understand that once you have owned all the tools that there are to own. Like training wheels on a bicycle, the tools of the craft are a necessary teacher for the student to recognise their own potential of practicing magick and of altering their own worlds. We will now cover the most important tools in the craft.

The Besom

The besom is the best cleaning tool of all the options that Witches have to cleanse a space. It can seem like an ordinary grass broom, but to the Witch, this besom can remove all baneful energy from a place, and it does. Many Witches and Wiccans know of sage, they know of holy water, but they do not know of the powerful ally that the besom makes. Not only is the besom a powerful cleanser of the negativity but it is also a bridge between worlds. When the besom is laid down on the ground it becomes a doorway. This doorway is then used in rituals such as handfasting or at Beltane celebrations.

The Wand

The Wand and the Athame have the same duties. They draw and extend the power of the practitioner; they target and focus that energy to a precise pinpointed location. The wand is used, according to Gerald Gardner himself to call nature spirits and those spirits who are threatened by the sight of the Athame. The Wand is masculine in nature, but this will also depend on the tree from which the wand was harvested. The Willow for example is a feminine tree and will cause the wand to display the feminine attributes of the Willow tree as well as the masculine aspects of it being a wand.

The Athame

The Athame is masculine. It is a black handled knife with a double-edged blade used, like the wand, to extend and draw power to and from the practitioner into a focused area such as the perimeter of the circle. It is also never ever to be used to cut anything except ethereal cords and doorways in the circle. The Athame is an astral tool and should be kept as an astral tool.

The Chalice

The Chalice is used as one of the representations of the womb of the goddess. The Chalice is kept on the altar and used in ritual for ale and libation, for the great rite or the condensed form practiced in Gardnerian rituals. The Chalice represents the element of Water on the altar.

The Censor

If you are fortunate enough to own a censor such as the ones seen in the Catholic Church, then that is wonderful. They are excellent tools for space cleansing and preparing by Air. A censor is a closed incense dispenser that hangs on a chain and can be swung to and fro by the practitioner. The censor can be replaced and is more often replaced by an incense holder. It governs the element of Air which is masculine.

The Pentacle

The pentacle, as mentioned in the previous chapter on The Altar, is a representation of the element of Earth and it is a representation of the goddess. The reason that the pentacle is crafted from a natural element such as wood, is because it lends further strength to the fact that it is a tool of the goddess. In Wiccan altars the pentacle is positioned in the centre of the altar because as detailed in previous chapters, the goddess is the origin of all conscious life. Wicca sees the goddess as the origin of all life and therefore the pentacle is the key to opening and closing the altar.

The Cords

Every coven has cords of dedication and initiation. The cords are plaited cloth or rope in varying colours to denote placement and hierarchy. If you are a solitary practitioner, you may create your own initiation cord and use it when you are doing ritual. Originally, they were called cingulum which meant 'belt'. If the practitioner were to leave the coven, the cord would be cut. This would sever both the physical cord and the etheric cords that the practitioner had to the coven and its members. Every coven is different, and colours can vary greatly.

The Robe

Like the magical name, the robe is another trigger into the divine witchcraft nature of the practitioner. The robe allows the mundane to be forgotten and when worn, allows the practitioner to stand fast in their magical personas. The robe is not essential but a helpful tool for all practitioners whether neophytes or experienced. In Wiccan ritual the robe is an essential part of the group mind. Most Alexandrian

Wiccans do not use the robe and are seen to be skyclad instead, viewing the nude body as a temple of the gods.

The Boline

The Boline is the white handled sickle shaped cutting blade. The boline is used for all types of mundane cutting. Examples of cutting things on the mundane would be string in a magickal working, herbs for the cauldron, sheets of paper or anything else. The boline is not used for cutting anything on the astral or on the ethereal plains.

The Cauldron

The cauldron is the womb of the goddess. The cauldron contains Awen, it contains the void of potential. It is the most significant representation of the goddess in any ritual. There is no item more likened to the aspects of the feminine divine than the cauldron. The cauldron is used to mix and charge our spells, it is used to burn and banish, welcome in and bless. The cauldron is the eternal goddess, we take our magick, place it in her womb to manifest and we await the birth of our will and her will to be done.

Chapter 4 – Grimoire of Correspondences

The Witch's world is filled with understanding the vibrations and the spirit inherent in each thing, place and creature. A witch makes it their goal to understand these energies to be able to use them in manipulating or altering energy as they see fit. It is this knowledge that the world found to be dangerous, for in the wrong hands, this knowledge can be disastrous.

Even with the understanding and the knowledge of these vibrational signatures, the witch is not a god. You must still answer to the greater powers and you must still ensure that there is always a balance or nature herself will ensure that for you. The natural order of things is no fable and it always bounces back to its original state if the witch is unable or unwilling to follow through with the magick embarked on in the first place.

Correspondences are simply an account of thousands of other accounts of witches and practitioners of the occult. These are the records of years of similar findings of how certain things react and how they behave when used for certain purposes. For example, the knowledge that Orris Root is used extensively in magick to attract permanent romantic love into one's life is not just a fable. This knowledge has been recorded by thousands of practitioners over many years and when the findings are similar, they are kept, being a truth within the landscape of Witchcraft and the occult. It must be noted though, that if you are drawing love into your life, for example, ensure that you have an open space for something new to enter. Declutter, cleanse and make space for the new magick to enter your life and never ever do it when it will cause harm to another being.

GODS, GODDESSES AND SPIRITS TO WORK

WITH IN THE BEGINNING

There are thousands of pantheons to choose from. In these pantheons and branches, there are spirits, gods, goddesses and allies from across the veil. There are many who will seek to assist a practitioner in their magickal pursuits without asking for anything more than simple respect and momentary devotion, but there are also those who wish to have a hefty payment in return for their assistance. Before you choose to invoke or evoke a deity or any entity, make doubly sure that you know their history and their lore, their methods of working and records of interaction with practitioners before you even attempt to invite them into your life.

Witchcraft is not child's play; it is not about thinking a salt circle can protect you from being irresponsible. You must practice responsibly and that means understanding who and what you are interacting with and willing to accept the consequences to yourself and to those around you, and that includes the spirits that you choose to interact with.

Another important adage to the Gods, Goddesses and Spirits to work with is the common question on spirit guides and who and what they are. Our spirit guides are generally accepted as those spirits who have passed on and who have made a spiritual soul pact to come back and assist those on earth from the astral. A spirit guide may or may not choose to show themselves to you. Some may communicate through hunches, or feelings, some may communicate through noises and sounds, others may communicate in your dreams or in visions and through meditation. It is also very common to have a *silent* guide whom you never even knew was there.

Guides are not malicious and will never cause you or your family any harm. A spirit or entity that causes harm is something completely different and that is a whole different subject. A guide is a spiritual entity whose compassion and sense of betterment for humanity has driven their soul back into service of those who are still incarnated here on this plane. There are also different spirit guides:

Animal Guides

Animal Guides are extremely common, and almost every person who is in contact with their spiritual side will know what their animal totem is. You can also have more than one animal guide throughout your life. Some animal guides may come to you once and never again. Animals have extremely valuable lessons to teach us and even the sighting of a bee in the morning when you are frantically running around is a sign from the animal kingdom to slow down a little and remember to connect to your inner peace.

Temporary Archetypal Guides

These are guides that show up in a different form to who they are. It may be the form of a Celtic warrior with blue paint running down their face that shows up in a pathworking or meditation. It may be an old woman with far too many wrinkles on her face to be human. They show up in certain forms that will resonate with a part of your soul and nudge you onto the right path or assist you in a time when you need them the most. These guides will never show their true form, unless it is one of your life guides that you have not listened to, who have now sought different ways to reach you. Mostly they go from person to person and only remain where they are needed.

Ancestral Guides

It is not uncommon to have a loved one come back to guide you. This is referred to as a soul pact, and even though the person has passed on, perhaps even before you were old enough to understand how much they loved and cared for you, they will come back to guide you from the astral. Ancestral guides are found in dreams, visions, meditations, pathworking's and even when you're standing in the kitchen alone.

Spirit Guides, Ascended Masters and the Angels

Spirit guides come in all shapes and forms. Many people attest to having angels by their side, or Jesus, Krishna or some of the other ascended masters. Spirit Guides of this nature are usually found with people who counsel many people at any given time. Reiki Masters, Healers, Lightworkers, Charity Doers and Spiritual Teachers usually have an ascended master or well-known spiritual guide at their side. However, it is not only those in the spiritual healing arts who can have the ascended masters. You too can have an ascended master come into your life to show you your purpose and often you then have a large amount of important work to do within humanity.

What should you do with a spirit guide?

When a spirit guide shows up in your life, it is wise to listen. It is also wiser to discern whether they are in fact a guide or a rampant spirit seeking to cause harm. Asking the intention of your guide is not disrespectful and if it is your guide, it will always be met with a heart-centered answer. If you have indeed made a connection with your spirit guide/s, then it is a wonderful thing to setup an altar or place in your home where you simply acknowledge them and leave them gifts or notes. Do not mistake this with worship. Your spirit guides will never ask you to worship them, and you will never have to. However, it is nice to simply acknowledge them and thank them for their wisdom and guidance.

Having a notebook dedicated to their messages is something that will come in handy even after your guides are gone. A spirit guide notebook that contains all the messages that you receive, from your totems, to your ancestral guides, to the temporary archetypes that come into your life. Sometimes the visions or messages do not make sense at that time but come six months later and you're paging through the book, and a lightbulb goes on setting you onto your right path.

Connecting with spirit is tricky for the human mental filter to consciously grasp. Everyone is not always in *spirit-mode* and if they are, they are usually called flighty or said to have their head in the clouds. It's almost near to impossible to remain in spiritual union 24/7 and for this reason we have our trusty notebooks, our sacred spaces and dedicated sacred time.

The following list is a 'safe' list of spirits and deities that have a compassionate heart toward the human condition and should not cause any malicious acts or harm toward you, so long as you offer the respect and the devotion and as long as your heart is calling them and not an egotistical power driven intention.

Gods for the Neophyte

OILS, RESINS, INCENSES

There are thousands of various incenses, resins and oils on the market today. For the aspiring witch, many of them will be bought and stocked up on, however learning to make them yourself, is by far one of the greatest tools to add to your knowledge box.

One of the best companions for this section in its entirety is Scott Cunningham's *Incense, Oils and Brews*. It never fails one and always has substitutes and warnings when the ingredients are poisonous or if the incense tends to be a little over the top.

Resins and oils are really self-explanatory and do not leave one with much room but to use store bought resins and oils. Incenses on the other hand, leave a lot of room to play. For the sake of beginners, the method below is for loose incense. Whilst making loose incense may seem like a simple one, it is actually a very delicate one.

What you will need:

- A bottle of seed oil.
- Sawdust, wood chips, bark shavings.
- 3 different dried herbs or crushed resin.
- 1 essential oil.
- Self-lighting coals.

Directions:

For the sake of explaining this method, the following recipe will be used:

Divination Loose Incense Recipe

What you will need:

- Holy Basil leaves (1 cup).
- 2 Teaspoons of Sandalwood powder.
- 3 Tears of Frankincense.
- 2 drops of Patchouli essential oil.

- 2 cups of seed oil (Pomace Oil)
- 2 cups of wood chips.

Directions:

- Mix together the dried herbs and the resins. It may be necessary to use a pestle and mortar to crush the resins into a powder. A coffee grinder does work wonders.
- Now add the wood chips to the dried ingredients.
- Into a single cup of seed oil, drop your 2 drops of patchouli oil.
- Now begin pouring the oil mix into the dried mix. The consistency that you are looking for is (when you squeeze it, it must make a stiff ball, however the second you let go it can crumble.)
- Pour the oil until the above consistency is achieved.
- This recipe should last 3 – 4 months.
- When you are done. Light the coal and drop a pinch of your amazing divination incense on the coal, allow it to burn. Drop more as needed.

HERBS, TREES, FLOWERS

Besides the resins, oils and incenses making use of the plants, flowers and trees. We must understand that the plant kingdom is its own world. It has a spirit deva protecting every plant, flower and tree. There is so much magick within the plant kingdom and this is one place that fascinates almost every single witch. There are however many of them who do not make use of the natural world and that is also alright. However, if you choose to use the plant kingdom, make sure that you always show respect to the relevant spirits, and do your homework. Always do your research! Many plants look like others, and whilst the one is a healer the other can be a killer. Also, unless you have a botany background, do not, for the love of the Goddess, go and ingest anything without consulting a doctor.

Do not believe everything that you read on the internet. For a personal story, the shamans where I studied, taught us to diet a plant for a week or longer. This meant no food only water. I took up learning about the deva of Mugwort. Well, a week later it was quite a bloody mess. I had ruptured my intestine from the dose of Mugwort, which was not even that high. However, I learned immediately that the spirit of Mugwort is not kind to the stomach if you overdo it. One cup of Mugwort tea in a 2-week period is fine. Further than that, she is going to go into your body and mess things up. The internet prescribes approximately 3 cups a day. This is ludicrous and an acquaintance who listened to the internet's advice, went ahead, drank 3 -5 cups a day, attempting to strengthen her psychic awareness and what happened was a hospital trip.

On the subject of psychic awareness. You are already in tune with the universe, dear soul, why is it that you feel that if you burn 100 tears of frankincense and drink a field of Mugwort tea that you are going to become more psychic. Your intuition came with the package at birth. It takes practice, not poisoning your system or burning the house down. Besides, anyone who has ever had the psychic visions that I speak of will know, that if they not appearing yet, they will and some days you will wish that you were back in the *hunting for a psychic strength remedy* phase. For the sake of magick, here are a few trees, flowers and herbs for your magickal practice.

MAGICKAL TREES

Birch	New Beginnings
Rowan	Protection against psychic attack
Alder	Stability
Willow	Goddess, Emotions, Harmony, Lunar magick
Ash	Crossing the veil, integration
Hawthorn	The Hag, The underworld
Oak	Stability, The God
Holly	Fatherhood
Hazel	Divination
Apple	Love
Bramble	Learning
Ivy	Perseverance
Blackthorn	Spiritual leadership
Elder	The Goddess
Elm	Healing, third eye
Gorse	Fertility
Heather	Luck
Aspen	To petition death for time
Yew	Transformation
Mistletoe	Truth

Magickal Flowers

Oak flower	Bravery
Gorse flower	Banish depression
White Chestnut flower	Mental clarity
Water Violet flower	Self-confidence
The monkey flower	Release fear
Agrimony flower	Standing in your own truth
Rock Rose	Anxiety
Centaury flower	Inner and outer strength and willpower strength
Knawel flower	Decision making
Policeman's Helmet flower	Harmony and peace
Chicory flower	Release of unwanted people
Vervain flower	Harmony and loosening of thoughts
Old man's beard flower	Stability and grounding
Heather	Combat loneliness
Plumbago flower	Trust and community
Felwort flower	Combating doubt
Olive flowers	Energetic boost
Rock water flower	Relaxation

COMMON MAGICKAL HERBS

Adders Tongue	Healing
Anemone	Protection
Angelica	Exorcism
Balm of Gilead	Love and passion
Benzoin	Purification
Sea Oak	Psychic Power
Hart's Thorn	Legal matters
Swallow Herb	Protection and Happiness
Foxtail	Protection
British Tobacco	Visions
Dragon's Blood Palm	Exorcism, Potency, Love
Holly	Dream magick
High John the Conqueror Root	Success, money
Pearl Moss	Financial abundance
Jacob's Ladder	Mental clarity and control
Summer's Bride	Prophetic Dreams
Maple	Money, luck in gambling

Mizquitl	Healing
Meadow Rue	Divination
Brandy Mint	Psychic powers and prophetic dreams
Wild Senna	Love
Sacred Bark	Legal matters, dispelling quarrels
Palms Christi Root	Protection
Cinchona	Protection
Copal	Purification
English Elm	Love
Ava Root	Visions
Job's Tears	Wishes fulfilled
Mugwort	Prophetic dreams and visions
Shepard's Herb	Divination
Pistachio	Breaking love spells
Dog Grass	Lust and passion
St. John's Wort	Happiness
Moonwort	Open sealed doors
Yerba Louisa	Purification of the self and the home

CRYSTALS AND STONES

Crystals, like herbs, have a vibration, an energetic blueprint that, when placed close to you, will affect your own vibration and energetic system. Sometimes the vibrations take time to take effect because of the emotional baggage that you are carrying and sometimes a certain vibration will work so fast with you that you will not be able to believe your eyes.

Below are some common, easy to find crystals that have a wonderful effect on the human energetic system. Remember that the crystal must call you, and you must feel the pull. This is an old witch's tale, but it does work. Sometimes you only realise why a certain crystal pulled you, months after you purchased it.

Fluorite	Mental clarity and controller of emotions
Garnet	Protection and banishment
Hag Stones	Divination, psychic enhancement and dream work
Hematite	Grounding and protection
Green Jade	Financial prosperity
Red Jasper	For a 'return to sender' effect
Witch's Amber	Divination
Lapis Lazuli	Psychic awareness and divination
Lepidolite	Protection against nightmares
Malachite	Protection (always use in conjunction with a rose quartz)
Mica	Astral projection
Moonstone	Divination and psychic awareness
Obsidian	Protection and grounding
Opal	Astral projection, healing and psychic awareness
Petrified Wood	Past life issues and regressions
Sapphire	Love, power and psychic awareness
Selenite	Reconciliation with old lovers
Sodalite	Wisdom

Topaz	Weight loss
Bloodstone	Spiritual and physical strength

DIVINATION

Divination – the magical art of foretelling future events as well as current events through the use of various tools. Tarot, oracle, playing cards, crystal balls, runes, candles, water, fire, birds, pebbles and bones all use the art of intuition and insight. There is no magic trick involved in divination. There does need to be a certain level of practice behind the person divining and also a 100% level of trust between you and the choice of divination method.

That is all there is to it. Oh, and of course your divine connection. You cannot read without your divine connection. Without the soul in the practice there will be no message for the person receiving the divination. To become good at divining for other people, you need to practice. If tarot is not working for you, try an oracle deck, if that doesn't work, try something else. The secret is the giddy feeling to learn the divination method.

Personally, Tarot, Lenormand, and scrying are my choices for divining. Fire scrying can be one of the most incredible and frighteningly accurate experiences. Water scrying is a little more peaceful and gentler on the soul. The other factor that will come with practicing divination is mediumship. The spirits will begin to talk, sometimes they won't stop and other times they will disappear for months on end.

The important part is that you learn to go with the timing and the flow of your inner soul clock and the clock of the universe. Nothing will ever remain the same, your practice will always change, alter and move into the direction that it needs to be.

Divination is an imagination of the divine game at play. So, choose your method wisely and always use your chosen method with respect and reverence.

RUNES OF THE ELDER FUTHARK

When studying the runes from the Nordic pantheon, it is imperative that you understand the mythology behind the runes. You should also know the deities involved and that each rune is an entire world by itself. The elder futhark is the oldest known magical system. It only became a writing system after the need for communication through a written form, before that it was magic. Each rune, each Aett, each combination is an entire universe, and the runes are not free from teaching lessons.

It is said that the gods still whisper through the symbols and with enough contemplation and devotion you will hear them whisper to you. The runemasters were called Vitki and they were women. Women who carried their runes wherever they went in cat skin pelt pouches.

A Vitki would study a single rune for a year or more, and only once the lessons were done, would the practitioner move on to the next.

Here is the rune poem stating how Odin received the runes. Translated from Old Norse (Aelfric, 2017):

Veit ec at ec hecc vindga meiði a
netr allar nío,
geiri vndaþr oc gefinn Oðin,
sialfr sialfom mer,
a þeim meiþi, er mangi veit, hvers hann af rótom renn.

Við hleifi mic seldo ne við hornigi,
nysta ec niþr,
nam ec vp rvnar,
opandi nam,
fell ec aptr þaðan.

I know that I hung on a windy tree
nine long nights,
wounded with a spear, dedicated to Odin,
myself to myself,
on that tree of which no man knows from where its roots run.

No bread did they give me nor a drink from a horn,
downwards I peered;
I took up the runes,
screaming I took them,
then I fell back from there."

For all the rune meanings, studying the Anglo-Saxon rune poems translated by Dickens will help you immensely on your journey. For the sake of this book, only the English translation will be added in.

Feoh
Wealth is a comfort to all men;
yet must every man bestow it freely,
if he wish to gain honour in the sight of the Lord.

Ur
The aurochs is proud and has great horns;
it is a very savage beast and fights with its horns;
a great ranger of the moors, it is a creature of mettle.

Thorn
The thorn is exceedingly sharp,
an evil thing for any knight to touch,
uncommonly severe on all who sit among them.

Os
The mouth is the source of all language,
a pillar of wisdom and a comfort to wise men,
a blessing and a joy to every knight.

Rad
Riding seems easy to every warrior while he is indoors
and very courageous to him who traverses the high-roads
on the back of a stout horse.

Cen
The torch is known to every living man by its pale, bright flame;
it always burns where princes sit within.

Gyfu
Generosity brings credit and honour, which support one's dignity;
it furnishes help and subsistence
to all broken men who are devoid of aught else.

Wynn
Bliss he enjoys who knows not suffering, sorrow nor anxiety,
and has prosperity and happiness and a good enough house.

Haegl
Hail is the whitest of grain;
it is whirled from the vault of heaven
and is tossed about by gusts of wind
and then it melts into water.

Nyd
Trouble is oppressive to the heart;
yet often it proves a source of help and salvation
to the children of men, to everyone who heeds it betimes.

Is
Ice is very cold and immeasurably slippery;
it glistens as clear as glass and most like to gems;
it is a floor wrought by the frost, fair to look upon.

Ger
Summer is a joy to men, when God, the holy King of Heaven,
suffers the earth to bring forth shining fruits
for rich and poor alike.

Eoh
The yew is a tree with rough bark,
hard and fast in the earth, supported by its roots,
a guardian of flame and a joy upon an estate.

Peordh

Peorth is a source of recreation and amusement to the great,
where warriors sit blithely together in the banqueting-hall.

Eolh
The Eolh-sedge is mostly to be found in a marsh;
it grows in the water and makes a ghastly wound,
covering with blood every warrior who touches it.

Sigel
The sun is ever a joy in the hopes of seafarers
when they journey away over the fishes' bath,
until the course of the deep bears them to land.

Tir
Tiw is a guiding star; well does it keep faith with princes;
it is ever on its course over the mists of night and never fails.

Beorc
The polar bears no fruit; yet without seed it brings forth suckers,
for it is generated from its leaves.
Splendid are its branches and gloriously adorned
its lofty crown which reaches to the skies.

Eh
The horse is a joy to princes in the presence of warriors.
A steed in the pride of its hoofs,
when rich men on horseback bandy words about it;
and it is ever a source of comfort to the restless.

Mann
The joyous man is dear to his kinsmen;
yet every man is doomed to fail his fellow,
since the Lord by his decree will commit the vile carrion to the earth.

Lagu
The ocean seems interminable to men,
if they venture on the rolling bark
and the waves of the sea terrify them
and the courser of the deep heed not its bridle.

Ing
Ing was first seen by men among the East-Danes,
till, followed by his chariot,
he departed eastwards over the waves.
So the Heardingas named the hero.

Ethel
An estate is very dear to every man,
if he can enjoy there in his house
whatever is right and proper in constant prosperity.

Dæg
Day, the glorious light of the Creator, is sent by the Lord;
it is beloved of men, a source of hope and happiness to rich and poor,
and of service to all.

Ac
The oak fattens the flesh of pigs for the children of men.
Often it traverses the gannet's bath,
and the ocean proves whether the oak keeps faith
in honourable fashion.

Æsc
The ash is exceedingly high and precious to men.
With its sturdy trunk it offers a stubborn resistance,
though attacked by many a man.

Yr
Yr is a source of joy and honour to every prince and knight;
it looks well on a horse and is a reliable equipment for a journey.

Ior
Iar is a river fish and yet it always feeds on land;
it has a fair abode encompassed by water, where it lives in happiness.

Ear
The grave is horrible to every knight,
when the corpse quickly begins to cool
and is laid in the bosom of the dark earth.

*Prosperity declines, happiness passes away
and covenants are broken.*

THE TAROT

The tarot we know today is from the great philosophical mind of Edward Arthur Waite. Together with the illustrations from Pamela Colman Smith, we received what is known as the Rider-Waite Tarot. There are thousands of websites and books promising to teach you the tarot in under 2 hours or in 10 days or some other ludicrous claim. Tarot needs practice and there are 78 cards in a traditional tarot, following the Rider-Waite system, 56 of those are known as the minor arcana, and 22 cards attributed to the major arcana.

The tarot is a story using archetypal imagery, occult symbolism and numerological correspondences to bring an entire universe in a single deck. Some decks that have modern imagery manage to bring this story to life very well, others do not at all. It sounds so boring to begin with a traditional Rider-Waite deck, however when you get into the symbolism and the remarkable amount of information that is contained within each card of the tarot, your interest will be renewed. If it is not, then perhaps tarot is not for you.

If for example you want to learn the tarot but funds are not great, then make sure to visit the website: www.learntarot.com. The author of the book, which is given away for free, and the course and the cheat sheets that we have added below, is Joan Bunning. She has assisted millions of aspiring tarot readers with an excellent point to start their journey, completely free of charge.

The Major Arcana

FOOL (0)	MAGICIAN (1)	HIGH PRIESTESS (2)	EMPRESS (3)
Beginning Spontaneity Faith Apparent Folly	Action Conscious Awareness Concentration Power	Non-Action Unconscious Awareness Potential Mystery	Motherhood Abundance Senses Nature
EMPEROR (4)	HIEROPHANT (5)	LOVERS (6)	CHARIOT (7)
Fatherhood Structure Authority Regulation	Education Belief Systems Conformity Group Identification	Relationship Sexuality Personal Beliefs Values	Victory Will Self-Assertion Hard Control
STRENGTH (8)	HERMIT (9)	WHEEL OF FORTUNE (10)	JUSTICE (11)
Strength Patience Compassion Soft Control	Introspection Searching Guidance Solitude	Destiny Turning Point Movement Personal Vision	Justice Responsibility Decision Cause and Effect

HANGED MAN (12)	**DEATH (13)**	**TEMPERANCE (14)**	**DEVIL (15)**
Letting Go Reversal Suspension Sacrifice	Ending Transition Elimination Inexorable Forces	Temperance Balance Health Combination	Bondage Materialism Ignorance Hopelessness
TOWER (16)	**STAR (17)**	**MOON (18)**	**SUN (19)**
Sudden Change Release Downfall Revelation	Hope Inspiration Generosity Serenity	Fear Illusion Imagination Bewilderment	Enlightenment Greatness Vitality Assurance
	JUDGEMENT (20)	**WORLD (21)**	
	Judgment Rebirth Inner Calling Absolution	Integration Accomplishment Involvement Fulfilment	

The Minor Arcana

WANDS	**CUPS**	**SWORDS**	**PENTACLES**	
ACE	Creative Force Enthusiasm	Emotional Force Intuition	Mental Force Truth	Material Force Prosperity

	Confidence Courage	Intimacy Love	Justice Fortitude	Practicality Trust
TWO	Personal Power Boldness Originality	Connection Truce Attraction	Blocked Emotions Avoidance Stalemate	Juggling Flexibility Fun
THREE	Exploration Foresight Leadership	Exuberance Friendship Community	Heartbreak Loneliness Betrayal	Teamwork Planning Competence
FOUR	Celebration Freedom Excitement	Self-Absorption Apathy Going Within	Rest Contemplation Quiet Preparation	Possessiveness Control Blocked Change
FIVE	Disagreement Competition Hassles	Loss Bereavement Regret	Self-Interest Discord Open Dishonour	Hard Times Ill Health Rejection
SIX	Triumph Acclaim Pride	Good Will Innocence Childhood	The Blues Recovery Travel	Having/Not Having: Resources Knowledge Power

	WANDS	CUPS	SWORDS	PENTACLES
SEVEN	Aggression Defiance Conviction	Wishful Thinking Options Dissipation	Running Away Lone-Wolf Style Hidden Dishonour	Assessment Reward Direction Change
EIGHT	Quick Action Conclusion News	Deeper Meaning Moving On Weariness	Restriction Confusion Powerlessness	Diligence Knowledge Detail
NINE	Defensiveness Perseverance Stamina	Wish Fulfilment Satisfaction Sensual Pleasure	Worry Guilt Anguish	Discipline Self-Reliance Refinement
TEN	Overextending Burdens Struggle	Joy Peace Family	Bottoming Out Victim Mentality Martyrdom	Affluence Permanence Convention

	WANDS	CUPS	SWORDS	PENTACLES
PAGE	Be Creative Be Enthusiastic	Be Emotional Be Intuitive	Use Your Mind Be Truthful Be Just	Have an Effect Be Practical Be Prosperous Be

	Be Courageous Be Confident	Be Intimate Be Loving	Have Fortitude	Trusting/Trustworthy
KNIGHT Positive	Charming Self-Confident Daring Adventurous Passionate	Romantic Imaginative Sensitive Refined Introspective	Direct Authoritative Incisive Knowledgeable Logical	Unwavering Cautious Thorough Realistic Hardworking
KNIGHT Negative	Superficial Cocky Foolhardy Restless Hot-Tempered	Overemotional Fanciful Temperamental Over refined Introverted	Blunt Overbearing Cutting Opinionated Unfeeling	Stubborn Unadventurous Obsessive Pessimistic Grinding
QUEEN	Attractive Wholehearted Energetic Cheerful Self-Assured	Loving Tender-hearted Intuitive Psychic Spiritual	Honest Astute Forthright Witty Experienced	Nurturing Bighearted Down-to-Earth Resourceful Trustworthy
KING	Creative Inspiring Forceful Charismat	Wise Calm Diplomatic Caring Tolerant	Intellectual Analytical Articulate Just Ethical	Enterprising Adept Reliable Supporting Steady

THE BLACK MIRROR

The black mirror is not a toy, or a tool for those who do not know how to protect their home, their loved ones and themselves. The black mirror is however a strong doorway to the other side or across the veil. It is a *'one witch'* tool, and no one should even know where your black mirror is.

To craft a black mirror, insure that you use a mirror and not just a piece of glass. Follow the instructions below very carefully and use the black mirror in protective circle, always.

What you will need:

- A round mirror
- Black water-proof paint
- A paintbrush
- A few pieces of quartz crystals
- A brick
- A cement place where you can crush the crystal
- A black velvet cloth, big enough to cover the mirror three times
- The Dark moon
- A bag of sea salt
- Candles

Directions:

- Cast circle, making sure you have everything that you need inside the circle.

- Spread sea salt around the perimeter of the circle.

- Repeat the following chant:

"Oh, divine Goddess of the void and black moon,

I seek to access the veil beyond as you do,

Grant me the honour to attune,

To traverse the spiritual landscape beyond the veil,

Through this black mirror I now downscale

The universe as is your domain."

- Now crush the quartz crystal, or if you have crushed it prior to this, then place it to one side.

- Paint the black mirror until the coat is thick and no part of the mirror shows through.

- Sprinkle the clear quartz crystal pieces across the wet paint.

- Now hold your receiving hand to the black moon, and your gifting hand over the black mirror, just like the position of the magician tarot card.

- Repeat the following over and over again until the hair on your body rises up and you know that this mirror has been attuned.

"Attune to,

Black moon,

Black mirror through."

The black mirror is the black or dark moon. At zero percent illumination the void is there for us to see. The dark moon is really used for far more than banishing, but please use it with caution because as Nietzsche said:

"And if you gaze long enough into an abyss, the abyss will gaze back into you."

CRYSTAL BALL GAZING

Crystal ball gazing is a form of scrying. The crystal ball itself has no magical ability. When scrying, what is happening is that the images from your mind's eye are being projected onto a surface. A scryer is able to project his/her images onto any surface of their choosing. However, a crystal ball, made of clear crystal quartz will strengthen and empower the gifts of the practitioner to a percentage that is directly proportionate to the size of the crystal ball.

Many practitioners believe that a glass ball and a crystal ball are the same thing, they are not. A crystal ball has inclusions that show that the ball is in fact made from clear quartz crystal, whereas a glass ball is perfectly clear. If you are fortunate enough to come across a

Victorian Era scrying ball, they are made of glass and cut in angular patterns, like how a diamond is cut. These prove to be one of the best devices when choosing to crystal gaze.

The Lunar Calendar

The Dark Moon

The Dark Moon - The time of Cord Cutting Rituals, Infinity Cord Cuttings, Dark Magick that seeks to delve into the separation of anything that does not serve the highest path that you seek. This night is the night of endings to make place for the magick that will happen on the New Moon. This is the night where we seat ourselves alongside the depths of the wisdom held by the Crone and we perform magick of destruction before creation. This is the night of facing the void, crossing the veil, communing with those that have passed on, meditating on the shadow aspects of the self and of our own lives.

This night beckons purification rituals, rituals of banishing and protection, rituals of destruction, magick found in the void, and spell work that hearkens to the darkness within. The Dark Moon, just like the Full Moon is an Esbat of great importance. It should always be prepared for during the waning phase of the moon and every witch can benefit from the workings of Dark Moon magick. Prophetic Magick is also especially potent on the Dark Moon. Scrying, Tarot Reading, and any other forms of divining are recommended on this night, however, make triply sure that you protect and prepare for what you shall find on the night of the Dark Moon. No magick on this night is for the faint hearted.

Dark Moon Deities: Kali, Hecate, Cerridwen, Morrigan, Badb, Nemain, Hella, Kalma, Lilith, Nephtys.

New Moon

Appearing just after the dark moon, New Moon Magick is where you set the intention, spell good fortune and cast spells of growth, prosperity and health. Even though the actual moons strength is not that great, it is the first sliver of new beginnings. Any magick that incorporates growth, light and positivity are encouraged during this time. The New Moon is also an excellent time for divination into queries of the future aspects of life. It is wise to begin positive spell work during this time and strengthen it toward the full moon where the final working is done.

If you cleansed, banished or performed magick during the waning and Dark Moon then this is really the time to fill the gaps that were emptied. The New Moon provides the witch with a new start. It is the night to begin again. Call on the Maiden and create what you desire. Just like the Sabbats use the Sun, so the Esbats use the moon. Make sure you do not miss this night of powerful magick potential.

Deities to call on: Persephone, Aega, Coyolxauhqui, Kuan Yin, Lasya, Sadarnuna.

Waxing Crescent Moon

The Waxing Crescent is sometimes preferred over the New Moon for starting your spell work, but only because you can actually see the moon up in the night sky. If your magick began on the New Moon, make sure to increase its power by reinforcing the magick throughout the waxing moon until you reach full moon. The Waxing crescent is a time for setting your goals to manifest on the full moon, or in two or three full moons time. It is the time to sew good intentions positively project healing and wellbeing into your life. The entire scope of the Waxing Moon, from the New Moon until the Full Moon is a time of renewal, of second chances and of growth and prosperity. It is a fruitful time, and so should all your magical workings be the same!

Waxing Gibbous Moon

The Waxing Gibbous is a time to project heightened magick into the universe. The power of the moon is great, and influences can be felt quite strongly already. Re-energising and re-affirming your New Moon magick are an excellent idea. It is also a great time to cut your hair, ensuring its speedy growth. Love Magick is also extremely successful if performed during this phase of the lunar wheel.

Financial matters that were dealt with on the new moon, should be revisited and empowered. The waxing Gibbous is a moon of success and the first sign of the mother aspect of the Goddess emerging. It is now a time of working with the Mother, and/or the Maiden aspects in your magick.

Full Moon

The Full Moon, the time of great magick and wish fulfilment. An old tale whispers secrets of how a single heart felt desire spoken out loud to the great Mother in the sky will come true by the time she shows her belly again. This night all magick of growth, of empowerment, of love, of money, of spiritual enlightenment, of mental clarity, direction and receiving is performed. It is a highly important Esbat and a large degree of witches never miss this evening. It is also the evening of performing Drawing Down the Moon and making healing poppets. It is an especially brilliant night for women or men seeking feminine inspiration to bask in the moonlight and feel the presence of the Goddess.

Scrying on the night of the full moon is something which is always magickal and provides many answers to the seeker without much effort. Protection amulets, mojo bags, healing poppets, witches' besoms, tools of the craft and moon water are all created and blessed upon this especially magickal night. The Mother Goddess is in her full power and she makes it known, many humans feel the effects of the full moon and many of them feel as though they are crawling out of their skins. Witches know how to balance, calm and utilise the full moons energy wisely.

Deities recommended on the full moon: Diana, Cerridwen, Seline, Gwaten, Kuan Yin, Sarpandit, Sefkhet, Rhiannon, Ina, Ishtar, Andromeda, Isis, Ameterasu, Danu, Ernmas, Gaia, Lakshmi, Ma'at, Nuit, Triple Goddess, Shakti, Venus.

Waning Gibbous Moon

The Waning Gibbous is the time to analyse your life. Shadow work begins here. The dark mother aspects are venerated, and we begin to take a good hard look at every aspect of our lives in detail.

Deities to use during the waning moon: Morrigan, Kali Ma, Cerridwen, Macha, Badb, Shakti, Ishtar, Chandi

Last Quarter Moon

The Last Quarter is a stronger dark energy. It is likened to the feeling of bathwater running out whilst you are still in the bath, this is that first pull and heaviness that you feel. The Last Quarter signals the first appearance of the Crone, She and the Dark Mother now lend aid to your magick. It is not yet time to cut cords, but it is time to clean out the unnecessary. It is time to reorganise and to revaluate your life, your modes of thinking, your actions and to go inward. The Last Quarter is excellent for introspection work. The remaining light of the Mother will guide you through your shadow work in a loving manner.

Waning Crescent Moon

The Waning Crescent sees the last of the Dark Mother becoming the Crone, her wisdom now at nearing its peak. Creation of 'Witch Bottles', banishing magick and all manners of cord cuttings can begin being planned for to take place on the Dark Moon. It is a great time to walk the road of the shadow self along-side the Crone. Ask her for wisdom, ask her to reveal in the darkness that which needs to come to the light. Problems which are obscure can be magickly placed before the crone and answers will be found in scrying. The last of the light in the moon lends aid to the darkness and creation of dark altars, veneration to the Crone aspect of the Goddess and the energy within is performed. Hexing can also be performed under this moon, but also remember - with great caution and understand the consequences.

Chapter 5 – Pathworking's for the Witch

<u>The pathworking – Into the Celtic Fray</u>

Breathe in deeply and hold your breath

Now exhale as hard as you can.

Blow out all your frustration, blow out your insecurities, blow out your fear.

Now breathe in deeply again and hold your breath

Blow out all your anxiety, your mistrust, your pain, your anger, your resentment,

Breathe in deeply, hold your breath, close your eyes

Breathe out as hard as you can and relax.

You're standing on the top of a balcony with two marble staircases leading down the left side and the right side. The marble beneath your feet is white with flecks and streaks of black running across its surface. You place your hand at the top of the chrome railing, you feel the coolness beneath your fingertips, you feel the security of its support. You take your first step. The light behind you is luminating the stairs beneath you. The rough rock walls with their striations cause shadows deceiving your eyes. You continue down the spiraling staircase, the warmth of the descent engulfing your being. You take another few stairs down watching the shadows become less as the light begins to dim even more. You can now see the lantern at the bottom of the staircase.

The candlelight brings you a sense of comfort. You feel eager to see what lies ahead. There are a few stairs remaining before the landing where you can just make out the oak door that's copper binds have a green hue from years of ageing. You reach the door. Its handle is a round copper ring. You grab hold of the handle and tug as hard as you can, and the swollen wood gives way. Behind the door are three rough carved stone steps and in the glimmer of the light you can see the spiderwebs, their strands as thick as wool, sticky and glistening in the flickers of light. As you reach forward the webs cling to you, the ever-present thought of what created these lingers in the back of your mind. But nothing living seems to be moving amongst these strands. You press forward grabbing the web and desperately trying to remove it from your body and your clothing.

As you step forward the light seems more and more intense. As you break through the last metre of web, the illuminating moss that covers this cave shines a gentle light on the underground pool of water. Sitting beside it is a hunched figure, staring intently into the reflecting waters. Without turning they acknowledge your presence by lifting their hand and motioning you toward them. They offer you a place by their side on the soft feathery moss. The natural heat of being so deep underground warms your body. The coolness of the spiderwebs no longer seems to concern you. As you stare into the pool of water, the reflection of your new-found guide stares back at you. They slowly slip a wooden tube from within their cloak and place it before you.

You notice that the one end has been closed by a red wax seal. With mere hand gestures they instruct you to remove the seal and you pull an ancient parchment out. As you unroll the parchment, you notice the language upon it is not something you immediately recognize but eventually the lettering forms an image that is so clear in your mind. A message of love, trust, self-worth and pride. In this darkest place you have found the answer to your question. You sit quietly beside your spiritual guide who nods in agreement that you have achieved the lesson that you came here seeking. Once again, they motion you to roll up the parchment and place it back in the tube. They slowly take this from you and push it into your pocket, and silently motion you to leave this place of sanctuary for now. As you turn your head you notice the obstacles that you faced getting here no longer exist.

The passageway of webbing is now open, the candlelight from the oak door illuminates your path back. You notice the rough stone that you tread on, now shines with the footsteps of mother of pearl. The rainbow hue tells you that this is a path that you can come back to tread as often as you desire. The warmth clings to you as you head toward the oak door which is wide open and without obstacles. You slide your feet onto the first of the marble stairs and you notice a faint in the distance above you. You begin ascending the marble staircase, the light now growing stronger and clearer. You begin to recognize the fragrant incense from before.

As you once again reach the balcony you find the people that you love and trust eagerly awaiting the message that you have brought from your guide. They embrace you with love and acceptance knowing that the journey that you have just taken has opened you to the beauty of your own soul and to the beauty of others. The gatekeeper ushers you out slowly snuffing out the candles onto the balcony. The outer door opens, and you see before you a large elder tree and kern. This is your doorway to return always to the Celtic fray. Breathe in deeply and start to feel your physical body. Slowly move your fingers, wiggle your toes, and when you are ready open your eyes.

Without saying a word, write down your experience in your notebook.

Pathworking – Meeting your spirit guides, gods and goddesses through the sand

Breathe in deeply and hold your breath

Now exhale as hard as you can.

Blow out all your frustration, blow out your insecurities, blow out your fear.

Now breathe in deeply again and hold your breath

Blow out all your anxiety, your mistrust, your pain, your anger, your resentment,

Breathe in deeply, hold your breath, close your eyes

Breathe out as hard as you can and relax.

You are on a beach, the waves are lapping over the sand, back and forth, back and forth. Watch the waves cover the sand and make it perfect again. I want you to bend down and begin writing the number 30 on the sand, allow the wave to take it away, now 29, 28… 27, watch how each time the sea water removes the number… write the number 26, 25, 24… watch how the sea dissolves these numbers and how calm you are feeling right now. Write 23 in the sand, watch the wave take it away, 22, 21, 20… again the waves wash away the numbers and leave the sand bare. Now write 19, 18, 17, 16… and again watch the numbers disappear. Write 15, 14, 13, 12,

11... and allow them to be washed away by the cleansing sea water. Write 10, 9, 8, 7, 6, 5... and allow the healing sea water to wash away the numbers, leaving you even calmer than before. Now write 4... and let the number be washed away, 3... and let the number be washed away, 2... and let the number be washed away, 1... and let the number be washed away...

Watch the next wave come in and when it disappears there is a trapdoor in the sand, quickly before the next wave washes it away, open it, climb in and close the trapdoor. The room you find yourself in is lit by candlelight. On the walls there are marking, symbols and shapes, all drawn in red paint. You may go and inspect them if you so wish.

There is an archway on the left side of the room, walk towards it. Before you, in the middle of the archway is a jelly like substance, creating a portal. Step through this substance across the veil and into the land of the spirits, the gods, the goddesses. This is the forgotten land, the holy land. In front of you is an entire array of structures. There is a being sitting on a chair in front of these structures. Go toward this being. Look at them intently. Are they motioning anything? Remember their clothing, their face, their hair, their eyes.

They are holding a black box on their lap. They give you the box. You take it and open it. Look at the gift inside. This is the one gift that you need at this moment in your life. Thank the being for the gift. Ask the being to reveal to you a being that you can call on for help during this phase of your life. As you ask this, another being walks up to you. Remember their clothes, their hair, their facial features and anything specific about them that stands out. The second being speaks to you, listen to what they have to say – (Long Pause) – Thank both beings for their time. There is a paper on the floor with a pencil, pick it up and give it to the second being, ask them to write their name on the paper, take the paper and look at the name, remember it. It makes sense to you, and you know this being. Thank them both again. Turn around and see the beach in the distance. Walk toward the sea. When you get to the ocean, allow the waves to lap over your feet. Feel the cold, refreshing water cleanse your feet and know that you are always welcome here.

Smell the incense in the room. Allow yourself to return to your body. Wiggle your toes, your fingers and scrunch your nose. When you are ready open your eyes and write down everything that you have experienced even if you think it makes no sense, it will in time.

Chapter 6 – Using Ritual?

A Basic Standard Wiccan Ritual

"Smudge all who are present before entering the circle.

Anoint all who are present inside the circle area.

Both High Priestess and High Priest kneel before the altar.

Priestess places bowl of water on pentacle, places tip of Athame in water and says:

"I cleanse and consecrate and bless thee O creature of Water that you may be fit to dwell in our sacred Space. In the Names of The Lady of the Moon and the Lord of the Wild, I cleanse, bless and consecrate thee. So, mote it be."

All respond:

"So, mote it be."

The High Priestess replaces the water bowl. The High Priest places the bowl of salt on the pentacle, places tip of Athame in it and says:

"I bless thee O creature of Earth that you may be fit to dwell in our sacred space. In the Names of The Lady of the Moon and the Lord of the Wild, I consecrate and bless thee. So, mote it be."

All respond:

"So, mote it be."

The High Priestess now picks up the water bowl and holds it up with both hands at eye level. The High Priest takes a little salt on the Athame or in hand and drops it into the water, then stirs anticlockwise with finger or Athame saying:

"Water and Earth combined – blessed be"

All respond:

"Blessed Be."

Bowls are returned to their places. High Priestess picks up the Incense burner, adds incense, points Athame at coals and says:

"I cleanse and consecrate and bless thee O creature of Fire that you may be fit to dwell in our sacred Space. In the Names of The Lady of the Moon and the Lord of the Wild, I cleanse, bless and consecrate thee. So, mote it be."

All respond:

"So, mote it be."

The High Priest points Athame at smoke rising from burner and says:

"I cleanse and consecrate and bless thee O creature of Air that you may be fit to dwell in our sacred Space. In the Names of The Lady of the Moon and the Lord of the Wild, I cleanse, bless and consecrate thee. So, mote it be."

All respond:

"So, mote it be."

The High Priestess now combines the fire and air and says:

"Fire and Air combined – blessed be."

All respond:

"Blessed Be."

Circle Casting done by High Priestess

"I conjure thee O circle of Power that you may serve as a meeting place of love, joy and truth. To serve as a barrier between the world of men and the mighty ones. Keeping out all that is bane and containing all that is of love. To serve as a vessel and focus of the Intent of all gathered here. In the names of The Lady of the Moon and the Lord of the Wild, I conjure thee."

High Priestess picks up the water and salt mixture and walks the circle saying:

"With Water and Earth, I cleanse, bless and consecrate this place that it may be fit to serve as sacred space."

The High Priestess places the bowl back on the Altar. The High Priest picks up Incense burner and walks the circle saying:

"With Fire and Air, I cleanse, bless and consecrate this place that it may be fit to serve as sacred space."

The High Priest then places the burner back on the Altar, they both turn to the coven / group or if solitary just out loud and say:

"The circle is cast, and we are between worlds, where night and day, joy and sorrow, life and death, meet as one. So, mote it be."

All respond:

"So, Mote it be."

Universal Invocation

"Hearken to my call, all which was, is and will be. I call the all-knowing, all seeing Universal Soul, that from which everything comes came and to which everything must return. Come! Enter every heart and mind in this circle, uplifting each individual Spirit to join, for a moment in time, with the All. Hail and Welcome the Universal!"

The Element of Air

"Lords and Ladies of the watchtowers of the East, Elemental Spirits of Air, I do summon, stir and call thee. Bring to our circle your insight and protection and bear witness to our rites. Hail and welcome!"

The Element of Fire (S.H) The Element of Earth (N.H)

"Lords and Ladies of the watchtowers of the North/South, Elemental Spirits of Fire, I do summon, stir and call thee. Bring to our circle your courage and protection and bear witness to our rites. Hail and welcome!"

The Element of Water

"Lords and Ladies of the watchtowers of the West, Elemental Spirits of Water, I do summon, stir and call thee. Bring to our circle your love and protection and bear witness to our rites. Hail and welcome!"

The Element of Earth (S.H.) The Element of Fire (N.H)

"Lords and Ladies of the watchtowers of the South/North, Elemental Spirits of Earth, I do summon, stir and call thee. Bring to our circle your strength and protection and bear witness to our rites. Hail and welcome!"

Invocation of the Goddess done by the High Priestess

The invocation is specific to the ritual. It depends on which Goddess has been chosen or if a general invocation the Goddess is applicable.

Invocation of the God done by the High Priest

The invocation is specific to the ritual. It depends on which Goddess has been chosen or if a general invocation the Goddess is applicable.

Statement of intent. This is the intention of the ritual explained to all who are present in the ritual and what part each person will play.

In a standard Wiccan ritual, a mini form of the Great Rite is used to bless the cakes and ale:

The Cakes and Ale are consecrated. The High Priest kneels in front of the Altar facing the High Priestess. He holds the chalice of ale or fruit juice up to her. She lowers her athame held in both hands, point downwards into the wine while she says:

"As the athame is to the male, so the cup is to the female; and conjoined, they bring fruitfulness and blessings; they become One in truth."

To consecrate the cakes, the High Priestess kneels before the High Priest, holding up the plate of cakes before him. The High Priest traces an invoking pentagram in the air over the cakes and says:

"Oh, Queen most secret, bless this food unto our bodies, bestowing health, wealth, strength, joy and peace and that fulfilment of love which is perfect happiness."

The High Priestess replaces the plate on Altar.

OFFERING LIBATION

The High Priestess and the High Priest make the offering to the Gods.

The High Priestess holds the cup up to eye level and says:

"As all things proceed to us from the Goddess and the God, so must some return to them in recognition of their love and favour. For the Gods and we are each dependent upon the other, and all must have their due. Blessed Be!"

All respond:

"Blessed Be!"

The High Priest holds up the plate to eye level and says:

"Oh, gentle Goddess of the Moon and Lord of Death and Rebirth, accept this token not as a sacrifice, but as token rendering of our appreciation, our love and our respect. Blessed Be!"

All respond:

"Blessed Be!"

Give Libation into the cauldron / bowl that you have set aside for this purpose, it will be given to the earth when the ritual is completed.

Both the High Priestess and the High Priest now share the chalice of ale and the cakes in perfect love and perfect trust. The High Priestess turns to her coven and says:

"We now share fellowship of the soul with one another and the gods."

The High Priest takes the plate and the High Priestess takes cup and they move anti-clockwise around the circle. They take the cakes and ale to each coven member in turn and offer saying:

"I offer you this cup/cakes in perfect love and perfect trust."

The coven member sips the ale or eats the cakes and says:

"I accept in perfect love and perfect trust. Blessed Be."

Once the cakes and ale have been completed the entire circle is taken down, entities are dismissed and bid farewell. This process is as follows:

The Release of the Universal Spirit

"I thank the Seen and the Unseen, the All, for your presence and love in our circle this night. Leave with us that feeling of connection, oneness that you bring to our souls. I ask that you continue to touch our lives every day. Hail the Universal!"

Dismissal of the Goddess done by The High Priestess

Dismissal of the God done by The High Priest

Dismissal of the Element of Earth (S.H)

The Element of Fire (N.H)

"Lords and Ladies of the watchtowers of the South/North, Elemental Spirits of Earth, I do thank thee for bringing your strength and protection to our circle tonight. Hail and farewell!

Dismissal of the Element of Water

"Lords and Ladies of the watchtowers of the West, Elemental Spirits of Water I do thank thee for bringing your love and protection to our circle tonight. Hail and farewell."

Dismissal of the Element of Fire (S.H) The Element of Earth (N.H)

"North Lords and Ladies of the watchtowers of the North/South, Elemental Spirits of Fire, I do thank thee for bringing your courage and protection to our circle tonight. Hail and farewell."

Dismissal of the Element of Air

"Lords and Ladies of the watchtowers of the East, Elemental Spirits of Air, I do thank thee for bringing your insight and protection to our circle tonight. Hail and farewell."

Release Circle

Ritual is done. Feasting and other grounding exercises can now be done."

Why Build on the Standard Wiccan Ritual?

The standard Wiccan ritual is a ritual devised by Gerald B. Gardner, it has been modernised by the Gardnerian lineage covens and altered to suit a modern world. The standard ritual is laid out as it is to ensure that there is a perfect balance throughout the ritual. It ensures that all bases are covered for cleansing, protection and provides the neophyte practitioner a safe space within which to practice their workings.

The standard Wiccan ritual requires nothing, but your own *'theme'* attached to it and the change of deities and attributes requested from the elemental guardians. Ritual architects such as Doreen Valiente, who was most probably responsible for the skeleton edit of this ritual, know how to ensure that there is balance throughout. If you wish to write your own ritual and change the order of the ritual mentioned above, then by all means do so, however, you will notice that the balance may be a little out, or you are left feeling *'off'* after ritual.

Even though the above ritual is a coven ritual outline, the exact same applies in a one-man ritual. The only difference will be that you will have to do all the work yourself.

A NON-WICCAN NORDIC RITUAL WITH PRE-

RITUAL TALK AND EXPLANATION

Pre-Ritual Talk and Explanation

The old Norse way was very different to our own understanding of the world of the gods today. In the ritual journey that we will embark on in an hour or so, we will be joined with the gods in the old ways. We will see them through the gifts of wisdom known as the runes. We will be invoking the man-god who gave his mundane sight for the sight of the gods and through his own journey he, himself became a god. Not many who follow the old ways believe that the great Odin was a human like you and me, but the fact is that each and every one of you have the gods within you. You have the potential to follow the same path to enlightenment just like Odin did.

Odin, it is said, in the poetic sagas and edda's (which are considered as holy texts to those who follow the old norse ways) speak of Odin hanging on Yggdrasil (the old Norse world tree) for nine days and nine nights. It says that no one fed him mead or gave him bread, this leads us to believe that he either suffered the fasting out of his own will or it was done to him. During this time, right before death he was given the wisdom of the magic of the runes. These are known as the elder futhark. The runes have been changed much and today we have a younger futhark, we have a gothic set, we have the Germanic runes and even those Icelandic variations.

Odin returned from his ordeal / journey with only one eye. This, I personally believe is more of a metaphor, in other words he gave up the mundane sight for the spiritual sight. So, he had the runes, he had travelled through the nine worlds of Yggdrasil and he had survived. He passed this knowledge on to worthy rune readers, which I might add, were mostly women. Men were not seen by the Nords as possessing the gifts of fortune telling and women travelled in groups of nine plus one from town to town practicing the art of Seidhr. This is a form of trance. These women were known as Volva's and Their runes were kept on red strings on their belts in cat skins and they provided valuable advice and direction to the people. It was only through Germanic influence that men became bearers of the rune knowledge and were known as Runemasters.

In our ritual, each one of you will be given a set of runes. In our first working we will charge our bag of runes; we will have them charged and consecrated by the old gods and we will set our intentions on them. It is imperative that this bag of runes never be touched by another and never read for anyone but yourself. These are your personal tools and must never be given away, when you have given the study of them up, then bury them deep in mother earth and they will be cleansed until found by another or returned through rot back into the earth.

In our second working we will draw a rune from the bag of odins runes. This rune that you pick will answer a question that you ask and will give you direction. The HP and HPS will lead you through deciphering the message. This rune has a hole for you to wear for the duration of the time its guidance is needed. Again, this amulet is yours alone. When the time comes, and you will feel it, you will bury it and allow its magic to return to the earth.

Now, we also invoke Frigga, Odin's wife or divine consort. She is the mother of the Nordic way, she is the divine aspect of all motherhood, and she overseas fairness and fertility, marriage and all of the gods. She is also the goddess of Seidhr. She will be the balance in the ritual.

She will bring the unity required and she will bring the divine influence and gentleness out of Odin. Odin is an ancient energy – he is taken lightly by many, but a wise shamanic energy like his is never stable. It is Frigga who balances him and who channels this divinity from him without the necessary need for any sacrifice.

On the subject of sacrifice, for cakes and ale, it was customary to have a boar slaughtered in Odin's honour. Instead of an entire boar we will have a holy bread baked in the old way. This bread and these cakes and ale will seal the bond between you and the old gods in perfect love and perfect trust.

Any questions?

Let us robe up and go journey with the gods…

Ritual

Robed and ready.

Ritual space is cleansed.

Hold hands.

Grounding

Take up magical identity

Stand and breathe.

Chant softly: "Gods within, divinity awakening"

Both the person who will be anointing and the person who will be smudging will go into circle with HPS and smudge, anoint and then fetch HP smudge and anoint.

Rest of group is smudged and anointed and enters ritual space.

HPS and HP kneel before the altar.

Pentacle is turned upright.

HPS: Bowl of water on pentacle, athame in bowl of water. Says:

"I cleanse and consecrate thee, oh, creature of water, that you may be fit to dwell in sacred space. In the names of Odin and Frigga, I cleanse, bless and consecrate thee. So, mote it be."

All present repeat: "*So mote it be*"

HPS lifts water bowl to eye-level and HP takes a pinch of salt and says:

"*Water and Earth combined. Blessed be*"

All present repeat: "*Blessed be.*"

HPS lights candle with flameage. Points athame at the fire and says:

"I cleanse and consecrate thee, oh creature of fire that you may be fit to dwell in this sacred space. In the names of Odin and Frigga, I cleanse, bless and consecrate thee. So, mote it be."

All those present repeat: "*So mote it be.*"

HP picks up the incense burner lights the incense from the flame of the blessed candle and motioning to the smoke says:

"I cleanse, consecrate and bless thee, oh creature of air, that you may be fit to dwell in our sacred space. In the names of Odin and Frigga, I cleanse, consecrate and bless thee, Oh creature of air. So, mote it be."

All who are present repeat: "*So mote it be.*"

The HPS now lifts the incense, and says:

"*Fire and air combined. Blessed be.*"

All who are present repeat: "*Blessed be.*"

Get ready for circle casting:

Circle of members in the middle. Facing outward. Hum "Om"

HPS casts circle:

"I conjure thee, oh circle of power, that you may serve as a meeting place of love, joy and truth. You are cast to serve as a barrier between the world of men and the mighty ones. Keeping out all that is bane and keeping in all that is of love. You are cast to serve as a vessel and a focus of all the intent of each individual gathered here. In the names of Odin and Frigga, I conjure thee, oh circle of power.

HPS cleanses the circle. Picks up water and salt / Holy water and walks widdershins saying:

"With water and earth combined, I cleanse... bless... and consecrate this space that it may be fit to serve as sacred space."

HP empowers the circle. Picks up the incense burner with incense and walks widdershins saying:

"With fire and air combined, I empower and strengthen this circle, that it may be fit to serve as sacred space."

Both HP and HPS stand at the altar and declare:

"The circle is cast. We are between worlds, where night and day, joy and sorrow, life and death, meet as one. So, mote it be."

All present repeat: *"So mote it be."*

All present make circle in centre of the circle and hands on top of one another holding, trusting and leaning outward. The four callers of the universal standing at the four points in the circle.

Universal invocation shared between four:

"Hearken to my call, all that was, that is, that will be. I call the all-knowing, all seeing, Universal soul, that from which everything comes, came and that to which everything must return. Come! Enter every heart and mind in this circle, uplifting each spirit to join for a moment in time with the All. Hail and Welcome the Universal Spirit."

All present repeat: *"All Hail the Universal Spirit of the All."*

EAST invocation of Air

"Lords and Ladies, of the watchtowers of the EAST, elemental spirits of Air, I do summon, stir and call thee. Bring to our circle your clarity, insight and protection and bear witness to our rites. Hail and welcome Air."

All present repeat: *"Hail and Welcome Air."*

NORTH invocation of FIRE

"Lords and Ladies of the watchtowers of the NORTH, elemental spirits of FIRE, I do summon, stir and call thee. Bring to our circle your courage to face the unknown and your desire to venture into the void of possibility, bring with you your protection and bear witness to our rites. Hail and welcome FIRE."

All present repeat: *"Hail and Welcome FIRE."*

WEST invocation of WATER

"Lords and Ladies of the watchtowers of the WEST, elemental spirits of WATER, we do summon, stir and call thee. Bring to our circle your perfect love and perfect trust and your protection and bear witness to our rites. Hail and welcome WATER."

All present repeat: *"hail and welcome WATER"*

SOUTH invocation of EARTH

"Lords and Ladies of the watchtowers of the SOUTH, elemental spirits of EARTH, we do summon, stir and call thee. Bring to our circle your stability, your direction and your intertwined connection to Yggdrasil and bring also your protection and bear witness to our rites. Hail and welcome Earth."

All present repeat: *"Hail and welcome Earth."*

HPS now invokes Goddess aspect Frigga:

"Friiiiiggggaaaaaa, Friiiiggggggaaaaaa, Friiiiiggggggaaaaaa... Mother of many, seer beyond the realms of gods and men. Bosom holding all beyond time and space. Mother of the gods see into our hearts this night. See into our souls. Mother Frigga we call on you to enter into this sacred space prepared for you and your consort. Join us. Hail and Welcome Mother Frigga."

All Present repeat: *"Hail and Welcome Mother Frigga."*

HP now invokes God aspect Odin:

"Odin... Ooooooh....dddddd...iiii...nnnnn... Odin! Come down from Asgardr, come down to join us in celebrating and learning your wisdom that you hung on Yggdrasil for. Come lend your wisdom to our workings, come lend your sight to our souls. Join your consort Mother Frigga in our sacred space prepared for you this night. Hail and welcome great father Odin!"

All present repeat: *"Hail and welcome Great Father Odin."*

All seated.

HPS now speaks:

"Welcome dear ones. We are now between worlds and joined in sacred space by our Great Father Odin and Great Mother Frigga and the elemental spirits of the four quarters. This is sacred space, and this is safe space. Tonight, we will be given wisdom from the gods. Each one of you will be handed a pouch of runes. They are a gift from the gods. For our first working we will take up the runes in our hands and we will hold them for a while, making a connection with them. You also have a paper in your bag with general guidelines to the meanings of each rune. Do not read the paper, simply place your hands on your runes and feel them. This will be done in silence. We will then charge them by raising energy to the chant of "Gods within, divinity awakening." The chant will peak at awakening. Our second working will be direction from the gods. The HP and HPS will come around and you will ask either HP (Odin) or HPS (Frigga) for direction, guidance. You will then be picking a rune from the bag and either HP or HPS will offer guidance. This rune that you pick will be an amulet for you to hang around your neck. After your guidance is received and everyone has had their chance you will be handed a string and we will then charge the amulet with the chant: "Gods decree, so it shall be" peaking at "it shall be."

Working is done.

Cone is handled both times by HPS. Intentions for first workings are sent into the bags of the members present. Intentions of second working into the amulets. Excess sent into the earth.

Cakes and ale.

Mini Great Rite performed by HP and HPS:

HP holds chalice up to the HPS kneeling before her. The HPS holds the athame up and places it into the chalice whilst proclaiming:

"As the athame is to the male, so the cup is to the female, and conjoined, they bring fruitfulness and blessings, they become one in truth."

HPS kneels before the HP and holds the cakes up to him... in this case it will be the boar bread on a wooden board. He proclaims:

"Oh, queen most sacred, bless this holy boar baked for the gods unto our bodies, bestowing, health, wealth, strength and peace and that fulfilment of love which is perfect happiness."

HPS holds the chalice to eye level and proclaims:

"As all things proceed to us from the goddess and god, so must some return to them in recognition for their love and favour. For the gods and we are each dependent upon each other. All must have their due. Blessed be."

HPS gives libation in the cauldron

All present repeat: *"Blessed be."*

HP holds the cakes up to eye-level and proclaims:

"Oh, gracious goddess Frigga, and mighty father Odin, accept this token not as a sacrifice but as a token rendering our appreciation, our love and our respect. Blessed be!"

HP gives libation in cauldron.

All present repeat *"Blessed be"*

HPS and HP share mead and boar bread in perfect love and perfect trust.

HPS proclaims to coven: *"We now share fellowship of the soul with one another and the gods."*

HP and HPS move widdershins offering cakes and ale in perfect love and perfect trust.

"I offer you this sacred boar bread / mead in perfect love and perfect trust. Blessed be."

Each member responds with:

"I accept this sacred boar bread / mead in perfect love and perfect trust. Blessed be."

Release energies:

Universal Released.

"I thank the seen and the unseen, the All, for your presence and love in our circle this night. Leave with us that feeling of connection and oneness that you bring to our souls. I ask that you continue to touch our lives every day. Hail the Universal"

***(no farewell as the universal is within us always.)

God released by HP

"Great Father Odin we thank you for your sight, your wisdom and your loving guidance. Stay with us on our journeys through Yggdrasil and in our pathways if we choose to pursue the knowledge that your runes hold. For now, we bid you farewell. Hail and Farewell Great Father Odin!"

All present repeat: "hail and Farewell Great Father Odin."

HPS releases Goddess aspect

"Divine Mother Frigga, we thank you for bringing your gentleness into our rites and for guiding the energies and the flow of wisdom. Guide us in the future if we choose to pursue the knowledge that the runes hold. For now, we bid you farewell. Hail and farewell Great Mother Frigga."

All present repeat: "Hail and Farewell Great Mother Frigga."

SOUTH dismissing EARTH

"Lords and Ladies of the watchtowers of the SOUTH, elemental Spirits of Earth, I do thank thee for bringing your stability, your direction and your intertwined connection to Yggdrasil as well as your protection. Hail and Farewell EARTH."

All present repeat: *"Hail and Farewell EARTH."*

WEST dismissing WATER

"Lords and Ladies of the watchtowers of the WEST, elemental spirits of Water, I do thank thee for bringing your perfect love and perfect trust and your protection. Hail and Farewell Water."

All present repeat: *"hail and farewell Water."*

NORTH dismissing FIRE

"Lords and Ladies of the watchtowers of the NORTH, elemental spirits of FIRE. I do thank thee for bringing your courage to face the unknown and your desire to venture into the void of possibility, as well as your protection. Hail and farewell FIRE!"

All present repeat: *"hail and farewell Fire."*

EAST dismissing Air.

"Lords and Ladies of the watchtowers of the EAST, elemental spirits of Air, I thank thee for bringing your clarity, your insight and your protection. Hail and farewell Air."

All present repeat: *"Hail and farewell air."*

Release the circle.

Enjoy the feasting like a Nordic Warrior.

Chapter 7: Spell work

Today, there is a spell for everything. From getting a new boyfriend, besides the spells to get rid of current ones, there are spells to change your eye colour and to lose weight. The line between reality and hopefulness is very thin, and there is the humour in it all, magic is everywhere. Let me use an example: If you say to yourself, "I have a headache." And you do this for the next 15 – 30 minutes. You will without a doubt end up with a headache or a raging migraine. It depends on your level of imagination, your intention, focus and the strength of your willpower.

Now no-one wants a migraine! So why can the same principle not apply to a million dollars? The answer is that it can. The secret is that you know beyond a shadow of a doubt that you are worth the migraine, capable of receiving a migraine, and that a migraine is a very possible thing. The million dollars has only been a wishful thinking episode and perhaps left to the things of daydreams. There are so many blockages in the mind concerning money, love and health that we think that magic is only for those gifted in the occult arts. It is not. Everyone practices magic every single day. All you have to do is to believe. You need to believe it so hard that your subconscious mind begins to program your daily life onto the path of success, of healing and you need to distance yourself from the non-believers, the ones who will not support your goal. This is also why the witch's pyramid has "to keep silent." At the end.

We are all subject to being mentally changed by the world around us. If your desire is great but your environment does not support this desire, its best you either silence yourself and let no one know about the magic that you are working, or you change your environment to suit your desire. You need to understand that everything that you read, everything that you listen to, everything that you subject yourself to does alter your life to run in line with that. Why would you purposefully subject your life to a situation or to people who do not have your best interests at heart? You wouldn't. So, why do so many people do it? They do it because of fear. You will never achieve a single successful spell if you have doubt or fear. There needs to be absolute trust in the power of the universe and absolute trust in the power you hold inside of you to change whatever it is that you are willing to change.

To quote Frank Herbert:

"I must not fear. Fear is the mind-killer. Fear is the little death that brings total obliteration. I will face my fear. I will permit it to pass over me and through me. And when it has gone past, I will turn the inner eye to see its path. Where the fear has gone there will be nothing. Only I will remain."

Remember this quote, for this is exactly what fear is. Fear nothing and you will accomplish great things. What is stopping you from the greatest success that you can dream of?

SPELLS FOR LOVE

A charm bag to draw love to you

What you will need:

- A square piece of rose red cloth
- A sprig of Rosemary
- A pinch of Orris Root
- A handful of Caraway seeds
- A pinch of Cinnamon
- A photograph, item or piece of hair from the person you are wishing to attract.
- The waxing moon phase.
- A large white board to work on.
- Red String.

Directions:

- Place everything together on the white board. Place the items neatly next to each other and then place both your hands palms facing downward over the items.

- Repeat the following:

"In the name of The Lord and The Lady,

In the great name of love,

I activate, empower and charge each item with drawing intimacy,

With drawing divine passion mirrored above."

- Now place the caraway seeds, the cinnamon, the orris root and the sprig of rosemary into the red square.

- Take the hair or the photograph of the one you have your eye on and close your fist, hold it to your heart and repeat the following as many times as you feel is necessary:

"By the grace of the powers that be,

You shall love me eternally."

- Place their hair or the photograph on top of the items in the red square.

- Fold the four corners together so that you can make a pouch.

- Tie this pouch with red string and whilst you do this repeat the following:

"Love to me, come fast and swift,

By full moon next you shall give me the gift,

Of a lover's heart, of a lover's soul,

Our divine union made to last, mine to be the control."

Carry this pouch on your person and when you see the one you have your eye on, do not be shy, speak to them and make sure to use a sentence with the word union in it. It does not matter how you use the word. Just make sure it is said.

A lover's quarrel box

What you will need:

- A small black box.
- Sheets of white square paper.
- The quarrel.
- A red pen.

Directions:

- Write down the quarrel or the disagreement that you have had with your partner on the white piece of paper.
- Fold the paper as many times as you can and whilst you are folding it, repeat the following:

"Smaller and smaller, quarrel away,

Gone to the wind, forgotten today,

Once I toss you in the void,

Gone you will be until the end of my days."

- Throw the folded quarrel into the black box and let that box be the place where you place any quarrels or disputes, arguments or problems.
-

The Cowrie Full Moon Baby Boomer

The origin of this spell is unknown; however, it has been passed down through the line of witches and works every time there is someone that has difficulty in falling pregnant.

What you will need:

- 23 Cowrie shells – the small ones are fine.
- 99% illuminated full moon, and the night of the 100% illuminated full moon.
- Your partner.
- Money to buy one pair of booties.
- 2 pieces of your hair, 2 pieces of your partners hair.
- Red string.

Directions:

- Before attempting a steamy night, it would be necessary to set everything up first.
- Place the cowrie shells under the bed in the figure 8 eternity symbol. Make sure that you do this on the first full moon night. It is the second night of the full moon or 100% illumination that your baby will be conceived.
- Once you have placed the cowrie shells in their pattern, walk the figure 8 on all sides of the bed, do this as many times as you can, place both your hands on your womb and repeat:

"A soul I draw to me, open I am, child come to me, mother I am."

- Now go immediately and purchase a pair of baby booties. In the one bootie place your hair, in the other place your partners hair, tie them both together with the red string. Repeat the following as you do so:

"Welcome little one, made from dad and mom, a soul so precious, my own to be, a soul so precious, the time to give life to the seed."

- Place the booties in the middle of the figure 8 under the bed. Make sure it will be undisturbed until you and your partner make love.

SPELLS FOR ABUNDANCE

An Abundant Home Spell.

What you will need:

- 13 fresh peppermint leaves.
- 2 sticks of Cinnamon
- Boiling Water
- A blue bucket
- A mop or a cloth if you will be cleaning on your hands and knees.

Directions:

- Place the peppermint leaves into the bucket one by one, repeating the following:

"Peppermint, fresh and inviting, bring to me the abundance so exciting."

- Add the cinnamon sticks into the bucket and repeat the following:

"Cinnamon sights set on gold, bring in riches young and old."

- Add the boiling water on top of the ingredients and allow to steep for 3 minutes. When done, top up with cold water.

- Mop the house now from the front door to the back door walking backwards, whilst you do this hum this chant like a little tune:

"Welcome in abundant things, welcoming you in, welcome in a life of kings, welcoming you in."

- Repeat this spell once in every waxing lunar phase, make sure you do this spell on the waxing moon only.

There's Always Money in My Wallet Spell

What you will need:

- Cinnamon essential oil
- A blue candle
- Any amount of money, it must be a note, not coins.
- Your wallet

Directions:

- Take the note / paper money and rub cinnamon oil on it. Repeat the following:

"Money, money attract more of you, copied and doubled and tripled to hoard.

Money, Money, attract more of you, there is nothing I cannot afford."

- Carry on repeating the chant above as you light the candle. Drip the wax onto the note, three drops of wax are enough.
- Carry on repeating the chant as you place the note into your wallet.

Watch the money multiply!

A Spell of Happiness

What you will need:

- Yourself
- A paper
- A pen
- A rubbish bin

Directions:

- Write down the sadness, all of it, pull it from your mind and allow it to flaw through your arm into the ink and onto the paper.
- Write down everything that you are sad about, and if you do not know why you are sad, do not stress, just write.
- When you are done, you may be feeling a little tired.

- Take up the paper, hold it to the sky and repeat the following chant:

"Depro paper, keeper of that soot in mind, be gone with you, terrible swine!"

- Tear the paper into tiny pieces, be aggressive about it.

- Take a nap. This step is just as important as the ones before. When you wake you will feel much better!

SPELLS FOR HEALTH AND HEALING AND PROTECTION

Creating your own protection mojo bag

herbs, crystals and items that signify your guardians or those you trust to protect you are used in gris-gris or mojo bags. A mojo bag is a combination of items that work together to serve a single purpose. In magick the saying, "keep it simple stupid" really works. So today we will be making a powerful protection bag.

What you will need:

- 3 herbs for protection
- 1 essential oil for protection
- 1 crystal for empowerment.
- A square piece of black cloth (black for absorbing negativity)
- Spit / a bit of your hair / a fingernail clipping
- Red ribbon / string
- 1 black candle

Create your sacred space, burn some sage or other cleansing herbs to cleanse your space and ready it for your work. Remember to always cast circle and call in the spirit guides and deities if you have forged such a relationship. Light your black candle and begin your working.

Use the chant below to empower each item that will be added to your mojo bag. Add each one into the bag and then close your bag by folding the four corners together.

Chant:

"Creature of perfection and power,

I call on your ability to protect and empower,

_____, I awaken your protective vibration this instant,

Make me (or another if you are making it for someone else) resistant,

Protect me, shield me, shield all that I hold dear,

Far or near,

Protect and diffuse any negativity,

As I will, so mote it be!"

Take your red string and spin it tightly around the bag to secure it, leaving enough for the nine knots mentioned below. Visualise the powerful protection emanating from the mojo bag. Begin knotting the red string and with each knot follow the rhythm of the following chant, repeating the words as you tie the knots.

"By the knot of one, this spell has begun
By the knot of two, my words are true
By the knot of three, it comes to be
By the knot of four, powerful protection in this core
By the knot of five, the spell is alive
By the knot of six, the spell is fixed
By the knot of seven, this power is now driven
By the knot of eight, all harm now dissipates
By knot of nine, complete protection is mine!"

Take your magickal protection bag and bury it at your front gate / front door in a pot plant or keep it on your person.

The Draining of Negativity Spell

What you will need:

- **A bath**
- **Lavender Oil**
- **Valerian Tea**
- **Yourself**

Directions:

- This spell can be done without the tea and the lavender; however, these two plants help immensely in this spell. It is effective by itself as well.

- Run enough water to cover your body.

- Drop 4 drops of Lavender essential oil into the bathwater.

- Climb into the bath.

- Valerian is known as the confidante in the herbal kingdom's deva properties, whilst you lie in the water, tell the valerian deva all your pains, your angers, your frustrations. Everything and sip the tea each time.

- When you are done, pull the plug out.

- Lie flat in the water.

- Feel the tug of the water as it drains out of the bath.

- See the negativity leave, down the drain!

Repeat this spell whenever you feel the need to.

DRAWING DOWN THE MOON FOR THE SOLITARY PRACTITIONER

What is Drawing Down the Moon?

Drawing Down the Moon, or alternatively Drawing Down the Goddess is both a practice taken by a High Priestess within ritual in the bounds of circle, or a ritual practice on its own performed by a solitary practitioner.

> *"I am the womb:* **of every holt,** *I am the blaze:* **on every hill,**
> *I am the queen:* **of every hire,**
> *I am the shield:* **for every head,** *I am the tomb:* **of every hope."**

Excerpt restored by Robert Graves, The White Goddess (Graves, 2013)

Drawing Down the Moon is in all its aspects the action of invoking the goddess in her entirety into oneself. Whenever we call her into ourselves, or whenever we invoke her, we call it Drawing Down the Moon. The original ancient call has been lost, changed and rewritten so that we are only left with fragments of the original call. However, the three laws of magick are: Focus, Intention and Will. Beyond all tools, talismans and space if you have these three laws you have any ritual and magick ritual in its core essence.

The act of Drawing Down the Goddess is a spiritual state of encompassing the feminine aspect of the universe in all its magnificence. There is really no more to it except the finer details of invoking a certain aspect of her, which has only risen to popularity in modern pagan circles, calling it Drawing Down the Moon as well. The original ritualistic act was in order to bring her down in her entire form. It was not done by an unskilled practitioner due to the incredible force that the vessel or practitioner would have to withstand. The control would be paramount, and it is imperative to understand that this ritual, whether practiced as High Priestess or solitary practitioner is not for the untrained mind.

The Goddess was drawn into the practitioner so that she would be able to commune with others in the circle who could not see, hear, touch or feel her. She would only be invoked by a skilled High Priestess and the very rite of invoking her at this level was an honour of the highest magnitude.

Today, Drawing Down the Moon is practiced by anyone who has a mind to invoke the goddess. The rite itself has been watered down and it has been altered to suit the practitioner. It is common practice to be seated under the full moon and perform the ritual. The original function was to channel her essence to the people so that She could directly commune with them, today it is simply to feel her essence, or the essence of her many archetypes.

The Solitary Rite

Begin with a cleansing bath, use music and incense to allow you to enter into the frame of mind needed for sacred space. If you wish to add oils or herbs to your bath, mugwort, wormwood, sage is excellent. Alternatively, a cup of herbal tea containing mint, Vervain, mugwort, wormwood and some honey to taste is brilliant to open yourself to the art of the rite you are about to perform. (If you are pregnant do not ingest or bath with these magical herbs at all, you will cause serious harm to your unborn child.)

Remember to take a journal and pen/pencil into the circle. Writing down your thoughts once you have invoked the Goddess's wisdom which is not easily obtained beyond ritual.

Now that you are cleansed, open circle. You are allowed to wear a flowing dress, your ritual robe or go skyclad if you so wish.

Breathe deeply three times, stand with your feet shoulder apart and hold your hands, palms facing upward to the full moon and repeat this invocation:

"Ancient Mother,

Goddess above, threefold darkness and light in one,

Lover of the fiery sun,

Mother of the unknown,

Mother of the earth,

Power of the pitch black

Power of the hearth,

I call to thee,

Come to me,

Breathe in me,

Let my eyes see,

My heart believes,

Great Goddess I call to thee,

Come to me,

We are one.

Come to me,

We are one.

You are in me,

We are one."

You may now write in your journal and perform any working that you prepared. Once done, make sure to say farewell to the Goddess and close ritual space as per normal. Doing this ritual on every full moon is a fantastic way to connect with the primal feminine energy and does wonders for both male and female practitioners alike.

A Final Word of Advice from an Ol' Witch.

It is with much love that this book was written, with the added intention that you, the practitioner on this path of the wise soul, will find hope, inspiration, direction and your own voice. There are so many directions that you can go into, so many avenues for you to explore and so much that you can accomplish, and you will, if you set your mind to it.

Remember the three laws of magic, focus, will and intent, for together they are the recipe for a life of happiness and stability. Always think before you act and keep a journal or ten. Always write down everything. Collect images that you love, build a library of you. Even months after writing something, you can look back and see how you have grown. Reading and researching is a large part of the witch's path, and you do not need to have your nose in a book all the time, but one book a month is the least that you should be reading. Knowledge is indeed power. Power does not belong to the rich and famous or the ones who are influencers, it belongs to the individual, each individual. If practicing magick is your happy place, then that is the avenue you must travel.

Try as best as you can to write your own chants and your own spells. If you have the focus, the will and the intention then you cannot go wrong, and please, never harm anything for the sake of getting your way, there is no point in causing pain and nothing, but your own inner torment will come from it. Love the gods, show them gratitude and spend time in devotion and the world will be your oyster. You will know happiness like never before. Lastly, remember to love yourself, because you, dear soul, are perfect!

Merry meet, merry part, and merry meet again!

WITCH BOOK:

INTRODUCTION

IF THIS BOOK CAME YOUR WAY...

...Then it must be for a reason.

Perhaps you always felt a close connection to Nature and her elements, a connection you couldn't quite put into proper words. All you know is that you feel most like yourself when you're out into the deep woods or by the open sea; when you can smell the rain in autumn or see the flames dance on a winter night. All you know is that there's a secret rhythm to the changing of the seasons, the phases of the Moon and the way the light fluctuates; a rhythm that you can dance to. You don't even have to know the steps.

This book is for you.

Perhaps, like so many of us, you grew up in a Christian family... but always struggled to connect. Not with Christianity's core message of love and forgiveness which is absolutely fine, but with its mainstream, religious rules and teachings. (So many things to feel bad about and repent for! Surely, we've been brought to this Earth to play, learn and have fun?) But your struggles haven't made you secular or worse, cynical. You're still looking for something to believe in, something bigger than you. Something that allows you to be your true, whole self.

Yes, dear one, this book is for you too.

Perhaps you've started walking your Pagan path already. Slowly but surely, you're soaking up every occult thing you come across. And there are so many occult things to come across in this day and age! You've bought some cute crystals at Etsy, followed a couple of witchy accounts on Instagram for inspiration and was thinking of getting your first deck of tarot cards. You're still unsure what it all means though; how it all fits together. You know you're interested in the spiritual... but can you call yourself a witch yet?

Sister, this book is definitely for you!

On the other hand, perhaps you've been on this Path for a while now. Perhaps your momma or your nanna have been teaching you rituals and spells ever since you were a little one... Perhaps these brilliant women, in their wisdom and love for you, never even called them "spells": just some movements to do, some words to say or herbs to brew when you want to help ease a loved one's pain, help your flowers grow and have prosperity at home... You have a lot of practical knowledge and skills that stem from family lore but you haven't felt the need to dive into the theoretical part of it yet.

You'll be pleased to know: this book is for you as well.

Merry meet, one and all.

In [Book Title TBD] we won't be taking any sides. We'll discuss both the Light and the Sacred Night; both the Yin and the Yang; both the theory and the practical, everyday aspects of the Path. We'll offer insights into what it means to be a Pagan, a Wiccan and a Witch — and how you can be either... or all three.

In this book, we'll talk about the past and how the journey of magick started.

We'll talk about the present and how magick is once again awakening all around us (you've felt it too, haven't you?).

And we'll talk about the future. The Earth's future but you own future too, no matter where you're coming from. We'll talk about how your magick can and will change your life, if you let it.

Throughout this book, you'll notice that as the seasons, so will our tone change. Sometimes we'll be serious: we'll warn you about all the things that could go wrong with a spell or a magical object. Other times, we'll be as lighthearted as a robin singing his song on a Spring morning. We'll urge you to not take yourself and your craft very seriously.

Nature and Magick are never just one thing — they keep changing, evolving and adapting. So will this book. So will you, in your Path. And later on, when you return to this book to reread a spell or brush up on a ritual for a Pagan holiday that's fast approaching, perhaps you'll notice things you didn't notice the first time around; you'll spot little details that escaped you, or see things you've tried for yourself and would now do a bit differently.

That's how it should be.

Your only authority on your Path, at the end of the day, is you.

We're just here to show you the way.

The way back to our ancestors and their lost, ancient teachings — but also the way forward. So that you can use that knowledge in a modern context and understand the unique blessings and struggles of this digital era we're living in.

Because although some things are much better now (hey, we're not getting burned at the stake anymore, for one) other things have also become a lot more complicated. Surely, our Pagan forefathers and foremothers never had to deal with things like "protecting your aura from electronic fields" or "struggling to align with Nature when you live in a crowded city"...

But worry not. At the end of this book, you'll have all the answers you need. At least, all the answers you need in order to start asking the real, magickal questions — the ones only you, your familiars, your matron/patron deities and your guiding spirits can answer.

The first part of this book is about Paganism.

We'll talk about what Paganism isn't (because people, throughout the ages, have had so many misconceptions about it!) and what it really is. We'll explore its rich history and its diverse present, all the way from 35,000 BCE to today. We'll see how Pagans have been exalted, hunted and burned at the stake, tolerated and then exalted again as the Wheel turns. At the end of the first part of the book, we'll go through all the things that make or break a Pagan, so that you can decide what applies to you.

The second part of this book is about Wicca.

Once again, we'll talk about what Wicca isn't (hint: it's not the same thing as Paganism, as many outsiders believe) and what Wicca really is. We'll take a look at how it started and how it has evolved to this day; we'll go through the most important Wiccan rituals and beliefs. By the end of the second part of the book, you'll know if Wicca is for you.

The third part of this book is about you.

Yes, you.

You who may or may not belong to the other two categories. You who may have a penchant for herbal magic, a knack for predictions of the future or a sixth sense when it comes to communicating with spirits. No matter what your unique gift (or gifts), we'll talk about ways to hone it; to do and be better, every day.

Yes, there will be spells. Use them wisely.

There will be tarot cards. We'll talk in as much detail as we can about what they symbolize and how they can help you in your divination practice as well as your wellness and self care rituals.

There will also be ingredients for you to create your unique blend of magick; instructions on how to manifest the energies you most desire in your life; insights on how to use other divination tools like runes or numerology without second guessing yourself; suggestions on how to celebrate Pagan holidays.

If this book came your way, then there must be a reason.

It's time for you to start reading and find out what that reason was.

PART 1: PAGANISM

CHAPTER 1: WHAT PAGANISM ISN'T

"History is written by the victors."

This is a famous saying by Winston Churchill who, while definitely not a Pagan or otherwise connected to the teachings of this book, certainly knew a thing or two about shaping narratives for political gain. "History is written by the victors" means that the winners of any conflict, be it military, monetary or social, are the ones who get to tell the story from their point of view; the ones who get to define what the "truth" is.

How is this relevant to a book about Paganism and magic, you ask?

Oh, it's very simple: when it comes to the prevailing of religions and the power they hold in society, Paganism has unfortunately lost. It took many centuries: Paganism started losing ground around the 4th century CE, and was almost completely wiped out within the following centuries in Europe. (The timeline was a bit different for other continents, with the Americas and Africa maintaining their Pagan traditions for longer, until the so called "Age of Discovery" and with the Arabic part of Asia being Islamized around the 7th century CE.)

Many people remained Pagan, sure, but they did so in secret; in fear of punishment, torture, even death if their secret came out. Punishment inflicted by the practitioners of the winning religions, the ones whose traditions were now considered the norm.

And the winners of that particular conflict were the practitioners of Christianity.

So, Christianity has gotten to define history. Even if in many an occasion, "defining" history meant blatantly distorting it; even if it meant spouting lies about what once was the dominant faith of the people or appropriating traditions as the victors saw fit.

This is not an exaggeration, it's simple facts. If you're doubting what you just read, or simply never thought of Christianity as the "victors" in a conflict that shaped history and reality itself, ask yourself this question: What year is it?

Is it, perhaps, 2019?

If you live in the Western world, the answer is yes.

But 2019 years since what?

What event is globally considered so important that has defined even the way we measure time itself? That has divided the flow of history in "Before" and "After"?

(Hint: it's someone's birthday.)

Perhaps you're starting to get it now?

Christianity has won — and because of that, history has been rewritten.

Because of that, even now, when you call yourself a Pagan openly, most people will feel unsettled (even if they're polite and will do a good job hiding it). Because of that, even now, the word Pagan is somehow associated with things dirty, wrong or unholy. Despite the fact that, by the very definition of the word, being "a Pagan" is literally the most natural thing any human being can be.

That's why the first thing we need to talk about in this book, **is what Paganism isn't.**

To clear any misconceptions people (even you!) may still be carrying deep inside, perhaps without even realizing. And to arm you with the arguments you'll need, next time you come across someone who feels offended, frightened or just unsettled by the mere word "Pagan".

Are you ready? Let's begin setting history straight, shall we?

PAGANISM IS NOT ABOUT WORSHIPING THE DEVIL

This is a long story that will make much more sense once we delve into the origins of Paganism in the next chapter. But for now, all you need to know is this: Paganism is as further away from devil worshiping and satanism as can be. In fact, Modern Satanism, is (by its own definition) deeply a-spiritual and secular so once again the opposite of what Paganism is.

Let's repeat it once more: Pagans don't worship the devil. Never had, never will. Why? Because they don't believe the devil exists — not in the sense most people think of the devil, that of the antagonist of God and master of all evil, anyway. That devil is a Christian invention.

Certainly, the idea of an absolute evil that antagonizes the absolute good can be found in many religions. But the idea that Pagans worship the devil/absolute evil, is basically propaganda created in the early years of Christianity, to scare people away from Paganism.

Yes, many Pagan gods, deities and creatures of Pagan lore have horns. But so do goats. Are goats evil? The mere idea is laughable, isn't it? And yet, any depictions of horned Pagan deities (like the

Greek god Pan, satyrs or fauns) have been reinterpreted by Christianity as diabolical...

We'll get more in depth into the how and why that happened, in the next chapter.

PAGANISM IS NOT LOCATION SPECIFIC

Every single civilization on Earth has its own Pagan traditions. Although when we say the word "Pagan" most of us think in European/Western World terms, the truth is that the Pagan traditions of Native Americans, Africans and Aboriginal Australians are by no means any less rich or important than their European counterparts. (If anything, they're probably richer because they had more time to grow roots in people's consciousness, as Christianity reached these places much later than it did Europe.)

That's why Paganism today is such a diverse practice: every practitioner carries his or her own local traditions and there is an endless well of knowledge to tap into.

Now, isn't that beautiful?

PAGANISM IS NOT THE ENEMY OF CHRISTIANITY — OR ANY RELIGION, REALLY

Being a Pagan doesn't make you hate Christians. (Although for many years, the exact opposite could have been said to be true.)

More importantly, Paganism is not a religion: at least not one, single religion, with common characteristics among its practitioners and a well-defined dogma as most organized religions are. The Pagan mindset, although not always polytheistic (since every place has its own traditions), is fundamentally about accepting and understanding that there are many forces out there: there shouldn't be one single authority to overrule them all.

Today, you'll see many Pagans also embracing Christian, Jewish or Buddhist traditions. That's because they know we are all children of Nature and are all, at the end of the day, talking about the same thing in different words. For a true Pagan, there are no victors and losers: life is complicated and circular — and what goes around comes around.

Paganism is certainly coming back around today, isn't it?

History may be written by the victors, but myths and legends are written by the oppressed; to transfer traditions and beliefs from generations to generations, disguised as fairy tales. And when it comes to the human psyche, myths and legends are much more powerful.

CHAPTER 2: THE HISTORY OF PAGANISM

I know what you're thinking.

"History is boring. Who wants to read all that anyway? Where are the spells?"

Am I right? Are you thinking something like that?

Here's the thing, dear one.

No one is forcing you to do anything you don't want to do. No one is forcing you to read anything you don't want to read. In fact, you can skip ahead to the third part of the book, where all the practical, fun stuff await, where you'll learn how to do real spells...

But wait. I have to warn you of the consequences, if you choose to do that.

To perform any spell, even the simplest one, you need to understand and respect the forces you're working with. If you don't understand them, nothing will happen — no matter how long you chant or how many fancy ingredients you've gathered. If you don't respect them... well, then you're risking angering some of them and inviting serious repercussions in your life.

(I've seen first-hand what happens when people try to cast love spells with no idea what they're doing or without acknowledging all the forces at play… These people only end up tying their own emotions and lives to that other person, the recipient of the spell, who still doesn't care about them. They are unable to get over that person; they spend their lives in frustration and misery. And that's just a mild example of a spell gone wrong.)

Imagine walking into a chemistry lab to perform an experiment. Would you ever do that without knowing the periodic table first? Without understanding what every element does and how they tend to interact together? Would you conduct any of your experiments without wearing gloves, a lab coat or even goggles?

Definitely not — unless you want your lab to explode.

That's why, as a Pagan, a Wiccan and a Witch, understanding your history is important. Your ancestors, the people who have walked this Path before you, have suffered a lot. They were persecuted, demonized, colonized; they had to adapt, to find inventive ways to stay true to their beliefs. That only made their magic stronger.

You're one of the lucky ones. You don't have to suffer (although sometimes, life will serve you some suffering if there are lessons to be learned and you're refusing to learn them). You just need to soak up their wisdom. To learn and understand who they were, what they've been through and how it all fits together.

That's why this history lesson is important. For your own good, please don't skip it.

THE DAWN OF PAGAN WORSHIPPING

Let's backtrack a bit. In the previous chapter, "What Paganism Isn't", we mentioned at some point that Paganism is not a religion.

Well, it isn't. At least not in the sense that we've learned to understand religions through the lens of Christianity, Jewdaism, Islam and Hinduism (and to a lesser extent, Buddhism): as set systems with a formal dogma and rules that anyone who consider themselves a believer is expected to abide to — and all those who don't are infidels that need to either be dealt with, converted or at the very least frowned upon.

If you ask historians today, paganism is more accurately defined as a sum of numerous different "cults"[1], operating without a written religious doctrine or a formal version of what is considered the "right, official way" to worship. Did each "cult" was sure their beliefs were probably more to the point than the beliefs of other "cults"? Yes, probably. Did they go to war about it? Not really. Of course there was fighting and wars in the Pagan world; brutal wars in fact. We're not here to claim that Pagans were all peace-loving people. But spreading one's deities to another region was never very high among the reasons two clans or kingdoms would fight each other.

There's a simple reason for that: ancient Pagans understood that no god or goddess on their own could be the ultimate source of authority over everything and everyone. They accepted contrasting forces, within Nature as well as within their belief systems — that's why it was easier for them to accept other people's beliefs. Even if, in many occasions, they would make fun of each other's gods (or believe that a war would be won because their gods were ultimately stronger than those of their opponents).

Another reason is the lack of organization that comes from having a formal creed. There were sacred texts, certainly, but Pagan beliefs were mostly spread through word of mouth; through the tales the elders would tell the young while gathered around the fire, the rain storming outside. Myth, legend and folklore were intertwined (and often indistinguishable) with stories about how the world and the gods came to be. And along with the person who would do the retelling every time, the story would change slightly.

That doesn't mean Pagan beliefs are a collection of fables. At least not in the sense you think of fables today as something "not true". But

---

[1] Cameron, Alan G. (2011). The Last Pagans of Rome. New York: Oxford University Press, p. 26-27

they were certainly more dynamic and less "set in stone" than the beliefs of the dominant religions of today.

Why? Well, you need to consider the time all this happened.

We did say this would be a bit of a history lesson, didn't we?

Paganism predates the written word. In fact it wouldn't be wrong to say that Paganism, in its various expressions depending on the corner of the globe you look at, has been the first spirituality system humanity ever came up with.

Now, notice how we said "they first spirituality system" and not "the first religion"?

Historians, anthropologists and religious researchers alike have been trying forever to pinpoint what was "the first religion" known to man — some of them for historical purposes, others with the motive to prove that their own religion was the first, ergo, the "original" one. But here's the thing: human evolution doesn't exactly work that way. Same was as it is now proven that there was not one single "cradle of civilization" from which we all emerged, there was never one single "original religion" as well.

When humanity was still relatively new to this planet (and there weren't so many of us around) we were probably more similar to one another than ever. We all faced the same threats to our survival: wild animals that could hunt and kill us if we strayed too far from the fire, harsh winters that made it impossible to find food, droughts that made our crops die, diseases that ravaged us from an early age making it necessary to have a strong body and do everything as young as possible... It wasn't very easy being human back then, was it?

No, it wasn't. We needed help to get by. To make sure our crops would survive, our children would grow up strong and our fire wouldn't die out in the middle of the night. So we looked for help in the only places we knew: the magnificence of Nature — and the support of one another.

We developed our own explanations for natural phenomena: the changing of the seasons, the sudden burst of lightning, the winds that sometimes wouldn't come when we wanted our ships to sail. In awe of Nature and her manifestations that were so much more powerful than us, we came up with names and backstories for all these supernatural entities that were clearly all around us; for all these forces of Nature that could save or ruin our lives.

And guess what? The names of these deities may have been different from one another, depending on what part of the world you were in, but their essence wasn't. It doesn't matter if she was called Aphrodite, Venus, Freya, Oshun or Xochiquetzal: people believed in a goddess that protected love, lust, childbirth and women. Almost every Pagan culture has a goddess of fertility, a goddess of home and a goddess of love (very often, the three are one and the same); a god of the sun and a god or goddess of the underworld; a god of war and a god or goddess of wisdom. These gods and goddesses were believed to interact with one another the way forces of Nature do: sometimes favorably, other times causing chaos.

Let's hop on a time machine and examine a bit more how it all started, shall we?

The year was 35,000 BCE.

We still mostly lived in caves, but we'd mastered the art of moving around in boats, as well as the art of using plants for healing. We lived in small communities in what was back then Eurasia and venerated the circle of life, from birth to death. Archaeological finds from that era up until 26,000 BCE, show burials of bones stained with red ochre, which most of them agree it likely was for spiritual purposes. Red ochre symbolized the body being returned to Mother Earth, the Great Goddess — and entering the circle of rebirth through blood.

Already back then, the Divine Feminine was present in the human psyche. That's when the first "Venus figurines" first started appearing in graves all across Eurasia[2].

Yes, you got that right: the first recurring artifact to be found across all human civilization, was not a depiction of power and war (like Zeus' lightning bolt or Thor's hammer) or of exalted wisdom (like the Star of David) or even of sacrifice and martyrdom (like the Christian cross). It was one that revered the female form and celebrated life and fertility. Carved from stone, ivory or formed in clay, these Venus figurines all had large breasts, full bellies and hips and exposed vulvas. Although modern historians are still not 100% in agreement as per the exact purpose of these figurines, the general consensus is that they were probably emblems of fertility, success and the Mother Goddess.

Isn't it interesting that our first statues, collectively as a species, celebrated Nature and honored life through the female form?

It makes sense, if you think about it. What was Earth, back then, if not the Great Mother who nurtured us all and provided us with food and warmth to survive?

Of course, Earth still is the Great Mother. She hasn't changed. It's us who changed a lot throughout the millennia, to the point that we forgot we owe everything to Her; to the point that today we think we could deplete her resources completely and then hop on to a spaceship and colonize some other unfortunate planet...

But let's not get carried away yet! We still have a lot of ground to cover in this trip through time.

From about 10,000 BCE to 100 BCE, different ancient civilizations flourished.

---

[2] Dixson, Alan F., and Barnaby Dixson. 2011. "Venus Figurines of the European Paleolithic: Symbols of Fertility or Attractiveness?" Journal of Anthropology 2011, p. 1-11.

And their diverse Pagan traditions flourished with them.

Humanity's oldest temple (that we've discovered so far) is believed to have been in use between 9,000 BCE and 7,000 BCE, in the Southeastern Anatolia Region of Turkey. It's called "Göbekli Tepe" which is Turkish for "potbelly hill" and is thought to be a pilgrimage site where people honored Nature and its creatures (pillar carvings of various animals as well as people have been found there). It's also thought that the site functioned as a cosmogonic map of sorts, for the locals to understand how they were all connected — both to the landscape that surrounded them and to the cosmos. The archaeologist behind this discovery believes that the people who built Göbekli Tepe were practicing shamanism and worshipped deities that were much later found in ancient Mesopotamia…

A millennia or so later, again in Anatolia, at the proto-city settlements of Catalhoyuk, people seemed to use figurines that once again exalted the feminine body — only this time, there were also phallic symbols and hunting scenes. Mother Nature was still at the core of spiritual beliefs, but powerful individual expressions of her (like the sun or the mountains) were slowly emerging as manifestations of male deities.

You can see the common theme, right?

It was all about the embodiment of Nature in physical structures and forms: female and male; human and divine. We'd started mapping not just our inner duality but also our relationship to the animals, the stars and the cosmos.

And this was not only the case in Turkey, but all across the other side of Europe as well.

Around 3,000 BCE, some of the most intriguing structures started appearing in Ireland and what is now the United Kingdom. The first one, Newgrange, was a huge circular tomb, tightly surrounded by a stoned circle (almost like a crown would surround a king's head). It has carvings from rose quartz and is positioned in such a way that, when the Sun rising on the day of the Winter Solstice, its rays hit directly the tomb's entrance and flood the inner chamber with light. Winter Solstice in general, was one of the most important times of the year for Pagans: when the longest night of the year was over, and there was once again hope for spring and renewal. The walls of Newgrange are adorned with spirals; a symbol of renewal and eternity. It was believed that gods resided inside! Although archaeologists cannot agree on why Newgrange was built (do they ever agree on anything?), the two most possible explanations are that it was either part of a religion that venerated the Sun and how it moved in the sky, or the dead and their passage to underworld. If you take into account the dualities we've already seen in earlier temples, it was probably both: a celebration of like (the Sun) and death (the Underworld). We'll see something similar when we talk about the pyramids in a while.

Newgrange certainly wasn't the only structure in that corner of the world that was built perfectly aligned with a solstice or an equinox… You may know one of these other structures.

It's Stonehenge.

Stonehenge was initially built around 3,100 BCE — although it continued evolving until 2,600 BCE. A wooden circle is thought to have originally existed within the stone circle, with the wooden posts later replaced with its current standing stones. Although the stone circles look rather abstract and minimal today, back then its architecture was quite complex: it had an altar, a cremation cemetery, a portal and subtle engravings on its stones show symbols like a dagger and an ax. To this day, no one knows how its builders managed to move the huge monoliths around, but we do know that they made sure they were perfectly aligned with the midsummer sunrise and the midwinter sunset of that time.

Stonehenge is considered to be a place of immense power. It's no accident that the ancients built their temples in the places they did, perfectly aligned with the elements of Nature. It is believed that they followed invisible "ley lines", energy lines from within the Earth that made some locations more magically potent than others[3]. That belief was especially strong among the Celtic Druids — and it's something many modern Pagans believe to this day.

But let's get back to our time machine, this time to visit ancient Egypt and the Pyramids.

Ah, the Pyramids! One could write a whole book about the Pyramids and still not manage to scratch the surface of their complex spiritual importance... but we can at least try to figure out how it all fits together in this ancient Pagan puzzle, can't we?

Around 2,635 BCE, the oldest surviving Pyramid was commissioned by a Pharaoh and started its construction. One hundred years later, the Great Pyramid of Giza had been completed — and a hundred years after that, around 2,494 BCE, the Pyramid Texts were composed; one of the oldest religious texts that have survived to this day. This marks an era when Paganism, at least in the more developed parts of the ancient world, was beginning to acquire a more well-defined shape. This is roughly around the time when the first pantheons started appearing; different gods and goddesses, each "responsible" for a specific domain of Nature and human life. These pantheons are first encountered in Mesopotamia, Egypt and Greece, but later become common among Pagan religions in China, South America and Africa as well.

You could almost say that what started with simply worshipping Mother Nature, evolved to worshipping some of its manifestations... to worshipping the different conditions of human life. There are several common threads throughout these pantheons, that we've briefly touched before and will discuss more in a later chapter. Because we're not done with the Pyramids yet!

The Pyramids are perhaps the best example of the duality of Paganism: combining the worship of the Sun and its light, with the

---

[3] Doyle White, Ethan (2016). "Old Stones, New Rites: Contemporary Pagan Interactions with the Medway Megaliths". Material Religion: The Journal of Objects, Art and Belief, p. 346-372.

veneration for the dead and their shadow kingdom. They were all built on the west side of the Nile, which was considered the domain of the dead and were given names that were all somehow associated with the light of the Sun. The structures themselves speak to that underlying duality, with their broad base that reached under the earth and their pointy edge towards the sky… The idea is the same as the idea behind a witch's conical hat really: to create a cone of power. Some believe that the power was so strong that the pyramids were designed as a resurrection "machine" for the Pharaohs to come back to life!

Now wouldn't that make a much more interesting movie than all those mummy horror films?

Speaking of fascinating stories that are not being told often enough: the Minoan civilization. Established around 2,200 BCE in ancient Crete, with its epicenter at Knossos palace, the Minoan civilization was actually considered the first advanced society in Europe. Now you may have heard the tale of the Minotaur, the mythical half-man, half-bull monster that lived inside the maze… but did you know that the Minoan civilization was fundamentally matriarchal, with women in equal positions as men, very often being naked from the waste up like men?

Yes, naked female breasts in ancient Crete were not a taboo[4] as they seem to be in today's Instagram… And this has its roots in the Pagan mentality of viewing the woman body as something to be celebrated and aspired to; something strong and primal not delicate and hidden away in shame. In fact the most important goddess of the Minoans, the goddess of the snakes (who is believed to be an earlier version of goddess Athena) is always posing proud in figurines, with her breasts uncovered while otherwise dressed in an exquisite gown, one snake in each arm. Why snakes? They were always a symbol of wisdom, but also of change and rebirth; of shedding one's skin. (We'll elaborate more on Pagan and magical symbols on a later chapter.)

---

[4] Nikos Kazantzakis. At the Palaces of Knossos. London: Owen, 1988.

But to get back to the pyramids for one last time: Egyptians were not the only ones who built them. Around 1,200 BCE, the Olmecs in Central America started building pyramids too — once again to venerate the dead. Later on, around 250-900 CE, the Mayan pyramids were built...

Isn't it fascinating to see how, in such ancient times, humanity was pretty much in agreement about the truly important things in life? Not sameness, as each culture gave its own spin on things, but an agreement nonetheless. Modern humans could definitely stand to learn a thing or two from ancient Pagans in that regard (and many others).

Next stop on our journey: the first sparks of monotheism appear around the world.

And guess what? It coincides with the first versions of written creed...

From 2,150 until about 600 BCE, sacred scripture are beginning to emerge throughout the known civilization. First in Sumeria, with the Epic of Gilgamesh, a king chosen by the gods to save his people, who along the way spurned the gods and learned the secrets to immortality. Then in India, around 1,700 BCE, the first one of the Vedas (the oldest scriptures of Hinduism) was composed; it talked, among other things, about a supreme god. This kickstarted the Vedic age, the formative period of the Indian civilization. Around 1,250 BCE, the Upanishads were composed: these later Vedic texts contain some of the central concepts that then evolved to Hinduism and Buddhism.

Then, around 600 BCE, the Torah was compiled. Torah was the first of the sacred Jewish books that created the Hebrew bible: they spoke about how the Jewish were god's chosen people and they had to endure a lot of suffering and live by certain strict laws. It was believed that the teachings of the Torah were given to the prophet Moses directly by Yahweh, the god of the Jews (that later evolved to the God of Christianity) and he wrote them down.

Around the same era, a bit further away, the emperors Darius and Xerxes are making Zoroastrianism the official religion of their expanding Persian empire. Zoroastrianism was all about the fight between the absolute good, a supreme god called Ahura Mazda ("Wise Lord" in Iranian) and absolute evil, as preached by the spiritual leader Zaratustra.

Confucius in China also compiled his first book during that same time. Shu Ching, written in the form of speeches from a king to his ministers, discussed ideas about the morality of government, venerating the ancestors and not doing to others what you don't want others doing to you[5]... (A lovely message, to this day.) A hundred years or so after that, Buddha was born.

It would be another 400 years or so until the birth of Jesus Christ...

MAKING THE WORLD A MORE MONOTHEISTIC PLACE

Well, that was a looong trip through time, wasn't it? You practically witnessed the dawn of spirituality and religion in fast forward within a few minutes... It's okay if your head is spinning!
Take a few moments to breathe.
It's now time to unpack all these things we just learned and understand them a bit better, in terms of how they affected Pagan beliefs and the way the world works today.
Basically it can be condensed into one sentence: as people moved further away from Nature, building intricate cities and creating laws where the will of the king had to be venerated, monotheism started taking over. And in every single case, the ultimate god was considered to have male characteristics (not in the sense of having a male body, but in the sense of propagating male, patriarchal values). Was that an accident? Not really! The kings and emperors of ancient civilizations (with the exception of Classical Greece that had already invented democracy by then), were men, following a bloodline that was believed to have been blessed by the gods. So they needed an ultimate "overruler", an authority that could bypass all others and that people would obey.

---

[5] Medhurst, W. H. Ancient China. The Shoo King or the Historical Classic. Shanghai: The Mission Press.

That authority, normally, it had to look a bit like them.

So you go from a place in the collective human psyche where the female form is venerated as a manifestation of Mother Earth and the Primordial Goddess, to a place where man-made texts and laws are considered to contain the only truth. A truth that, conveniently, always involves a male-like being, usually older and wise, ruling over everyone — sometimes benevolently, others through fear.

Can you see what's happening here? We went from honoring Nature the notion that we are made of nature and should live in alignment to that nature (cue all those buildings aligned with the rays of the sun), to believing we are somehow greater than Nature and that we should live in alignment to a divine wisdom (even if we have to suffer or follow strict rules). It's a fundamental shift, the repercussions of which we are experiencing to this day. Because what is blatant capitalism and the burning of the Amazon's rainforests for profit if not the evolution of the monotheistic idea that we are somehow "better", "chosen" and that we "deserve" to take everything we want since our way is the only correct way?

Just think for a second how the Bible starts: "In the beginning was the Word, and the Word was with God, and the Word was God[6]."

If you honestly believe that a superior, male-presenting wisdom created Nature, then you're going to lead a very different life than those who believe that Nature IS the superior wisdom. If you think that wisdom and male authority trumps female power and the miracle of childbirth, then you're going to have a very different society than the ancient Minoans where women had their breasts uncovered. If you believe that one god is all you need, then you'll have a very different way of managing disputes and expanding your kingdom than the ancient Greeks who had 12 gods (6 male, 6 female) and even saw monarchy as something that could be debated — at least until Alexander the Great came along.

Of course, the counterargument can also be made: didn't these empires flourish as much as they did precisely BECAUSE they believed their one and only god told them to march on? Because they had explicit laws and rules and sacred scriptures instead of relying

---

[6] Old Testament: The Book of Genesis.

on an oral tradition and more or less only fighting each other for resources? Isn't this the reason polytheistic societies like those of the native Americans and Africans fell prey to the European colonizers who believed they were on a sacred mission to christianize the world? Didn't organize religion also bring about a society that was able to expand exponentially?

Probably. But this is not a book about how to best colonize the world or rule over your fellow humans. There have been enough books like that, written throughout the ages. As a species, we're not that much better off for it — especially if you were unlucky enough to be born in the areas of the world that were colonized, looted and enslaved by these "wise" believers in monotheism who brought their "civilization to the primitive world".

This is a book about understanding where we all came from: the womb of the same Mother Earth. Whether we've turned our backs at it or not, Paganism is a part of our psyche. Our bodies are still a manifestation of dualities. Childbirth is still a miracle. And the appreciation of feminine power is finally returning.

Dear one, this is a book to help you understand that what you believe, shapes your world.

And for a very long time, our world has been shaped by people who have turned their backs to our Pagan past and to our common, Mother Earth.

It's time to take our world back, don't you think?

But first, let's talk a bit about how the word "Pagan" came to be.

"They are crazy, these Romans[7]"

---

[7] English translation of the phrase, « Ils sont fous, ces Romains ! » from the comic book Astérix by René Goscinny and Albert Uderzo, first mentioned in Astérix et Cléopâtre, p. 10, p. 23.

Have you noticed something from our trip through time? The word "Pagan" was never used by the ancient people to define themselves and their beliefs.

That's because that word didn't even exist yet: it was first coined around 300 CE.

Incidentally (just kidding, it wasn't incidentally at all), that was the time when the ruler of most of the then known world, the Roman Empire under the emperor Constantine, declared Christianity as its official religion.

There are many reasons why that happened, depending on who you ask.

The main (read: Christian) narrative says that in the decades that followed the death of Christ, the work of the Apostle Paul and his letters reached people in every corner of the Roman Empire, creating pockets of early Christianity. Although Christianity was persecuted and illegal, secret Chrstian societies started growing despite their very often violent deaths in Roman arena, torn asunder by lions... Christians suffered, but it only made their faith stronger — until the emperor Constantine saw the light and converted to Christianity himself.

We've all seen this movie, haven't we? Some variation of it always plays on TV around Easter...

As always, the truth is slightly more complicated.

The Romans didn't care so much about Christians per se. Judaism was a formal religion under the Roman Empire — as it was easier for the Romans to control larger territories if they allowed their subjects to keep their ways and customs. So unless Christians did something to challenge Roman authority (or were accused of doing so by someone who had a bias against them for personal reasons), they were mostly left alone.

Yes, Romans were a bloodthirsty bunch and people were thrown to the lions in the arena, there's no denying that. But it wasn't just Christians who suffered this horrible fate: it was basically everyone who would break the Roman law and wasn't highborn enough to be granted a more dignified death like beheading.

Around 200 CE, emperor Decius believed that the Roman Empire needed to strengthen its roots to avoid infighting and present a united front to the many threats they were facing (like the Goths). So he made sacrificing to the Roman gods a law of the Empire — as well as providing proof of having sacrificed to the gods. This led to many Christians who lived under Roman rule to not be able to comply… and as a result become persecuted. Interestingly enough, Decius' ruling of "mandatory sacrifice" didn't do much to stop the Goths from winning battles against the Romans. He himself died in battle.

Around 300 CE, emperor Constantine tried a different approach. Not only he granted Christianity a legal status and stopped the persecutions, he eventually declared it the official religion of the Roman Empire. The thing is though, historians today are still not sure if Constantine's motives were sincere or political: there was something about that new Christian religion, that unwavering belief that comes from monotheism, that just seemed to organize people better under a cause than it did the (by then used to a luxurious and hedonistic lifestyle) Romans who still worshipped the Roman pantheon. There are many sources that claim Constantine used Christianity as a way to promote obedience to his imperialistic policies, turning the figurehead of the emperor to that of someone who's executing God's will on Earth — and that he remained secretly Pagan until he was baptized on his deathbed.

We've all seen enough *Game of Thrones* episodes to know this is not unlikely.

In any case, it was under Constantine's rule that Christianity first became a source of power and authority. Of course, it wasn't an easy task to pull off, convincing the Romans to give up their gods and goddesses. That's where the word "Pagan" comes in.

For the first time ever, a word was needed to describe all those who haven't converted to Christianity and still believed in the old gods and goddesses. That word had to be inclusive enough so as to capture all the different beliefs that fell under the would-be-Pagan umbrella, but also subtly derogatory to make it clear that Christians were now the first-class citizens.

Words like "hellene" (to signify those who worshipped the Greek-Roman pantheon) and "heathen" (meaning the one who dwells on the heath) started being used. But "Pagan", from the Latin word for "rural/rustic/villager/relating to the countryside/non-military" (paganus), seemed like the perfect fit — and eventually became interchangeable with "non-Christian". Why?

If you understand Constantine's reasons for the official switch to Christianity as a way to "rally the troops", then it's easy to see how people who still opted to practice the old religions started feeling ostracized. It became easier for them to start living a more rural life that didn't get them in the crosshairs of the now-Christian population that lived in the more urban areas; living closer to nature where they could practice their beliefs in peace made sense. Another reason is that according to Constantine's imperialistic vision, all Christians were considered "milites Christi": soldiers of Christ (and of the Roman Empire, it goes without saying).

It bears repeating, dear one: Pagans didn't choose the word "pagan" to describe themselves. It was a derogatory term applied to them by those in power — fueled by political propaganda and propagated by ignorance. Not unsimilar to the way the name "Indians" was given to native Americans by the colonizers (first by mistake, then to signify their inferiority to Europeans).

History is written by the victors, didn't we establish that?

Of course, the same way Rome "wasn't built in a day", so Christianity didn't take over the Roman Empire completely overnight. And although the now-called Pagans certainly didn't feel like they had more in common between them than before (for instance, a Norse Pagan would never consider themselves of the same tribe with a Celtic Pagan or a Greek Pagan), slowly they started realizing that living under Christian rule meant they would either have to hide themselves, or rebel and suffer the consequences.

Many of them chose the latter — while others practiced their craft in secret, "hiding" Pagan symbols in everything from actual Christian churches to little home decorations.

They didn't always have to hide their symbols though. In a bizarre twist of fate, many Pagan symbols and traditions were actually incorporated into canon Christianity. Especially when it came to Christmas. Many Germanic/Scandinavian and Celtic rituals and symbols, from kissing under the mistletoe (a holy plant in both Scandinavian and Celtic lore) to burning the Yule log (a Norse Winter Solstice tradition) and even decorating fyr trees with lights and presents (another Norse tradition, to honor Odin) were eventually incorporated into Christmas celebrations. But that happened a bit later.

For now all you need to know is that the date of Christmas itself, we owe to Pagans. Yes, really.

It was during those early days, when the Church had to convince people to give up their Pagan ways and join the reinvented, all-Christian Roman Empire. Suffice to say it wasn't easy, especially when it came to the bon viveur Romans. Romans liked their parties and never missed an opportunity to celebrate. For instance: upon the Winter Solstice, which as we've seen was a big deal for all Pagans, the Romans and Greeks traditionally celebrated Saturnalia — the birth of Saturn/Kronos.

Originally celebrated on December 17, the birth of Saturn was a week-long, lavish celebration where people would roam the streets sans clothing, carol singing, binge drinking and exchanging gifts. Shops and businesses would close, food and drink would be aplenty... There was no easy way to convince a whole nation to forego a party like that, especially when that nation was the Romans! So the Church declared the birth of Christ to be celebrated on December 25 and made it "8 days of Christmas" — so that people could start celebrating on the 17th as they were used to. Brilliant, right? It was that "8 days of Christmas" that slowly evolved to the "12 days of Christmas" of today.

And transferring Christmas in December (we say "transferring" because most historians now believe Christ was born in the Spring) didn't just placate the Romans[8]. It helped the Zoroastrians adapt as well, as the birth of Mithra, who was also called "The Invincible Sun" took place on December 25. And of course it fit all the other Pagan cultures who viewed the Winter Solstice as a day of hope and love, where the Light is reborn....

Hey, nothing wrong with that. A new religion comes along and incorporates rituals, symbols and beliefs from the old religions to keep people happy. It's a good thing, right?

Unfortunately, it didn't stop there.

As many people back in the day tended to combine their newfound Christianity with many of their Pagan practices (like sacrifices, divination, Pagan festivals, believing in omens etc), the Church needed to draw a line in the sand, of sorts. They needed to convince people that the Pagan ways were wrong and evil, instead of what they really were at the time, aka politically inconvenient. And the way to do that was by taking some key Pagan practices and symbols and vilifying them.

To get back to the misconceptions about Paganism discussed on the first chapter: the reason people have this idea that Pagans worship the devil, is because the Church took some of Paganism's most popular deities and use their physical characteristics to create the image of the Devil; the antithesis of God; the absolute evil. Who were these deities?

Mostly Pan, the Greek god of nature and wild animals, who was depicted as half-man, half-goat, with horns sprouting from his head. Pan was never evil: he was a fun-loving being who embraced the joys of nature, virility and sex, although his temper would often cause panic (yes, that's where that word comes from) to his opponents. He

---

[8] William Walsh, The Story of Santa Klaus, 1970, p. 62.

was worshipped in the outdoors and was often depicted in statues and paintings with an erect member...

You can see, perhaps, why the newly founded Christian church would not like that?

Pan symbolized everything (interestingly enough "everything" is literally what the name Pan translates to in Greek) this new religion wanted to break free from: sexual freedom, a close connection to nature, a reverence of the naked body. Jesus Christ's message at its core may have been one of love and forgiveness, but the framework around Christianity was still very much influenced by Judaism (Christianity was considered the "continuation" of Judaism anyway, it is commonly accepted that both religions believe in the same God). And Judaism, as we've seen, preached piety and suffering in order to be accepted in god's kingdom after death.

Abstaining from temptation, was Christianity's main theme. And nothing was more tempting than the fun-loving gods of Pagans who preached being laissez-faire and celebrating your body and your desires, as well as your connection to the animal world...

Another such "offender" was Cernunnos, the horned god of the Celts and the Gauls. Cernunnos is depicted with antlers on his head and always surrounded by wild animals (among them stags, snakes, bulls and rats, all symbols of wisdom and virility). In contrast to Pan though, Cernunnos is peaceful, sitting calm and cross legged — something historians believe symbolized his dual nature, embracing both human wisdom and empathy and animal power, presiding over both Nature and the Underworld. Yes, those Pagan dualities again... Aren't they beautiful?

Cernunnos is worshipped today by modern Wiccans (more on that in the next part of the book).

Anyway, perhaps you're starting to get it now. Horns, a symbol of fertility and abundance, were connected with evil. Women who were free and shameless about their sexuality, were called witches (or whores, with the example of Mary Magdalene in the Bible being "saved" by Jesus and repenting for her sins). What was once a revered connection to Nature and its magnificence, the female body, started becoming a thing of shame that had to be hidden and only viewed by specific men (like a woman's husband).

Male sexuality was also stifled (there are no winners in this game of oppression). Men were supposed to only engage in "carnal relations" with their spouses with the goal to procreate, whereas homosexuality was considered a perversion and abomination...

The most heartbreaking thing? There are still people out there, so many centuries later, that still think in those terms. That are so far removed from their primordial Nature they can't see we are all unique — and perfect just the way we are.

But we should continue our journey through time, dear one.

Dark stuff happened in the Dark Ages

From about 500 CE to 1,500 CE, Europe went under what is now known as "the Dark Ages". During that time, to be accused of being a pagan (or a witch, as these terms were all piled under the same "non-devout Christian" accusation) was not just derogatory. Certainly, pagans were thought to be unclean, hedonistic, savages even — but most importantly they were considered sinners in the eyes of the One True God of Christianity. Sinners that had to either convert, or die brutal deaths. Charlemagne, king of the Franks, the Lombards and eventually emperor of the Romans, who's also called "Father Europe" because he "united and christianized the continent" personally hunted down the Pagan Saxons in order to christianize Saxonia (what is now England) chasing them on horseback on a river to give them the chance to "get baptized or die".

And we called Romans bloodthirsty a while ago when they were throwing Christians to the lions.

Around 800 CE, Pagan traditions were only practiced in secret as the official religion of the continent was for the most part Christianity. Yet, Paganism didn't die out.

The Vikings saw to that.

Also known as "the Old Norse religion", Norse paganism was practiced in Scandinavia (and among the Germanic tribes that descended through Europe) since 500 BCE. The Norse/Germanic pantheon had many similarities with the Greek/Roman pantheon: a group of gods and goddesses, closely connected to nature and to animals, none of them completely good or completely evil. Even the trickster god, Loki (who is compared to Hermes/Mercury), had moments of heroic redemption for every bad prank he pulled to the other gods[9]...

Yes, exactly like in the comics and in the superhero movies. Isn't it funny how our modern pop culture celebrates so many Pagan elements? It was about time, perhaps!

The Viking Age, from around 700 CE to 1,000 CE, brought Christianity and Pagans at a clash throughout Europe. As Scandinavians left their calm, farm lives, boarded ships and started invading the European shores, they brought with them tales about Odin's wisdom, about Thor's power and Freya's beauty. They were the enemy, certainly, ransaking villages and looting churches — but form some people they were also a reminder of a different way of life; a life that was more free (and for women, certainly more equal). Christian women finding Vikings attractive and laying with them started being a frequent occurrence (with many illegitimate children born along the way) so the Church and the kings of Europe had to portray the Vikings as filthy, uncivilised animals who (you guessed it) worshipped the Devil.

Regardless, at the height of their military expansion the Vikings reached as far south as Sicily and as far West as the then unexplored America — and part of their Pagan beliefs came with them and grew roots in these new places, embedded with the local folk customs.

Remember when we talked about the Yule Log and decorating trees at Christmas earlier?

---

[9] Neil Gaiman, Norse Mythology, 2017, Bloomsbury Publishing PLC.

Even the myth of Santa Claus, riding his sleigh in the sky, is for the most part inspired by Odin (the AllFather of Old Norse Pantheon, often compared to Saturn or Zeus) riding his 8-legged flying horse, Sleipnir, visiting children at night and leaving gifts (or coal if they were bad) for them inside their boots. Although St Nicholas did live around 200 CE and gave a lot to the poor, as did Agios Vasileios, the Orthodox Christian version of Santa Claus around 300 CE, their figures eventually melted together with legends around Odin and his gift giving and ended up in the version of Santa Claus we have today.

(Who only started wearing red at the beginning of last century, thanks to a Coca Cola advertisement, but that's another story.)

But while West and Central Europe was discovering a unique balance of combining Pagan beliefs with a Christian official facade (to get a sense of how extended this intermingling was, just pay close attention to the symbols you'll find carved in old churches: you'll find everything from Thor's hammer there to vulva-like depictions of fruits and flowers, that echoe the symbols used to honor goddesses in many Pagan pantheons), the East was another story.

Byzantium, the continuation of the Roman Empire that became independent since the Church schism in 1054 CE, was a highly theocratic society that prosecuted viciously not just any perceived Pagans but also any different versions of Christianity (they were called heretics). Meanwhile, in the Arab world, any Pagans had converted to Islam around 700 CE.

And speaking of Islam: Paganism was not the only thing Christianity tried to stifle. Islam, back then, didn't have the militant approach many practicioners of this religion have today. On the contrary, they were probably more civilized and kind than the Europeans (and we owe a lot to Islamic scholars who translated most Ancient Greek texts and brought them to the surface once again), who launched eight Crusades to "drive the non-believers away from the Holy Land".

But that's what happens when you believe there is only one God out there; that yours is the only right one and that all others are impostors. In a way, it wasn't the Christians' fault either: they were bound to be geared like that ever since they turned monotheism into a way to control countries and armies...

Dear one, we need to jump ahead a few centuries now. And what comes next is not pleasant, not at all. But it needs to be discussed.

After all, this has been a long trip through time that's now reaching one of its most crucial moments for your understanding of what it means to be a Pagan...

It all started with a book, published in 1486 CE.

The book was called, "Malleus Maleficarum[10]".

Now, you may have noticed that we haven't really addressed witchcraft at all so far. Rest assured we will do so in the next part of the book. For now, all you need to know is that witchcraft has been around for millennia. It wasn't always considered good or bad: in many cultures, sorcerers were viewed as healers/holy people who would help with the crops and soothe illnesses. In others, sorcerers worked with kings and queens to consolidate their power and help them vanquish their enemies, the same way today modern presidents would have advisors on certain matters.

But witchcraft was also a part of everyday life. The first written mention we have of it comes from 2,000 BCE, when in the Babylonian code of law in Ancient Mesopotamia, the Code of Hammurabi[11], it is mentioned a process for a man to cleanse himself from a spell another man has cast on him by jumping into the holy river...

Notice how this was about men, not women, casting spells at each other?

---

[10] Malleus Maleficarum, Heinrich Kramer & Jacob Sprenger, translated by Montague Summers, 2011, Martino Fine Books.

[11] Bryant, Tamera (2005). The Life & Times of Hammurabi. Bear: Mitchell Lane Publishers.

Although the near Eastern antiquity has some great lore pertaining powerful female sorceresses, among them Medea (who first appears in Hesiod's *Theogony* but has been immortalized in Euripides' tragedy by the same name) and Circe (who bewitched Ulysseus' men in Homer's *Odyssey*), witchcraft wasn't really gender specific in the Pagan world in terms of who practiced it. In fact, in Africa, in the Yoruba tradition, witchcraft-practicing men were considered more common and dignified than women (who were viewed with suspicion if they practiced it).

When it comes down to it though, most deities connected to witchcraft, from Hecate in Greece to Freya in Scandinavia, were female. And perhaps that made the difference in the eyes of Christians who were looking for scapegoats... Because women, in the Middle Ages, were a much easier target than men, socially — especially if they were unmarried or widows.

But here's the thing: witchcraft was forbidden in Europe since 900 CE, considered "a trick of the devil" (yet another attempt to stifle Pagan traditions). Most people either didn't believe witches were real, considering them a fable and superstition, or knew better and stayed silent. In many parts of Europe, where the Pagan roots were still strong, witchcraft was considered a minor offence and if someone was caught they were expected to do some penance and that was it.

For the most part, practitioners of the Craft could still do rituals in secret or operate under the radar. But Heinrich Kramer changed all that.

A monk of the Dominican Order, Kramer was obsessed with witches all his life. In one of his visits in the Tyrol region of Germany he got into an altercation with a woman called Helena Scheuberin, who didn't approve of his methods and was audacious enough to speak her mind. (The horror! Can you imagine, dear one? Speaking your mind as a woman in the Middle Ages?)

Kramer brought this woman, along with six other local women, to trial for witchcraft, citing her sexual life as one of his arguments.

Thankfully the local bishop was a reasonable man and sent Kramer home telling him he was crazy.

Kramer, seething at this insult, wrote "Malleus Maleficarum" (or as it is alternatively known, "The Hammer of Witches") as an act of revenge against the bishop and all those who refused to believe that "magic is a real threat" — but also revenge against women like Scheuberin who dared to speak their minds. In this book, Kramer provided detailed instructions on how to identify witches who, according to his arguments, were mostly women.

He didn't stop at identifying them: Malleus Maleficarum also offers excessive details on how to hunt them, interrogate them and punish them.

Sounds crazy, right? Something today we'd view basically as hate speech… But Kramer took his book to the Pope, the Pope liked it and gave it his seal of approval… The book became so popular, it was a bestseller in Europe — surpassed only by the Bible. And as a result, more than 80,000 women were burned at the stake or otherwise tortured to death between 1500-1660 CE under charges of "witchcraft". Who were these women? Were they witches?

Some of them, perhaps. But most of them were just unfortunate enough to have been born at a time and place where just being a woman, especially unmarried or a widow, was enough to draw suspicion on you (especially beautiful women who were thought to reject the sexual advances of powerful men). And if this horror wasn't enough, innocent animals were also burned with them. Mostly cats, who also had the misfortune of being associated with the Devil — probably due to the fact that Freya, the Scandinavian goddess of beauty who was also a witch, rode a chariot carried by flying cats… If you're feeling sick to your stomach, it's only normal. Those were horrendous times indeed. But do you see know, dear one, how far we've come? Do you see why being able to joke about being a witch on Instagram is disrespectful to all those women who died for the mere suspicion of being one?

I hope you see that. I hope you see how lucky you are to be able to make this choice and live your magickal life out in the open.

So where does that leave the Pagan world of old?

Well, depends on where in the world you look — and how eurocentric you are (as many of us, unfortunately, still tend to be).

Pagan traditions in Africa had been flourishing since time immemorial; each tribe (and later on, country) of this vast continent having their own beliefs, passed down from generation to generation through word of mouth. Many of these beliefs and pantheons, like the Yoruba religion of Nigeria and the Vodun religion of Benin, Togo and Ghana, came with them to the Americas around 1500 CE when the colonization and slave trade destroyed so many lives... Although in slavery though, these people found strength in their Pagan beliefs (very often also practiced in secret as their masters wanted them to convert to Christianity) and in time these traditions were embedded with local beliefs. Vodun in particular, became the base for practices that are alive and well to this day in Haiti, Cuba, Brazil, Puerto Rico and Louisiana.

A whole book dedicated to the Yoruba and Vodun and their branches wouldn't be enough to do justice to these rich, Pagan traditions... But we'll try to cover some of their symbols and beliefs in the third part of the book, dear one. For now it's enough to say that the colonizers may have enslaved so many people from the African continent but they failed to enslave their minds and spirits... and the colonizers' descendants are now buying magic potions and tarot sessions from their descendants on Instagram. Ain't life a funny thing? Balance always gets restored, although it may take a few generations.

But let's get back to Europe, for a moment. As the Middle Ages gave way to the Renaissance, Paganism started winning ground again — as did a strong revival of magic. How did that happen? Weren't witches supposedly all burned at the stake? Well, now. Have you forgotten that the true practitioners of witchcraft were always women AND men? The rituals and the traditions stayed alive, only they became more theoretical and esoteric, out of fear of retribution. Soon, during the era of Romanticism (from 1780 CE to 1850 CE), artists and writers found themselves drawn back to Nature, as well as to the aesthetics and folklore of Pagan medieval times and an idolized version of Ancient Greece and its pantheon.

Witchcraft and magic, Vikings and their Norse gods and goddesses, became a source of wonder. Although, of course, given the times, it was mostly wealthy white men who dabbled with magic or expressed that wonder — as the repercussions for them were close to nonexistent...

LET'S TALK ABOUT SALEM, SHALL WE?

Which brings us to the hot topic of Salem, Massachusetts.

In 1692, witch hunting had subsided in Europe — but the freshly colonized New World (only 80 or so years had gone by since the first American colony was founded in Virginia) was still a bit slow in adapting trends. So when two young girls were (as it is now believed) poisoned by a hallucination inducing fungus, mass hysteria quickly ensued believing witches were responsible for cursing them... leading to the Salem witch trials.

During the Salem witch trials, 200 people were tortured and coerced to confession of using witchcraft to harm people. One of them, Tituba, an enslaved woman, confessed that she was a witch (all the rest maintained their innocence, until their tragic deaths). 19 people were burned at the stake, 5 of which men. Witch burning took over in a few other states as well, before thankfully dying out. Ironically enough, it is today acknowledged amid the magical community that there were no real, practicing witches in Salem back in the day... but many of them have moved to that area since some theatrical plays and TV shows of the middle of last century started showing a more appealing face to magic and gave Salem its moniker as "Witch City".

Nowadays, those women and men who burned at the stake in the Salem Witch Trials are considered martyrs in the local magickal community. If anything, magick is celebrated in Salem (although through a glamorized lens, associated with overspending in witch memorabilia).

One cannot help but wonder how Kramer would feel about that...

Hopefully his spirit has moved on and learned better than to torture women by now.

Chapter 3: Paganism Today

We're almost at the end of our historical journey. We've seen the rise and fall of Pagan civilizations, we've seen the prosecutions and the mandatory conversions to Christianity; we've also seen the tide beginning to change and Paganism becoming cool again.

In a way, we are now at the most important part of our journey of understanding.

In this chapter, we're going to talk about how the 19th and the 20th century gave us so many of the tools, rituals and frame of reference we're using today as modern Pagans, Wiccans and Witches. We're going to talk about how things like spirit consultations and tarot cards came to be and how the secret societies shaped ceremonial magick. Yes, magick with a k.

You'll see, in a while.

Are you ready, dear one?

Paintings, revolutions, occult societies

Remember how we talked about the age of Romanticism earlier, where white men (mostly artists at first) started expressing an interest in all things occult? Perhaps reading this book so far will have helped you realize this: behind most trends associated with Paganism, either pro or against it, the motives are usually political.

This case is not that much different.

During the 19th century, the Western world changed a lot. Several revolutions, starting with the French in 1789 and then the Greeks who revolted against the Turks after a 400-year occupation and succeeded to gain their independence, changed the face of Europe. Around 1848, revolutions across Germany, Austria, Hungary, Italy, Denmark and Poland created new national, independent states from the ashes of old kingdoms and empires. There was a feeling of returning to one's roots and traditions, of defining what makes a nation unique and separate from its neighbors. It may not come as a surprise that this return to folk traditions in order to foster a feeling of national identity and pride, awoke many Paganism practices as well!

It happen more organically than you'd expect. For instance, writers started realizing the tremendous wealth of their national mythologies and started compiling and retelling fairy tales and myths of old (is there anything more Pagan than that?). It was during that time for instance that the Brothers Grimm wrote their (originally much more grizzly than the watered down versions we are familiar with today) fairy tales and Elias Lönnrot compiled Finnish mythology into an epic poetry work, *Kalevala*[12].

Paintings and music soon followed. Before you know it, witches and ancient goddesses, rituals and mythical creatures were depicted in paintings of prestigious painters, lauded in poems and theater plays following in the Shakespearean tradition. [It needs to be said: William Shakespear was a Pagan admirer way before it was cool, during the most difficult century for Paganism between 1500-1600 CE. He included Greek mythological characters, Pagan gods and goddesses and the practice of witchcraft in many of his works. Astonishingly enough, his sorcerers weren't always female, or always evil. Hmm, could he be onto something?]

---

[12] Friberg, Eino; Landström, Björn; Schoolfield, George C., eds. (1988), The Kalevala: Epic of the Finnish People.

This fascination with Pagan practices may have started with fairytales and art, but it didn't stay in that theoretical realm for long. The 19th and 20th century also herald the beginning of many secret societies and sects that either practiced witchcraft in some form or theorized about it.

The Hermetic Order of the Golden Dawn

The most interesting secret society of the time was probably The Hermetic Order of the Golden Dawn or simply, Golden Dawn. At some point they were so famous in Victorian England, they weren't that much of a secret at all. They even made the news often.

To understand them a bit better, we first need to talk about Hermetic traditions in general. Yes, this is going to be another trip through time — but rest assured it will be a brief one.

After the death of Alexander the Great (who managed to conquer most of the then-known world within his short life, before dying at 33 years old in 323 BCE), the Kingdoms of Babylon, Egypt and the Near East in general were never the same. Certainly, the people who lived there were still mostly locals, but since their rulers, the heirs of Alexander, were of Greek descent, every aspect of life, culture and religion was glimpsed through a Hellenistic lens. Since the Egyptian Pantheon had many similarities to the Greek one, that last thing wasn't so hard to do either.

That's when Hermes Trismegistus ("thrice great") started being worshipped. Hermes Trismegistus was basically an amalgamation of Hermes (the Greek god of communication, or Mercury as it became his Latin name) and Thoth, the Egyptian god of wisdom. Old Thoth temples were now used to worship this "new and improved" version of the god and quickly his worship became a big thing during that time period.

How does that affect the 19th century Europe, you ask?

Well, the texts written based on that worship, the Hermetic texts, were basically instructions on how to perform witchcraft in a sophisticated and philosophical manner[13]. Created (mostly) by men, for (mostly) men. They combined astrology practices that were very popular with the Babylonias of the time, with alchemy (the practice of turning a substance, say coal, to another substance, say gold) and animistic practices (like spirit conjuring and animating statues, yes, really, it was based on the belief that everything has a soul). Most importantly, these Hermetic texts were written in a way that cauterized systemic religion and geared towards personal development; towards making one's self ascend to something greater, an existence that goes beyond the physical.

These Hermetic texts maintained a prominence throughout the ages. Some Christian scholars saw Hermes Trismegistus as a foreteller of Christian God; the early Muslims believed he built the pyramids of Giza – he's even mentioned (not by name, but implied) in the Quran. So although of course these texts were considered Pagan of origin, they were not condemned like other Pagan texts were during the Middle Ages. On the contrary, the Hermetic texts gained great notoriety in Europe, especially because of their dialectic on how to control Nature (which was a big thing back then). They helped a new generation of people who combined science and a quest for knowledge with occult wisdom, like Italian philosopher and wizard Giordano Bruno, emerge. In fact, even Sir Isaan Newton studied these Hermetic texts to help him "understand the world better." Yes, the guy who brought us the law of gravity was also a low-key wizard.

But then again, everyone who was someone was a low-key wizard back then. Which brings us full-circle to the creation of Golden Dawn[14].

In a way, Golden Dawn was an evolution of Freemasonry: its three founders were all Freemasons and the organization followed the tenets of Freemasonry in terms of creating different grades of hierarchy and initiation; different "Orders". But whereas in

---

[13] Yates, Frances A., Giordano Bruno and the Hermetic Tradition. University of Chicago Press, 1964.

[14] Runyon, Carroll (1997). Secrets of the Golden Dawn Cipher Manuscripts. C.H.S.

Freemasonry the focus is mostly on creating bonds of fraternity and helping each other in distress (providing along the way "secrets" that can benefit and improve the lives of its members), in Golden Dawn the focus was in studying the Hermetic texts and practicing ceremonial witchcraft and metaphysics experiments. Plus, unlike in Freemasonry, women were allowed in Golden Dawn. Perhaps because of that, around 1895 CE the secret organization was so well established in Victorian England that had more than 100 members, many contemporary celebrities and artists (like the poet Yeats) among them.

One of these celebrities of the time was Aleister Crowly.

THE PART WHERE ALEISTER CROLEY DESERVES A BOOK OF HIS OWN

Crowley was many things: a poet, a painter, an author, a world traveler; a mountaineer and (according to some sources) a spy for the British Intelligence. He's influenced Yeats; written poems for the painter Rodin, whom he knew; wrote articles for Vanity Fair and prominent astrology columns of the time; performed sex magick with movie stars; got deported from two countries; impregnated several women most of whom not married to him; had many male lovers; faked his death with the help of Portuguese writer Fernando Pessoa... Crowley was, originally, "fascinated" by Adolf Hitler — at least until he realized the extent of the threat of nazism and condemned Hitler and his practices by calling him "a black magician".

Yeah. It does make you wonder how Hollywood hasn't turned his life into a movie yet. (Although the name Crowley has been used in several TV shows to describe fictional demons.)

He's also the reason we write magick with a k: he started writing the word like that based on its more archaic spelling, to differentiate it from the common parlor tricks of stage magicians and illusionists (like Houdini) who were also starting to become popular during that time.

Aleister Crowley joined the secret society of Golden Dawn in 1898 and progressed until the Second Order, at the grade of Adeptus Minor. His mere ascendance to that final grade caused such conflict within the Golden Dawn ranks, the society's founder was practically kicked out for helping him ascend. Why? Well, Crowley was a divisive figure — he enjoyed being one.

It wasn't just his open bi-sexuality, promiscuity and drug abuse that made him polarizing in the eyes of his Victorian contemporaries. It was mostly the fact that he believed he was a prophet of an ancient Egyptian being, destined to guide humanity into the "Æon of Horus". The Aeon of Horus, in contrast to the Aeon of Osiris which Crowley thought humanity was currently experiencing (where patriarchy and monotheism ruled) or the older Aeon of isis (where Crowley saw as that time in humanity where matriarchal values and the worship of the goddess were more prominent) was supposed to usher in a new era for mankind. An era of ascendance and self-realization — a philosophy that was very close to the core message of the Hermetic texts.

Even more polarizing, was how he got this idea.

Apparently, after spending some time in Scotland and traveling to Mexico and India, where he studied Buddhism and Hinduism, Crowley and his then wife honeymooned in Egypt, where they visited the pyramids. (Remember how we elaborated on the power of the pyramids on the previous chapter and how they were built to connect the sun with the underworld and act as chambers of resurrection?)

Apparently they had some kind of profound experience there, because soon after they turned their rented apartment in Cairo into a temple where they invoked Egyptian deities. His wife, Rose, started getting messages from spirits and informed Crowley that there were beings who waited to communicate with him. A few weeks after that, Crowley himself was contacted by a being he called Aiwass, who apparently dictated him a book, from beginning to end, which Crowley finished writing in three days.

The Book of the Law became the basis for Thelema, the religion Crowley later on founded. The premise of Thelema is "Do what thou wilt shall be the whole of the Law[15]," urging people to live only according to their own True Will and use magick as a tool for self-actualization. Crowley's book and religion became a tremendous influence both to his contemporaries and to the students of magick, the occult arts and self-actualization that came after. It is rumored that the founder of Scientology, L. Ron Hubbard, was deeply inspired by Crowley and involved in Thelema. It is also widely acknowledged that Crowly and Thelema inspired Gerald Gardner to found Wicca... but more on that in the next part of the book!

Apart from Golden Dawn, which the disagreement about him caused a schism in some of its temples, Crowley founded and participated in other esoteric orders, like the A∴A∴ and the German-based O.T.O. (Ordo Templi Orientis), through which he preached and propagated Thelema. The religion was spread to the US and Australia besides Europe and by 1920 Crowley had established an Abbey in Sicily where he lived in communion with his followers and participated in various rituals that very often included sadomasochistic versions of sex magick, influenced by his studies in Tantra yoga. He also created his own tarot deck, the Thoth tarot deck, where the Major Arcana cards follow a different order — he felt that the popular Rider-Waite tarot deck was more intended for laymen and less for actual occult students.

(We'll cover more of this on the third part of the book where we'll discuss the Tarot.)

The press of the time didn't see eye to eye with him. One newspaper in particular, loved to publish defamatory stories about him — they called him a Satanist, an advocate of human sacrifice and "the wickedest man in the world". Although he often thought about suing that paper, Crowley's lifestyle and his lifelong struggle with his heroin addiction always left him strapped for cash. He ended up having to accept bizarre work offers (from advisor to rich people to

---

[15] Crowley, Aleister. The Equinox of the Gods. New Falcon Publications, 1991.

astrology column writer) and welcomed notoriety as a means to keep spreading the word of Thelema.

In his "autohagiography" (like an autobiography, but for self-proclaimed saints and we're saying this with as little irony as possible) Crowley explained that his ultimate vision was one of restoring Paganism to a purer form. After his extensive studies in various Asian occult traditions and religious philosophies, he wanted to combine "oriental wisdom" with the Hermetic philosophy and ceremonial magick of the Hermetic traditions.

Regardless of how one feels about Aleister Crowley and his approach to witchcraft, his charisma and influence cannon be debated. His legacy to this day is that of a man who awoke the thirst for occult knowledge in the 20th century; someone who inspired people to study and try to understand magick.

Magick with a k, of course.

Honoring the Past, Redefining the Present

After Alister Crowley's Thelema rose in popularity, modern Paganism really caught on — first in Europe and then in the US, Australia and South Africa. Also called "neo-Paganism", this new wave of honoring and following the old Pagan traditions quickly became as diverse as its practitioners. It turns out, dear one, that it's the most Pagan thing to do.

So what does it mean to be a Pagan in this day and age — that may be the Aeon of Horus or just the Aeon of Instagram?

It really depends on how you see yourself in relation to your ancestors. For instance, many modern practitioners or Paganism and Witchcraft are indeed direct descendants of the Yoruba and Vodun practitioners of old, who came to the Americas when they were brought into slavery by the colonizers. But the ancestry line of European Paganism is not as easy to identify — and this is an important subject that we'll cover in the next part of the book, when we talk about Wicca and Witchcraft.

What it boils down to is that some Modern Pagans are trying to revive the old religions (picking a single religion that believe is closer to their heritage or personality) as faithfully as they can, by even dressing the part, whereas others prefer to borrow different elements from many different Pagan practices of old and create their unique blend of Paganism. The first are called reconstructionists, the second are called eclectic.

Wicca, which we'll go into detail later, is an example of a new Pagan religion with eclectic elements, as it combines shamanic practices of Native Americans with Celtic Druidry and Thelema ceremonies. There are also the practitioners of Crowley's Thelema to this day, those who practice modern Druidism or Hellenism, those who practice Odinism (Norse Paganism) or Heathenry (Germanic Paganism with a contemporary twist), those who practice Stregheria (an Italian version of Wicca, focusing on local medieval traditions of witchcraft).

Some modern Pagans will also combine elements from monotheistic religions such as Buddhism, Judaism and Christianity, not feeling that one clashes with the other. I personally know many fellow Pagans who believe in Angels (Archangel Michael in particular) and pray to both Madonna, the Holy Mother of Jesus (who many historians argue that her sanctification and worship was a way to entice Pagans who were used to worshiping Goddesses), wear the Cross and have Pagan altars dedicated to gods and goddesses... Does that sound weird to you?

If it hasn't been clear in this book so far, we don't believe one way of going about it is inherently better than the other. You'll need to forge your own Path and decide what's included in it.

We'll talk about it more in our next chapter.

Chapter 4: How Do You Know You're a Pagan

How do you, indeed?

If that long, 2-chapter history lesson taught us anything, dear one, apart from the fact that burning people at the stake is as bad as throwing them to the lions, is that there is no set or "authentic" way to be Pagan.

Being Pagan is being in touch with Nature — and the only constant of Nature is change. As the Wheel turns, so do our beliefs, our habits and our priorities. With new seasons comes new understanding. What you consider the core of your Pagan identity today there's a big chance it won't be the core of your Pagan identity a few years from now or further down the line.

Trust on this to happen.

So… what? Abandon all attempts at a definition? Of course not!

History, at least the abridged version of it we attempted to embark earlier, has taught us that a Pagan is someone who perseveres; who adapts. The person who speaks their mind even if they know the situation may not be in their favor (like Helena Scheuberin who stood up to Kramer). The person who knows that rational thought and scientific research is all well and good, but it's not all there is. The person who is not afraid to go against the grain, think outside the box or even make the box disappear altogether! The person who most of all, understands that Nature is a manifestation of our Divine Mother and for that deserves our utmost respect and protection.

(Is Greta Thunberg a Pagan, you ask? I don't believe so, dear one. But she does share and preach some very fundamental Pagan values and for that, we salute her.)

But seriously, no Pagan would ever do anything to hurt Nature for no reason: sure, Pagans used to cut down trees to chop wood for fire or to build their houses, but they were always careful not to chop too many trees in one area, because they knew the consequences once the first heavy rainfall fell. Pagans liked profit as much as the next man, but they knew that if they overextended themselves or completely depleted their resources they would be the ones to suffer. So many modern humans seem to have forgotten this — it's mind blowing, really!

A Pagan understands balance. A Pagan understands there are things bigger than our egos or our wallets or our rational explanations for things. A Pagan will never be dismissive of the dark when out in the woods, because although they know they're probably perfectly safe, they still feel a sense of awe for all the energies out there. They do not wish to disturb the night if they don't have to. They don't need to prove their superiority to Nature. They know better.

We've been talking a lot about Nature, it's true.

Can't you be a true Pagan and live in a city?

Of course, dear one! What did we say about no set or "authentic" way of being a Pagan?

Many Pagans nowadays still choose to live in the big cities. They thrive from the hustle and bustle, the energies of the different people they meet, the openness of diverse cultures and the many opportunities to celebrate. Yes, a Pagan likes to celebrate when it's time to celebrate.

That's not to say that to identify as a Pagan you have to be a party animal who'd make even the Romans blush. But all Pagans understand that our bodies come from Nature and we have to respect them, to give them their due. And that is true both when it comes to our sexuality and to our relationship with food.

Would a Pagan ever go on a diet, you ask? Probably not, at least not to adhere to some society's beauty standards. But they would most definitely change their eating habits in order to feel better/stronger/lighter or whatever better health looks like to them. Plus, all Pagans respect food too much to ever associate it with guilt. Even if they consume animal products (which many of us choose to abstain from) they do so consciously and with respect to the life forces that have been sacrificed for their nourishment. Some Pagans even prefer to hunt their own game.

Guilt, as mentioned earlier, is another key word here. Guilt has been the driving force behind many monotheistic religions: guilt, fear and promises of a better life after death if we're being pious enough in this one. Of course Pagans will experience some guilt throughout their lives (we are human, after all). But their guilt will come from their own actions or lack thereof: from things they did or didn't do, mostly to other people. This is a different guilt than the guilt inflicted on people by society or religion, for all the things they are not allowed to do in order to be "good".

To get back to the sexuality part, not all Pagans are as promiscuous and hedonistic as medieval gravures would paint us to be. Some are still experimenting; some are in long, committed relationships; some have chosen a solitary path or prefer platonic relationships. But whatever they do, they understand that sex is a part of life. Sacred, sometimes. Mundane, other times. A taboo, never. This kind of morality, of denying one's urges to appear pious in front of a god or a society that would judge them, is just not interesting to a Pagan. We make our own moral code, based on what feels right to each of us.

Are Pagans bad? Well, some of them are, dear one. Being a Pagan does not exempt you from certain aspects of humanity and not everyone you'll meet out there has your best interests at heart. Trust this to be true as well. But the point of this chapter is for you to understand that all kinds of people can be Pagan. The question then becomes: what kind of person are you?

And what kind of Pagan will you be?

Hopefully, you'll be someone who listens to their heard, always. Someone who sees the wonder in the everyday and makes no excuses for their path and their choices. Someone who knows there are things out there we will never be able to explain but also someone who will never stop being intrigued by the unknown; the hidden; the occult. Someone who honors their ancestors; those who came before us, whose sacrifice and wisdom has paved the way for our existence.

Someone who may or may not combine elements from different Pagan paths to craft their own. Someone who may or may not practice magic, but who definitely knows magic is all around us. To paraphrase the song, "I feel it in my fingers, I feel it in my toes."

Yes, that song is about Christmas. But we already established Christmas were more or less invented by Pagans, didn't we? So it's kinda ours to steal.

PART 2: WICCA

CHAPTER 1: WICCA THEN AND NOW

Welcome back, dear one. It has been quite a ride, reading about Paganism, hasn't it?

Now that you understand what it means to be a Pagan (and hopefully have started thinking about the kind of Pagan you'd like to be), it's time to discuss Wicca. Wiccan is part of Modern Paganism; it's one Path you can take out of many. The reason why we've chosen to focus on Wicca more than on other forms of Modern Paganism in this book, is because Wicca is the largest Modern Pagan religion (followed by Neo-Druidism). It's a diverse Path that has changed and enriched so many people's lives all over the world…

Perhaps, dear one, it will also change yours.

But first things first: what exactly is Wicca and how it came to be? This is what we'll attempt to answer in this chapter.

Gerald Gardner and the Ghost of Aleister Crowley

We briefly mentioned, in the first part of the book, about the effect Aleister Crowley had in the occult community of the late 19th and early 20th century — to the point that he and his religion, Thelema, served as a major inspiration for the founder of Wicca, Gerald Gardner.

(I do hope you haven't skipped that part of the book, there's important information there that will help you understand the rest of the book... You haven't? That's the spirit, keep reading!)

Who was Gerald Gardner then?

Frequently called the "Father of Wicca", Gardner's interest in the occult can be traced in the years he spent as a civil servant for the UK in Singapore, where he became fascinated by the magickal practices and traditions of the locals. After retirement and a brief respite in Cyprus where he wrote a novel, Garner returned to England where he lived near the New Forest, a historical woods in Southern England that's been proclaimed a royal forest since 1079 CE. There was a significant occult community in the area and Gardner eventually joined an occult organization called the Rosicrucian Order Crotona Fellowship.

The Rosicrucians, a bit similar to the Golden Dawn, was an esoteric organization seeking "knowledge that is hidden to many". One of the differences with Golden Dawn however, is that their practices apart from Hermetism, Kabbalah and alchemy also include mystical Christianity.

Gardner wasn't particularly impressed with the Fellowship, especially with their Grand Master's claims of being Pythagoras reincarnate (among other things). When one of the Fellowship's leaders in 1939 sent a letter to every member claiming that war would not reach Britain and the very next day the Crown declared war on Germany, Gardner was practically convinced there was no real power or wisdom within that organization.

Through this organization though, Gardner made an acquaintance that changed his whole life.

The Father of Wicca recounts[16] him and the Fellowship visiting the house of a local woman one night, where he went through a ceremony of initiation skyclad (naked). There, he heard the word "Wica" — which he recognized as an old form of the word "witch". Back then, there was a historical theory made prominent by archaeologist Margaret Murray: that the persecution of witches in the 1500-1600 CE was an organized attempt to erase from history a pagan religion devoted to a Horned God[17]. (Which wasn't entirely wrong, but it made the mistake of painting all the different Pagan traditions and beliefs with the same brush, as well as assuming the women who were burned at the stake were actually witches and not mostly victims of patriarchal and social violence.) In any case, when Gardner heard the word "Wica", he was convinced that Murray's claims were true and that the coven he'd visited was a continuation of that ancient Pagan religion that had survived the brutal witch burnings of the Middle Ages...

He became fascinated with this group. Despite him always being very open to the press (to the point that he has been accused by his contemporaries of being a publicity w**re), he never revealed the ceremonies he witnessed with that coven — apart from one ceremony that was meant to ward off the Nazi invasion to England. The witches, according to Gardner, formed a circle in the woods one night to raise a "cone of power" to send to Berlin...

Could it be that it was witches who helped the allies win WWII? There is no way to know, dear one. Certainly, stranger things have happened throughout the course of history.

---

[16] Gerald Gardner, (1954). Witchcraft Today. London: Rider.

[17] Murray, Margaret A. (1921). The Witch-Cult in Western Europe. Oxford: Clarendon Press and Murray, Margaret A. (1931). The God of the Witches. London: Faber and Faber.

But let's get back to Gerald Gardner.

His eclectic interest in different occult practices, specifically esoteric Christianity, led him to become an ordained priest of the Ancient British Church. He also joined ADO (the Ancient Druid Order) with whom he attended rituals at Stonehenge. (Remember the importance of Stonehenge and the way it was built? Its draw to Pagans still remains strong to this day...) Gardner didn't stop there: he joined the Folk-Lore Society, the Society for Psychical Research and, ultimately, the O.T.O., after meeting Aleister Crowley.

Gardner's fascination with Crowley has been the subject of many biographies and historical research... A fascination that seems mutual, considering that Crowley, right before he died, issued a charter decreeing that Gardner was to undertake one of the most important positions in O.T.O. after his death. By that time, Gardner had already started creating his version of Wicca rituals based on his observations of the New Forest coven — and as these rituals worshipped the Divine Female alongside the Horned God, he had initiated many High Priestesses to the Craft. Crowley, according to Gardner, was thinking about joining Wicca but he disliked the idea of "being bossed about by women". According to other sources, however, he was initiated in Wicca in secret and has in fact written many of the rituals that are attributed to Gardner himself.

It's a bit of a headache at this point, isn't it, dear one?

What we need to take away from all this is that the need to find kindred spirits has been ever present throughout humanity's history. Isn't that one of the reasons you picked up this book?

These two, clearly powerful and emblematic men, were looking for answers all their lives and did no small amount of experimenting to find them. They both envisioned a more self-actualized humanity, and they both felt the need to "dress up" their practices and rituals with something bigger than themselves: in Crowley's case the Egyptian god that was revealed to him in the pyramids, in Gardner's case, the uncovering of a secret cult that had survived for centuries... Regardless of whether their claims were 100% truthful or not (as historians remain sceptical on both counts), these two men practically created a Modern Pagan revival that helped thousands of people to find their place in the world; people who felt alienated by Christianity and monotheism.

Of course, like most emblematic figures, both men were very polarizing. They both joined secret organizations (in Crowley's case, Golden Dawn, in Gardner's case the Rosicrucians) where he caused a stir with the rest of the members and ultimately struck out on their own. Gardner may not have been called "the world's most wicked man" by the press (although there were some headlines that he was preaching "devil worship"), but he was called a "hack" and a "fraud" by many, due to his tendency to overextend the truth — especially when it came to his formal qualifications, where he always claimed he had more degrees than he actually had.

After Crowley's death, Gardner believed he would be his successor in O.T.O but when that didn't happen he decided to focus on the witch-cult he (believed he) unearthed in New Forest. He was adamant in his mission to revive the Old Religion and awakening people's interest in witchcraft and wrote many books about it (including detailed rituals that usually involved ceremonial nudity, scourging and incantations) that gathered a lot of attention. His most popular book, Witchcraft Today, was prefaced by Margaret Murray who basically endorsed him and supported his claim about the coven being the descendants of those witches who didn't die in the Middle Ages.

Gardner formed his own coven in London, where he initiated many people into the Craft, many of which moved on to spread the word of Wicca in the US and Australia in the following decades. Sadly, he had a falling out with many of his former friends and priests/priestesses of Wicca, who left what is now called "Gardnerian Wicca" to start their own Wicca traditions.

THE GARDNERIAN LEGACY AND THE MANY BRANCHES OF WICCA

Since we talked about the "Father of Witchcraft", it would be only fair to talk about the "Mother of Modern Witchcraft" next, right? Her name was Doreen Valiente.

Valiente met Gardner in 1952 (when she started corresponding with him after having read articles about him and Wicca) and was initiated into the craft in 1953. She rose quickly through the ranks and became his coven's High Priestess — to the point where she revised Gardner's Book of Shadows, removing Aleister Crowley's influence (most of it, at least) and added an emphasis to Divine Femininity with Goddess prayers[18].

Valiente ultimately grew weary of Gardner's love for press and attention and left Gardnerian Wicca along with her followers. She experimented with different Wicca branches that had started to emerge by then (more of that in a while), joined the Pagan Front and the Witchcraft Research Association and wrote various magazine articles and books promoting Wicca. A big departure of Valiente from the Gardnerian tradition is that she believed anyone could be a Wiccan, no "skyclad" initiation by a Wiccan High Priest or Priestess needed.

In a way, dear one, the fact that you're able to read this book and learn some Wicca rituals, we both owe to Daphne Valiente. And for that, we give thanks to the Mother of Modern Witchcraft.

One of the Wicca branches Valiente worked with briefly was Charles Cardell's.

Starting as Gardner's friend and coven member, Cardell had a huge falling out with him — to the point where he wrote many defamatory articles about Gardner. In those articles, among other things, Cardell claimed he was the one to first use the term "Wicca" and to this day his followers are called "Wiccens". His version of Wicca included

---

[18] Valiente, Doreen (1989). The Rebirth of Witchcraft. London: Robert Hale.

worshipping a Horned God called Atho and in his publications he antagonized both Gardner and Valiente. Yes, he fell out with her as well. (Valiente actually was disappointed by Cardell being dishonest, when he tried to convince her that some contemporary items he possessed were magical relics from Pompei...) But it was Cardell's way of falling out with everyone, it seems: he also fell out with another Wiccan friend, Raymond Howard, who even took Cardell to court accusing him of hexing him.

Doesn't that sound awfully like the two men from the Code of Hammurabi, casting hexes at each other? It's fascinating to see that, for all the wisdom Magick can bring into one's heart, we are ultimately humans and our egos can always get the best of us...

Anyway, Raymon Howard himself continued the Coven of Atho — he even claimed he had a 2200 years old statue of the god (which was later revealed he'd carved himself).

Another important Wicca personality of the time was Eleanor "Ray" Bone, who is known as the "Matriarch of British Witchcraft". Bone created many covens and furthered the practice of Gardnerian Wicca (also believing that the New Forest coven was the continuation of an ancient tradition) evolving it into what is now also called British Traditional Wicca. Bone had a fall out (as it seems to have been the early Wicca fashion) with Alex Sanders, who went on to create his own version of Wicca called "Alexandrian" that includes more elements of ceremonial magic and Qabalah. Alexandrian Wicca is more technical, with more rigorous training and ceremonial practices, but also more eclectic and less hesitant in borrowing techniques from other traditions. In fact, their motto is "if it works, use it". Contrary to Valiente's tradition though, in Alexandrian Wicca you have to be initiated by another witch — it's not an open club.

Let's take a breath, dear one, shall we?

So many names, and so many of them fighting one another! You may have started feeling that Wicca is not very inviting — and that's definitely not the case. You have to consider that back then, in the 60s and 70s, rediscovering the Pagan ways felt (and was) revolutionary.

Everyone wanted to make their own mark into this new movement. In the end, that's a good thing.

It's through all these different, often conflicting, viewpoints, Wicca became what it is today: a vibrant religion with many different branches, where there is something for everyone...

In the United States, the Gardnerian and Alexandrian Wicca traditions were combined into what became Blue Star Wicca, that still emphasizes initiation but also accepts solitary practitioners and people who are both polytheists and monotheists. Blue Star Wiccans are all about giving back to the community and including a lot of music and singing in their rituals — they also have initiatory tattoos. Blue Star Wicca is still practiced as a Wicca branch in the US.

In Canada, the Odyssean Wicca is most prominent (they chose the name to imply the "spiritual journey" one must go through). Odysseans follow the British Traditional Wicca but in a more eclectic way. They have a public Wiccan priesthood and a very rigorous training system (like in the Alexandrian tradition), not accepting new students easily.

Another notable Wicca branch is Zsuzsanna Budapest's Dianic Wicca, also in the States. Dianic Wicca is the only version of Wicca that's female-only: they only worship the Goddess (in contrast to the duality of a Goddess and a God in most Wiccan traditions) and do not accept men in their covens. They've also borrowed many elements from the folk magick traditions of Italy as well as various healing practices from many cultures. It may sound weird and a bit sexist perhaps, but Dianic Wicca is first and foremost a welcoming place for women who have been victims of violence or abuse and are looking for a way to reconnect with their inner power...

Told you there' something for everyone in Wicca, dear one.

WICCA TODAY

After reading through all that you may be wondering: what, exactly, is Wicca today?

What do these Wiccans believe in?

The answer to that may be slightly different depending on who you ask (and what tradition they follow). Wiccans, like all Pagans, have an inherent dislike of homogeneity. Each Wicca branch prefers marching to the beat of their own drum (sometimes literally) and although Wicca is recognized as a religion, there is no central authority figure like a Pope or an Orthodox Patriarch. Although Gardner's and Valiente's texts are widely spread, along with the texts of other writers such as Starhawk or the earlier works of Charles Godfrey Leland (his book *Aradia, the Gospel of Witches* was actually the seed for Margaret Murray's and Gardner's theory of an existing ancient coven), many Wiccans will also study sacred texts from other religions, like the Bible or the Torah, or even create their own, eclectic mix of traditions.

But for all their distinct personalities, there are some broad lines all Wiccans adhere to.

First of all, Wicca is an Earth-based religion — which means there is an inherent respect of Nature and a belief in a cyclical view of the time (the Wheel of the Year). Apart from Dianic Wicca, all other traditions believe in the duality of a Goddess and a God, who are basically the yin and yang expressions of all energies in the Universe: some people perceive these gods as abstractions or even Jungian archetypes, whereas others consider them as real as a devout Christian considers God. The gods of Wicca have a loving relationship between them and evolve with the seasons. The male forms of god in Wicca change on a yearly basis, celebrating virility and strength in Spring with the Horned God (or similar deities) and fatherly love, protection of the family and wisdom with the Oak King (or similar deities) in the Winter. The triple nature of the Goddess as Maiden, Mother and Crone is also celebrated monthly and associated with the Waxing, Full and Waning phases of the Moon.

As Wiccans nowadays come from so many different ethnic backgrounds, local deities are incorporated in people's beliefs as manifestations of the Great Goddess/Female Energy or the Great God/Male Energy. However, Wiccans are also encouraged (and the author of this book finds this very important) to educate themselves on other cultures' pantheons and decide if they feel any connection to the deities of these pantheons — and include them in their worship if they do. So for instance you can be a Wiccan who lives in Australia but worships Odin (from the Norse pantheon) and Artemis (from the Greek pantheon). Or you can be a Wiccan who lives in Greece and worship Hekate (the ancient Greek Goddess of Witchcraft) because it's part of your heritage, but also worship Kali (from the Hindu pantheon) and Mawu (the creator goddess from the Yoruba pantheon) because they're badass ladies and you feel a connection to them.

Wiccans don't believe any god or goddess will mind sharing your affections, dear one. Or, if you decide to only worship one God or Goddess, or not worship anyone in particular and just be in awe of Nature, that's perfectly alright too.

Regardless of what you believe or don't believe in, most Wiccans have some set celebrations that they observe throughout the Wheel of the Year. These are the four Sabbats (Samhain, Imbolc, Beltan and Lamas) that continue the celebration of ancient Pagan festivals that marked the changing of the seasons, as well as the four Esbats (Yule, Ostara, Midsummer and Mabon) that correspond with the solstices and the equinoxes. In Wicca tradition, the year actually begins after Samhain, so the first day of the new year is considered November 1st — although they will also gladly celebrate with their non-Pagan friends on January 1st.

What about heaven and life after death, you ask?

If you ask ten Wiccans about their views on afterlife, you'll probably get ten different answers. Many Wiccans believe in some version of rebirth or reincarnation, because of their belief in the cyclical nature of the universe. Others will believe in some version of elevated spirit existence (like heaven or Valhalla) after death whereas others prefer not to think about it at all. The thing everyone will agree on is that this life is not a trial or a test so that we can be granted access in some paradise when we die. Our life in this world and our physical existence matter, our body matters and we owe it to ourselves and to our gods to take care of it and live a life that's as happy and fulfilled as possible!

To that extent, there is only one sacred law among all Wiccans: "an ye harm none, do what ye will" (you can encounter this phrase in different variations, but the meaning remains the same). This phrase is basically Gardner's adaptation to Crowley's Thelema law "do what thou wilt" but the idea behind it is not new. As we've seen in the first part of the book, Confucius offered a similar advice in his texts several thousand years ago... This phrase is included in a poem called the Wiccan Rede[19], which was first circulated around the '40s with the intention to pass on the old Pagan ways and traditions. Most Wiccans consider it sacred, in the sense that they will get back and consult it every now and then. The Rede talks about the Goddess and the God, the Sabbats and Esbats, about plants that are suitable for magick and about the energies of the Moon. But its core, is the Wiccan law of non harming anyone, delivered in verse.

This Wiccan law means that it goes against Wiccan beliefs to harm any other being, both humans and animals or plants — that's why you'll see many Wiccans espousing a plant-based diet and you'll probably see zero Wiccans advocating violence of any kind. Wiccans value peace. We also never, ever, use our magick to harm or hex people.

Which brings us to another key question you may have: do Wiccans cast magick spells on a daily basis? Do they even practice witchcraft at all?

That, dear one, we'll discuss in the following chapters.

---

[19] "The Wiccan Rede" (Full Version) as depicted in The Celtic Connection website, https://wicca.com/celtic/wicca/rede.htm

Chapter 2: What Wicca Isn't... and What It Can Be

Now that we've touched upon the history of Wicca and the way it's been practiced today all around the world, it's time to clear up some issues and misconceptions that often come up.

Wicca is not the continuation of an ancient religion

"We are the descendants of the witches you could not burn." I'm sure you've seen this motto somewhere, dear one. It's been featured in everything from t-shirts to posters people have held in various demonstrations. It's a very valid sentiment, certainly.

But in most cases at least, it's just that: a sentiment.

We're not saying there are no legacy witches and Pagans out there. People who, for generations, they've worshipped the old gods and goddesses and performed various spells and rituals that were passed on from their elders. While these people, "legacies" let's call them, certainly exist, they are not the bulk of what makes modern Paganism or Wicca.

Yet, we've already seen how Margaret Murray and Gerald Gardner believed there was a secret religion and practicing covens that had escaped the witch burnings... Where did that belief come from? For the most part, it started back in 1899 with Charles Godfrey Leland and his book *Aradia, or the Gospel of the Witches*[20].

Leland was a writer and folklorist from the States who met a woman in Tuscany. That woman, whom Leland called Maddalena, claimed to be a witch — and she gave him access to lore and texts that were allegedly the sacred texts of her coven. After eleven years or working together, this woman gave Leland a manuscript she called Vangelo (which is Italian for "gospel") that narrated the story of local Moon Goddess Aradia who was worshipped among her coven apparently since medieval times. Leland basically translated her manuscript in English; that's how his book came about. Although the book was more or less ignored until the mid-20th century, the post-war renewal of interest in the mystic and the occult made the Gospel of Witches one of the most prominent texts, affecting people like Murray and Gardner.

Now, there may very well have been a coven in Tuscany that Leyland came across, just as there may very well have been a coven in New Forest that Gardner came across. People have been practicing witchcraft, whether solitary or in covens since time immemorial; the witch burnings certainly derailed the movement and spread terror, but it is unlikely that they shuffled out witchcraft completely (since, as we've seen, the witch burnings were mostly targeting women). But does that make the Italian witches and the English witches practitioners of the same "Old Religion"? Not really.

As we've seen, ancient Pagans always considered themselves different from their Pagan neighbors. There was never one "Pagan religion" or one way of practicing witchcraft. So what Leyland and Gardner came across, is proof that witches exist — but that's about it. Any attempts to create a common narrative, an unbroken line that

---

[20] Leland, Charles Godfrey (1899). Aradia, or the Gospel of the Witches. David Nutt.

goes back to the Middle Ages, were probably wishful thinking and a way to increase the credibility levels of their teachings (at least in Gardner's case). It helped create Wicca back then, that's for sure.

But we know better now.

Now we can accept Wicca for what it truly is: an eclectic reconstruction of mostly Celtic Pagan traditions, with elements from ancient Greek, Hermetic and shamanic traditions, that's also open to influences from local pantheons.

Does that make us less authentic or real? Definitely not.

Think about it in Harry Potter terms, dear one: there are pureblooded wizards and witches, like the Potters, the Malfoys and the Weasleys… but there are also wizards and witches born from "Muggle" families, like Hermione Granger, who have more talent and magical skills than most purebloods, despite being first generation. (Harry Potter is fiction, but the analogy still stands.)

The fact that you don't come from a magickal family (that you know of) doesn't mean you're cut off from magick. You know why? Because no one, ever, is really cut off from magick.

Magick, witchcraft, and honoring Nature like she deserves, have been embedded in our DNA ever since we lived in those caves and created those fertility Goddess statues we talked about in the beginning of the book. Wicca is just a modern, more organized way to access and honor all that. It is a continuation of what our ancestors believed in, in the sense that we are all humans and we all share the same common thread of existence.

WICCA IS NOT ABOUT WORSHIPING THE DEVIL

We've already seen why equating Paganism with devil worship is not just wrong, but historically inaccurate as well. This is even more true in the case of Wicca.

One of the cornerstone deities/god archetypes in Wicca is the Horned God. The Horned God draws mostly from the Celtic God Cernunnos (but also from Pan) to celebrate a non-toxic version of masculinity and male energy. The Horned God is strong and fertile, helping the Goddess create new life — but he is also fair and kind, a protector to all beings.

We are taking back the depictions of horned beings that Christianity has vilified; we are reclaiming them and reassigning them the status once had: that of beings who symbolize good luck, abundance, strength and fertility.

Now, we've already seen that the devil is a Christian invention. A way to create a strong antagonist for God and convince people that being a Pagan should be avoided at all costs. Although today many Wiccans include elements of Christianity in their beliefs, we need to make this clear: if you ever meet a Wiccan who tells you they worship the devil, rest assured they're most definitely not really Wiccans. Why? Two reasons.

First off, this idea of an "absolute evil" is mostly a human construct. It's not something you'd ever encounter in Nature. There are destructive, chaotic energies all around us, that's for sure, but they're never 100% "bad" or "evil" because Nature doesn't have morality in the human sense. More importantly, Nature is never just one thing. Every destructive energy contains within it the seed of new creation — and the phrase "it's always darkest before the dawn" is popular for a reason.

Secondly, remember how we said that Wiccans don't necessarily agree on many things when it comes to their beliefs but they all agree on one sacred law? Remember what that sacred law is?

"An ye harm none, do what ye will."

Exactly. Wiccans believe in never hurting another being — that's why we also never make sacrifices that include shedding a creature's blood, like many ancient Pagans did and some modern Pagans do to this day. So it stands to reason that someone who abhors hurting others would definitely not worship a deity (made up by Christianity or not) that is all about being evil and hurting others.

Doesn't that make sense, dear one?

WICCA IS NOT "WITCHCRAFT LITE"

This is perhaps the most weird misconception of them all.

There is this belief, circulating in some circles, that Wicca is a "watered down" version of witchcraft, a "white-washed" way of practicing the Craft. This belief is often found among Pagan (non-Wiccan, of course) circles but also among people whose only interaction with witchcraft is what they've seen in shows and movies.

So where does this belief come from?

It starts with the name "Wicca", dear one.

See, back in the 50s when Gerald Gardner first started spreading the word, the name he used to describe this new version of the Old Religion was mostly "witch-cult", "witchcraft" or "Craft of the Wise" (or just Craft). Some times, he would circle back to the word Wica (with one c) that he heard during that New Forest coven ceremony. In fact, remember how one of his followers-cum-rivals, Charles Cardell was thought to first use the term Wicca with two c? Regardless of who were the first to use it though, Wicca with two c didn't appear until 1962, so a good decade after it was first founded.

By that time, Gardner had already been called "devil worshipper" by the press once or twice…

It's crucial to understand that time were different back then. The name Wicca, although an archaic word for witch/wizard ("wiccacraeft"), it sounded less offensive and dangerous to the broader public than if Gardner had continued calling this the "witch-cult". Simply by not calling it Witchcraft, he managed to attract people to it who might have otherwise been too scared or biased to explore it. Which is funny if you think that it's the same word, only an older version of it! And yet, it's understandable: this may not have been the Middle Ages anymore, but witchcraft was still illegal and had real ramifications for people who were accused of practicing. Truth be told, it still is, in many parts of the world. Going for the safer option was a smart move!

But there's also another reason we're calling ourselves Wicca: by using this older version of the word, it's like Wiccans are stating their intention to honor and continue old Pagan traditions.

So… does that make Wiccan less deserving of being taken seriously than people who call themselves witches or wizards? Definitely not.

"Don't mistake my kindness for weakness," as the song goes. Songs can be wise, can't they?

That being said, being a Wiccan and being a Witch are not always synonymous. We'll explain more in the next chapter, hang on to your broom dear one!

CHAPTER 3: ARE YOU A WICCAN OR A WITCH?

Now that we've seen what Wicca is (and isn't) all about, it's time for the tricky part.

Perhaps you've heard in your witchy circles people saying things like "I'm no Wiccan" (because they believe that being a Wiccan is somehow less than being a "real" Witch). Or, if you are new to all this, you've probably followed a few witchy accounts on Instagram or YouTube, to get inspiration. And at some point, you may have come across people talking about how being a Wiccan versus being a Witch and how the two are not the same...

Did that leave you super confused? After all, we did just say that Wicca is another word for Witchcraft, so what's the difference if any?

Patience, dear one. We will explain everything.

The difference between Wicca and Witchcraft is that the first is a religion (or spirituality, if you will) whereas the second is a practice. And as any kind of practice, it may also be tied to a religion or spirituality — or it may not. Below we will attempt to unpack this in a three-fold way: we'll see how not all Wiccans are Witches, how not all Witches are Wiccans and how you can be both, if you so desire!

Not all Wiccans are Witches

When Gardner first started his "witch-cult" of his, the focus was mostly on rituals (many of which, as we've seen, were taken from Crowley's unique brand of ceremonial magick). Gardner's first acolytes and initiates were all deeply interested in the occult, most of them had a background in ceremonial magick from other secret organizations and were highly geared towards the practical aspects of the Craft; namely, raising power from the elements and deities and performing spells (although they didn't really call them "spells"). Sure, it was tightly knit with the worshipping part (which usually involved nudity and scourging) but the end goal was always to raise power to achieve a certain goal.

However, Wicca today is officially a religion — albeit one with an eclectic theology and no real central authority. As the people who practice Wicca now come from all corners of the world and from all sorts of different backgrounds, perhaps it will come as no surprise that not all of them are practicing witches.

What does that mean, practically?

Think of it as a luscious field, rich with flowers in full bloom: you may choose to walk among the flowers every day, rejoicing by their colors and fragrance, perhaps take a few photos or cut a few every now and then for your vases... but otherwise leave them be. Or you may choose to harvest the flowers: use their petals for teas and herb mixes; make soap or candles by combining them with essential oils; boil their stems for their medicinal properties; even dry them out and grind them into colorful dust you can use for your makeup! So many things one can do with flowers... At the end of the day though, the field is the same. The flowers are the same. It's just the way you choose to use them that changes — and the way you choose to use them, at the end of the day, boils down to what kind of person you are and what brings you the most joy.

Is it starting to become clearer now?

Simply enjoying the flowers doesn't make you a better or a worse person than the person who chooses to work with them. It just makes you, you.

It's the same thing with non-practicing Wiccans.

They can still reap the rewards of living a healthy life and happy, in tune with Nature and in communion with the gods and goddesses of their Pantheon. They can partake in the magickal energy all around us without having to work with it and shape it for specific results…

Want another analogy? Think about it as a party. (After all, Pagans know how to celebrate.)

Now, at this party, there will be alcohol offered freely. You can drink that alcohol and be merry… or you can use that alcohol to make intricate, sophisticated cocktails that you will then drink and be merry or even offer to others. It's basically the difference between a party goer and a mixologist: they're both going at the same party, it's just that the latter has a bit more work to do! And making cocktails can be their hobby, their way of meeting new people, their way of making a living or simply their way of keeping their wits sharp and learning new things!

Are we saying then that non-practicing Wiccans are lazy? Waiting on the practicing ones to do all the work? No. In fact, they both need each other.

At a (Christian) church, you have both the priest and the flock. At a piano recital, you have both the pianist and the audience. At a theater group, you have both the director and the actors. None of these groups of people are lesser than the others — they just have a different focus, discipline or specialization.

You don't have to be a virtuoso pianist or even know how to read the notes to enjoy music!

So what do non-practicing Wiccans do then, if they're not practicing magic? In a way, they do: they're practicing the rare and precious magic of living their lives to the fullest, with an open heart, a respect for Nature and with awe for the gifts each new day brings…

But seriously, non-practicing Wiccans are worshipping the Goddess and the God (in any variation they choose). The way they worship is still a matter of personal preference: some will pray twice a day and light candles, others will quietly smile every now and then, knowing their gods are with them. Most, will do both, depending on the day and how busy they are with other things! Yes, that's right, Wiccans also live in the mundane world, where bills need to be paid and loved ones (who may or may not be Wiccans as well) need to be nurtured...

Sometimes, they won't have time to do much. But as long as they're living their lives with the intention to never harm anyone and be happy, they're still enjoying those proverbial flowers in that field.

NOT ALL WITCHES ARE WICCANS

Which brings us to the opposite end of that argument. As we've seen, people have been practicing witchcraft, in their own way, for many millennia. Definitely way before 2000 BCE (when, as we've seen in the first part of the book, we have the first written mention of practicing witchcraft in the Code of Hammurabi). And the way they've practiced witchcraft, has been as diverse as them — and always in conjunction with their local Pagan beliefs[21].

For example, someone who practiced witchcraft in ancient Africa, say in what we now know as the Yoruba tradition, didn't necessarily followed the same rituals and rules of conduct as someone who practiced witchcraft in ancient Mesopotamia or ancient Scandinavia. Certainly though, there are certain broader methods of performing witchcraft that we know were used in many different cultures.

One of these methods is spellbinding: the art of imbuing an object (or a human being) with a specific intention — also known as "hex" when that intention was malevolent. Spellbinding could be done by carving symbols in a candle, a rock or a piece of wood; by tying ceremonial knots in a ribbon or a piece of cloth the "victim" of the spell would be wearing; by placing spelled objects in that person's vicinity; or simply, by chanting words and incantations.

---

[21] Leo Ruickbie, Witchcraft Out of the Shadows: A Complete History, Robert Hale; New edition (April 1, 2012).

Another is divination, the art of seeing the future. This also has been practiced in a variety of methods, across different cultures. (We'll talk all about it in the next part of the book!)

Another is spiritual communion: conjuring or communicating with non-corporeal beings that can either be ancestors' spirits (ghosts) or extra-dimensional beings (what people refer to as "demons", "angels" or even deities). This was done either to get help from the beings for problems to community was facing, or for selfish reasons such as to get revenge on one's enemies or inflict fear and amass power.

Healing, either achieved through energetical touch (what we would call "reiki" today) either through herbs, tinctures and poultices (through knowledge that we'd today call homeopathic or herbal remedies), has always been a big part of witchcraft as well. Healers were always revered and sought-after in ancient times, usually called things like "wise ones" or "white witches". Sometimes though, whether because they made a mistake or simply because an illness was too far gone for them to cure (or, in more rare cases, were sabotaging the treatment for their own gain), healers would get blamed by their communities and accused of everything from failing crops to contagious diseases.

Truth be told, most acts of magic are at their core neutral. They become "good" or "bad" based on the intention with which are yielded. In a way, magic is a bit like money: you can be a generous philanthropist or a ruthless billionaire that profits over other people's hard work. That doesn't mean money is inherently good or bad by itself, it depends on how you use it.

Historically, witchcraft has been associated with sacrifices. Most often animal sacrifices, but also human in some cases. It sounds horrible, I know! But does that make every sorcerer/practitioner who ever made a sacrifice "evil"? Not necessarily. You need to consider the historical era and the mindset around this. Human life, although cherished as a miracle in a collective level, on a personal level didn't mean as much as it did today — especially if we're talking about the life of someone who wasn't wealthy or powerful. Sometimes, people truly believed that by sacrificing one human to appease the gods they could save their whole village... That doesn't make them evil, it just makes them tragically misinformed.

Sacrifice, in a way, is always necessary to create magick. You need to give something to get something, it may sound like the lyrics of an R'n'B song but it's actually true on a cosmic level as well. You can't create something out of nothing. That being said, a sacrifice doesn't have to involve spilling anyone's blood for the spell (any spell) to work: it can be an energetic sacrifice, a way of giving thanks and committing yourself to serve the energies/deities or a symbolic sacrifice (like cutting some of your hair, pouring wine or milk on the earth, or burying an object in the ground). Wiccans who practice magick understand that, as it is closely connected to the Wiccan Rede and the Wiccan law of doing no harm.

But not all people who practice witchcraft today are associated with Wicca or adhere to that law. People who follow Crowley's religion for instance, Thelema, believe that "the full of the law is do as thou wilt". Many non-European practitioners of witchcraft, for instance those who practice branches of Yoruba or Vodun, may include small animal sacrifices in their practices. Does that make them evil? If you believe that, dear one, then I hope you're not eating meat...

The point of this chapter is not to scare you off, but to show you that not all people adhere to the same moral codes. This applies to all aspects of life, as well as witchcraft. So when you meet a Witch, be mindful but also please be considerate: some people may even find it insulting to be confused with Wiccans, as they are very proud of their own magical traditions.

In the end, you should respect everyone you meet along this Path — but put your trust in the people who have earned it. That being said, it's not unheard of for Wiccan witches and non-Wiccan witches to work together or use each other's services. Especially in our day and age, when there are so many practitioners out there and you can access their services or merchandise online... That's not a bad thing.

As long as you're not hurting anyone, or hiring someone non-bound by the Wiccan Laws to do the hurting for you. For example, if you're a Wiccan, it's not okay to do a spell to "get back" on someone or put a hex on someone, and it's definitely not okay to pay a non-Wiccan to place that spell or hex for you. (That would be like saying you're a vegan and then paying someone to kill and eat animals in front of you, so that you get the satisfaction! No sane vegan would ever do that, as they're vehemently opposed to causing any animals harm…)

But as long as your motives are pure and your heart is open, then by all means, do mingle with your non-Wiccan, modern Pagan community. There are so many vibrant traditions out there and so many things to learn, dear one!

You can definitely be both a Wiccan and a Witch

So as we've seen, being a Wiccan and being a Witch are not mutually inclusive. Now it's time for the good news: they're not mutually exclusive either! You can totally be both a devout Wiccan and a badass witch, if that's what you want. How?

It's simple, dear one.

Just keep the Wiccan Law forever in your heart, whenever you practice spells or rituals. Make the "an it harm none" your internal moral compass that will help you navigate tricky situations or decide whether a specific ritual or a spell are a good fit for you. For example: if you practice divination as a Wiccan, and you're doing tarot readings for other people, you should refrain from answering questions that would motivate or empower people to hurt others.

(So, if a client asks you "how can I make my lover leave his wife" or "how can I make my rival at the office lose the promotions so that I get it myself", kindly explain that you cannot answer questions like that as they clash with your beliefs. Most people will understand, and not persist. If they do persist, it's a sign they shouldn't be your clients anyway.)

But basically, that's your only limitation as a Wiccan Witch. If you're not hurting anyone (directly or indirectly), then there is no spell, ritual or practice that is out of your reach!

Here are some ways you can be a kickass Wiccan Witch:

-You can use the power of plants to help a loved one feel better or protect yourself and your home from bad energies.

-You can work with crystals to increase your psychic powers and intuition or augment the vibrations of your home.

-You can use cooking spells to whip up meals and confections that will make your loved ones happy, while at the same time protecting them from the inside.

-You can work with the Elements to protect yourself and your loved ones from anyone who would cause you harm or to manifest intentions that would help you live a better life.

-You can commune with plants and animals, to nurture them and help them grow and heal. In return, they can help you with your Craft, acting as familiars or omens.

-You can commune with spirits, of the ones who have passed or of ones you have a connection with, to gleam answers, get help or even help them find peace (although that's not recommended for beginners, you need to know what you're doing!)

-You can work with your sisters and brothers to raise a collective power to help Mother Earth heal or protect your homeland in case of emergencies (hey, if it worked for the coven Gardner witnessed trying to protect Brittain from Nazi invaders...).

-You can work with everything from plants and crystals to divination and deities in order to nurture your relationship and enhance a loving atmosphere at home. (Be careful though: this does not mean creating something that does exist, making someone fall in love with you or tying someone energetically to you even if they want out... This will surely backfire!)

-You can use all these tools mentioned above to heal yourself, physically and emotionally and enjoy your life more.

-You can get in tune with the waxing and waning phases of the Moon, to help things grow in your life or let go of things that are holding you back.

-You can protect yourself from people who mean you harm, from people who soak up your energy or from places that have a bad aura.

Does that sound exciting, dear one? Are you eager to get started? Of course you are!

This is what this next part of the book is all about. On Part 3: Everyday Magick, we'll get acquainted with all the basic tools and rituals you're gonna need to have in your arsenal, as you get started on your witchy Path. We'll then dig a little deeper on the different ways to practice witchcraft, so that you find the one that better speaks to your personality (along with a few go-to magickal tips for each type). Then, as promised, we'll talk about divination and tarot cards and help you get started with your first divination readings. Once we've covered all that, it's time for some seasonal spells and getting you better acquainted with the Sabbats and Esbats — and what kind of magickal energies abound in each one...

Bear in mind, dear one, that this is just the tip of the iceberg. If you're serious about your Path, you'll never start learning and growing. You'll get back to the same spells, change the words or some of the ingredients; you'll come up with new ways to do tarot readings; you'll start new Sabbat traditions of your own. As you know, us Pagans are infamous for doing things our own way! So please, don't feel the need to treat the book as the ultimate authority: the ultimate authority is you. If something described here (or in any book) doesn't feel right to you, then trust your gut. As long as you're not hurting anyone, of course!

(Disclaimer: You won't find any spells or rituals in this book that break the Wiccan Law of "do no harm". We're kosher that way. Sorry... but not really sorry, why would you want to do harm?)

Okay, that's it. Enough about theory and history lessons. Although of course they had their usefulness and brought you were you needed to be and develop a sense of understanding, now it's time for the real fun to begin!

PART 3: EVERYDAY MAGICK

Chapter 1: Basic Tools and Rituals

Welcome to the third and final part of this book, dear one!

They do say all good things come in threes, don't they? Yes, they do, especially when "they" are Wiccans. After all, "Mind the Three-fold Laws you should, three times bad and three times good," according to our Wiccan Rede[22]!

So if you're itching for some magick and practical knowledge, this part of the book has your back. We'll start

Choose the Tools That Work for You

---

[22] "The Wiccan Rede" (Full Version) as depicted in The Celtic Connection website, https://wicca.com/celtic/wicca/rede.htm

We've all seen those vintage images of witches riding their brooms, dressed all in black, a tall conical hat on their heads and a black cat on their tails...

A quick scroll on Instagram today, reveals a slightly (but not a lot) different image of what it means to be a witch: we see women with long, flowy hair somewhere in the woods, surrounded by cauldrons, wands, crystals (so.many.crystals), tarot cards, pendants, altars, herb jars and gourds, spellbooks, skulls and feathers, candles... Did we mention cauldrons?

Do you really need to go to Diagon Alley with a full list, like Harry and his friends before school season at Hogwarts, to be able to call yourself a witch? No, not really. In fact, every single one of the tools we'll discuss in this chapter as "basic", you could substitute for just your brilliant mind and your strong intention to manifest your desires! So why then, bother with objects at all?

It's not about capitalism or consumerism (although of course, it doesn't hurt to support small, independent witchy creators). It's mostly about your psychology. See, when you're first getting started on your witchy Path, it's only natural to *want to look the part*. You have all this self-doubt creeping in, that impostor syndrome whispering in your ear that "there's no such thing as real magick, you're just pretending", that gnawing fear that you don't really have what it takes or that you wouldn't even know where to begin... It can all be overwhelming, dear one.

That's where all these tools come in.

When you don't trust yourself and the power of your own heart and mind as well as the power of Nature (where witchcraft truly resides), these tools and objects will help you get into the zone and relieve some of the pressure: you may not fully trust yourself yet, but somehow you trust in them. Like talismans, magickal tools and objects give you something tangible to focus on. Something to hold on your hands, something to look at, something to smell or even something to taste. It's much easier than just looking at a blank wall...

Think of it as painting. It is known that, to create great abstract paintings, you first need to know how to sketch in a naturalistic way.

That's exactly what Pablo Picasso did: his early sketches of birds, when he first went to art school, were so realistic you thought they would fly away! But when he grew into his art, he created the cubist, abstract forms he's become famous for.

Like Picasso, you too need to learn the rules in order to be able to break them or realize you never really needed them in the first place...

So, without further ado, here are your witchy essentials to get your started!

Book of Shadows
Ah, the Book of Shadows! You've seen it in TV shows, from the 90's Charmed to its recent reboot and everything in between... You know how it's supposed to look like by now: old, sturdy, with a leather cover in a dark color, a pentacle or a triceta (more on sacred symbols later) engraved in the front, containing precious spells... But given that you're not a legacy witch and you didn't accidentally find one in your attic, how do you go about acquiring one? Can you just buy it on Amazon or Etsy?

Yes you can — but please don't.

The Book of Shadows is supposed to be your depository of spells and witchy knowledge. If you are not a legacy witch, then it's supposed to start with you, grow and evolve as you grow and evolve. So in the beginning, your Book of Shadows can just be a nice, blank notebook! It doesn't have to be expensive, or contain any magickal symbols (although of course, if you find one that you absolutely love how it looks, you should go ahead and buy it). In fact, it's considered a much better practice if you make your Book of Shadows yourself.

You can start with a plain notebook in a color that speaks to your Craft: it can be black or brown, sure, but it can also be white, purple, grey, green, gold... as long as it's a color that speaks to you and makes you want to spend time with it! It's better that you don't buy it online, either. Spend some time in an actual bookstore, touch some notebooks: see if any of them makes your hands tingle or if you have a gut feeling about a particular one. It doesn't matter how it looks, you can always customize it later.

Got your notebook? Great! Now, to make it into your Book of Shadows.

As with every new item you buy to use into your Craft (or any second-hand items of clothing or furniture you purchase), you'll first need to purify it; to make sure there are no lingering negative energies on it. To give it a clean slate, energetically speaking! So go ahead and purify it.

(We'll explain more about purifying in the next part, about rituals.)

Then, you can decorate your Book's cover and back with symbols that speak to you. This can be anything from the Pentacle to the triple moon symbol, to the alchemical symbols for the Elements. You can even press flowers or glue crystals onto it. Just let your imagination soar!

Once you're happy with how it looks, it's time to start writing in it.

Traditionally, the first thing you should write in the first page is your name (your given name, or the name you've chosen for yourself as a Witch) and the date when you decided to start following your Path. Then, depending on which specific pantheon or deities you feel a closer connection to, you can also dedicate your Book of Shadows to Them.

If you identify as a Wiccan, it would be an excellent idea to copy the full version of the Wiccan Rede on the second or third page. There are a few different versions of the Wiccan Rede available online, but perhaps the most commonly used is featured on the official website of wicca.com. Feel free to visit their website and look for it yourself[23], or find it here:

---

[23] "The Wiccan Rede" (Full Version) as depicted in The Celtic Connection website, https://wicca.com/celtic/wicca/rede.htm

The Wiccan Rede

Bide within the Law you must, in perfect Love and perfect Trust.

Live you must and let to live, fairly take and fairly give.

For tread the Circle thrice about to keep unwelcome spirits out.

To bind the spell well every time, let the spell be said in rhyme.

Light of eye and soft of touch, speak you little, listen much.

Honor the Old Ones in deed and name,

let love and light be our guides again.

Deosil go by the waxing moon, chanting out the joyful tune.

Widdershins go when the moon doth wane,

and the werewolf howls by the dread wolfsbane.

When the Lady's moon is new, kiss the hand to Her times two.

When the moon rides at Her peak then your heart's desire seek.

Heed the North winds mighty gale, lock the door and trim the sail.

When the Wind blows from the East, expect the new and set the feast.

When the wind comes from the South, love will kiss you on the mouth.

When the wind whispers from the West, all hearts will find peace and rest.

Nine woods in the Cauldron go, burn them fast and burn them slow.

Birch in the fire goes to represent what the Lady knows.

Oak in the forest towers with might, in the fire it brings the God's

Insight. Rowan is a tree of power causing life and magick to flower.

Willows at the waterside stand ready to help us to the Summerland.

Hawthorn is burned to purify and to draw faerie to your eye.

Hazel-the tree of wisdom and learning adds its strength to the bright fire burning.

White are the flowers of Apple tree that brings us fruits of fertility.

Grapes grow upon the vine giving us both joy and wine.

Fir does mark the evergreen to represent immortality seen.

Elder is the Lady's tree burn it not or cursed you'll be.

Four times the Major Sabbats mark in the light and in the dark.

As the old year starts to wane the new begins, it's now Samhain.

When the time for Imbolc shows watch for flowers through the snows.

When the wheel begins to turn soon the Beltane fires will burn.

As the wheel turns to Lamas night power is brought to magick rite.

Four times the Minor Sabbats fall use the Sun to mark them all.

When the wheel has turned to Yule light the log the Horned One rules.

In the spring, when night equals day time for Ostara to come our way.

When the Sun has reached it's height time for Oak and Holly to fight.

Harvesting comes to one and all when the Autumn Equinox does fall.

Heed the flower, bush, and tree by the Lady blessed you'll be.

Where the rippling waters go cast a stone, the truth you'll know.

When you have and hold a need, harken not to others greed.

With a fool no season spend or be counted as his friend.

Merry Meet and Merry Part bright the cheeks and warm the heart.

Mind the Three-fold Laws you should three times bad and three times good.

When misfortune is enow wear the star upon your brow.

Be true in love this you must do unless your love is false to you.

These Eight words the Rede fulfill:

"An Ye Harm None, Do What Ye Will"

Isn't it beautiful, dear one? But if you choose not to copy paste the full version, just make sure to write the Wiccan Law, "An Ye Harm None, Do What Ye Will".

That's the most important part after all!

Okay, now that you have your Book of Shadows purified, adorned and inscribed, it's time to begin using it. How do you do that? There are many ways:

-You can start by writing down spells, as you learn them.

-You can write the meanings of tarot cards (you'll find them in the next chapters!) or design your tarot spreads.

-You can write about your dreams, if you felt were prophetic, and return to that page later to see if something came about.

-You can make pages for all the major Wiccan celebrations, include rituals for these celebrations and seasonal spells and prayers.

-You can create a table of correspondences for the rest of your tools (as in, what each color stands for, what you should be using each crystaf for etc), so that you have everything at hand.

-You can write prayers for the Goddess and the God.

-You can draw Pentacles as mandalas (draw them without thinking, as you meditate on things).

-You can write recipes for magickal foods, elixirs or potions.

-You can write your desires, how you would ideally want your life to evolve, what are your intentions for this part of your journey... Feel free to revisit and adapt this part later on!

Your Book of Shadows should be private to you and kept somewhere safe. Think of it like your journal: you wouldn't want people to go about reading your journal, would you, dear one?

Altar
Just like your Book of Shadows is your journal, your altar is your witchy office: the place where you'll do your worshipping, your spell casting, your divination practicing... Of course like everything else on this list, you don't necessarily need an altar: your whole house can be your altar — or your nearest grove, forest or beach (see more on Nature, later in this chapter). But having a specific space just for you, where you can get your witchy vibes on, it will be very inspiring and liberating, especially at first.

So, your altar then. It really depends on your living arrangements: how discreet you need it to be (if say, you have roommates that are not exactly into the occult), how big of a space it can take.

An altar can be anything from a desk, to a shelf, to a side table — even a cupboard or a chest that you can keep closed when there are prying eyes about! There's no steadfast rule on what your altar should be made from either, but it's best to choose natural ingredients like wood or a flat stone surface. Remember to purify it before you start using it!

If you look for the hashtag #altar on Instagram, you'll find close to one million posts that could help you get inspired on what your own altar could look like... but remember that there are no set "rules" about what you should include or not. Only guidelines, and your best judgement.

Traditionally, on your altar you can have any statues or symbols of deities you worship (if you're eclectic in your beliefs, this could also include a statue of Buddha or Madonna). You can have your Book of Shadows, your tarot card decks (or any other divination methods you use) and your candles. It's also considered a good idea to include representations of the Elements and place them in the appropriate Directions:

-a pentacle, a rock, a crystal, a plant or a green candle for Earth (North)

-a bell, a feather, an athame or a yellow candle for Air (East)

-a wand, a cauldron or an orange/red candle for Fire (South)

-a chalice, a small jar filled with salt water, a sea shell or a blue candle for Water (West)

-a statue of a deity or a white or purple candle for Spirit (Center)

(We'll talk a bit more about the Elements, their Directions and further correspondences on the next part about rituals.)

Wondering what some of these things mentioned above are and how to use them? Let's go through the rest of the list of your essential tools and you're find out!

Cauldron

Perhaps one of the most "cliche" tools associated with witchcraft out there. How many times have you seen witches in anything from paintings to Shakespearean plays, stirring potions in a bubbling cauldron? And usually the ingredients they keep adding are quite elaborate... Who has the time to find "eye of newt" in this day and age? Definitely not a Wiccan who would never use the body parts of an animal so flippantly!

Energetically, a cauldron symbolizes transformation through fire; rebirth. You don't actually have to boil anything in it (depending on where you live it may not even be safe to do so): you can just use it as a safe place to have your tea lights and candles and experiment with adding spices and herbs to them as they burn.

Athame

In sharp contrast to the cauldron, athames are actually not publicized enough: not many people who are not actually practicing witchcraft know about them. (Perhaps it's better that way?)

An athame is a ceremonial knife, usually with a white handle (made of ivory or bone). There are athames you can buy online, or you can use any hand-carved old knife, as long as you purify it.

Very important: you're not supposed to use your Athame to cut anything physical, so please don't use a knife you use for cooking or eating! Athames are symbolical "cutting cords" and redirecting energies: you can use them to carve symbols on candles, create pentacles on air or basically use them as you would use a wand. In fact, most witches prefer athames from wands, as their sharp edge is a better conduit for energy than the blunt edge of any wand.

Speaking of which…

Wand

I know, dear one. Wands are cool and bring out your Harry Potter fan…

But contrary to popular belief, you don't actually need a wand. The wand is you, your arm or your fingers (or your athame). Despite that fact, many witches choose to have wands on their altars, as they are a good symbol of power, fertility, masculine energy (it is a phallic symbol after all) and they represent the element of Fire when you are not able to have something flammable around.

When it comes to choosing your wand: please don't buy it online.

The best thing you can do is take a walk in the woods or find a fallen branch somewhere. Carve the branch yourself, to the size and shape it feels right: you can add symbols, hang ribbons or attach crystals to it... It needs to feel comfortable and warm in your hand when you hold it!

You can use your wand in spell casting, in creating Pentacles on air (just like your athame) or to perform a symbolic Rite that combines masculine and feminine energy, by placing your wand inside your Chalice.

Chalice

The chalice symbolizes the Element of Water in your Altar, as well as feminine energy.

Any cup, glass or mug can be your chalice — although traditionally, it needs to be made from clear materials that reflect the light, like glass or crystal.

You can use your chalice to sip wine or water in ceremonies, to purify water and crystals or even to contain your runes, flowers, sea shells or anything else that brings to mind femininity!

Pentacle

We've been talking about Pentacles a lot, haven't we? And for good reason: a Pentacle is to Wiccans what the Star of David is to a Jew or the Holy Cross to a Christian. It's a manifestation of divine energy and a reminder of the things we believe in the most.

The Pentacle is practically a five-point star inside a circle. It is created to contain all five Elements: Earth, Air, Fire, Water and Spirit, each one represented in one of the star's five points. The circle symbolizes the World (both Above and Below). What the Pentacle is saying in plain English is that everything is contained within this world: all the elements, as well as Divine Spirit, all working together as part of the same grand design…

In slightly less philosophical terms, the pentacle is a super strong symbol of protection. Many witches and Wiccans have it engraved on the altar, or crafted from stone or wood. Some choose to wear it as a necklace (or a tattoo). In your altar it also symbolizes the element of Earth.

A silver bell

Also known as "the voice of the Goddess", a silver bell can be a beautiful way to ground yourself and meditate at the beginning and the end of a ritual. It's considered to clear the energies, and accentuate your intentions — very much like ringing a bell brings the students back to the classroom or announces guests at your home!

You can experiment with how many times you ring the bell, as each number is considered to bring about different energies. (We'll get more into numbers later on.)

In your altar it symbolizes the element of Air.

Candles

Candles are probably the simplest form of magick — so simple, they're even used in mainstream Christianity! Think about it: what is lighting a candle to pray if not a spell of sorts?

Candle magick is such an extensive field, it would require its own book. I urge you to find books on candle magick and read up, dear one!

At this point, what you need to know about candles is that similar to the bell, they can clear the energy of a space (immediately purify it) and they can also carry your intentions on their flames, sending it from the earth up to the sky as the smoke rises…

You can use candles to honor your deities or ancestors; to meditate before or during a ritual; to celebrate a particular Pagan holiday; to carve symbols or intentions and burn them as spells. Once you figure out what color to use for each occasion (consult the part about colors later on), you can use for everything from love spells to divination and fertility spells. You can use your athame to carve runes, names or symbols on their shaft; you can burn small pieces of paper (as symbols of things you want to let go of); you can place them on top of effigies (as symbols of things you want to keep burning bright); you can drip their wax to seal your intentions or spells.

Just remember to be safe and always put them out afterwards! When you do, remember to thank them as you blow — they deserve it, candles are the most hard-working witchy tools!

Crystals

Crystals are pretty. They're also powerful and healing — if you know how to use them properly.

The problem with crystals however, is that you don't really know where they came from: how exactly they were mined and if the people who mined them were exploited or given a fair wage... As a Wiccan who believes in not harming anyone, directly or indirectly, you need to be mindful of these things. It's better to buy crystals only locally, and when possible from people who were directly involved in mining them.

That being said, crystal magick is another extensive field you can look into if you want: there's practically a crystal for any kind of energy you'd like to emulate[24]!

To begin with, here are some crystals you can start experimenting with:

---

[24] Scott Cunningham, (1987), Cunningham's Encyclopedia of Crystal, Gem, and Metal Magic.

-clear quartz, for clarity, spirituality and intuition

-rose quartz, for love, happiness and affection

-amethyst, for protection, wisdom and intuition

-selenite, for intuition, psychic powers and divination

-pyrite, for power, courage and protection

-black onyx, for honesty, power and protection

Crystals on your altar usually symbolize Earth, but depending on their properties they can symbolize other elements as well. You can use them as energetical batteries, to charge your tarot cards, your Book of Shadows or spells; you can carry them with you for protection; you can place them around your house for protection and good vibes; you can use them to sanctify the water on your chalice. Some witches take that last part one step further and like to bathe with their crystals in the bathtub — but that doesn't really do anything besides looking cool on Instagram and pissing the crystals off.

Because yeah, your crystals have personalities and they don't like being mistreated. You should also remember to charge them every now and then: place them on a window sill so that they can get fresh energy from the sun or the moonlight.

Plants, herbs, flowers and essential oils
Every flower and plant out there has some magickal (and medicinal) properties that can help you with your Craft. This is also a field that you may end up studying your whole life and still discover new properties by trial and error. You can use herbs to burn as incense (see also the next part about sage); you can brew plants and flowers for teas and potions; you can include plants and herbs in cooking spells; you can anoint your candles or your skin with essential oils that bring out a specific quality…

There really is no boundaries to the things you can use your herbal arsenal for!

Scott Cunningham, one of the greatest writers of Wicca, has written an excellent book about the magickal abilities of plants that should be part of every witch's book collection [25]. But just as a quick reference, here are some popular, easy to find and safe to use plants you can start including in your witchy repertoire:

-basil, for love, wealth and protection

-rosemary, for protection, healing and love

-rose, for passion, love and luck

-cinnamon, for success, healing and love

-jasmin, for love, money and prophetic dreams

-sage, for wisdom, banishment of negative energies and protection

-mugwort, for astral projection and prophetic dreams

-lavender, for serenity, peace and a good night's sleep

Salt, sage and palo santo
We've already seen how sage can be used to banish negative energies. In shamanic traditions of Native Americans, they'd use to burn sage to purify the air or someone who may be carrying negative energies. Modern witches and Wiccans use sage to protect and purify, along with salt and palo santo. As a general rule, sage tends to remove all vibrations, both positive and negative, reinstating an energetic clean slate.

But as far as protection and purification goes, salt is perhaps the strongest of them all. (Those superstitions about throwing salt over your shoulder or creating a salt circle to keep ghosts out of a room

---

[25] Scott Cunningham, (1985) Cunningham's Encyclopedia of Magical Herbs.

have been popular for a reason.) No bad energy can break through a salt circle or a salt bath. You can purify your tools, from your Book of Shadows to your candles and crystals by burying them in salt for a while (from a few seconds to a whole night or more, depending on the situation). You can also just sprinkle a bit of salt around your altar, or carry a few grains of salt in your pockets (or place them with some lavender under your pillow to ward off nightmares).

Palo santo is a gentler alternative, as it does not remove any positive vibrations, only the negative ones. For extraordinary results, you can combine all three.

Broom (yes, really)

You're not going to use it for flying, please don't try. Now that we've gotten this out of the way, brooms can be used to energetically clean your space and ward off malevolent spirits. Traditionally they're called "besoms".

Keep your besom in a corner facing your front door, for good luck.

Yarn and ribbons

Knot magick is a very interesting field. The idea behind it is that you can meditate and tie knots on a ribbon or yarn to remove obstacles or manifest your intentions. (That's more or less how prayer beads and worry beads came to be!)

Many witches always have ribbons in all colors at the ready, to use depending on the occasion and the spell. You can also hang them in your hair or in your house, for protection.

As for yarn, you can use it to make your own "Witch's Belt", also called a Cingulum. Basically you need to take eight yarn colors, one to represent each Sabbat and Esbat and you slowly braid them together throughout the year: you start with the ribbons of the first three Sabbats and Esbats until you have a braid, then you create two more braids as the following celebrations come... and in the end you braid all three braids together.

The Cingulum is to be worn as a belt over your ceremonial robes to amplify your power, but many Witches also choose to wear it wrapped around their wrists as a bracelet as well.

Ceremonial robes

Yes, we said "ceremonial robes". But they definitely don't have to be black, or like a Halloween costume. Your "robes" can basically be anything from a loose, comfortable long dress, to flowy yoga pants and a shirt if you're less into the theatrics. It's nice if it touches the earth, as it provides you with a tangible connection between Above and Below, but the most important thing is that you feel clean, special and comfortable when wearing them! For that reason, it's better to have a particular type of clothing you only use for your Craft and not for your everyday life.

Many witches (especially ones that follow Gardner's practice) will work their Craft naked, however this may not always be the most practical or viable option!

Nature

Yes, Nature is your ultimate tool. Being a Witch is all about understanding and living according to Natural Law. In fact, Nature could easily replace most of your tools mentioned here.

For starters, when you're out in Nature you don't need representations of the Elements to work with; you are literally surrounded by them! You can take water from a running stream, a lake or the sea; you can get barefoot and dig your toes on the ground or in the sand to draw energy from the earth; you can recharge by spreading your hands open wide towards the light of the Sun of the Moon; if you want to redirect energy, fallen branches can be your wand; if you're near the ocean, the salt of the water works as a protection shield and a natural purificator.

Just be careful with lighting a fire in Nature. Do it respectfully, safely and always put it out afterwards.

UNDERSTAND YOUR BASIC RITUALS

Okay, dear one, now you've got your tools at the ready. So… how do you go about using them?

There is literally no end to the rituals and spells you can start practicing daily with these tools. But first you need to master a few simple rituals that will serve as the basis you can build upon.

Meditation

Meditation is truly a witch's best friend — although we may not always have called it that.

The practice of meditation was first recorded in the Vedas around 1500 BCE (see the first part of the book for more info on the Vedas) and was well developed in Taoist China and Buddhist India around 600 BCE. In the Western world, meditation (in the form we know it today) became popular around the 1960s-70s, as part of the renewed interest in the occult and in oriental wisdom. But the thing is, witches always meditated. They may have called it "stepping between the worlds" or "opening up their Sight" or simply spending time alone in Nature, but the premise remains the same: to be able to tap your inner Power, first you must quiet your mind.

There are currently many great apps in the market that can help you turn meditation into a daily practice but perhaps you don't need them. Try lighting a candle and just sitting for a while, looking at the flame and focusing on breathing calmly. Let the world around you slowly melt and disappear. You'll notice that with time, it will become easier to slip in and out of this deep state of mind — and it's a state of mind (or, non-mind) you need if you're to do any work on your Craft.

Purification

We touched upon this briefly in the previous part about tools: purification is a very important ritual that can be performed on anything from witchy and non-witchy objects to people and spaces.

To purify something you need tools such as: salt, sage, palo santo, water and fire (and sometimes, crystals).

There are many purification techniques, depending on the situation:

-You can take a purifying shower (or stand out in the rain for a few seconds), letting the water wash away any lingering negative energies and feel your body being returned to a state of infinite possibility and power.

-You can burn a sage bundle or a palo santo stick, and smudge yourself, an object or your home. It is common to move your hand around in such a way that you create shapes with the smoke, usually Pentacles or the symbol of infinity (looks like the number 8 lying down).

-You can place the object, or your hands, in a bowl full of salt for a few moments or minutes. Let the Earth work its magick.

-You can, carefully, place the object or your hands over the flame of a candle — high enough so that you don't get burned, obviously! The idea is that the element of Fire will purify and transform any lingering negativity to new, vibrant energy.

-You can place some sage leaves on your chalice and fill it with water. Let the water sit for a while and the leaves to be soaked in. Then you can use this water to purify yourself or objects. (A little here will go a long way: just dip your fingers on the sanctified water and use them to tap some of it on your third-eye chakra, or on the object you want to purify.)

While performing any of these rituals, you can chant something like "remove the negativity of yesterday, bring only good vibes this way".

The words don't matter that much, use words that come naturally to you. It's the intention that counts, and your intention should be to purify this object or yourself.

Raising Power

Raising Power is like supercharging yourself with energy, so that you can redirect that energy towards the spell or ritual you're performing — or even towards that part of your body that is hurting or that area of your life that could use some improving.

Raising Power is much easier done with more witches, by joining hands and forming a circle. (With more people, it's easier to raise more energy and redirect it towards big threats, such as the amazon forest fires or wars and famine.) But if you're a solitary practitioner as so many of us are, you still have some very powerful allies you can work with to raise Power for your spells and rituals! Who are these amazing allies? The Elements.

Earth

The element of home and stability, the one that keeps you grounded and helps you find your True North. Earth is a great element to work with for spells/rituals that involve matters of home/career/finances.

Air

The element of inspiration and communication, of change and renewal. Always look in the East when working with Air. A great element to work with when you want to get a message across, or for matter that involve writing/talking to people/social life/traveling/studying.

Fire

The element of passion, creativity, sex and jest for life. Fire, residing in the direction of the South, is a great Element to invoke for sexual spells, but also anything that has to do with work projects you are passionate about or with spells to reclaim your power.

Water

The element of love, emotions, sensitivity; of surrendering and letting go. Water resides in the direction of the West and will be your perfect ally for anything from love and fertility spells/rituals to work on divination and healing.

Spirit

The element that binds them all together, existing in the Center, simultaneously inside and outside this world. Use spirit in protection rituals, to invoke deities or to bring your other spells/rituals full circle and give thanks.

Whenever you want to work with a specific energy/element, the simplest way to do so is to turn your body to face its Direction and light a candle in its honor. But it's considered a better idea, at least in the beginning, to combine all the elements (in the order that were mentioned here) moving clockwise in a circle with one of your arms extended — you can use a wand, an athame, a sage bundle or just your finger.

Once your ceremony/spell is over, do the same thing anti-clockwise to give thanks and release the energies/elements.

Invoking the Deities

How do you invoke a god/goddess?

This is a complicated matter and you should only embark on it once you feel comfortable that you understand and respect what this god/goddess is all about. Otherwise, at best nothing will happen and at worst you're risking making some deity annoyed...

So please, do your research, find the god/goddess you identify the most with or feel closer to (these are often called Patron or Matron deities) and develop a relationship with them — don't just call on them when you need something! Worship them during your daily life as well, send them love, light candles in their names and give them offerings. The same way a devout Christian would think about his or her favorite Saint, or about Jesus and God themselves.

Once you know what you're doing and who you're doing it with (and why), make your invocation with a clear, steady voice and state your intention. Use their formal names, or the names they have been called by their worshippers (for instance, Odin, is also called the AllFather). Mention the realms in which they rule and the areas of life they can affect them most.

Don't expect something to happen instantly. Sit with the intention for a while, meditating on the presence of your Patron or Matron deity. After a while, give thanks and release them.

It's only good manners, dear one!

Protection
Throughout your spells and rituals, you'll need to make sure you are protected from any negative energies from within, but also any restless spirits that make venture to enter from without. Creating a circle with the power of the Elements works as a protection shield, but you can also create a literal circle with a rope or salt on the ground and step inside it.

A smart and convenient way to always be protected is to purify a piece of jewelry (preferably silver or containing crystals) and invoke the Elements and deities to bless this jewelry and imbue it with Power. Then, you can wear it or hang it from your doorstep (or over your bed) whenever you want to feel safe and protected.

Chapter 2: Find Your Witchy Flavor

What kind of Witch are you? No, this is not a Buzzfeed quiz, it's a serious question.

In a similar way that doctors can be general practitioners or specialize in a particular field of medicine field (like oncology or gynaecology), you can decide to be a Witch that tries a bit of everything... of find your specific witchy flavor. Although finding that (and polishing it) will be your lifelong Journey, in this chapter you can get a brief understanding of the most prominent witch types — at least the ones that do not violate the Wiccan Law of doing no harm.

Elemental Witch

In a way, we're all Elemental Witches. We all need the Elements, especially Spirit, to draw Power from. But an elemental witch usually has a special connection to one of the elements — and that affects her Craft.

For example: have you always felt an affinity for fire? Do you find it easy manipulating candle flames with your energy or mind? That may be a sign that you're an Elemental Witch. Be careful though: the

Elements are very powerful and you'll need to learn to control yourself around them because accidents do happen. (I once knew a Witch with an affinity for Water who managed to accidentally flood her apartment... twice!) You need to remember to balance yourself and your surroundings so, for instance, if Fire is strong within you, make sure you're surrounded by calming waters often.

Sea Witch

A sea witch is in a way an Elemental Witch with an affinity for Water — but her Power is supercharged by the ocean. Did you always feel a connection to the sea and the waves? When you're in a bad mood, do you find it easier to heal when you're by the oceanside? Has swimming or diving always felt like second nature to you and you've never felt any fear towards sea creatures? You may be a Sea Witch! It would be worth exploring the lore of supernatural creatures with ties to the ocean, like mermaids or selkies — you never know what you may discover about yourself!

Green Witch

Another denomination of an Elemental Witch, this time with an affinity for Earth. Green witches have what we call "green thumbs": they're most at their element in the woods or at their garden, helping plants, flowers and trees grow and flourish. A green witch's home can start resembling a jungle after a while, once all her herbs are repotted and her flowers have bloomed...

Does that sound like you? Great! Being a Green Witch is a very useful skill and one our planet desperately needs!

Kitchen Witch

Kitchen (or hearth/home) witches are basically a Green Witch's close cousin. You too have an affinity for all earthy things and love working with plants and herbs — only you prefer the comfort of your own home and the warmth of your stove to the woods. A Kitchen

Witch uses her Craft to nurture her loved ones through food, pays special attention to pets and kids and turns even simple tasks like cleaning the floor to opportunities for magick.

HEDGE WITCH

This is a term that's been thrown out a lot. It has taken to mean "a witch with no official training, mostly doing her own thing[26]" but traditionally, hedge witches are thought to exist a bit "in between". To cross over the "hedge" between the worlds and visit the realm of spirits. If you ever had experiences in the astral plane or it's always been easier for you to see spirits and interact with them, you may be a hedge witch.

Tip: if you are a hedge witch, please make sure to double down on your protection. Use every tool available to you to make sure no destructive spirits will ever "catch a ride" with you, okay?

TECH WITCH

This is a new category, but one that's gaining ground. A tech witch understands that technology runs on electrical currents and magnetic energy and can use these energies to her benefit. Have you always been particularly lucky around electronics (that may not have been working properly for other people but always work for you)? Do you always manage to find internet even when the people next to you are struggling? Do you feel "seen" by the apps you download? You may be a tech witch!

---

[26] Mandy Mitchell, (2014) Hedgewitch Book of Days: Spells, Rituals, and Recipes for the Magical Year, Weiser Books.

DIVINATION WITCH

Every type of witch, even the ones who are not featured here (because they violate the Wiccan Law of doing no harm), usually practices some kind of divination. But a true divination witch usually has some kind of inherent foresight — either in the form of dreams or in the form of interpreting omens that come her way.

Divination is a fascinating field that everyone can learn and benefit from. In the next chapter, we'll talk in depth about it!

CHAPTER 3: DIVINATION 101

Ah, to gaze upon the future and get answers on what's to come!

Admit it, dear one: you couldn't wait for this chapter to arrive.

(Perhaps you even skipped a couple of chapters to get here? Hopefully you didn't. There's much to learn in those chapters as well.)

Divination has been a companion of witches and Pagans since the beginning of time. The word itself, deriving from Latin, means both to "be inspired by a god" and to "foresee, foretell". In the ancient Pagan world, seers or "manteis" (in Greek) were revered and their counsel sought after, from both kings and commoners. Very often, seers would be brought onto the battlefield, to read the omens. That could mean either looking out for any incidents like birds flying or the clouds dissipating that could be interpreted as positive or negative, or sacrificing animals and studying their entrails for hidden messages from the gods. In many cases, a general would not attack unless they got the "go" from their seers. (Sometimes these seers would lie, having been bought by the opposing forces.)

If seers interpreted signs, oracles were thought to commune with the gods directly. The most famous oracle of the ancient world was the Oracle of Delphi, in Greece. In fact, it was once considered "the navel of the Earth" because of the importance that was placed in the prophecies Pythia (the priestess of the god Apollo who operated the oracle) would deliver to people. There is no clear verdict among historians on how these prophecies were given: some said she would inhale the vapors that emerged from a chasm between the rock and reach a state of lucid dreaming; others claimed she communed directly with the gods and spoke in tongues, or in obscure poetry verses. Most, however, agree that her prophecies were enigmatic — and have been interpreted differently by different people more than once, usually with dire consequences.

Consider this a cautionary tale, dear one.

When you start asking questions about the future, the answers may not come in the form you expect. You need to be prepared to read between the lines and think outside the box.

It wasn't just ancient Greece though that relied heavily on divination. From the Aztecs who worshipped Tezcatlipoca, the god of sorcerers and magic, to the Ifá divination system of the Yoruba that required an initiated priest/priestess called Awo, giving insights on the future and the will of the gods was a fundamental part of Pagan life. Seers would study animal entrails but also the movements of living animals, natural phenomena such as clouds and thunder, liquids such as coffee or tea, parts of the human body (like the palm of your hand or your iris) or use tools such as rocks, runes, cards and bamboo sticks. They would also gaze upon reflective surfaces such as mirrors or river streams or study the flames and the embers of a fire...

Anything, really, can be used as a divination tool — and it probably has been.

Of course, divination was officially forbidden in the early days of Christianity in Europe, along with all other Pagan practices, but that didn't mean people ever stopped using it. In fact, it's kinda forbidden in many countries even to this day — and yet divination practices are actually booming. All you have to do is log into Instagram and you'll come across anything from tarot cards and runes to people reading tea leaves and palms.

But where does it really come from? Can tea leaves actually tell us the future?

It doesn't work exactly like that, dear one.

To practice any kind of divination, you need to open yourself to messages — both from your subconscious and from the spirits and deities. You need to bring yourself to a state that's both focused and relaxed, almost meditative — but sometimes it can also work wonders to be under the influence of substances (not that we're advising that). That's what Pythia was doing after all, when she was inhaling those "vapors" back in ancient Greece... But maybe don't tell your professors at school that!

Ultimately, how you'll practice divination is, like many things in the Pagan world, a matter of personal preference. So if slaughtering a lamb and studying its entrails is not exactly your cup of tea (pun intended) keep reading: you'll find some of the most common divination methods below. It's usually advised to experiment with a couple of them, so that you can find the one that fits you best.

Disclaimer: you don't have to practice Divination to be a "good" witch or Pagan. If the thought makes you uncomfortable or afraid, please listen to yourself. It means you're not ready yet. And if that's the case, please feel free to skip this chapter and go straight to the chapter about seasonal spells. But if uncovering the secrets of the future thrills you even just a little bit... then please, keep reading!

FIND THE PRACTICE THAT SUITS YOU

In this day and age, a Witch is spoiled for choice when it comes to divination practices.

Some of us practice only one method that we feel "speaks" to us more, others like to combine different methods or try different things depending on our mood and the seasons.

Let's go through the most common divination methods together, shall we?

Astrology

The art of looking at the position and movement of the stars in the sky to make predictions about the future has been around since the ancient Babylonians — and became especially popular in Ptolemaic Egypt through the Hermetic texts (as we've seen on the first part of this book, when we discussed the origins of secret organizations like Golden Dawn). It's true that since the revival of Pagan practices after the 19th century, astrology has become both extremely popular and mainstream, but at the same time it's also considered a "less than" spiritual practice. Perhaps it's all these astrology hotlines out there?

Regardless, the art of astrology is not for the faint of heart. Truly understanding the movements of the planets, how they interact with one another and how this interaction can affect one's natal chart and future is an intricate process — not recommended if you're just starting on your path and need some answers fast! (Please, don't call a hotline.)

On the other hand, because astrology is such an intricate technique, as long as you do the calculations and you consult the charts and timetables, there is usually not a big margin for error — or variations in personal interpretation. So you can feel more "secure" in your predictions.

Cheiromancy

Also known as palmistry, the art of reading one's palm to ascertain the future has been practiced all over the world — and every culture has its own explanations for what every line, peak and valley of your palm really means. Very popular among Roma fortune tellers, palmistry to this day also has a "parlor trick" flair among modern witches and sceptics alike.

Palmistry is easier to learn than astrology, as there is a finite number of lines and features in one's hand and identifying their meanings is relatively simpler. The only "problem" with palmistry is the fact that the features of one's hand doesn't really change that much over time. So although it may be a potent tool for one-time readings, if you rely on it frequently it may give you a sense that everything is predetermined and that there's no room for growth.

And who wants to feel like that?

Cleromancy

One of the most diverse techniques out there. People throughout the ages have casted anything from lots, dice, coins, runes (as in Old Norse Pagan traditions), yarrow sticks (as in the Chinese I-Ching tradition), oil palm kernels (as in the Ifá tradition of the Yoruba) and even marbles.

Although the Ifá tradition is usually practiced by people who share the Yoruba heritage, the I-Ching is open to anyone who will take the time to study it. There are books that showcase the meanings of each throw (there are 64 hexagrams that you can create by throwing either yarrow sticks or coins) in detail [27]. Like astrology, once you understand the process there is not much room for "error" although the interpretations can be quite poetic and abstract.

Runes, basically the old Germanic/Scandinavian alphabet, has been used for both writing and divination purposes since around 150 CE. Rune divination is actually one of the best practices for witches who are just getting started! The word itself means "secret" or "hidden" and the way it works is you carve each letter of the alphabet (there are 24) in tokens — that are traditionally made of wood but can be made of stone as well. Each rune, apart from symbolizing a letter, it also symbolizes a word: for example, the rune D, Dagaz, means "day" but also "good luck" and is considered to denote spiritual growth. Note that if you order a set of runes online, one of them will be blank; this is not a mistake. The blank rune, also called "Odin's

---

[27] The Complete I Ching - 10th Anniversary Edition : The Definitive Translation by Taoist Master Alfred Huang, Inner Traditions Bear and Company.

rune", symbolizes infinite potential. Talk about creating your own future!

Dowsing

A type of divination using a Y-shaped rod, traditionally used to locate water or metals. Nowadays, most people use pendants for dowsing divinations: judging by the way the chain of the pendant moves if the answer to a question is "yes" or "no". Dowsing can be an impressive divination technique, especially around ley lines and places with strong magnetic energy… but it can also be manipulated easily by the practitioner moving their hands just so.

Ouija boards

The flat boards that feature the letters of the alphabet were used as a parlor trick when first invented in 1890, but became a more "serious" divination method during World War I. Ouija boards are supposed to help you communicate easier with spirits during seances (where the spirits supposedly move the needle towards the letters they want to form words with) but like pendulum dowsing they can be easily manipulated by the person who holds the needle as well.

Prophetic dreaming

Oneiromancy is a vast field, with several books written on the subject — so we should keep it short here. In short, having prophetic dreams can be an overwhelming experience, especially if you're still new to your Path. Can you trust your prophetic dreams to come true? Especially when they're usually about bad things… And there are so many different definitions out there…

Breathe, dear one. Prophetic dreams can be a powerful tool, but only if you use them as a tool and you don't give them any dominion over your waking life. Make sure to always have a journal near your bed, so that you can write down your dreams every morning (or, since we live in 2019, use an app to take notes). Then, study their meaning later in the day, when you will have calmed down and their hold on you will have dissipated a bit. Please know that even if you dream something very bad (that's happening to you or a loved one) it doesn't mean it will take place exactly as you dreamt it. Take it more like an indication of the current energies, and work to send good vibrations and healing to the person you dreamed about.

If the dream was about you and you don't like what you saw, murmur "I give this dream no power over me" a few times, until you feel back in control of your own destiny.

Scrying

Ah, all these movies where fortune tellers look at crystal balls and see the future (or scam their clients). Scrying is an ancient and extremely difficult technique, recommended for advanced practitioners. Any reflective surface, from mirrors to crystals and water streams can be used for scrying — there is really no guidebook for scrying, as it's your intuition and the guidance you may receive from spirits and deities that will affect what you See. So please, don't spend hours looking at crystal balls, disappointed at the perceived lack of your abilities: scrying takes a lot of practice and a very specific state of mind.

A good start to get in that frame of mind, dear one, is to start meditating daily. Empty your mind, perhaps looking at the flame of a candle or a specific marking on a wall. After a while, you'll notice you're still looking at it without "really looking at it". That's the type of "soft but focused" looking you need to use when scrying. You'll get it right, eventually.

Tarot cards

Is it you, or are tarot cards EVERYWHERE lately? It's not you, dear one.

Tarot cards, also known as cartomancy, have been used for divination since around 1750 CE, in Italy and France — but soon became popular throughout Europe. Back then, the preferred decks were the Tarocco Bolognese and the Tarot of Marseilles, but the usage of tarot cards in Victorian secret societies such as the Golden Dawn (see first part of the book) increased the creation of tarot deck designs and started a competition between occultists about whose tarot deck version is considered the "best". We've already seen that Aleister Crowly created his own tarot deck, the Thoth tarot, but the Rider-Waite tarot deck (that draws inspiration from 19th century occultist Eliphas Levi) was back then and remains to this day the most commonly used tarot deck.

Tarot cards are perhaps the best way for beginners on the Path to practice divination and sharpen their intuition. Trust that your life will change once you incorporate daily tarot card readings in your schedule! Not because the Tarot cards have all the answers and will tell you what to do (definitely not, nobody has ALL the answers) but because their suggestive imagery is strong enough to guide your intuition but also soft enough to let you draw your own conclusions and hone your skills. Start by pulling one card a day — and reading the detailed guide below!

UNDERSTAND THE TAROT CARD MEANINGS

Tarot cards have changed a lot throughout the ages — nowadays there are hundreds of cool versions of tarot decks out there! You should definitely do some research to find a deck that speaks to you, but it is recommended, dear one, to start with the traditional Rider-Waite tarot deck. Once you unlock the meanings of the traditional cards, you'll be better equipped to understand modern tarot decks.

So buckle up, as we embark on a journey through the Major and Minor Arcana of the Rider-Waite tarot deck. Ready? Great!

The Major Arcana consists of 22 cards, numbered from 0 to 21. These cards depict the major events in a person's life; the stages of our journey through life. In fact, many believe that if you put all the Major Arcana cards one next to the other, they tell a story. Try it out; it will help you understand their narrative better.

But for now, let's examine the cards one by one, shall we?

Card Number: 0
Card Name: The Fool
The Fool describes new adventures — and the hubris with which we sometimes undertake them. The card shows a young man striking out on his first adventure, full of excitement for what's to come and cheered on by his loyal dog. The sun shines brightly on him: we can't help but share in the boundless optimism of this image! The ignorance and confidence we sometimes display at the beginning of a journey can be beneficial: there are some tasks so arduous we would never take them on if we knew better. He carries his belongings at the end of a wand, which symbolizes the energy, creativity and strength The Fool is bringing with him in this new journey. If successful, we will develop new skills, new perspectives and make new friends along the way… But The Fool also reminds us to be cautious, dear one. When starting a new chapter in our lives, too much confidence can be just as bad as too little. Imagine if we tripped and fell before we even began!

Card Number: 1
Card Name: The Magician
The Magician reminds us we have everything we need in order to succeed. We simply need to look around us. The card shows a highly-skilled individual who knows how to harness his full potential, straddling the space between the internal and the external realm. He extends his hands in opposite directions to remind us that, "as above, so below". (Isn't that as Pagan as it gets?) The Magician is surrounded by tools that symbolize the four elements: a sword for Air, a wand for Fire, a cup for Water and a pentacle for Earth. Holding a white wand in his one hand and pointing at the lush flowers blooming around his feet, he declares his ability to control his own Destiny. An Ouroboros around his waist and the symbol of infinity crowning him like a halo, are here to remind us of the eternal nature of The Magician's inner power — and our own. If we don't believe in own our ability to shape our life as we desire, we will never manifest our full potential. This card can also be a warning that we've been relying too much on other people and failing to take full responsibility for the lessons the Universe is serving us.

Card Number: 2
Card Name: The High Priestess
The High Priestess connects us with our feminine energy and reminds us to sit still and trust our intuition. We will realize we knew the answer to the question that's been troubling us, all along.

She is an invitation to go deeper, connect to our spiritual self and listen to the messages from our subconscious: sitting at the entrance of the Temple of Sacred Knowledge, where only the truly wise can enter. She is flanked by two columns, one black and one white, symbolizing again the Pagan duality (day and night, male and female, yin and yang). Her clothes are flowy like water and simmering like the Moon which graces her feet. The Moon is also present in the crown she is wearing, shaped after its three facets: the crescent, the Full Moon and the waning moon; the three faces of the Goddess. A cross in her chest and the scroll in her hands show that The High Priestess possess the secrets to divine knowledge but does not offer access to them freely. With this card, it is possible that we will find that secrets are being kept from us. It can also show that we've been hesitant to act.

Card Number: 3
Card Name: The Empress
The Empress symbolizes fertility and motherhood: she is exactly the Divine Feminine worshipped by our ancestors so many millennia ago... The card is showing her nesting amid a lush forest, sitting on a throne of comfortable red cushions, adorned with the symbol of Venus. A crown of twelve stars graces her blond hair and her long robe is embellished with pomegranates, for fertility and abundance. The river of Life is flowing near The Empress' feet and she stands as beautiful and benevolent as the trees surrounding her. Now is a great time to give birth to new creative projects and see them blossom and grow. We should express our affections and nurture the creatures surrounding us, be they humans, animals or plants — but not overdo it. Too much water can kill a plant, as too much affection can spoil or suffocate a person. Are we over-infantilizing someone, believing they need us more than they actually do?

Card Number: 4
Card Name: The Emperor
The Emperor is calling us to be as confident in our strength as he is. He rules bravely, with fierce determination. The card shows him at the feet of a craggy mountain, sitting on his austere throne — the only embellishment being the four heads of rams, symbolizing his success in battle and his association with Aries. The Emperor is, after all, a warrior King: he may be holding they symbols of the world of the living he is ruling (the Orb and the Ankh), but he wears the full body armor of a Knight underneath his red cloak. We are called to ascertain our dominion over a situation, or to protect those dear to us, never failing to establish order where we need to. Although, like every stern ruler, we may not always be beloved when we find ourselves in positions of power. Are we holding the reins too tight?

Card Number: 5
Card Name: The Hierophant
The Hierophant is the ultimate teacher; the mentor figure we need to guide us through moral dilemmas, the education institution who can help us unlock our potential for knowledge and understanding. Like The High Priestess, The Hierophant is also sitting at the entrance of a Temple, flanked by two marble columns. But his realm of knowledge is not just the subconscious: he equally rules the conscious, subconscious and superconscious, something made apparent by his three crowns, three papal robes and the three-cross scepter he is holding. The Hierophant is presiding over the traditions and customs that allow our society to function, the keys to the kingdom of men on his feet. Kneeling before him are two of his acolytes, their heads traditionally shaved in the style of Capuchin monks, symbolising piety. We can emulate the values of The Hierophant and assume a mentoring role towards others, sharing our hard-earned wisdom. But we should be careful to not be blinded by our own beliefs or becoming too attached to our own habits. "Different" doesn't always have to mean "a threat".

Card Number: 6
Card Name: The Lovers
The Lovers represent the divine pairing, the balanced union of perfect opposites. In this card, The Lovers stand completely naked, facing each other as equals. They're in the Garden of Eden: behind the woman, the Tree of Knowledge is ripe with fruit but the Serpent, symbolizing temptation is circling it. Behind the man, a tree made of flames represents his fiery passion. The Lovers are blessed and protected by the Archangel Raphael, who is sending them a gust of wind to facilitate communication. A radiant Sun, symbolizing happiness, shines on them both. In our own lives, The Lovers symbolize all these relationships, be they romantic, platonic or even professional, that complete us and bring harmony into our lives. But this card is also a warning not to linger too long in indecision, or stay in relationships that no longer serve our growth.

Card Number: 7
Card Name: The Chariot
The Chariot reminds us to be in the driver's seat of our life, reigning in any external hindrances and charting a clear course towards our goals. Like the warrior in this card, who stands ready for action. He has no horses to reign in: at the feet of The Chariot, a black and a white sphinx, symbolizing opposite forces, are resting. But the warrior will move The Chariot through the power of his will, represented by his white wand. Cosmic symbols, from the Sun on his head to the Moon on his shoulders, assure of his success and remind us we don't have to rely on excessive strength to triumph. We just need to keep our eyes focused on where we want to go and we will surpass any obstacles along the way. As long as we don't forget our true path in life!

Card Number: 8
Card Name: Strength
The message of the Strength card is not to stifle our basic instincts or ignore our desires. Like the woman with her hands on the lion's mouth depicted on this card, we too need to lovingly acknowledge our raw emotions (the lion) and then rise above them. With her hands wrapped gently around the open mouth of a fierce lion, the woman proves that Strength is much more than mere physical might. Her long white dress, adorned with flowers, speak to the purity of her intentions and her inner beauty. The symbol of infinity over her head shows her endless potential. Showing compassion, both to ourselves and to others who need our help, is what true Strength means. But we shouldn't become too confident in our own abilities, or care more about how people perceive us than about how we can use our gifts to help them… That's not strength, dear one, that's pride.

Card Number: 9
Card Name: The Hermit
The Hermit asks us to take a step back from our busy schedules, in order to see the bigger picture. Perhaps we have been focusing too much on being surrounded by other people and material comforts, and we have forgotten who we truly are at the core of our being. In the card, The Hermit stands alone on the summit of a snowy mountain, his only source of light being the Six-Pointed Star inside his lantern, a symbol of wisdom. Covered in simple gray robes, The Hermit may be old but he possesses knowledge and authority, represented by his long wooden staff which supports him as he carefully makes his next steps. Spending some time alone, reading or meditating, may be all we need in order to return to the outside world all the wiser for it. But we shouldn't withdraw too much into our own shell. No one is happy being alone forever.

Card Number: 10
Card Name: Wheel of Fortune

A harbinger of good news and serendipity, the Wheel of Fortune is here to remind us that no matter how trapped we may be feeling in our current situation, change is always just around the corner. The Wheel of Fortune, adorned with the alchemical symbols for the four elements and surrounded by a serpent (for evil), Anubis (for the dead and the living) and a Sphinx (for wisdom), represents the circle of life. Just like life, The Wheel of Fortune contains both the good and the bad, forever spinning in mid-air. At the four corners of the sky, winged creatures symbolising the fixed signs in astrology (Aquarius, Scorpio, Taurus and Leo) illustrate our ability to find stillness and control even amid frantic change. We shouldn't hesitate to embrace that change: the Wheel of Fortune favors the bold. But we should also remember that goes around comes around. Have we been attracting good karma into our lives?

Card Number: 11
Card Name: Justice

As the Wheel of Fortune brings us karma, so does Justice make sure that our actions have the consequences they deserve. Seated between two grey pillars, holding the scales on one hand and an upright sword in the other, Justice is the manifestation of law. Cloaked in regal red, with a squared crown representing rational thought and her white shoes declaring her pureness, Justice combines logical assessment with the need to listen to one's intuition. A purple veil hanging between the two pillars, implies that Justice is here to deliver the wisdom of a Higher power. Whether we are waiting on some personal or professional assessment or we are dealing with legal matters, Justice reassures us that, if we have been truthful and virtuous, we have nothing to fear. But if we are quick to judge a person or a situation, we should ask ourselves: would we apply the same standards to us?

Card Number: 12
Card Name: The Hanged Man

The Hanged Man asks us to let go of what we previously thought possible, or inevitable. Hanging by his right foot, The Hanged Man has chosen this fate on his own volition: as his free left foot shows, he can disentangle himself at any time. The Hanged Man seeks clarity and is willing to suspend himself from the Tree of Life in order to gain a different perspective. His red pants and blue shirt symbolize a balance between his passions and his controlled emotions, whereas his yellow shoes and his vibrant halo are symbols of his brilliance. His state of surrender is teaching us patience and alerts us that the time is not right yet to make any big changes. If we "hang in there" a little bit more, answers will surely come. But let's be honest with ourselves: do we perhaps love to play the martyr? Drawing attention to the sacrifices we've endured for the greater good?

Card Number: 13
Card Name: Death

Don't be afraid, dear one! The Death card's message is kind and necessary: we shouldn't resist change. As the sun sets Death rides on his white horse, his banner of a five-pointed flower representing change. A skeleton in a black armor, Death is at the same time inevitable and indestructible: no one can escape the change he brings, although many (from a bishop to a child) will try. In the river behind him, a black boat is heading towards the Towers of the setting sun, already carrying the soul of the fallen king who sleeps peacefully and eternally underneath Death's horse. Knowing that transformation is one of the most important aspects of life, Death wants us to embrace the closing of a certain chapter. It's the only way for us to start a new, better one. As long as we don't hold on to grief more than we really have to...

Card Number: 14
Card Name: Temperance

Temperance is a reminder for the need of diplomacy: we need to listen to both sides of the argument and to put strong feelings aside in order to overcome our differences. With one foot firmly on the ground and the other dipped in the water, the angel of Temperance is here to balance the elements and bring harmony. Simultaneously feminine, masculine and genderless, Temperance is delicately pouring water from one golden cup to another, representing the eternal flow between the conscious and subconscious mind, but also the need to temper our emotions. At the end of the road behind the angel the Sun burns bright, as Temperance paves the way to Enlightenment. It's by being equally open to other people's feedback and our own intuition, that we will manage to achieve harmony. As long as we don't use diplomacy as a way to avoid taking a stand.

Card Number: 15
Card Name: The Devil

The Devil is a warning that our worst instincts (jealousy, cruelty, greed, insatiability) may be getting the best of us, trapping us in a prison of our own making. Once free and comfortable in their nakedness, the lovers are now chained at the feet of The Devil. With the torso of a man, the feet of a goat and the wings of a bat (we should remember here that the Pagan symbols in this deck are sometimes used through a Christian lens), The Devil is a representation of what happens when our more animalistic side takes over. Looming over his victims on a pedestal, The Devil raises one hand in salutation while setting fire to the man with the other. Although he seems to have complete control over the lovers, their chains are loose and their hands are free: they could choose to liberate themselves at any time. Just like the lovers who are loosely chained however, we too can break free from our bad habits if we decide to. We don't have to completely surrender our sense of self-control just to have some fun. The Devil invites us to savor everything life has to offer, but the task of determining the cost is up to us.

Card Number: 16
Card Name: The Tower

The Tower requires us to embrace the change. When lighting strikes The Tower in this card, everything will be illuminated; no secrets will remain hidden. This sudden upheaval is happening so that we can be freed from any structures, relationships and bonds that do not serve us anymore, even if we were oblivious to their problems until now. The Tower appears to be a solid construction at first glance — but if we look at its base, it becomes clear that it was built upon uneven and shaky foundations. Amid the chaos wrought by the lighting, two people are falling from The Tower's windows in desperation. Surrounding them, 22 flames lit up the sky (for the 22 steps in the Major Arcana journey), symbolizing that this upheaval is too part of life and cannot be avoided. We need to jump from the crumbling structure in order to be saved, not freeze in panic or try to pretend this is not happening.

Card Number: 17
Card Name: The Star

The Star is here to light our way and guide us towards a better day. Just as the angel of Temperance had one foot on the ground and the other immersed in water, so does this naked woman, kneeling gracefully under the light of The Star. But while Temperance poured water from one cup to the other, in The Star the woman is opening the circuit; using two clay urns, she is taking water from the pond with her right hand and watering the earth with her left. Behind her, a bird perched upon a lush tree represents inspiration. Above her, seven smaller stars symbolize the seven chakras of the human body. An indication that the odds are in our favor, The Star urges us to start dreaming big once again and having hope that our dreams will be fulfilled. We should never be too jaded to believe in happy endings!

Card Number: 18
Card Name: The Moon
The Moon is here to guide us when not everything is as it seems. We can find our way through any uncertainty, as long as we accept the limitations of our rational mind and trust our intuition and subconscious. Ruler of the realm of mysteries, The Moon shines its light on the creatures of the night, bringing forth dualities in all things: the twin towers of Good and Evil are indistinguishable from one another; the tame dog is barking at The Moon like his wild brother, the wolf. Amid this dreamy landscape a crawfish steps slowly out of the waters to follow the path towards the unknown, beyond the towers and the mountains in the distance. Just like in dream logic, believing in things we may not entirely understand may be our safest way forward. We will need to embrace this period of uncertainty and not let our fears and anxieties get the best of us.

Card Number: 19
Card Name: The Sun
As his light helps the crops grow strong, so does The Sun's influence in our life brings us all our heart's desire. The dark night of The Moon is now but a distant memory: It's a new day and a brand new start. Four sunflowers, representing the four suits of the Minor Arcana, emerge from behind a gray wall whereas in front of it, a small naked child is riding a white horse, symbolizing innocence, vitality and nobility. The child waves a banner in the color of blood, representing renewal, new life and happiness. Health, prosperity and success in our endeavors; a happy family and home; new creative projects that will bring us the recognition we've been craving: nothing is impossible under the nurturing light of The Sun. We should be grateful for all our blessings, dear one.

Card Number: 20
Card Name: Judgement

Judgement comes to remind us to take stock of our actions and recognize our failings. As the Archangel Gabriel blows his trumpet, the dead are rising from their graves: men, women and children, naked and smiling, all extend their hands towards the Archangel in bliss. Hanging from the Judgement's trumpet, a square white flag with a red cross represents the four stages of life and the sacrifices needed in order to achieve purity and rebirth. There is still time to atone for any mistakes; to see our efforts rewarded and a conflict concluding favorably. Judgement, ultimately, represents forgiveness: forgiveness we need to extend toward others, but also to ourselves. Judgement will not be in our favor if we are not truly humble.

Card Number: 21
Card Name: The World

The World signifies our achievements, when we have come full circle and can reap our rewards. As the angel, the eagle, the lion and the bull (the four representations of the fixed signs of the zodiac) stood at the four corners of the Wheel of Fortune, so they stand now at the four corners of The World. A dancing woman, naked but for a purple cloth that represents wisdom, is constantly spinning within a circle of laurels, symbolizing evolution and success. Holding two white wands similar to the one The Magician held, the woman is bringing the magic full circle: everything has manifested as it was supposed to. We are content and complete, at peace with the people and the situations surrounding us. This perfect harmony is a time to rest and just be happy, before we start planning our next adventure. Can we pack it all up and try again?

Now that you've mastered the Major Arcana, it's time to dive into the Minor Arcana.

The Minor Arcana consists of 4 suits: Pentacles, Swords, Wands and Cups. Yes, dear one, they look a bit similar to the playing cards: there are number cards from Ace to Ten and then Pages, Knights, Queens and Kings for each suit. Only here the goal is not to collect as many Kings or Aces as possible as you do in poker. It's to understand the significance of this, the more "mundane" part of the tarot cards that speaks to everyday situations.

Ready to start?

Pentacles

The Pentacles suit is associated with Winter (that's why it's usually mentioned first) and with the element of Earth. Cards of this suit speak mostly about "earthly" matters such as money, material security, work, matters of the home, generosity and materialism.

Ace of Pentacles

Emerging from a cloud amid a grey sky, an aetherial hand surrounded by a halo is holding the Ace of Pentacles like a generous offering. The coin, its bright yellow color representing both material treasures (gold) and divine knowledge, contains an engraved pentacle: all four elements of life on Earth, bound together by Spirit. Underneath the divine offering, we see a garden with blooming white lilies — a symbol of innocence and purity, but also of abundance. A gate made from rose bushes, representing morality leads a yellow path toward the mountains in the distance and the higher knowledge that awaits there.

The Ace of Pentacles, like all Aces in the Minor Arcana, signals a new beginning. The Pentacles being the suit of Earth, this new beginning will most likely involve our career or our finances. It's a great time to make investments or start a new job, but this card is also a good sign when it comes to health issues or moving to a new home.

But the Ace of Pentacles can also imply a materialistic streak in our personality and a tendency to play it safe. Do we care about money a little too much?

Two of Pentacles

A young man wearing a very tall red hat, representing a passionate connection between his own thoughts and the divine inspiration that comes from the sky, is balancing the Two of Pentacles in his hands. Standing on one leg, the man holds the two coins intertwined in a green cloth, shaped like the infinity symbol: his balancing act is both rooted in the present and adaptable to chances, but also of a timeless quality. Behind him, the sea seems quite turbulent, with two ships performing their own balancing act, riding the waves high. It is a symbol of the man's turbulent thoughts and subconscious, but the fact that he is actually standing on firm ground, wearing green shoes, means that he is currently thriving despite the challenges.

Like the man in the Two of Pentacles card, we too are currently thriving — although it probably takes a lot of multitasking. Whether it's working two jobs and having two sources of income or simply weighing our options and budgeting wisely between our needs and wants, the Two of Pentacles is a sign that we are currently in perfect balance.

The Two of Pentacles however is a volatile card: the tables can be overturned very easily, leaving us feeling overwhelmed. Have we taken on more responsibilities than we can handle?

Three of Pentacles

A young man is working as an apprentice stonemason at a cathedral, where the Three of Pentacles are carved in the stone. He momentarily stops working to acknowledge the two people beside him: a priest and a nobleman dressed in a colorful outfit. They are holding the plans for the design of the cathedral and they seem eager to discuss them with the stonemason. Despite his more modest clothes implying a lesser social status than the other two men, the stonemason is standing on a bench and is being looked up to, indicating that although they all come from different walks of life, this construction is a teamwork where practical skills are necessary and held in high esteem.

The Three of Pentacles means that we will need to work with a team in order to achieve our goals — we shouldn't hesitate consulting people who come from a different background than ours. The Three of Pentacles is also a sign that we are honing our skills and getting valuable experience. We are on our way to greatness.

But the Three of Pentacles can also mean we are relying too much on what other people think about us, or about our work. Would it be better to shut down the outside noise and just focus on our work?

Four of Pentacles
A man, sitting on a stone bench overlooking a city, has a firm grip on the Four of Pentacles. One of the coins is balancing on his head, over his golden crown, while the others are stomped underneath his feet and held close to his chest, representing an unwillingness to part with wealth or material comforts. His black fur coat over his red cloak is keeping him warm, but it is also a symbol of how his wealth has isolated the man from all the people in the city behind him. The position of the man's hands around one of the coins resemble Ouroboros (the snake that feeds on itself), further indicating a closed system with no space for outside influences.

The Four of Pentacles is certainly a positive card for our bank account. It denotes financial stability and material comforts, a luxurious home where we are being surrounded by beautiful things. The card also speaks to our ability to save money, often to a great social cost, like avoiding going out with friends in order to not overspend.

But the Four of Pentacles is also a great warning that we have become too greedy and stingy with money. Are we losing our inner joy just to add a few more coins into our savings?

Five of Pentacles

During a snowy night two raggedy beggars are passing outside a church, the Five of Pentacles gleaming with light from its stained glass window. The beggars are scarcely clothed, partially barefoot and one of them is using clutches, a representation of the many adversities a person can face in life. The church window has a warm glow and its decoration with leaves, flowers, and a candelabra holding the Five of Pentacles, symbolizes the possibility of safety and abundance that is currently being denied to the two poor passers by. It is also possible however that the beggars are so preoccupied with their own struggles, they don't notice that salvation is within reach.

The polar opposite of Four of Pentacles, Five of Pentacles warns us about hard times and financial adversity. Perhaps we will be faced with unexpected fees to pay, or spent a period of austerity to compensate for previous overspending. Although a worrisome card, the Five of Pentacles is mostly here to remind us that hope and help are always within reach, we just need to know where to look.

But the Five of Pentacles can also be a warning of a more dangerous kind of poverty: the emotional one. Have we been isolating ourselves from the beloved people in our lives, those who are our true source of wealth?

Six of Pentacles

Almost like in a continuation of the story depicted in Five of Pentacles, here the two poor beggars seem to have found mercy and charity under the protection of the Six of Pentacles. Wrapped in warm cloaks, they are kneeling in front of a man who is handing them out coins with his right hand while holding a scale with his left — suggesting an evening out of resources and, perhaps, karma. The scale is almost in balance but not fully, hinting that it is better to always err a bit more on the side of giving. The city with its high rising towers in the background brings to mind the rich ruler of Four of Pentacles, only this time the wealthy man has left the isolation of his rich and secure home to help out the less fortunate.

Whether we identify more with the giving or the receiving aspect of Six of Pentacles, this card is here to remind us that both are necessary in life. We shouldn't be too proud to ask for help, or too cold hearted to help others. It doesn't have to be about money even: charity takes many forms.

The Six of Pentacles however can be a perfect example of how good intentions, sometimes have bad results. Is constantly giving to someone making them too dependent on us?

Seven of Pentacles

After raking leaves for what seems to be really long time, a man is currently resting on his rake, admiring the pile of leaves that is blossoming with the Seven of Pentacles. He looks slightly despondent and tired, as if he can do nothing more at this point but wait, although upon closer inspection we can see there is more work to be done -- and more to be gained by doing it. The man is wearing two different colored shoes, a symbol of being halfway there.

The Seven of Pentacles represents that lack of energy we feel toward the end of the working week, when the reward of the weekend is within sight, but not there yet. In a broader sense, Seven of Pentacles represents the need for patience. We have been working hard and perhaps we haven't yet seen the result we would like. But the best is yet to come if we just keep going.

The Seven of Pentacles also warns of our tendency to be distracted, when a task becomes repetitive and boring. Is it taking us longer to finish our work because our head is not in the game?

Eight of Pentacles

A man wearing a work apron and straddling a bench, an allegory for him being "on top" of the situation, labors hard with etching the coins in Eight of Pentacles. He is very present, focused and diligent in his craft and he has already finished a stack of pentacles who are now attached to a tree, suggesting growth. His red trousers and shoes represent his passion and determination, while his blue shirt shows he is calm and serene in his work. A town is visible further away, a further representation that, unlike his Seven of Pentacles counterpart, this man has left all distractions far behind.

The Eight of Pentacles is a sign we are in the "zone", taking pleasure in our work and in the reputation we are building for ourselves. Apart from actual work matters (a possible promotion that comes with its share of extra responsibilities and a raise), this card may also represent our ability to think practically, use the tools that we have in any given situation and ultimately excel at anything.

But the Eight of Pentacles also warns us about the dangers of workaholism. Have we become too enveloped in our work that we've forgotten to have a life?

Nine of Pentacles

A lavishly dressed woman enjoys the bounty of her vineyard, surrounded by the Nine of Pentacles. She holds a hooded falcon in her left hand, a symbol of her intellectual superiority but also of her self control. The gold and red colors of her clothes represent an enviable financial and social standing, whereas her light touching of the grapes and the coin suggest that the woman is not too concerned about money. Further financial stability is implied by the large house at the back whereas in front of her, on the ground, a small snail signifies that this luxurious life took her a while, but her patience has finally been rewarded.

Like the woman in the NIne of Pentacles, so are we able to create our own safe space, exactly as we want it. Whether it's an actual home, an unconventional relationship or an allegory for our own state of mind, the Nine of Pentacles is here to remind us that we already have everything we need in order to be happy.

The NIne of Pentacles however can also represent a tendency to show-off. Are we living beyond our means simply to impress other people?

Ten of Pentacles

An old man is sitting in the company of two dotting dogs, a couple and a child just further away: it's a family gathering, accentuated by the Ten of Pentacles. The old man's vividly decorated robe suggests his many accomplishments, with patterns of vines and grapes speaking of a luxurious lifestyle. He is petting one of the dogs while the child is petting the other, indicating a family that is bonded together by trust and loyalty. They all seem to be inside a castle's walls, a symbol of prosperity at home and financial security.

Like all the cards with the number ten in the Minor Arcana, the Ten of Pentacles represents the culmination of our efforts; our hard work being rewarded. Whether it is a much wanted promotion or a source of income that will really make a difference in our lives, the Ten of Pentacles speaks of abundance and prosperity. If we are considering moving to a bigger house, this card is a very positive sign that we should.

The Ten of Pentacles, although an inherently positive card, can also be a sign that we are using our newfound wealth (or our family's wealth) in an immoral way. Are we trying to buy ourselves special treatment?

Page of Pentacles

Standing on a green and luscious hill, the Page of Pentacles is admiring his fortune. Dressed in brown and green, to signify stability and prosperity, the page has nonetheless a vibrant red hat on, a sign that he is passionate and proud of his new achievement. A small grove of trees to the left and a plot of freshly plowed land on the right signify a fertile ground for new developments and a good potential for success. There may be difficulties ahead, implied by the mountain range lining the horizon, but for now the Page of Pentacles is in a good place.

Like the Page of Pentacles, so will we achieve the most when we combine ambition with diligence. Whether it's making plans for the future, studying hard or choosing to help and support a friend, the

Page of Pentacles reminds us that good things will come as long as we stay loyal, grounded and kind. We don't have to rush progress.

The Page of Pentacles however can also be a warning of sometimes being too timid for our own good. Are we not being as supportive and proud of ourselves as we are toward others?

Knight of Pentacles

The Knight of Pentacles is sitting on his black steed, a golden pentacle in his right hand. He's positioned on a hill overlooking his surroundings, a newly plowed land spreadings out at the foot of the hill. The Knight of Pentacles looks determined and calm, as if carefully considering his next steps. While the other knights of the Minor Arcana have plumes and wings on their helmet, this knight has green leaves, suggesting that his ambition is to preserve and protect what he already has, rather than go hunting for more.

The Knight of Pentacles is the perfect embodiment of the phrase "slow and steady wins the race". By being efficient and reliable, we will achieve better results than if we'd stormed into a situation without thinking things through. There's nothing wrong with having a routine.

The Knight of Pentacles however can also exasperate people with his seemingly slow pace and lack of apparent progress. Being a creature of habit is one thing, but are we being too stuck in how we're used to doing things that we don't see there is a better and faster way?

Queen of Pentacles

The Queen of Pentacles sits on her ornate throne, amid a lush forest. Her throne is carved with patterns of cherubs, ram's heads and fruit, symbols for fertility, abundance and love. Rose bushes are hanging over her and flowers abound by her feet, further depicting this queen's affinity for abundance and her love for things that bring joy to the senses. A red rabbit near her feet is a sign of her maternal and protective nature. The combination of red, green and white in her dress, along with the blue mountains and the yellow sky, symbolize that the Queen of Pentacles is the sum of many different qualities, a complex character who can best be understood as mother who will do anything to provide a safe and comfortable home for her children.

The Queen of Pentacles may represent our relationship with our mother, or some other female figure in our lives who always supports and nourishes us. This card also speaks to the supportive and nourishing aspects in ourselves and our ability to "turn a house into a home". It's overall a positive card, especially with regards to practical and domestic issues.

But like any overly doting mother, sometimes the Queen of Pentacles can be overbearing. Are we smothering our loved ones in our certainty that we know what's best for them?

King of Pentacles

Secure and proud within his castle walls, the King of Pentacles sits on an ornate throne decorated by four bulls; a symbol of steadfastness, willpower and virility. His long robe is richly decorated with vines and grapes, a depiction of success and abundance. Grapes are lying by his feet as well, scattered among luscious greens and flowers. He holds a sceptre in his right hand for cosmic power and authority, and a pentacle coin in his left for material manifestation. His left foot is resting on the head of a beast he's slain, suggesting a man of self-control.

In contrast to other Kings, the King of Pentacles can clearly appreciate the nice things in life — and he urges us to do the same. Whether he's representing a male mentor-like figure in our lives, there to help further our career, or our own steadfastness and ability to rise to the top of our field, the King of Pentacles is a very positive card. Success is here, and we should enjoy it.

But the King of Pentacles can be notorious for his inflexibility and resistance to change. Being steady and true to one's beliefs is admirable, but at what point does stubbornness become a hindrance?

Swords

The next suit is the Swords suit. Associated with Spring and with the element of Air, cards of this suit concern matters of the mind: our thoughts, worries, misconceptions, communication and ideas, the concept of truth and lies.

Ace of Swords

Emerging from a cloud amid a grey, downcast sky, an aetherial hand surrounded by a halo is brandishing the Ace of Swords. The sword is double-edged, a symbol of sharp wit and honesty, while a golden crown seemingly floats at its tip with a laurel wreath hanging from each side — all symbols of success, clarity of thought and divine inspiration. Three flames can be seen on each side of the sword, representing an equal distribution of knowledge but also a warning: truth will not always be easy, or pleasant.

The Ace of Swords is that "aha!" moment we have when everything suddenly fits together and makes sense. It can be a sudden revelation of something that was kept hidden from us: a shock at first, but we will become stronger and more successful for knowing the truth. This card also signifies a new, successful idea or project, as well as good developments in health related matters.

But like any double-edged weapon, the Ace of Swords can hurt both ourselves and those we point it against. Is honesty always the best policy? Or is sometimes saying nothing simply the most decent thing to do?

Two of Swords

With her back at the sea on a moonlit night, a blindfolded woman is seated at a stone bench. Her hands, folded in front of her chest, are brandishing two very long swords, each one pointing at a different direction. There are clearly two paths that the woman could take, but her blindfold forbids her to look at either. In the water behind her, two small and craggy islets symbolize possible obstacles, whereas

The Moon above acts both as an advice to listen to our intuition and a warning to not be fooled by illusions.

Two of Swords is a card that denotes our inability to make up our minds and move forward. The choices are there, and one of them is the right one for us — but to find it we need to spend some time gathering more information and not blindly jump to conclusions.

But like the woman in the Two of Swords card, we may also be responsible for our own lack of clarity. Are we too afraid to face the truth and make a hard choice, that we spend too much time in needless deliberation?

Three of Swords

Dark, grey clouds have gathered in the sky; a heavy rain is falling. The grim weather, a metaphor for the sorrow and grief that are to come, is contrasted by a bright red heart, pierced with the Three of Swords. The three wounds inflicted by the swords may represent the betrayal of a loved one, or heartbreak from the loss of a person or a relationship that was dear to us.

Although the Three of Swords is certainly not an auspicious card, its most valuable lesson is that our current pain and heartbreak can be used as a compass. They can point us, if not to where we need to be, at least to where we need to be away from. Because the message of the Three of Swords is very clear: we cannot carry on as we were, pretending we are fine.

But the Three of Swords can also indicate a love triangle that we are unable (and unwilling) to give up. Can our heart sustain two loves at once — and at what cost?

Four of Swords

Amid the calmness of a sanctuary, a knight lies eternally inside his tomb. On the wall above him, three swords are hanging vertically, a representation of the wounds he's suffered in the past. A fourth sword, placed under his tomb, signifies that his struggles have now ended: the knight's spirit is finally resting peacefully, something we can also gather from the position of his hands, as if he was in prayer. A stained glass window at the left part of the wall shows a depiction of a woman and a child in bright, warm colors, as if welcoming the fallen soldier back home in a loving embrace.

Four of Swords is all about the stillness that comes after the storm the Three of Swords wrought in our heart. Unlike the knight in the card though, we don't need to rest eternally. Whether we are talking about a literal nap amid a stressful working day, planning a vacation or simply taking a step back and trying to find inner calmness, thanks to the Four of Swords we will feel a sense of renewal when it's time to get back to the world again.

But the Four of Swords can also be a sign that we tend to take too many "breaks" from reality. Are we keeping ourselves hidden out of fear, to avoid getting hurt again?

Five of Swords
As the grey clouds dissipate revealing a blue sky, so is the conflict that took place in Five of Swords apparently over. A red haired man is in the process of gathering the fallen swords: he currently has two resting on his left shoulder, while picking up a third with his right hand. Two more swords are scattered in the ground, perhaps belonging to the two figures that are now walking away from the battle, toward the cleansing and healing waters of the sea. The man is looking at the two soldiers, but his look is indecipherable: are they his recuperating allies, or his vanquished enemies?

Five of Swords is a reminder that we always lose something in every conflict we choose to participate in — even when we have seemingly won. There is no honor to be found in needless fighting. Even if we believe we were on the right side of an argument, we should always remember to pick our battles.

But Five of Swords also represents our tendency to make ourselves miserable by getting hang up in past annoyances. Are we still behaving like a victim, lamenting something that's over and done with?

Six of Swords

A boat is being rowed in the calm waters, toward a peaceful-looking land. Riding on the boat is a woman completely covered in a yellow cloak, a symbol of the knowledge and wisdom that she has acquired through the many adversities she has faced. Next to her, a small child, depicts the innocence that is not yet destroyed. The Six of Swords are surrounding her, three in each side, acting both as a shield and a memory of the losses the woman and her child may have suffered.

As the boatman of Six of Swords is slowly and safely taking the family of refugees to a better place, so do we, slowly but surely, start to distance ourselves from a bad person or situation. Whether this takes the form of an actual trip, a bigger move to another place to live or simply an internal disentanglement from what has caused us harm, Six of Swords is definitely a welcome sight.

Although Six of Swords is a very gentle and positive card though, we should be careful not to confuse "moving forward" with "running away from problems". Have we left behind unresolved issues that are bound to catch up with us soon?

Seven of Swords

A man is seen leaving the military camp in a rush, a poignant red fez and shoes contradicting his otherwise humble clothing and betraying his fickle nature. He is carrying all the stolen swords he can manage (five of them are in his arms, but he has left two behind) obviously thinking he's gotten away with it himself. Unfortunately for the thief, a group of soldiers further away may have spotted him. The dark cloud gathering behind them warns that this theft will have heavier repercussions than the thief expected.

Seven of Swords is the card of secrets and deception — and of the small details that can "give us away" right when we thought we had managed to avoid getting caught red handed. Whether we are the ones doing the deceiving, or the ones being deceived, this card is always a warning to pay more attention around us and not take anything and anyone for granted.

The Seven of Swords can also signify a general lack of trust that has resulted from our less-than-ideal behavior. How can we demand the trust of others when we are not entirely trustworthy ourselves?

Eight of Swords

A woman, bound and blindfolded, is cautiously treading treacherous and slippery ground surrounded by Eight of Swords. She is using only her feet to feel her way forward; a slow, frustrating and impossible task. Behind her, placed on top of steep cliffs and overlooking the landscape, is a castle representing the days of comfort and security, now long gone. Yet the woman, much like the woman in Two of Swords, could simply choose to remove her bondage (which is nothing but a loose fabric) and free herself. It is clear that what's stopping her are not her external limitations, but her own limiting thoughts.

When the Eight of Swords appears, we need to arm ourselves with patience and, like the woman in the card, carefully put one foot in front of the other. Whether it's a relationship, a job or a financial situation that has us feeling powerless, the Eight of Sword reminds us that we can make it through — the only thing keeping us back is our own fear.

But the Eight of Swords can also represent the part of ourselves that wants to completely give in to a situation or a person, despite knowing it will probably cost us. Are we surrendering the control of our life to someone undeserving?

Nine of Swords

A person is sitting up in bed in the middle of the night, unable to sleep. We can't tell if it is a man or a woman, as they cover their face in their hands in desperation, a sign that they have lost themselves in despair — they can no longer stand to even look at the situation they find themselves in. Nine swords are hovering against the black backdrop, representing all the threatening thoughts looming over that person's psyche. The mattress of the carved, wooden bed is thin, providing little comfort, while the duvet is a patchwork of symbols: thorny roses and astrological signs, symbolic of the forces of destiny and the struggles of everyday life.

Nine of Swords is perhaps one of the least comforting cards; an embodiment of our worst fears. However, this card is here to remind us that these dark thoughts that keep us up at night are nothing more than that: just dark thoughts. Maybe right now we are feeling vulnerable and insecure, but these feelings will melt away the next day, when the sun comes up.

Nine of Swords is also a reminder not to face our demons on our own. When we are going through an existential dark night of the soul, isn't there someone we could call for help?

Ten of Swords
A man is lying face down in the mud, stabbed with the Ten of Swords. His red cape reminiscent of a bloodbath, represents his past victories which could not save him this time, while his yellowish hand is eerily twisted and lifeless. As to punctuate the sense of ending, the sun is yielding in the horizon, drowning in a heavy blanket of pitch-black sky. The mountains and the ocean however have a soothing blue color and the waters are still. There is silence and peace, at last.

Like all the suit cards with the number 10, the Ten of Swords indicates a finale, a curtain call. And despite the fact that this finale does not seem to be a very pleasant one, neither for the protagonist nor for us, we can find comfort in the fact that we have hit rock bottom. From now on, there's nowhere to go but up.

But the Ten of Swords can also signify our flair for melodrama. Have we really been stabbed in the back by others, or do we like to pretend so to excuse our own shortcomings?

Page of Swords

The clouds may be gathering in the sky and the wind blowing like crazy, but the Page of Swords is ready — his stance reminiscent of a baseball batter ready to strike. His thick hair, a symbol of youthfulness and vitality, is waving like a flag as the winds are gathering in strength. He may be on foot, but he is also unburdened by heavy armor, his simple robes allowing him to move swiftly and adapt. For now he has the high ground, standing on the green grass.

The Page of Swords is a great communicator, always bringing new ideas to the table. This card encourages us to speak openly and passionately about the things or the people who have sparked our interest. We may not be entirely sure yet how to bring our new exciting project to completion, or how to take the next step with that fascinating person, but our intention is set. And that makes all the difference.

The Page of Swords aptitude for communication however also makes him a talented liar. When we know that with very little effort, we can present a version of the events that serves our needs better, what's keeping us honest?

Knight of Swords

The sight of trees bending from the wind and the sharp edges of the clouds herald the coming of a storm. Unfazed, maybe even excited, the Knight of Swords is charging ahead with his sword raised — forward and upward, signifying progress and expansion. The plume of his helmet and the fiery mane of his noble steed are animated both by the winds of storm and the winds of the speed with which the Knight of Sword charges forward. The horse's saddle is decorated with flying creatures: butterflies and birds, representing speed, quick wit and freedom of thought.

The Knight of Swords is an unstoppable force that wants to take us along for the ride: when this card appears, there is no room for hesitating or seconguessing ourselves. Whether we want to grab the attention of a potential new love interest or achieve a professional milestone, the Knight of Swords is giving us the horsepower to hit our goal, fast. Where there is a will, there is a way.

But as the Knight of Swords does not seem to care about the well being of his horse while he marches on as fast as possible, so do we sometimes become insensitive to others in our hurry to get things done.

Queen of Swords

As if asking her subjects to rise up to the occasion, the Queen of Swords is raising her left hand, holding a sword upright with the other. Behind her the sky is accumulating clouds but the Queen seems to be rising above them. Her rational grey robe is adorned by the blue of the sky, representing emotional stability and clear thinking. Both her crown and the carvings of her throne depict winged creatures, from cherubs to butterflies, symbols of divine inspiration and the free flow of ideas. Flying above her head, a single bird symbolizes the holy spirit, making the Queen of Sword's judgement a fair and wise one.

Like the Queen of Swords, we too are expected to exercise a fair judgement in all things and use our communication skills for good. This card also represents a woman who can be our mentor, or the smart friend who always knows how to help us make it out of a tough spot.

But the Queen of Swords can also be a warning: do we consider ourselves too smart to mingle with other people? Being haughty will only bring loneliness in the long run.

King of Swords

With his face chiseled by a stern severity, the King of Swords sits on his throne. He is holding a sword in his right hand, but the blade is slightly tilted, as if ready to bestow a knighthood rather than attack. Hir robe, blue as the heaven behind him, represents the King's absolute control over his emotions and his total clarity of thought.

His cape however, glowing red on the inside, reminds us that we shouldn't be fooled by his calm exterior: this King is as powerful as the King of Wands, and will not hesitate to exert his power on others. His diadem and throne are adorned with butterflies and cherubs, symbolizing freedom of thought and divine inspiration.

The King of Swords usually represents that wise older male friend or mentor figure in our lives, who always seems to know what we should do, even when we are unsure of our own actions. But it also represents our inner voice of reason, for all those times when we need to put our head before our heart.

Like any powerful King, the King of Swords can be violent — although his weapon of choice will be words. But aren't words, when yielded with precision and bad intention, able to cut deeper than any sword?

Wands

The next suit is the Wands suit. Associated with Summer and with the element of Fire, cards of this suit speak to our fiery nature: our passion, our creativity, our sense of adventure and celebration, but also our power struggles and desires.

Ace of Wands

Emerging from a cloud, a white, aetherial hand surrounded by a halo, is holding a wooden stave: the Ace of Wands. The stave is still alive and growing: new leaves are sprouting while some leaves are being shed. The equal amount of leaves falling from each side of the wand represents a balance between the spiritual and the physical energies — and the equal opportunities that will be presented in both realms. In the distance, a castle behind some mountain peaks represents a journey that will be challenging, but worth it.

As the aetherial hand seems to be offering the Ace of Wands, so are we being offered an opportunity for renewal whenever we come across this card. Whether it is a new job opportunity, a project that will allow our creative self to flourish, or a newfound excitement about a person in our lives, the Ace of Wands is an indisputable sign to march forward.

But the Ace of Wands, although an inherently positive card, can also sometimes indicate a tendency to burn too bright, too fast. Are we too seduced by the prize (like the castle in the distance) that we underestimate the effort it will take for us to grasp it?

Two of Wands

Standing atop his castle walls surrounded by Two of Wands, a man is gazing towards the horizon. The castle, representing past successes and a reluctance to move forward, overlooks a beautiful but diverse scenery. Resting his left arm on one of the wands, the man is holding a globe in his right hand, symbolizing the infinite potential that awaits him once he ventures outside his castle walls. The man is dressed in fine robes in the colors of fire (orange and red), depicting his enviable current social status but also his zest for life.

Before embarking on our next exciting adventure, Two of Wands is here to remind us to take a pause for a moment and consider our best way forward. By taking inventory, focusing on our goals and applying careful deliberation, the success of our creative endeavors is all but assured.

But Two of Wands also warns us not to spend too much time on our comfort zone that we let an opportunity pass us by. Resting on our laurels may be comfortable, but does it also prevent us from winning more battles?

Three of Wands

Perched on the edge of a cliff, a man surrounded by Three of Wands is gazing at the sea, his red cloak depicting the victories he has achieved so far. Three ships, representing change and opportunities, are sailing in the horizon. The sky is yellow, representing knowledge, and the man is facing the sun — which is the source of all knowledge. The two wands on his right show the work he has done so far to get where he is, whereas the wand the man holds in his left hand symbolizes his plans for the future.

The Three of Wands indicates we've past the original phase of our journey or endeavor: we have ventured beyond our comfort zone (the castle in Two of Wands) and gathered valuable experience along the way. The future will bring expansion and success, as long as we are careful enough to keep planning ahead and flexible enough to change course as needed.

The Three of Wands however can also depict our tendency to "freeze" when something is not going according to schedule. When faced with delays, blockages and confusion, can we accept that all these hindrances along the way are also part of the journey?

Four of Wands
Rising high onto a golden sky, representing abundance, the Four Wands are joined together, creating a canopy of flowers. Underneath it, a couple dances in celebration, their hands holding flowers in the air. Both wearing white robes, representing purity, their cloaks are blue and red symbolizing the harmonious union of opposites. The couple stands in front of a grand castle, while more people are celebrating behind them.

Four Wands is the card of celebration — both literally and figuratively. In the literal sense, a wedding or a work party may be in our near future, where we are invited to attend and rejoice together with the people who are celebrating. But Four of Wands also represents all the things we have achieved so far, be they in our career or relationship, and the need to have rituals that honor our progress.

Four of Wands however, although a very positive card, can serve as a small warning not to be "all play and no work". Merrymaking is necessary when it is earned, but are we celebrating a bit too much, too soon?

Five of Wands

The Five of Wands are entangled in the air, brandished by five men holding them in opposite directions. The men are clearly interlocked in a conflict, all of them fighting multiple fronts at once, neither of them able to gain an advantage on the others. It is not clear, from their expressions, whether this is a friendly sparring match or an actual conflict — but their clothes, all in different colors, symbolize their dissimilar points of view.

The Five of Wands is here to remind us that a little healthy competition, at work or at any endeavor we are passionate about, can be a good thing as it motivates us to work harder. However, if we become too enamored with the conflict itself, we run the risk of forgetting what it is we were competing about in the first place.

The Five of Wands can also warn us of internal conflicts, that can make us lose our focus. Do we have so many contradicting thoughts and feelings that we've reached an inner impasse, unable to move forward toward achieving our goals? Are we being our own worst enemy?

Six of Wands

Surrounded by Six of Wands, a man is marching victorious. He wears a wreath on his head, symbolizing success, while another wreath is adorning the wand he is holding. Five more wands are raised by the crowd in celebration, as he gallops by. His horse is white, depicting purity and nobility, his green blanket symbolizing affluence and victory. The man's red cloak is a testament to his boldness and his pride in his achievement.

The Six of Wands is a very auspicious card, signifying that we have risen against the obstacles and now it's time to be rewarded for our endeavors. People will be looking up to us: we shouldn't shy away from accepting a leadership position, as we are clearly well-equipped to handle it.

But the Six of Wands can also mean that we are prone to "touting our own horn" a lot. When healthy pride in our accomplishments becomes vanity, we become blinded to the truth. In our attempt to impress the people around us, have we overplayed the importance of our own achievements?

Seven of Wands

Backed at the edge of a cliff, a man is fighting for his life. Holding a wand firmly with his both hands, he is pushing his opponents who are trying to overpower him from below, represented by the six other wands. His clothes (yellow, red and green) symbolize a combination of Fire and Earth; of passion and stability. Even though the odds seem to not be in his favor, he doesn't seem willing to accept defeat: as long as he doesn't back off, the battle is not lost.

Seven of Wands represent our inner courage and ability to "stand our ground" even when situations seem less than ideal. Staying committed to the path we have chosen and true to our convictions will get us through the adversity even if, at the moment, outside help does not seem very likely. It's always darker before the dawn.

The Seven of Wands however can also point to our infexibility and our inability to ask and accept help. Being constantly defensive will sooner or later exhaust us: not every battle can be won. Can we learn to let go when it's time to do so?

Eight of Wands

Like arrows, shot through the sky from a great distance, the Eight of Wands are on their way to land soon. Seemingly suspended in mid-air over a serene landscape, over a river which represents the flow of life, the wands are actually gathering speed by the second. Like the arrow of progress, the Eight of Wands are always pointing forward and, with no obstacles standing in their way, they will definitely land on their intended target.

The Eight of Wands, like a friendlier version of The Tower, represents change that will come suddenly into our lives: an unstoppable force we can only embrace and work with, not against. Sudden encounters and news from abroad should always be expected whenever this card shows up. In contrast to the Tower though, the Eight of Wands shows us that we have everything we need to navigate this change and make the situation work in our favor.

But the Eight of Wands can also be a warning against making too hasty decisions. When faced with a changing situation, are we perhaps reacting too spasmodically and losing our aim and focus? Even the most powerful arrow throw is useless if it is not aimed toward a specific target.

Nine of Wands
An injured soldier is holding on to his wand like a staff. Eight more wands are towering behind him and the soldier, looking weary and tattered, is glancing at them suspiciously. The tight belt around his waist representing his tight resolve, the man may be exhausted but he doesn't seem ready to give up. Maintaining an alert position, he understands that there may be another upcoming battle to fight, but perhaps that battle will be the last one.

The Nine of Wands brings us mixed messages: we are tired from our efforts, but hopeful that the attainment of our goal is in sight. Like the soldier, we too have come a long way and achieved a lot, very often at a big personal cost. So now that we are called to prove our worth once again, be it at work or at another creative endeavor we feel passionate about, we feel somewhat fed up. But we know we've come a very long way to give up now.

However the Nine of Wands can be a sign that our insecurity and paranoia are getting the best of us. Contrary to what we may be feeling right now, not all our colleagues or peers are "out to get us". Is our exhaustion making us see enemies that are not actually there?

Ten of Wands

Ten Wands are being carried by a man, who seems to be really struggling under their weight. Bundled together tightly, the wands are blocking the man's view: he is heading toward a village, a representation of reaping the rewards for his struggles, but he can't see how near or far the village actually is. All he can do is keep putting one foot in front of the other and trust he won't drop his precious bundle now that he's so close to completing his journey.

Like all the suit cards with the number 10, the Ten of Wands indicates completion. We have reached the end of a circle. We have achieved our goals — although perhaps we are too preoccupied by the many responsibilities that came with them, to be able to relax and take stock of our gains.

Ten of Wands also acts as a warning: have we taken on too much, risking a burnout along the way? Wouldn't things be much simpler if we just delegated our efforts and let others help us with the workload? Sometimes, sharing our success may be the only way to achieve it.

Page of Wands

Standing on a barren land, a yound and finely dressed man is holding a wand with both hands. He is focusing his gaze on the subtle growth of leaves at the wand's tip, the only source of fertile nature visible, representing the spark of new ideas and budding new interests in a world that perhaps is not ready for them yet. The man's golden hair are a symbol of his intelligence whereas the salamanders adorning his shirt signify transformation. He is on the cusp of discovering something magnificent and telling everyone about it.

Page of Wands speaks to our inner child, the one who is brimming with enthusiam while taking on a new hobby or when meeting a new person. Like the young man in the card, we too want to share our newfound interests with the world, but it currently seems like there is nobody around who would be interested in hearing us. Thankfully, the lack of audience doesn't dim our joy.

But the Page of Wands can also be a bit too restless and spontaneous for its own good. Are we starting too many new projects but failing to invest the time and seriousness needed to see them through to the end?

Knight of Wands

Riding on his orange horse, a symbol for his fiery nature, the Knight of Wands is determined and ready for action. The shirt over his glossy armor has the same salamander patter with the Page of Wands to indicate transformation — only here it seems a bit tattered at the end, a symbol of the Knight's bigger life experience compared to the Page. Holding his wand with one hand and his horse's reins with the other, the Knight of Wands is ready to jump to reach his destination faster. The mane of his helmet brings to mind flames, signifying his passion and urgency.

The Knight of Wands urges us to be bold and not hesitate. To "fall head over heels", whether it is for a new romantic interest, a new job or a new creative endeavor. No half measures will do, only fierce determination and going all in. The Knight of Wands is also an auspicious card when it comes to travel, new adventures and new beginnings in general.

But as the Knight of Wands can also come off as a bit too hot-headed, so can we, while caught up in our own storm, make mistakes of judgement or accidentally hurt the feelings of people around us. Can we temper our passion with the voice of reason to avoid falling headfirst into a blunder?

Queen of Wands

The Queen of Wands is sitting on her throne, adorned with symbols of pride, passion and happiness: lions, flames and sunflowers. She is holding a wand on her right hand and a sunflower on the other, balancing her more nurturing nature and her great intuition with her assertiveness, her rational thought and her ability to lead. A black cat sitting at her feet, hints to the fact that the Queen of Wands, although sweet and warm, can become a dangerous opponent if you cross her.

Like the Queen of Wands, we too are called to combine all the different aspects of our personality if we want to live our best life. Usually representing a female ally coming to our aid, to help us with a work-related or even a personal issue, the Queen of Wands can also represent our own inner female energy, who knows that beauty and intelligence are complementary forces, not mutually exclusive.

But the Queen of Wands can also serve as a warning that we have become too self-absorbed. Are we caught in the beauty of our own reflections and failing to face some of our flaws?

King of Wands

Gazing thoughtfully in the distance, the King of Wands sits on his throne. His long cloak, like the tapestry on his throne, is adorned with lions and salamanders that are biting their tails — symbols of infinity, transformation, strength and the ability to surpass obstacles. A small, live salamander rests safely at his feet, a hint at f the King's protective nature. On his fiery red hair, a golden crown shaped like flames represents passion and wisdom. The King of Wands is holding his staff with his right hand, while the left is resting calmly on his lap, signifying that he rules with effortless power.

The King of Wands usually represents a male mentor figure in our lives, there to help and guide us through professional and creative challenges. Combining bravery and determination with the wisdom of experience, the King of Wands is also our inner teacher: the accomplished part of ourselves who wants to spread his knowledge and help others.

But the King of Wands can also be overbearing and arrogant at times. Absolute power, even tempered with wisdom, can make us believe that we know what's best for people. Can we keep our ego in check while we help others flourish?

Cups

The last suit is the Cups suit. Associated with Autumn and with the element of Water, this suit is all about our emotional world: our powers of intuition, our need for romance, friendship, commitment, flirting and a happy ending.

Ace of Cups

Emerging from a cloud amid a grey, yet calm sky, an aetherial hand surrounded by a halo is holding the Ace of Cups like an offering. Overflowing with water representing emotional fulfillment and creativity, the Ace of Cups stands above a serene pond filled with lotus blossoms, a symbol of spiritual awakening and openness. A dove, carrying a wafer on its beak about to place it inside the Ace of Cups, signifies the Holy Communion and a a bestowal of blessings from above. Five streams of water running from the cup represent our five senses, uniting the spiritual with the physical realm.

As the aetherial hand seems to be offering the Ace of Cups, so are we being offered an opportunity for emotional rebirth. A sign that our feelings are being reciprocated or that a new relationship or creative project is on the horizon, the Ace of Cups is an inherently positive card. It's time to drink from the cup of life.

But the Ace of Cups can also imply a tendency to ignore our rational mind and make choices based only on our emotions. Can we be objective when faced with matters of the heart?

Two of Cups

Sheltered underneath the wings of the red alchemical lion, a representation of the attraction and harmonious coexistence of volatile forces, a man and a woman are offering the Two of Cups to one another. Gazing intently into their loved one's eyes, the couple is wearing wreaths on their hair, a symbol of their many achievements in life and the strength they each are bringing into this union. They are raising the Two of Cups in opposite hands, balancing the male and female energies, while the staff of Hermes between them signifies duality and good health. The couple clearly has the protection of cosmic forces and they are headed toward a happy life, on the little house on the hill.

The Two of Cups invites us to toast to a new relationship or partnership. Although predominantly a card that signifies our mutual decision to commit to our romantic partner, the Two of Cups is also a great sign for any kind of contract or agreement we are currently working on solidifying. When we find the perfect partner (romantic, platonic or professional), we become stronger together.

But the Two of Cups can be a warning that we tend to over-glorify our relationships. Are we glossing over potential problems in order to convince ourselves and the world that we have met our perfect someone?

Three of Cups
Three women, symbolizing the three Greek goddesses of charisma (Graces), are raising the Three of Cups while dancing under a radiant blue sky. The bearers of the Three of Cups, their long robes suggesting inner radiance, success and zest for life, are all crowned with wreaths and there is a plentiful harvest underneath their feet. Their hands are interconnected, a mark of their strong and harmonious bond, while one of the women is also holding grapes — an indication that these are clearly bountiful times, worthy of celebration.

A reminder to embrace the things that bring us joy, the Three of Cups invites us to unleash our inner Grace. On a more practical level, the Three of Cups speaks of all the exhilarating moments spent in the presence of good friends and enjoyable company. A party, birthday celebration or even a wedding may be in our near future when this card appears.

The Three of Cups however can be a warning that we have been oversharing, or relying too much to our friends and support system. Could we stand on our own and still radiate joy without being followed by our entourage?

Four of Cups

Under a sycamore tree, a man is sitting with his arms and legs crossed, a symbol of inertia and separation from the world around him. Appearing deep in contemplation, the man does not seem to notice or care about the lush green hill he is sitting on, or the gold cup presented to him by an aetherial hand emerging from a cloud. Three more gold cups on his feet represent all the things he has achieved or possesses already, and yet he fails to feel enthusiastic about.

The Four of Cups is a sign we don't quite feel content with how our life is currently unraveling. Although we may at first glance have everything we could possibly desire, there is an inner disconnect and an inability to accept life's many blessings. Just like the man depicted in the card, so are we being presented with an opportunity to chance our current situation for the better... if only we come out of our bubble, stop taking our blessings for granted and really look around us.

But the Four of Cups is also a warning that greed will get us nowhere. Do we constantly yearn for more in order to feel satisfied?

Five of Cups

A man wrapped in a black cloak, a symbol of loss and despair, is standing inconsolable near a river that flows incessantly, like the flow of emotions. With his body turned toward the water, the man does not seem to acknowledge all of the Five of Cups surrounding him. Three of the cups are emptied in front of him, their contents spilled on the ground as an allegory for emotional loss and suffering, but two cups are still standing behind the man — a symbol that the situation may not be as dire as he chooses to believe. At the far end, a bridge is promising to take the man away from this destitute situation and into a more positive place.

The Five of Cups may at first glance convey sadness and disappointment, but the card's true message is to stop focusing on what has been lost and be grateful for everything that is "still standing" in our lives. Only through a mentality shift that will allows to accept what we cannot change, can we move forward to bigger and better things.

The Five of Cups can also speak of a tendency to blame ourselves for situations that couldn't possibly have been within our control. Should we keep trying to punish ourselves for our perceived failings?

Six of Cups

Playing outside a castle, a symbol of comfort and security further accentuated by the presence of the guard in the back, two children are surrounded by the Six of Cups. Each cup is filled to the brim with verdant greens and white flowers, representing vitality and innocence. The boy, dressed in red and blue to convey his zest for life and inner calmness, is giving one of the cups to the little girl, as a token of friendship and appreciation. The girl is accepting the cup with white gloves in her hands, a further mark of innocence and purity.

The Six of Cups is a card of happy reunions and nostalgic trips down memory lane. Whether it speaks of meeting old friends or of rediscovering our inner playfulness, Six of Cups reminds us that it is important to look at the world through the wide, full of amazement eyes of a child.

But the Six of Cups can also imply a reluctance to "grow up" and change our habits. Are we so attached to how things and relationships used to be that we cannot see the positive aspects of starting something new?

Seven of Cups

Seven of Cups emerge from a cloud, bringers of a phantasmagoria that complete overshadows the man who is gazing at them. A different spectre is emerging from each cup: a human head or mask, for the man's public persona or potential partnership; a phantom, for the need to unveil the man's true spiritual self; a snake, for sexuality, knowledge and change; a tower, for security and stability; shiny jewels, for wealth; a laurel wreath, for victory and pride; a dragon, for the man's inner darkness. The man seems unable to choose which cup to pick, lost in the fantasies and illusions each choice represents.

The Seven of Cups is an indication that we are currently searching for purpose. Perhaps we are being presented with many choices, but neither of them is exactly right for us. If a situation or a person appears too good to be true, we need to consider whether perhaps they are.

The Seven of Cups also warns us: having an active fantasy is not a bad thing, but getting lost in daydreams about how things could potentially turn out, will get us nowhere. Has our head been stuck in the clouds for too long?

Eight of Cups
During a moonlit night, a cloaked figure is seen walking away from the Eight of Cups. In contrast to the Five of Cups though, this time the man's cloak is red — a symbol of determination and of the man's adamant belief something more exciting is waiting for him down the road. He has already crossed the river from where the Eight of Cups lie, signifying that his emotional detachment from the current situation has already begun. The Moon, representing the need to listen to one's intuition, seems to be looking down at the man who has a long and arduous journey in front of him.

The Eight of Cups is a sign that we are ready to embark on a path of personal growth and leave what no longer serves us behind. From ending a relationship or a work partnership to moving to a different appartment or simply quitting a habit that was bad for us, the Eight of Cups promises that change may be hard, but it will be worth it.

But the Eight of Cups can also be a warning we may be leaving behind things or people that are important to us, simply out of boredom. Are we being too quick to abandon ship?

Nine of Cups

A clearly rich man, wearing a red hat that represents his ambition and drive, is sitting on an ornate bench in front of a shelf where the Nine of Cups are being displayed. His arms crossed across his chest, the man's body language and self-contented face expression seem to convey pride of his achievements and a determination to maintain them. The blue cloth underneath the Nine of Cups symbolizes the man's inner calmness but also his conviction that he deserves everything he has gained.

The Nine of Cups is a sign that we will probably be getting what we wanted — whether it's material possessions or a fortuitous development in some area of our lives. Also called the "wish card", the Nine of Cups shows us that happiness is possible not just to attain, but to maintain as well. We need to have confidence, in ourselves and in the Universe.

But the Nine of Cups reminds us that in order to get what we really want, we should first be honest with ourselves about what that is. Should we be more careful what we wish for?

Ten of Cups

Framed by a halo and a radiant rainbow, a symbol of divine blessings and favorable circumstances, the Ten of Cups are floating in the sky. Underneath them, a happy couple are sharing an embrace, their hands held high as if saluting the beautiful day. Dressed in red and blue representing passion and emotional stability, the couple is clearly at that stage where their relationship is tested and true. Next to them, two children are playing, their clothes mirroring those of their parents. The lush, green scenery in front of them represents prosperity and happiness; a life that's nurtured by positive emotions the same way the trees are nurtured by the water of the stream.

Ten of Cups is one of the most positive cards to come across. We are surrounded by love and have achieved harmony in our relationships. A great card for marriage, having children or buying a house together, the Ten of Cups can also symbolize reaping the rewards of our efforts and basking in the appreciation of our community.

The Ten of Cups though can sometimes be an indication we are working hard to maintain this flawless facade in our relationship or marriage. Have we become obsessed with our pursuit of perfection?

Page of Cups

His back to the sea, the Page of Cups is inspecting the fish he has caught in his golden cup. The young man is dressed in pink and blue, representing a balance between his feminine, intuitive side, and his masculine, rational side. The lotus flowers on the Page of Cups represent his spiritual awakening, while the fish he caught on the cup symbolizes the birth of a new creative idea, endeavor or even a "hunch" the Page has — but is unsure what to do with it yet.

Just like the Page of Cups, so may we be feeling suddenly inspired and yet unsure what to do with our inspiration. This card is an invitation to nurture our creativity and try our hand in something new, perhaps an art-related hobby. A new flirt may appear in the horizon as well, and the Page of Cups reminds us to be sweet but also reasonable about it. It's not the time to fall head over heels yet, but it may be soon.

The Page of Cups can also serve as a warning of coming off as overly sensitive and childish. Do we really enjoy being perceived as the fragile flower?

Knight of Cups

His horse halting before crossing a stream, the Knight of Cups is holding a golden cup like a message to be delivered. Making his way forward slowly but elegantly on what seems to be a foreign land, the Knight of Cups features wings on his helmet and feet, a clear sign of his communication and diplomacy skills but also of his mercurial nature. Worn over his armour, the Knight's cloak is adorned with fish and running waters, representing intuition and inspiration, the red color an indication of this Knight's passion, idealism and charisma.

The Knight of Cups usually represents an offer we can't refuse, made by a very charming individual. Whether it's an invitation to a party, being asked out on a date or a professional opportunity, something exciting is definitely coming in the horizon. The Knight of Cups can also represent the progress we are making in our artistic endeavors: we're ready to share our work of art with the world.

But for all his charm, the Knight of Cups may not always be sincere. Are we being fooled by pretty words and failing to see the intentions behind them?

Queen of Cups

Her ornate throne placed right at the intersection of ocean and land to represent the different realms of emotion and reason, the Queen of Cups seems to be preoccupied by the trophy she holds. It's a cup, but closed (a nod to the subconscious) and adorned with religious symbols and two angels that seem to be guarding it on each side. Small mermaid children carved on her throne depict the Queen of Cups' motherly nature and giving soul, but also her potential for being overly dramatic and unpredictable. Her feet, dressed in blue slippers to signify calm emotions, do not touch the water: she is in control.

The Queen of Cups has been characterized many times as the "drama queen" of the Minor Arcana, but this is not always the case. This card invites us to pay attention to our emotions and intuitions, the deep reasons that are making us behave a certain way. We should not discount the messages our subconscious is trying to deliver: it is our intuitive nature that will set us apart and help us excel at a project or creative endeavor.

The Queen of Cups though is ultimately a card of emotions — and no matter how hard we try, we can't always keep them in check. Are we becoming blinded by them?

King of Cups

Whereas the Queen of Cups' throne was just on the ocean's shore, the King of Cups reigns right above it — but his feet, resting on his concrete throne, are never touching the water. Holding a golden cup in his right hand and a golden wand in his left, the King of Cups represents balance between the yin and yang qualities of assertiveness and acceptance. A fish-shaped necklace marks the King's creative personality, while the red details on his crown and cloak are a symbol of his power and ability to discern and make the most out of opportunities, further signified by the boat approaching behind him.

The King of Cups is a benevolent and generous ruler, who reminds us to always give first in order to receive. When this card appears, it may be an indication that we need to be diplomatic and not act based on our emotions alone, in order to secure success. The King of Cups may also symbolize a mentor, usually male, who can help us attain perfection in a project or endeavor.

The King of Cups however, especially in a love reading, can also represent a partner who is being a bit cold and reserved — or our own tendency to not show our emotions. Can we try wearing our heart a bit more on our sleeve?

CREATE YOUR OWN RULES AND RITUALS

You now hold the secrets of the tarot cards in your hands, dear one. Use them wisely. Understand your tools and their power — but also understand that power, ultimately, lies within.

For example: based on the type of tarot card reading you want to do, you'll find thousands of tarot spreads out there, some as simple as 3-card spreads, other as complicated as 15-card spreads. Don't be tempted to go for the complicated right away. Your intuition will work much better if you don't suffocate it with a barrage of images as you draw card after card after card.

Start small.

Begin by establishing a connection with your deck; it's a valuable tool and a partner in your work, so treat it with respect. Cleanse it with palo santo or sage, charge it with a selenite or a rose quartz crystal and make sure it's always dust-free. Light a candle, say a prayer to your matron deities, give thanks for the answers you will receive. And then, don't worry so much about what kind of spread you need to do: just pull a few cards that feel "right".

In general, you'll notice that as you're getting started on your divination techniques (and falling in love with the process) the temptation to add more elements, theatricality and well, props, will be immense. There are simply too many cute tarot cloths out there!

But at the end of the day, you don't need anything else but yourself, your intuition and the Goddess. If your intuition tells you to also draw a rune to clarify a tarot reading, go for it, no one will mind. If your intuition tells you to throw your cards on the floor like dice and see what comes up (or have your cat pick a card for you) then by all means dear one, go ahead.

The future is in your hands. It always has been.

CHAPTER 4: SEASONAL SPELLS

We've already seen how Pagans love to celebrate — and thankfully, the Wheel of the Year offers many opportunities for merrymaking!

In this chapter, we'll go through the major Wiccan Sabbats and Esbats and discuss the kind of energies that are present during each one, as well as some tips for seasonal spellcasting!

Are you ready, dear one?

SAMHAIN

Also called "a Witch's New Year", Samhain kickstarts the magickal Wheel of the Year. Celebrated on the eve of October 31, Samhain was one of the biggest old Pagan rituals that Christianity repurposed as All Hallow's Night and we all now celebrate as Halloween[28]. On Samhain, the veil between the worlds is at its thinnest, with spirits crossing over — so it's ideal for divination, spells to reveal ancestors' secrets and spells of rebirth.

An easy Samhain spell to try is making an extra plate of food for a beloved one that has passed (can also be a pet). Set it on the table along with a black or purple candle and give thanks. If you're celebrating with your family, honor the memory of the dead — if you're alone, talk to them. Once your dinner is done, take the offered plate outside and leave it for the spirits (a great idea to also leave a lantern alight all night long). Return to the table, with the candle still burning, and taking out your tarot cards (or your prefered divination method), ask the spirit of your beloved for guidance. Closing your eyes, let your hands be guided towards the right cards or runes to gleam their answers.

---

[28] Mandy Mitchell, (2014) Hedgewitch Book of Days: Spells, Rituals, and Recipes for the Magical Year, Weiser Books.

Yule

We've already discussed how Yule was celebrated in the Old Norse tradition and many of its Pagan customs have now become a part of Christmas. Yule falls around December 21, on the night of the winter solstice, the longest night of the year. Honor the Pagan traditions by gathering the whole family for a meal, let the Yule Log burn all night long (someone should take turns looking at it all night to make sure it doesn't go out) and hang mistletoe, the sacred plant of the Druids and associated with Freya, on your doorstep.

Yule is more of a time for celebration than it is a time for spellcasting. But there is one simple candle spell you can try: take a golden candle (to represent the birth of the Sun) and carve symbols with your athame to represent the things you want to awaken in your own life. The symbols can be as simple as a heart for love, or as complicated as the alchemical symbol for earth, to symbolize abundance — it's really up to you! Light your candle and sprinkle a pinch of cinnamon while it burns, for success on your endeavors. Chant four times:

"In this, the year's longest night,

light up the spark of new delight,

to the darkness shed some light"

Imbolc

Also known as Brighid's Day, celebrated on February 2, Imbolc is the time when Spring slowly starts awakening. This is actually a great time to dedicate yourself to your Craft: go out in the woods and see if you can find a branch to turn into yout wand; decorate your Book of Shadows and start using it; teach yourself to read the runes. Brighid loved poetry and writing, so try writing a magickal poem that contains the things you want to awaken in your life this Springtime. You can also make a wicker doll in her honor.

Candle magick is often used in Imbolc — choose a pale blue color candle and carve with your athame symbols of what you want to manifest. Do it in runes, to better appease Bridgid.

It's also a great idea to plant some bulbs in indoor pots, imbuing them with the intention of the things you want to bloom in your life.

OSTARA

Celebrated around March 21, Ostara officially marks the return of the Sun. It's one of those Pagan festivals that have been repurposed by Christianity, so you won't have trouble finding decorations for it: Ostara decorations are actually all about bunnies, little chicks and paste-colored eggs! (And yes, Ostara is where the word Easter comes from.) Feel free to paint eggs yourself, in the colors of the energies you want to bring into your life.

Ribbon magick is great for this Sabbat: pick ribbons in colors that symbolize the things you want to bring, change or manifest (green for wealth, yellow for happiness and creativity, pink for love etc) and after you purify them and imbue them with energy from the Elements, particularly Air, make knots on them and hang them from trees (or from your doorway if you're living in an urban apartment). As you tie them, chant:

"One knot to bring wishes my way

Two to be kind and let them stay

Three, four and five to open my door

Six to usher them in for evermore"

Beltane

Ah, Beltane! It's the second most important Pagan festival after Samhain — and its antithesis. Celebrated on May 1, Beltane is a feast of life, lust and sexuality. (Remember that maypole people used to dance around in villages of old?)

The best thing you can do in Beltane to be honest is drink and dance with friends, and find someone special to flirt with. Love spells are particularly strong around this time of year but only perform them to attract loving energy in your life, not a particular person (because bewitching someone to show interest in you goes against the Wiccan Law).

An easy and Wiccan-friendly love spell is to fill your chalice with wine (doesn't matter what kind, choose the one you love the flavor of), two strawberries, a sprig of basil and a pink quartz crystal. If you have a tarot card deck, you can also pick the Two of Cups card and place it under or next to your chalice. Leave it the glass near a windowsill, preferably somewhere where the moonlight can access it. On Beltane day, preferably before going out to party, pick out the strawberries and eat them slowly, consuming the loving energy. You can opt to drink the wine or spill it in the earth for your upcoming romance to root. Take the tarot card with you in your wallet.

Go out and have a magickal night!

Litha

Also known as Midsummer, Litha, the Summer Solstice, is celebrated on June 21st. Much like Yule, Litha is a time for celebration and eating out with friends, lighting bonfires and spend the day at the beach or near trees — leave the serious spellcasting for other Sabbats. That being said, Litha is ideal for flower magick.

Pick the flowers that symbolize the things you want to bring more of in your life (for instance, roses for passion, marigolds for happiness and marriage) and turn them into a flower crown that you'll wear for the day. And before you go to bed at night, leave a glass of milk outside for the fairies, to make sure your wishes are granted.

Shakespear knew a thing or two when he wrote about fairies in Midsummer Night's Dream.

Lammas

Celebrated on August 1, Lammas (also known as Lughhasadh) is a harvest festival dedicated to the Sun and to the god Lugh. This is a great Sabbat to awaken your inner Kitchen Witch and bake a loaf of magickal bread. The recipe you'll use for the bread doesn't matter, as long as you knead it by hand, manifesting your intentions with every movement. You can also use your athame to carve symbols on the loaf before you put it in the oven. Chant:

"Golden loaf of sun's reward

Bake my wishes as foretold"

Once the bread is out of the oven, still warm, take a piece with your right hand and eat it. You can accompany it with a glass of beer to further celebrate this Harvest.

Mabon

The second harvest festival, Mabon, is celebrated around September 21 on the autumn equinox. Mabon symbolizes the balance between darkness and light: you should light one black and one white candle (or just one grey candle) during this Sabbat.

Apples and pomegranates are considered sacred fruit during Mabon and you would be wise to consume both on this day. Save some of the apple seeds for your altar, to give as an offering.

Chapter 5: Final Words of Warning

All magic comes with a price. Isn't that what you see people saying in every fictional show or movie whenever anybody performs a spell?

"Price" may not be the right word for it. "Balancing act" is probably more accurate.

You see, dear one, every time you perform a spell or do a ritual, the ones you read in this book or others you will create and finetune on your own, you invoke a certain amount of Power. That Power may come from within you, and often does (although it's not recommended because then you're left completely drained and exhausted most of the time) but usually it is at least amplified, if not emanating, from the Elements, the Energies and the Deities you invoke.

You are taking something from this world, to shape it into something of your choosing and create something else. And because Nature hates a vacuum (scientists would agree to that) something else must be created to take its place.

Our world is not perfectly balanced as this above paragraph implies, that's true. Many times, balance takes a while to be restored — you may not even feel its repercussions in your lifetime. But restored it will be, eventually.

"Mind the Three-fold Laws you should three times bad and three times good."

This verse from the Wiccan Rede[29] describes in no uncertain terms that whatever energy you put out there, it comes back to you three times.

As we've seen, the Wiccan Rede is a Neopaganistic poem composed in the '60s to create some kind of a common code for the Wiccans — and the Three-fold Law is integral to it, as it is the

"An harm none, do as thou will" position. But the notion of getting back what you give is certainly not a novel one. Karma is a similar idea; the Hinduistic and Buddhist belief that one's actions and intentions shape one's future. Hinduism in particular has some other concepts similar to the idea of the Three-fold Law: Sanchita, Vartamana and Prarabdha, which talk about your accumulated works, your current work and your future endeavors as part of one chain of events.

Or, in plain English: who you've been influences who you are which influences who you'll become. It makes sense, doesn't it?

As for the "three times" part, we need to take into consideration how sacred the number three is to Wiccans, denoting the triple aspect of the Goddess as Maiden, Mother and Crone. Plus, the people who wrote the Wiccan Rede wanted to emphasize the importance of kindness and of doing good work, so getting three times more good things than you put out there sounds more motivational than saying "what you give is exactly what you get".

---

[29] "The Wiccan Rede" (Full Version) as depicted in The Celtic Connection website, https://wicca.com/celtic/wicca/rede.htm

If you are a Wiccan, of if you beginning to identify as one now that you've read this book, then I probably don't have to try any harder to convince you to follow this rule. If you are not though, or if this book made you realize you identify more with Pagans and/or Witches than you do with Wiccans, I need you to consider this very carefully.

You believe that you can co-create your reality, right? If you didn't, you wouldn't have gotten this far in this book. You believe that your intentions can shape your life and you can put out there the energies you want to put out there in order to live your life as you want it... right? Then ask yourself, dear one: if what you're putting out there is darkness (and not the Sacred kind), if what you're putting out there is ego and negativity, what do you think will fill your life?

We are what we do most often.

You may swear you're a good person until the cows come home, but if at the end of the day you're intentionally using magic to hurt others or to give yourself an unfair advantage then you will, sooner or later, get what's coming to you.

Please don't consider this a threat. It's not I, the author of this book, who will punish you for misusing magic. This book is not cursed. On the contrary, I've imbued it with only blessings and good wishes for you, to guide you in your journey (wherever that journey may take you). What I'm trying to say is that when you open yourself to negative energies, the negative energies listen. And they usually come — and bring some friends, in the form of unclean or restless spirits, with them.

Oh, they will entice you at first, make you feel powerful... that's how they operate. And then, they will convince you that you need them: that you need to accumulate more power or more of that thing you're currently after (Money? Attention? Affection?). After a while, even "more" won't be enough to really fill your soul. You'll get trapped in your own belief you can do everything and you'll keep tapping into your energy resources until you deplete them. Or, you'll keep serving these bad energies all your life (some people do) and then, when it's time to leave this realm for your next cycle of rebirth, you won't have learned anything. You'll probably have to be reborn under harsher circumstances, so that you can learn different lessons than last time.

That is not cruelty. It's not punishment or "paying the price". It is simply, unequivocally, Balance.

But it is this author's hope that you understand all this already. It is this author's hope that you've come into all this with good intentions, and you're leaving with even better ones. It is this author's hope that you'll use the things you learned in this book to make your life and the life of other beings (to the best of your abilities, of course) as full and radiant as possible.

It is this author's hope that you will be one with the Goddess, one with Nature and one with Yourself.

Be well, Pagans and Wiccan, Witches and Magicians.

Be kind, laugh often and make Magick. Always with a k.

Astrology Uncovered:
Introduction to Astrology

Twenty degrees up and down from the ecliptic and celestial equator, 12-star groups can be found and the name "Zodiac" was given to them in the dawn of times. This name allegedly comes from the Greek term "zodion", which means the "animal belt", and almost all of the names in it refer to animals. A common belief is that the names of the star constellations and their groupings came from the first hunters and nomads because they needed a proven method for orientation. When the age of agriculture arrived, determining the seasons of the year became necessary, and the motion of the Sun and Moon through heavenly constellations became determining factors for the meteorological and even political successes or failures.

Archeology has found firm evidence that the early humans from prehistoric times had an understanding of celestial movements and events. Many discoveries show that people of those ages carefully watched the sky and that they had precise calendars. Those calendars mainly portrayed the motion of the Moon, the Sun, and oddly, Venus and the star system of Pleiades. Why prehistoric men would have such an interest in aligning with the Pleiades or even Venus, no one knows, but this also raises another question. Why would prehistoric people even want to follow and measure the motion of celestial bodies to the extent that they were building huge systems of stones, and later on temples, to be able to track the Sun or other significant heavenly objects? Was it just for orientation, which is useful for hunting? Certainly not.

Astrology, together with astronomy because they were considered as one science, originated in Babylonia and Sumer. Both are considered one of the oldest natural science in the world. How come that the cradle of civilization had such knowledgeable astronomers/astrologers? If we forget about the official history for a moment and start speculating, could aliens, known as Annunakis, have taught them this art?

Scriptures mention that "angels" taught humankind the art of metallurgy, medical treatments and remedies. They even advised women how to start applying makeup and of course, they showed us how to "read the sky".

The whole area of Mesopotamia, including Babylonia, Sumer, and Assyria, is rich in archeological artifacts related to astronomical/astrological themes and many of them are dated older than 2000 BC. Babylonian priests were known for their superior knowledge about planets, stars, eclipses, and all geometrical aspects those bodies can form, which was used mainly for political predictions. Bear in mind that in those ages, there were no daily horoscopes published for the common people. Natal horoscopes were drawn just for the members of the royal families and astrology was also very useful for selecting the proper dates for building new cities or attacking enemies. This remained the norm almost until the last century because the natal charts of the "common people" were seen as absolutely unimportant.

Enuma Anu Enlil is the most famous archaeological artifact from these times. It is the compilation of 70 cuneiform tablets, which describe 7000 astronomical/astrological omens. During the following thousands of years, the science of mathematics was also developed, which was used for very precise calculations of the celestial positions and the creation of the first ephemerides. From Babylonian times, humankind inherited the habit of naming the planets after the gods and to associate them with mythical stories.

To this day, many modern astrologers claim that the original and most precise astrology called "Eden Astrology" can still be found in the areas of Iraq and Iran, but it is extremely hard to find astrologers who are practicing this art and who are willing to teach it, because astrology is outlawed in those two countries. Myth or truth, it's still hard to discover the answer.

Astrology was brought to Egypt around the 5th century BC by the Persians. However, Egypt was an extremely developed country in those times and it's hard to believe that they didn't know about planets and stars until the Persians came to conquer them. Whatever the case may be, Alexander the Great founded Alexandria and by the second century BC, this town became the location of the most famous university in the world. Ptolemy wrote an extensive work, *Tetrabiblos*, about the planetary characteristics, exaltations, triplicities, and many other basic facts. In those moments astrology, as we know it today, was born. Horoscope charts were made and analyzed in a very similar way as they are done today.

The knowledge about the stars was widely spread across the Greek territories and it was recognized as Chaldean (Babylonian) art. It continued to spread, naturally, over the whole Roman Empire and when the great kingdom fell, knowledge about astrology remained a secret

While the dark ages held power over Europe, the world of Islam continued the tradition of Alexandria's Great school. Many scholars went east, running away from rising the Christian dogma against natural sciences. The city of Baghdad became the new center of knowledge and many sciences in the forms as we know them today were founded there. The Arab world researched methodically so-called "fixed" stars and their influence on the life of our planet, and classified the system of calculating mutual relations between celestial bodies, which is known today as "Arabic parts".

When we look at the east, we are amazed by the levels of knowledge Indian or Hindu astrology achieved. The first notion of this art can be found in Vedas, which claimed to be the oldest known texts. By the times of Alexandria's greatest breakthroughs, Vedic astrologers had to deal with higher mathematics and very serious and precise astronomical observations. The legend goes that the ancient sage Bhrigu, one of the Saptarishis (seven sages who helped to create the universe), has all the horoscope charts of all people who were born and will be born on this planet.

Due to its close relation with astronomy Vedic or Hindu astrology deals with sidereal positions of planets and uses somewhat different types of aspects, while the meaning of all celestial bodies, zodiac signs and houses are the same as they are in the "western" school of astrology.

Chinese tradition is known for its concepts of yin and yang, and it uses somewhat different types of calculations, but astrology is present there from the ancient times and besides the popular Feng Shui, which deals with the energies of the Earth, Ba Zi art deals with heavens.

Over the Atlantic Ocean, Olmec and the Aztecs were known for their calendars and precise mathematical calculations when it comes to the position of our planets, especially Venus and, as you can guess, a constellation of Pleiades. However, later on, the Mayan calendar became the most recognized and famous calendar in the world.

Back in Europe, it didn't take a long time for astrology together with astronomy to rise again. Until seventeenth century, science was necessary if you wanted to become a doctor, for instance. All diagnostics and healing treatments were done according to the planets and stars. A Christian church wasn't so satisfied with this fact, but it was powerless due to the popularity and the cautious approach of astrologers in those ages.

However, when the era of humanism and education came, astrology was pronounced the occult science, or better yet, something which is not science at all. From that moment in time, it was separated from astronomy. An interesting fact is that Isaac Newton, the father of modern scientific thought, was the one to passionately love and study astrology.

A few hundred years have passed and astrology is back again. With the rise of modern psychology, astrology took a somewhat different turn, interpreting the planetary aspects through the inner or emotional states of human beings. Luckily, after decades of vague readings, astrology returned to its roots again, and as such, interprets the outer events and envisions the future.

Mistakes happen, indeed, but if the astrologer during the reading can see around 75-80% accurately your past, present and future events, challenges, losses, and triumphs, then you have found a quality consultant and you can count on that person to be your greatest ally for the planning of your future. Let's just not forget the words of JP Morgan: "Millionaires don't need astrologers, but billionaires do".

With this in mind and if you are interested in learning something more about yourself, you will find this book extremely useful, because it will help you to see clearly what are the meanings of the planets, signs, and houses in the horoscope chart and how to recognize your character, future challenges and even how to use those challenges for your success. This can be applied to all people and the most important part is that you will be able to predict the outcome of your relationships with others. You will also learn something about myths related to ancient gods and perhaps even have a little fun.

PLANETS

Through the eyes of astrology, our lives are determined by celestial bodies; such as, fixed stars, meteor showers, various flying objects and so on, but to be able to read astrological charts, you have to learn the basic traits of the main heavenly "influencers" and these are: Sun, Moon, Mercury, Venus, Mars, Jupiter, Saturn, Uranus, Neptune and Pluto, as well as the North and South Nodes of the Moon - Rahu and Ketu.

SUN

The ultimate deity in our little piece of this cosmos is the Sun. The Sun is the father of everything, the central body around which all others revolve. Its shine is the essence, the light, the life in us, and the energy source for photosynthesis, which is the basic metabolic process for plants and even for animals. We are all eukaryotes after all. Without the Sun, we are not able to exist. This is also the first god in any early religion and the founder of the yearly calendar because we have the spring and autumnal equinoxes, and the summer and winter solstices. Around those four points in time, all of our rituals were created and worshiped throughout the existence of humankind. Nothing else is so powerful and nothing else can create or destroy us like the Sun.

Its qualities are: center, masculine, warm and dry, royalty, generosity, responsibility, light, warmth, vitality, power, honor, glory, reputation, authority, healthy ego, stability, maturity, calm enthusiasm, goodness. If it's placed in an unfavorable position and in tense aspects with other planets, or points on the chart, it can result in: vanity, arrogance, narcissism, snobbism and so on.

The Sun, forming a beneficial aspect with the other planets, will always give the characteristics of someone who doesn't know about mean behavior, a person with classy manners, with good judgment, and a natural born leader. Its negative planetary aspects will portray a person who is pretentious, egoist, or untrustworthy; someone who ruins order or life itself.

The Sun is the king, a middle-aged man, rich, or in other terms, a very successful man. This star also represents the day of Sunday, the lion, cats in general, bees, royal and golden colors, castles, decorations, gold, glitter, expensive jewelry, blond hair in females, a man who loses his hair when it comes to males, France and all royal families. It is the vision and therefore symbolized with eyes. In male charts, it is mainly the right eye, in female charts – the left one. In the terms of medical astrology, the Sun is the heart, the spine and the bone marrow, vitamin D, and many claim that it is also vitamin A; all crucially important parts of body.

In the terms of music, according to Pythagorean ideas, this is the sound "do".

The conjunction of the Sun and Moon, and their placement close to the North or the South Nodes of the Moon and some fixed stars like the Pleiades, Hyades or Praesepe can show blindness. Positive aspects with the Moon bring unity between the will and emotions, and good relationships between parents. Negative aspects show the internal war between the masculine and feminine, between the father and mother in us, and metabolic turmoil.

If Mercury, or any other planet, is placed too close with the Sun, then it is considered as burnt, so in this case, reasoning is damaged by ego. In the other case, when Mercury is positioned a bit further, this describes a person with great intelligence and someone prone to leadership. Venus with the Sun in positive aspects will show an admirer of beauty and good manners. However, the opposite will indicate problems between emotions and pleasure on one, and ego pretensions on the other side. Mars and the Sun together in positive combinations will show courage and power, but in the negative terms, this is someone prone to conflicts and agitation.

The Sun and Jupiter point to the greatest ruler, the most spiritual teacher, genuine guru, but on the negative side this is someone who is gaining weight too fast, and someone who fights authority, creates obstacles, squanders money or other resources, and leads a shameful life. With Saturn, the Sun can represent a reputation earned by hard work and dedication, gains of properties and knowledge. In negative terms, this is the curse of the ancestors, the mark of trouble, of problems with the father or a fatherly figure, and a heavy burden to carry throughout the whole life.

Uranus and the Sun can form unusual psychology in a person and depending on the aspects, this can be a genius when it comes to scientific or technological breakthroughs, but it can also be someone with bipolar disorder or the plain "slave of fashion trends". With Neptune, the Sun gives the gift of art, especially poetry, knowledge of chemistry and biology, but the negative side can be shown as an inclination toward illusions of all sorts. With Pluto, this is the spirit with demonic powers which can create the highest good, as well as the lowest of the low.

MOON

Lady Luna is the mother. Yes, the Earth is our real mother, but when it comes to the projection of celestial bodies someone had to take the role of the mother and having in mind that the Moon depends on the Sun reflecting its light on us during the night, Lady Luna is perceived as the dark side of the light in us. This is not necessarily bad, but opposite to order and masculine rules.

The motion of the Moon had been the basis of counting days, or nights, and creating "months" known as the lunar calendar. The Moon needs around 28 days to complete its circle and this is the center point of the small cycle in us in comparison to the "big" cycle based on the motion of the Sun.

Its qualities are: cold and moist, reflects the light, feminine, distanced, moody, responsive toward outer stimulation, psyche, strong fantasy, dependence, softness, wonderings, changes, suggestible, subjective. And all of these traits could become positive, negative or even both at the same time.

The Moon is the day of Monday, the mother in general, mother holding a baby, baby, people in general, like a nation, women, middle-aged women, sea, water, lake, night, coldness, water retention, water overflow. The Moon represents everything soft and with big eyes, fish and water creatures, wolves, dogs, slimy insects, blue, silver and even white colors, pearls, isolated places, mirrors, Holland and USA too, lighter and softer hair and skin, left eye in the male chart, right eye in the female chart.

In medical terms, the Moon rules the stomach, breasts, and womb, and when the woman is pregnant, the "full womb". It regulates the flow of water in our bodies and the lymph system. Together with Venus, this is mother's milk in female charts and it's the quality of sperm in male charts. It can be any of the vitamins coming from the B complex and in music, it's traditionally considered to be the note "Fa".

Too close to the Sun or in square or opposition with it, the Moon is dried out. Emotions have been burnt for the sake of the ego, survival or due to bad psychological "inheritance" coming from parents or parental figures. The good aspects are softening the will and advancing in life in accordance with feelings, not just logic.

Mercury and the Moon are two very odd friends if they make mutual aspects. In opposition or square, those two celestial bodies imply the liar or the cheater, or deceiver. If this is not the case, the person's feelings and thoughts are harmonized and well guided. Good aspects with Venus lead to delicate and elegant tastes, enjoyment in romance and food, while the opposite brings some sort of "soap opera" in the native's life because emotions and sense of pleasure differ. So when I know that I shouldn't eat that cake or I shouldn't seduce that married man but I can't resist, then the whole drama is born and this can lead to some spectacular resolutions. Looking on this from the brighter side, this is how literature was born and is created today...and how it will continue to be created.

The Moon and Mars are very special when coupled. Negatively speaking, Mars destroys the Moon, people become senseless, especially women, cruel and extremely aggressive in some cases. It can also show pain, injuries, and surgical interventions. On the positive side, Mars can give the Moon persistence and tenacity to go through most difficult tests in life. Jupiter is all about gaining weight with the Moon, water plus fat, but it can also describe the purity of the mind and the soul.

Saturn and the Moon are performing great when positioned in auspicious types of aspects. Discipline is above feelings and the person is ready to suffer or to reshape its soul and body to achieve success. Negatively, this is loneliness, long, chronic diseases, troubles with older feminine figures in life, especially mother or grandmother. With Uranus, it can point toward magnificent and extraordinary ideas or plain madness. Although the aspects with Neptune can look similar, in this case, the person can be an exquisite chemist, doctor, poet or saint, or on the other side, the dark side of the Moon, the person can be a drug addict, someone lost in the world of inner illusions and a skilled cheater.

Pluto and the Moon? Resurrection, the hardest tests for the body, the edge of losing the soul, "I just came from hell" type of thinking, type of smile, type of revenge.

MERCURY

The mind, logic, logistics, operative memory, trickster, Jack of all trade and master of none, "trust me, I'm an engineer" type of showing off. "He" can "she" and "she" can return to "he" or the ultimate "it". Mercury is known as the messenger of the gods and it goes wherever no god or no man would even step. He or she is cold and dry and never further than 27 degrees from the Sun, which implies that logic is never apart from ego.

It represents communication, trading, short travel, marketing, streets, neighborhoods, hallways, markets, schools, offices, journalism, rumors, gossips, often "right to the point" references and information, healing, health and herbalism, nutrition, wheat, grass, seeds, nuts, vitamin C, small intestine, lungs, brain, nervous system, birds, insects in general, small animals; you can find Mercury everywhere. Wednesday is his day. In music, this is the tone "Mi" and in education, this is something you can apply in real life right now, a simple calculation, but very useful every time. The color orange, but it can change from honey to chestnut shades, also all pastel colors and shades of autumn leaves and fruits. From Belgium to Tunisia, from Brazil to Greece, you'll find him in many countries as the main ruler.

Mercury in good aspect with Venus is the skilled lover, sweet talker, and smooth operator. In approaching square or in a negative type of conjunction this couple points clearly toward a cheater or someone very unreliable, especially in a committed love relationship. This can also be the sign of rude or insolent language or even person's inner desires can look like this. With Mars, Mercury can lead someone toward enormous success in engineering professions, due to their mutual "fast thinker and skilled worker" symbiosis. In negative aspects, this is the sign of a very rude person, passive-aggressive, someone who had been beaten as a child and now beats others, problems with hands, palms, lungs, intestines.

Jupiter and Mercury's combination is the match made in heaven when paired properly by astrological aspects. Jupiter directs the soul toward the greatest heights of human achievements, purity of intentions and spirituality, while Mercury organizes the mind to be disciplined and fast when it comes to implementation of the noble Jupiter's teachings. The other way around is called total chaos of the mind. If you don't know exactly what this means, try to imagine an attempt to trade with God during meditation, and then try walking down the street with your eyes closed and your thoughts directed toward heavens. Some people can live like this, but not for too long, if someone else is not taking care of them all the time.

Saturn and Mercury together in the auspicious positions is the sign of a great mathematician, respectable and stable thinking and well spoken, especially as this person gets older. On the negative side, this is a problem with the speech or tongue, fear of speaking and expressing, loneliness when it comes to ideas and self-promotion and mind blocks.

Mercury and Uranus are known as the main trait of electricians, astrologers, geniuses and mad people. This is the basic model for electricity, in mind, in a body, in ideas. The conjunction of those two fast and furious celestial bodies frequently implies autoimmune diseases or neurological problems, or most likely both. In good aspects, this is the image of a spotless mind, but when bad times activate bad aspects of them, this is the clear danger of electrical stroke whether it comes from inside or outside sources. In those particular cases some medical diagnostic tools, like ultrasound or X-rays exams can damage such native.

A quality tarot card reader is known as someone with trines or sextiles between Neptune and Mercury. The same goes for a guitar player and if you add Venus to this formula, then you get the perfect musician, no matter what instrument is involved. Neptune is here to inspire, while Mercury serves to channel the message of intuition. If aspects between them are tense, this is the sign of a liar, cheater, or at least, messy speaker. Pluto and Mercury are indicating someone with heightened drama in communication or during usual daily obligations. This can also be the poisonous speech, but if positive, the person with this aspect can heal with just loud praying.

VENUS

She is pleasure itself. Is this good? Not necessarily, because Venus has the longstanding reputation of someone who challenged the almighty God or the Supreme Power or Energy (choose whatever you like the best) and was punished for her ideas and deeds. In western astrology, Venus is considered as a female planet, but traditional views look at "her" like Lucifer, the light bearer, someone who was most beautiful, skilled and intelligent among all angels. Those characteristics slowly, but surely led him to believe that he can be better than the God (Sun) itself and in the end, he was punished by being expelled to the underworld. Vedic myth concerning Venus differ somewhat, but the conclusion is the same. You will be punished if you start imagining your greatness greater than the Supreme Greatness. Vanity can be hell sometimes.

Venus is beauty, harmony, elegance, desire for material security, dancing school, wardrobe, court of law, garden, flowers, jewelry, shiny stones, fashion, sweets, especially chocolates, perfumes, assessors, romance, romantic literature, poetry, music, dancing, sheep, all small and soft animals. She is cold and moist by nature and her colors are blue, green, turquoise and even white. Her day is Friday. Her lands are Austria, Switzerland, Canada, China, Argentina and most of all, she loves beauty through an order.

Her organs are the throat, lower jaw, thyroid gland, neck, skin, and kidneys. She regulates the blood pressure and the levels of copper in blood. And her favorite sports, besides noble types of joy, like ballroom dancing, are qigong or yoga, disciplines known for their power of balancing and harmonizing inner energies. She is the queen of vitamin E, something necessary for the beauty of the skin.

Venus is "La", of course.

With Mars, this is the basic story of love, romantic pursuing and carnal passion. Negative aspects between them can cause havoc in a person's life, but on the brighter side, this is how art was founded in the first place. Jupiter and Venus are true love and devotion for spiritual teachings and, also, true love and devotion toward a good and useful sugar daddy, while on the negative side this is the sign that the person is not capable to budget for expenses or expenses tend to build up no matter what other safety actions are previously taken.

Saturn and Venus mean stability and tradition if positioned fine. However, on the other side, this is life without love, without true love, frustration, and coldness. Great for sculptors, horrible for lovers. Uranus and Venus usually meet through social media, airplanes or any other unusual place and time. There is the spark, there is the fire and there is one big nothing after. Disappointment usually lasts the longest, but the mistakes tend to be repeated in the case that the person has negative aspects between those two planets. In a positive way, this is the sign of exclusive taste, unusual, but lasting love with the pilot, astronaut, and scientist and so on.

Astonishing, gorgeous, wonderfully magical can be the voice of Venus when joined with Neptune. This is the fairy, the angel, the purest of the pure, the softest of the soft and the sweetest of all sweet things in this realm. But, when those two are in the tense aspects, this is the cheater of all cheaters, carrier of venereal diseases, or it can be shown as various missionaries trying to buy your soul using all sorts of manipulative psychological techniques. And this is, also, passion toward alcohol and frequently illegal substances. Venus and Pluto is the story of the Lord of the Underworld and his bride. Being positive or negative, this type of aspect always reminds us that there is a price we have to pay. The greater the pleasure – the greater the price will be.

MARS

He is our drive for life, for sex, for action. He is a warrior in every one of us. Masculine, his nature is hot and dry, his color is red, naturally and he is all about breakthroughs, "cut and enter" philosophies, so he can also be an expert when it comes to surgery. Of course, he is courageous, open, truthful and direct. He loves to reside in fighting places like dojos and open grounds too. Swords, guns, machines, advancing through deserts, through jungles, through mountains, there is always a war going on, and something and someone has to be conquered. Mars is the enemy to every other planet, except Venus. Her softness and femininity are his final defeat, but he can't resist her and he won't be able to resist her until the time runs out in this universe.

When negatively positioned or aspected with other celestial bodies, he is so hard to handle, heavy when it comes to polemics; annoying, destructive, full of injuries, verbal or physical fights with no particular reason or outcome, psychopath, murderer, dog or war; he can be everything.

His sound is "So", his vitamin K. He rules Tuesday, and in the terms of medical astrology he is the nose, the muscles, genitals, blood, and controls the levels of iron or red blood cells directly. His animals are all aggressive animals, no matter how small or big they are, especially males in animal species. Countries under his heavenly government are Germany, Japan, Israel, Syria, and Korea.

With Jupiter, he can become a warrior priest, military doctor, dignified expert, but when their aspects are negative this is the sign of agitator, manipulator, spitfire type of guy, always in conflicts with authorities, but it can be also beneficial for entrepreneurs if they manage to get "the rules of the game". His association with Saturn brings exceptional strength and discipline, gaining the fortune in the second part of life and longevity. However, if positioned in negative aspects, this is traditionally considered to be the hardest planetary aspect there is in the whole science of astrology. World wars are starting with this seal in heavens, and personal lives are filled with such hard challenges which can extend beyond human imagination. Car accidents, permanent disabilities, killing someone out of duty, accidentally killing someone, tough decisions, ruined happiness for the rest of a person's life.

Mars and Uranus bring a dash of gunpowder, electricity followed with an explosion. Great for engineering, technical breakthroughs, thinking out of the box, sudden turnarounds, but for a better solution. Negatively positioned, those two planets indicate strongly the danger of car accidents, electric shock, sudden attack, sexual deviations and aggression, criminal mind and similar fast and furious events and people. Neptune can bring magnificent insights regarding sailing, astrophysics, higher mathematics, hydraulics, and pneumatics. This aspect also gives great intuition when it comes to taking action and not taking action, proper place, and proper moment to strike or to pull back. Their negative traits bring the worst out of the person. This is the cheater, deceiver, criminal type of guy ready to do anything low to get what he needs. It also indicates alcoholic psyche, substances abuse, no matter whether those substances are legal or illegal.

Pluto and Mars fall under the special category because the position of Pluto has to be prominently placed in the chart to be active. But this is all about highest drama there is, childhood trauma which can't be healed followed by great inner transformation. Good aspects indicate enormous strength, the power to bare an unbearable, explosive, but creative mind. While the bad aspect shows sudden danger, sudden death, sudden victory.

JUPITER

This planet is a world of its own. Jupiter is almost like a little Sun in our system, with twelve satellites and the power to protect us from the outer cosmic bodies. He is all about expansion, education, broader views, religious teachings, long distance traveling, sailing over the open seas, archery, hunting, honor, noble tradition, synthesis of knowledge, law, and order, goodness, generosity. His day is Thursday, he is hot and moist and his color is bright yellow, but it can also be a bit darker, like saffron. Remember Buddhists or Hindi priests in their yellow or orange robes? This is the symbol for Jupiter.

In the terms of medical astrology, Jupiter is fat tissue and brain together with Mercury, liver and gallbladder, thighs, and buttocks, vitamin R. His animal is a horse or an elephant, but wild and free animals like deer or eagles all fall into his kingdom. It also loves to reside in woods and open spaces. His lands are Australia, Chile, South Africa, North Africa, Portugal, Scandinavia. According to Pythagoras's teachings, his sound is "Ti".

Of course, there are negative traits related to this planet; this is the main rule of the life itself. Jupiter can also gain weight fast, he can become overwhelming, endlessly unrestrained, vain, boring, manipulative and with a dirty mind or emotions. People often blame Saturn for their obstacles, and especially health problems. But at the same time, they tend to forget that no other planet can strike you so hard and fast with such expansion as Jupiter can do it.

In association with Saturn, this planet gives an exceptional and structured type of thinking and planning, achieving properties and wealth in general terms. These are constructive and systematic methods in business, agriculture, governmental tasks and in education. Those types of positive aspects are extremely significant in personal horoscopes, and astrologers in general tend to assume that all founders of main religions, like Buddha, Jesus, and Mohammed, had this aspect prominent in their natal charts. Negatively placed, energy exchanged between Saturn and Jupiter can lead to the loss of position or reputation, troubles with court cases and law, tendency for self-destruction, persecution, and serious problems for the father or grandfather of the person.

When you think about lottery gains, you have to associate Jupiter with Uranus in the heavenly formula for sudden success. This is also the image of the eccentric mind, unconventional thoughts, and often people's heroes during the times of war, and in some cases genius. Negative traits of this aspect are indicating a crazy person, someone who squanders his talent for worthless inventions, sudden losses, aggressive atheism, great problems caused by educated people.

Jupiter with Neptune is all about spirituality and the highest moral standards one person can acquire through life. This is the symbol for the accomplished saint who became the true role model for the masses, the teacher, and the avatar. A person with this aspect is not capable of distinguishing others related to their social levels, castes, races. The same person is deeply emotionally involved with suffering and resolving all problems regarding the suffering of people, animals, plants, the Earth itself. The negative side of this aspect can also show its grandiose or the wideness of evil because the person can become involved in a cult. This is the clear sign of someone who is the member or the leader of the religious sect, but political parties can be in play here also. Manipulation and humiliating perpetration, very twisted and often sick crimes are all present with this aspect.

Pluto with Jupiter can show the depthless quality of the mind. So-called "zeroing" when understanding is at its highest level that it negates itself. Singularity of spiritual thoughts, fast and strong transformation, resurrection, transmutation. Negative aspects between those two planets indicate horrible suffering due to religious beliefs, egoism and ecstasy, triumph through total destruction, victory through loss and vice versa.

SATURN

This is probably the most feared planet in the whole Solar system. It's known as the "Ring Pass Not" because planet Saturn with its recognizable rings was considered to be the border guardian of our sky and on the other side the mystery of the spiritual realm begins.

This celestial body is directly related to the flow of time, discipline, persistence, durability, seriousness, responsibility, reasoning, but it also governs properties, stones, especially precious pieces, old castles, graveyards, crypts, basements, top of the mountains, hard terrains in general, goats, hogs, mice, all small, but strong animals are his favorite pets, because they never give up.

Bulgaria, Tibet, India, Russia, Ethiopia, Iran, these are the countries marked by Saturn. His nature is cold and dry and it rules during the Saturdays. Prominent colors are black, of course, ashy shades, even purple or ultraviolet in rare cases. In the terms of medical part of astrology, this planet represents the bones, teeth and knees, skeletal system and our ability to stand upright. And it is also vitamin D, crucially important for the health of the bones. His sound is "Re" and he is portrayed as the old skinny man with prominent nose and ears.

The negative side of Saturn is a life full of obstacles, hunger, poverty, chronic diseases, deadly illnesses, freezing cold, endless waiting for things to get better, lack of resources, lack of love, lack of everything. The extreme pressure which can break or destroy many, but from exceptional ones Saturn makes exquisite jewels. Its symbol is the diamond because this is just the piece of coal which had to go through enormous pressures and temperature changes to become the hardest one and the most beautiful, most precious clear stone.

Together with Uranus, Saturn tends to preach about the ideas of socialism, communism, revolutions, how poor and insignificant rise against rich and royals to establish the new kingdom of equality. This usually happens through blood and new types of oppression. This can also indicate new ideas regarding science with results acquired through long and laborious research work. The negative side shows a longing for authority with unclear causes or outcomes, drastic behavior, damaged neurology and psyche, anarchism, eccentricity, problems with authorities or with the law.

Neptune and Saturn are good companions when it comes to the oil and gas industry, all things related to mining, especially underwater drilling, and excavations. This is also the sign of someone who can perceive the geometry of space or spaces together in the mind or in the speculative realms of geometry. Good for "serious" types of music, old instruments, legends, myths and ancestral teachings. It can lead some people to become the channel between the world of the dead and the world of the living. Negatively this aspect describes the liar, someone who doesn't just lie but twists the truth, especially in the political sense. Manipulation over masses through news or education, strange diseases, epidemics, death by stifling, nicotine or any other source of smoking addiction, asthma, cataracts.

Saturn and Pluto are considered to be the sign of an ancestral curse, black magic, dead bodies, massive destruction, investigation, archeology, forensics, sadism, ascetics. There are really no just good or just bad aspects between those two planets. Everything related to them is truly related to the greatest depths of our beings, the essence of the soul, reaching for the demon and dancing with him.

And this is the moment when we have exited the traditional heavens and discovered the new planets. Their influence wasn't so prominent before their discoveries, but from the point in time when we became aware of them, they incorporated into our lives and took the meanings and symbolism of our inventions too.

Planets outside the traditional astrology are mainly considered as the indicators of collective and social trends. They are more important for the political, cultural or technological changes than personal ones, but in some cases, when those planets make the direct aspects with traditional celestial bodies, then they can play major roles in the life of the native.

URANUS

Everything is sudden and everything is unusual when it comes to this planet. The gift of discoveries, technological breakthroughs, reforms of society and many more traits belong to Uranus. He can be the visionary, although his looks show someone coming from the plain origin. Newness through revolution is his signature. On the negative side, this is a person who is prone to collective trends and thought patterns, a destroyer of an aristocracy, the announcer of catastrophes and triumphs. Prometheus is his real name, for better and for worse. He rules over electricity, x-rays and IT technologies. And regarding traditional astrology, Uranus is seen as the "higher octave" of the planet Mercury. You can say freely – Mercury on steroids. Color is light blue, silver, any metallic shade.

In good planetary aspects with Neptune, this planet shows global trends, gifted mystics, faith, esoteric sciences, ideals of love and humanity, enthusiasm, heavenly music. Negative aspects bring out the fight against the norms and conventions, fall of idols and teachings, political fallacies, sexual disorders and adventurism which can lead to serious danger.

Pluto and Uranus together are never even close to the image of a harmless couple. This is the electricity combined with nuclear power, magicians, yogis, secret medicine, energy healing, scalar waves, tunneling through dimensions, mystical cults, poisoning, occult, psychiatrists, manias in all positive or negative sense of those words, although in those cases there is nothing even close to being considered as pure "positive" or "negative". It's just amazing in its creativity or destruction.

NEPTUNE

The god of the sea...of illusion. Traditionally seen as the higher octave of the planet Venus and therefore considered as something beyond beautiful, inspirational, delicate beyond perception, magically and sparkling rhythmical, glitter not gold. He also possesses the gift of demonic intuition, the gift of abstract thinking, higher philosophy related to natural sciences, diving into the depths of the sea, of the sky, cosmos, cells, biochemical processes. On the negative side, and yes, Neptune has a negative side as all other planets, this is the generic model of a liar, deceiver, a fraud, fake preacher, fake love, fake faith, fake education. It also had the tendency toward hoaxes, however, it's hard to fight with him. How can you fight fog? When and if got caught, he plays confused. All drugs are here, legal or illegal, all smoking tendencies, bacterial infections, poisoned water, poisoned air.

With any other planet Neptune achieves the miraculous initial success, enchantment and romance follow and then everything ends with disappointment, shame, dishonor, and blasphemy. Together with Pluto, this is poison, extremely high potency poison. Everything is ruined and covered with an indelible layer of pure venom which will last forever, like the consequence of nuclear explosion. In positive aspects, this is the sign of greatest mystic there is, a magician or someone who is dancing on the edge of divine devotion and total craziness.

PLUTO

The god of the underworld, many call him "fatum". He is the blackest of all black in color, he is the husband of the most beautiful woman and he rules over corpses. Without him, and her, the outer world can't be awakened, can't bloom and reproduce. On our ancestors, we all stand, from the roots we all grow. He is our origin, he is a resurrection, and he will be the end. Small, but dangerous like the energy in the single atom, like a nucleus, like nuclear. Pluto is considered to be the higher octave of the planet Mars and you can come pretty close to the right characteristics of this planet if you imagine it as the Mars with a genius mind and weapons powerful beyond anything else in the Universe...or perhaps Multiverse.

Pluto won't show its powers in any chart. It has to be positioned in angular houses (first, fourth, seventh and tenth) or to make a significant aspect with other planets. In those cases, you can see its powers, but even if you do, you'll wish you didn't.

NORTH AND SOUTH NODES OF THE MOON

North Node of the Moon is known as the Dragon's head and the South Node of the Moon is known as the Dragon's tail and those are traditional western names for the two calculative points in the sky. In Vedic astrology, those points are known as Rahu and Ketu and further on in this text, they will be addressed by those names, because this is widely spread all over the astrological world.

Rahu, as the North Node, and Ketu, as the South Node, are two opposite points in the chart and these points are the markers where the path of the Moon is crossing the ecliptic belt. These are not celestial bodies and they are always exactly 180 degrees apart from each other.

Myths associate Rahu as the head without the body, while Ketu is the body without the head. Rahu is something we have to process and learn during this current life, while Ketu is something we have already mastered through many of our lives, or in the previous life, which is important for this life in the terms of karma. Of course, if you believe in karma.

Those points tend to become very powerful when they are joined with planets in natal charts and they are capable of creating real havoc or powerful blessing, depending on other planetary aspects, and coming solar and lunar eclipses regarding transits.

Eclipses happen due to the fact that Sun and Moon are together on one of those two points or they are in opposition on the Rahu-Ketu axis. They bring changes; they take some things, issues, ideas or people we no longer need from us and present us with new events, people, issues, and ideas, whether we want this to happen or not. This is the nature of life, constant changes and growth through those changes.

Eclipses happening on the natal Sun can indicate a new direction in life, the danger for the father, while the eclipsed Moon can represent the danger for the mother or the soul of the native. Venus associated with Nodes will always bring unresolved issues into your love life and great instability with women, while similar can be applied for Mars, but in the terms of activity, men, enthusiasm. When the Nodes are placed together with Jupiter, a person will always seek higher knowledge, transform and adopt new teachings. With Saturn and Nodes joined in the natal chart, a person will feel cursed until the hard lessons about life, health, career, and discipline are mastered completely.

Association between Uranus, Neptune, and Pluto with Rahu or Ketu will always point in the direction of scientific, artistic or technological breakthroughs and those people will certainly have to go through many challenges, but at the same time, they will feel the strong, driving force to carry on and they don't give up on their dreams.

How to Read the Astrological Chart

Simply put, an astrological chart is the projection of the sky on the Earth's plane. Of course, that the Earth is not a plane, but this is not the question here because we approximate the image of the sky onto ourselves as if we were the center of the world. And if we "catch" the image of the sky at the same moment we were born, then we have the "natal chart". The same is applicable for the charts of the animals, buildings, companies, business deals, events like weddings, receptions and anything you can think of. These are all natal charts and they all describe the potential for good and bad events, which can happen further on, depending on some other factors.

The main one of those "other factors" are planetary transits. They are the most important fact in western astrology; while the Vedic school favors divisional charts, which is an arrangement of the planets and sensitive points in the chart calculated through some geometrical and mathematical rules. However, we will discuss the western or tropical school of astrology here. To avoid confusion, you should know that Vedic or sidereal astrology deals with sidereal positions of the planets in the sky, while western astrology deals with tropical positions or the projection of planets on the Earth's plane. In simple words, for example, the first day of spring is March 21st. We know this because day and night are equal and this is called the spring equinox. The Sun enters into the sign of Aries and the new cycle begins. You know that this is the equinox; you know that spring is here, but if you go to the observatory and look at the Sun through a telescope, you will see that Sun is still in the constellation of Pisces. This "effect" is happening due to the precession of the equinoxes; however, for now this concept is beyond the basics of astrology.

The most important thing you have to know is that both astrological schools are right, they have their precise prediction systems, which differ, but they both work. The quality of the prediction depends on the quality of chosen astrologer, not the school which is selected for the reading.

Let's get back to planetary transits. This is the term which describes the image of the current or upcoming planetary arrangement in the sky. If you, for instance, overlap the transit chart over your natal chart, you will be able to see the areas where you are challenged, blessed, where can you grow, in what to invest, from what or who to beware and so on. Sometimes the warning signs are extremely obvious if you know how to read those two sets of planetary arrangements together.

The same applies to your partner's charts, whether they can show the development and the outcome of love, business or any other relationship. All you need to do is to overlap those two charts and to read mutual aspects that the planets make.

GENERAL ASTROLOGY RULES

First, you have to know the meaning of each planet and the meaning of each astrological sign. Then you have to know the basic aspects planets make together.

The chart in the western astrology style is presented as a circle divided into 12 parts, each one representing astrological houses. The most important points are the Ascendant – Descendant (Asc-Dsc) line, which is a horizontal line in the chart and the Medium Coeli – Imum Coeli (MC-IC) line, which is showing the highest and the lowest points of your chart. Those are four of the most important points you have to pay attention to. Asc is your rising sign, describing just you. Dsc is how you deal with your love, business or any other partner and how you project yourself into the world. IC is your origin, while MC is your highest accomplishment.

A circle with the cross in it, it is so simple, and the whole life in it.

The image of your natal chart will look like this circle, but with the snapshot of the planetary arrangements at the moment you were born. This snapshot holds the potentials which will develop to a greater or a lesser degree, depending on upcoming planetary transits during your life. Whether those potentials and life's events are good or bad, you will know by reading the aspects the planets make.

Planetary Aspects

Whenever celestial body moves through the heavens, it creates a motion, therefore frequency, and therefore sound. Any relation between celestial bodies creates a mutual aspect and all together they make the music of the spheres. However, the aspects considered as the most important in astrology are conjunction, sextile, square, trine and opposition.

Conjunction happens when the two planets are placed close to each other so their influences are mixed. If there are three or more planets involved, then this is called stellium. Are the planets forming conjunction or stellium? This depends on their orbs of influences. Bigger bodies have greater orbs and for the Sun, Moon, Jupiter, and Saturn, this can extend to 15 degrees because they are big planets with great strength. Also, depending on the planets involved, conjunction can be considered as good or bad.

Sextile is formed between planets when they form the 60-degree angle between them looking from the center point of an astrological circle or a chart. Generally speaking, this is a good aspect and suggests that planets are active and can result in a positive outcome.

Square happens when two planets form a 90-degree angle in the chart and squares are often perceived as bad aspects because they can bring very challenging situations in our lives. But, at the same time, they force us to change and to grow in attempts to overcome or resolve our problems.

Trine is seen as the exceptionally auspicious aspect and it happens when two planets form a 120-degree angle between them. Although beneficial, trines can sometimes produce a lazy attitude, so there is really nothing just black and white going on in the sky.

An opposition is another "bad" aspect because two celestial bodies are forming 180-degrees angle and they are directly opposing each other. This is challenging too, causing open war between opposite sides, frictional, but at the same time, it provokes the search for a better option or solution.

ZODIAC SIGNS AND HOUSES

Now that we have learned the general meaning of planets and aspects in the chart, we should take the closer look at the astrological signs and houses. As you already know, the horoscope is divided into four sectors (remember the cross in the circle?) and twelve "houses" or main areas of life. In Vedic astrology, those houses are equal. Each one extends to 30 degrees. However, in the western school, this is not the case, because the geometry of the point on Earth where you were born, for instance, is calculated through various systems. This is something which is beyond the basics, but you should know that today, Placidus house system is mostly used and it shows the best results, except in the case that person was born in the areas of polar circles.

The main rule of astrology is that each Zodiac sign has the meaning of the same house. Translated, this rule can be easily explained looking at the signs. Aries is the first sign in the Zodiac belt, so the first house of any horoscope has the general meaning of the sign of Aries; the second house has the meaning of Taurus and so on until we reach to the Pisces or twelfth house.

For instance, you can be born in the sign of Gemini and this means that you were born between the 21st of May until 20th of June. However, if you were born, let's say, during the afternoon hours, your rising sign or your Ascendant could be placed in the sign of Scorpio. This is just an example; we will have to know the exact time to see where the Ascendant is placed.

Now, you have your natal Sun in Gemini, but your rising sign is Scorpio. This means that your first house is placed in the sign of

Scorpio, but at the same time, this means that you will have all the traits of Aries (first house) through the characteristics of Scorpio. In this case, also, the Sun is placed in Gemini, but in the eighth house of the horoscope, which again carries the symbolism of the sign of Scorpio. Add to this mix the position of your natal Moon and you will have the basic understanding of your character and appearance.

It can sound a bit complicated for an absolute beginner, but in time and with the little practice, you will start using those "double" systems, not even thinking about them while applying the rules.

Right now, have in mind that Hor, Horus or Hrs is the son of the god of time and this word can be found in many Indo-European languages and also in Egypt. Horoscope was the name for the priest who controls the measuring of the time. "Horos-scopein" means literally the clock watcher. Horoscope is all about the flow of time through the certain place, but is this the driving force through entire Universe?

Let's find out.

ARIES

Sun transits through Aries from the 21st of March until the 21st of April and during this period of time, the Sun increases its power rapidly, nature is awakening and suddenly we feel the urge to take action.

The sign of Aries or the first house in the chart is all about me, ego, will. The ruler of this sign is the planet Mars, which is diurnal (through daytime), this is also the male sign, the element is fire and the color is red. Aries is the cardinal sign and planet Mars rules Tuesday. Countries under this sign are Germany, Japan, Israel, Syria, Poland.

Aries is the image of the perfect soldier. He is strong, determined, a patriot, skilled in the art of war. He is also fast, with a rudimentary type of will, one-sided in his thinking, but honest and often naïve.

With the strong constitution and proper training – he is extremely dangerous. His favorite places are open spaces for sporting or martial arts activities, stadiums, city centers, all tall and new buildings made of steel and glass.

His feelings are fiery, passionate, easily affected, always above reasoning. His commitment to love can last for a very short or very long time, depending on the levels of passion he receives from his partner. In business, he needs some time to get the "rules of the game", but when he incorporates them then the breakthroughs are made. As a worker, he is very loyal, but tends to create tremendous stress and needs the time for relaxing after.

His best professions are related to sports, military, engineering, metallurgy, surgeries and any other type of duty where responsibility, clear line of command, order, and activity are necessary. He loves uniforms of any sort, no matter whether those uniforms are of the military and medical nature. He will equally enjoy the "uniform" of his favorite sports club, or him being dressed as a butcher, electrician, plumber or any other profession he is in.

There is no need to suppress this grandiose energy or Martian rage, especially when it comes to children born in the sing of the Ram. It's better to channel it through sports and activities in nature. Aries natives need to eat healthily, drink a lot of pure water and to spend their time in open spaces under the Sun. They should keep out of the stale atmosphere, small spaces, and boring environments.

Young women tend to be insecure because they are uncertain about the levels of their energy. They can be perceived as too strong and this ruins their chances for romance. And romance they want, indeed, like we all do. In this case, they feel better in groups and for them, and all other younger Aries natives, it's imperative to use the powerful inner drive creatively, because if they don't - they will tend to become members or even the leaders of delinquency groups.

Marriage for Aries people happens early and if their partner is calm in nature or prone to more feminine energies, this union will last for a lifetime because they need someone to be their safe fortress when they come back home. They are faithful because they are unable to lie and even if they fall in love beside their official partner, they will break this affair pretty quickly or they will divorce fast and remarry even faster. The sign of Ram is about honesty, even when it's based on naivety; about newness and rebirth. Strong outside, but very soft inside, the Ram is brave, interested in everything around him and careless like a baby.

The natives are not insensitive, as others could start to think; they are just bursting with energy and usually joy and precisely because they are so sensitive deep down inside, they cover their softness with the shield of sports, martial arts or membership of any organized group.

Sun exalts here in the sign of the Ram or in the first house of the horoscope because the Sun is the king and king just loves to show off leading his armies to war. This is the clear sign of very strong ego, self-sustaining type of thinking and living habits. In positive aspects with other planets, this is the characteristic of a psychologically strong native with a heightened sense of justice. However, when afflicted this Sun can show a tendency to become the dictator, he will certainly be inadequate when it comes to compromising and prone to quarreling, jealousy and simply unbearable. It can also indicate injuries of the eyes.

The Moon is seen as "too dried out" in this sign because the nature of the Moon is to be cold and moist and in those circumstances, the Moon is left on the hot and dry surface. A person with the Moon in the first house or placed in Aries will tend to have a short temper, sometimes brisk attitude and often be insensitive toward other's emotions. Injuries of the eyes (dry eyes) show in this case too, but together with the hurt feelings.

Mercury feels good wherever he resides, or at least he thinks so. This small planet of communication here doesn't know when to stop and words, words, words are spilled all around, often said in a rude manner or through an irritated tone. Agitator, a messenger in war, but good for sports, especially group sports like basketball, volleyball and similar activities.

Planet Venus is in detriment in the sign of Aries. This doesn't mean that she is losing her powers; it's simply the sign that she doesn't feel good here. Short hair, red hair, red lipstick, red clothes, sometimes sloppy and not so finely paired, sports shoes with the dress, elegant handbag with yoga pants, she can make great fashion designers cry out of sadness or a joy, depending on the positions of other planets. This is also the only position of Venus which indicates a turnaround in the game of love. Woman pursues a man, or in the case of male's horoscope, he waits to be pursued by a woman. For gay couples, this means that the one with dominant female's energy pursues the one with the dominant male's energy.

Mars is in his home here. Strong and powerful, but hard to handle. It also points into the direction of constant stress, even strokes, injuries of the head, especially the nose, redness in the face and body and often, scars. Blond and reddish blond, curly hair. Mars in Aries or in the first house rules the head - the skull (but without the lower jaw) and the hair.

Jupiter placed in the first house or in the sign of Aries shows joyous temperament, prone to weight gains, fatty cheeks and round eyes. An enthusiastic person, highly educated if other planetary positions are supportive and this is the image of the military priest or military doctor.

Saturn is in fall in Aries or in the first house. This indicates a very stubborn person, overwhelmed with life's changes. The danger of loss of hearing, injury to ears, problems with the upper teeth and even brain tumors. Stressful search for justice, for peace, for rest.

Uranus in Aries and also in the first house is the sudden explosion with long-lasting consequences. Unusual mind or methodology of thinking, "out of the box" solutions when Uranus is positively supported by the other planets, and a harsh and even crazy character in challenging positions. Use of the newest frequency types of technologies in engineering or as a weapon. Bipolar disorders, a pressure in the eyes, nervous breakdowns.

Neptune in Aries can be the true disaster. This is the planet of illusions, so in such dry theater of war operations, this planet is lost in alcohol and drugs. This can also point toward secret and popular "sports" among soldiers which include some sort of religious devotion mixed with drugs, most likely illegal ones. Generally, it can show problems with eyes, like cataracts, dementia, but also the talents for acting. In good aspects, this points toward hydraulics and pneumatics, new engineering technologies when it comes to water, oil or gases.

Pluto in Aries or in the first house is all about resurrection. Independent fanatic spirit, strong will and volcanic types of instincts. Demonic attraction and mad courage, black magic, fall, unique history.

TAURUS

The Sun transits through the sign of Taurus from the 21st of April until the 21st of May and during this time frame the Sun is stabilizing, everything in nature is ready for propagation. This is the time of quiet excitement, love, pleasure.

The sign of Taurus or the second house in the chart is all about mine, properties, belongings. The ruler of this sign is the planet Venus, which is here nocturnal (through nighttime) according to Ptolemy's Table of Essential Dignities; this is also the female sign, the element is the earth and the colors are brown and green. Taurus is the fixed sign and the planet Venus rules Friday. Countries under this sign are Ireland, Switzerland, Cuba, Tanzania, Cyprus.

Taurus is a female sign and that is why is easier to think of her as one very healthy and strong woman coming from the natural environment. She is slow and meticulous, but steady and she gets her work done. Someone might think that she is not so bright, but her slowness is far from being dumb. She knows the value of everything in every moment and this is why the sign of Bull is so important for monetary transactions.

She holds the keys to all rooms on her property and in every second she knows how much money her family possesses and where will expenses appear and how will the profits be made.

She is traditional and yes, she is the essence of value.

In medical terms, Taurus rules over the neck, thyroid gland, many hormones and lower jaw. Natives born in this sign tends to accumulate weight through life and if this is the case with women, many of them will have to starve their bodies to remain near the looks of a modern ideal of beauty. However, many of those women just give up and they enjoy this accumulation of everything, including fat.

Marriages last for a lifetime and many times love is being born out of the pure calculation, which is absolutely nothing bad in the eyes of one Taurus because substantial resources are the only guarantee for the happy ever after. How can we talk about love when I haven't seen your properties? How will I ever think of starting a family with you if you don't have enough money? What do you expect – to keep my future children hungry? These are all very realistic question one Taurus will think about even on the first date.

Children of this sign are peaceful and they desperately need the time spent outside in nature. You will raise them the best if you keep them playing on the meadow, in the woods, near the animals. And let them work all farmers' types of jobs or let them experiment in the kitchen. They won't all be involved in agriculture, but many of them will become the great biologists, especially botanists, builders, architects, exclusive cooks, animal trainers, veterinarians. But on the other side, this world of matter will make out of many of them respected bankers, investors, industrialists, high profile managers. Don't worry about their future, because they will be capable to raise their kingdom even if they don't possess a thing in the beginning.

The Sun generally feels good in the sign of Taurus or placed in the second house of the horoscope. This is all about incomes and all about earning money in style. However, profits are in most cases made through the land, farming, especially fruits and vegetables, although raising stock is also popular among these natives. Every business deal is checked first with parents, parental figures or a spouse. Tradition is important and respected through generations. Strong neck, strong voice.

The Moon just loves to be in Taurus. This is the place where the Moon exalts because it deals with security and family fortune. It's so easy to feel good when food is plenty, the land is fertile, stables are full of animals and rooms are full of children. Harmony and love. Big sensitive eyes, women tend to gain weight easily, especially in the second part of life, and there could be some problems with the thyroid gland. It's necessary for the person with any planet in this sign, especially the Moon, to walk bare feet on the ground.

Mercury is a bit slow here. It takes time to form the sentence, to think, to read. He doesn't even want to bother with those things when calculating profits and expenses are his favorite activities. Geometry is perhaps something too complicated to deal with, but when it comes to other mathematical areas like the stock market, Taurus Mercury can be invincible. When placed well, this indicates that the person loves to sing those old witty folk songs or the native has a natural gift for hip-hop reciting. Nice incomes from several small sources.

Venus is the fairy queen here. She is the best looking girl in the whole county and perhaps even further. This is her kingdom and she feels good in her body, in her home, in her properties, and with her own money. In many cases, she has a magical voice and singing is her natural talent. When receiving some negative aspects, this Venus can behave a bit like a sugar baby. Over the course of years, as her fortune increases, her weight will increase too. There are so many cases when a woman with this position is famous in the world of entertainment, has everything, but starves deliberately because her body accumulates everything. She adores designer's pieces in fashion, elegant clothes and extremely expensive handbags, shoes, and jewelry.

Mars is in his sign of detriment in Taurus. He doesn't lose his power, but he feels lazy and defeated by the fullness of life. There are no wars to fight in the rich land of eternal spring. He is like the soldier on his days off, so he just lies on the ground, looking at the sky or checking if any of the village girls walk nearby. He is also the great chef here and he is known for his meals made out of meat. Royal nutrition, yes, he also gains weight easily, but his body is big and covered in muscles. He loves woods and he finds his talents through working as a carpenter or peasant here. In the second house of horoscope, Mars creates expenses, usually for the home and personal items, but still expenses.

Jupiter in Taurus or placed in the second house can bring fortune, but this will happen only if the native is honest, educated and well prepared. This planet behaves like the omen from heavens here, but only if the ground is prepared in advance. Methodical techniques in agriculture bring success and methodical thinking goes the long way with Jupiter in the house of incomes.

Saturn in Taurus can indicate poverty in a very shallow sense of understanding astrology. This is happening because the influences of Jupiter and Saturn are misunderstood. Jupiter is the fortune, but the fortune in a spiritual or educational sense, while Saturn is the one to symbolize wealth in the terms of real, material properties. In this particular case the native can start poor and end rich, or the native can possess the ability to find cheap or to inherit something insignificant and turn it into a fortune. Great position for surface mining, archeology, sculpting, turning old peasant houses and farms into exclusive retreats. Good for banking also.

Uranus in Taurus is all about stock market changes, new agricultural technologies, disrupted currencies and economic crises. When Uranus is placed in the second house triggered by the other planetary transits it can create sudden gains or sudden losses of wealth.

Neptune in Taurus is all about trying to put down the heavens on the earth. In the positive context, this relates to art. A person is capable of making or singing heavenly music; this is innovation regarding sculpting and also amazing architecture. Someone might discover a geyser on the property, but on the negative side, this is extreme sensitivity toward chemicals and the danger of choking. Monetary gains through cheating.

Pluto in Taurus is great for forensics. This is all about digging bodies, digging knowledge, digging precious artifacts. It's also the demonic power of the Earth itself and some very weird ways of earning money while dancing on the edge of the law.

Gemini

The Sun transits through the sign of Gemini from the 21st of May until the 20th of June and during this time frame, the Sun is playful and communicative. This is the time of information exchange, sharing, exploring.

The sign of Gemini or the third house in the chart is all about the joy of belonging to a group, sharing, showing, marketing. The ruler of this sign is the planet Mercury, which is here diurnal (through daytime) according to Ptolemy's Table of Essential Dignities. This is also the male sign, the element is the air and the colors are yellow, orange and all pastel shades. Gemini is the mutable sign and planet Mercury rules Wednesday. Countries under this sign are Belgium, Iceland, Kuwait, Tunisia.

Organs under Mercury's or Gemini's government are hands, lungs, and brain (together with Jupiter). He is all about neurology, transport of information through the body, its logistics. These are the processes where the sign of Gemini is beyond being just shallow because it shows our capacity to breathe and to distribute the nutritious matter through the whole body.

Natives born under the sign of Twins in most cases have a sibling and very close relationship with them. Besides this fact, they are always surrounded by numerous friends and although those friendships are very changeable in nature, natives continue to grow the enormous circle of acquaintances. It's very important to know the proper person for a proper issue; this is the leading motive for any Gemini.

Their marriages or relationships are mostly far from being committed at least in their younger years. Later on, when other planets become dominant factors in their chart they can become faithful, but before this happens they have to live and relive the experiences of feeling joyous with multiple people. The usual case is two marriages, one which happened too early and was driven by passion and ruined by impatience, and the second one which happened when native started to feel old and realized that everyone around is in a committed relationship.

One unusual, but very common thing going on for young Twins is the fact that most of them have to go through very serious illnesses as babies and those health problems are frequently related to lungs or breathing in general. There is always some sort of drama going on in children's hospitals and after the hardest first year of life, everything that follows looks much better. Young Twins are very cheerful children, so joyous that you'll get often headaches just looking at them. They enjoy elementary school and all childish games and they want to stay in this protected land of childhood forever.

Just don't force them to learn about complicated sciences and thing of the past, because it will be extremely difficult for them to understand and totally useless for their careers. Good profession for Gemini natives is a journalist, marketer, teacher, instructor, reporter, editor, writer, seller, trader, lawyer. Others might complain that these are not so grandiose professions like being an architect or chemist, but without these professions, our world would stop. Someone needs to be the messenger between people and gods after all.

The Sun in Gemini or in the third house of the horoscope is all about the speech, imagination, skills, expertize, but regarding down to earth knowledge which is applicable in every day's life. This is also the game, the art of trading, exchanging any sort of information or assets, practicality, and intellectualism. Established in the sign of Aries and secured by Taurus, the Sun is now like a little child ready to explore the neighborhood. Everything is new and exciting and worth researching.

The Moon in Gemini or placed in the third house describes the restless soul and spirit. I want to be here and there, in the best case scenario, at the same time and I love to hear about this and that, mostly nothing important, but it doesn't matter. People with the Moon positioned like this love to drive around the city, frequent short travels and fast food places, especially the street sold foods. Their relationship with their mother looks like a teenager friendship and communication is flowing free, but mostly about non-essential issues.

Mercury in Gemini or in the third area of the chart is in his own place. This is the image of an investigative journalist, speculative trader, entrepreneur, marketer, someone who works with children, like teachers in elementary schools and kindergartens. It's all about the play of life, all about bubbling and chatting and building something new seamlessly out of nothing, i.e., magazines, newspapers, websites, nothing too deep. When positioned negatively, this Mercury indicates mental problems, Autism Spectrum Disorder or ASD, even bipolar behavior.

Venus in Gemini is the image of a girl or a boy, or whatever you like her or him to be. Also Venus and Mercury in close or tense aspects with Uranus can indicate a homosexual or bisexual person too. But more important for this Venus is her girly or boyish appearance. Her body is not developed fully like in a grown woman, her legs are long and thin and she is the moment of glory for the fashion industry because every piece of clothing on her looks exactly like when it's on the hanger. She is about parties and gossiping, about shopping and spending her time in cafes and in the city.

Mars in Gemini or placed in the third house is the evident sign for the entrepreneurial spirit. From every penny, he will make two, from any garbage information he will make pure gold. He will raise his empire on marketing, selling fog, selling some shallow educational stuff applicable in business. He will use his power in the world of communication and when involved in construction building he will focus on the downtowns of big cities – small and practical apartments, but in the heart of the world.

This Mars is also exceptionally good when it comes to martial arts instructors, someone who has to teach, explain and fight at the same time. These are strong fists too. And if positioned negatively, this is the small street criminal, punches or slaps.

Jupiter placed in the sign of Gemini is in his sign of detriment; the same applies for the third house in personal horoscopes. This planet doesn't feel good here, because the deep and broad knowledge it carries can't be expressed completely through the certain shallowness of celestial Twins. In good aspects, this indicates someone who is very talented in sports, especially group sports like basketball and some natives seems to grow very tall with this position. Negatively speaking this can lead to some cognitive problems, ASD again, because fats and neurology are not composed properly in the brain tissue.

Saturn in Gemini points to some verbal problems; the person seems too slow, not capable of verbalizing or expressing thoughts fast enough. This also indicates some misunderstandings with siblings, especially younger ones, troubles with lungs and neurology. This is good for building business in the later part of life, though.

Uranus in Gemini or placed in the third area of the chart is about disruptions of the speech or the ideas. Often bipolar, ASD which can be used in the world of new communication technologies, odd ideas, new solutions, out of the box type of thinking if other aspects are confirming the strength of Uranus. This is good for electricians, online speakers, TV reporters. It also indicates some sudden events in the life of native which will take place in the neighborhood or nearby, when other transits trigger this planetary placement.

Neptune in Gemini is the symbol for a great writer or a liar depending on other aspects, but it's usually both. Something odd can happen in the neighborhood, a person gets inspired while walking or talking with neighbors. Strange events inspire this person, they are mindful of mythical inspiration, this is great for poets and science fiction novelists. At the same time, a person with Neptune in the third house will always find a church or any religious temple near his/her home and he/she will go there frequently no matter what is his/her religious background may be.

Pluto in Gemini is cunning, sly, witty, and tricky above everything else. This is the omen for the magnificent manipulator, someone who does horrible things in a childish manner. They have unusual intelligence, but it is always accompanied with sarcasm.

Cancer

The Sun transits through the sign of Cancer from the 21st of June until the 22nd of July and during this period of time, the Sun is about nurturing, home and motherly figures. This is the symbol for taking care, being intuitive and sensitive.

The sign of Cancer or the fourth house has the main theme of inner protection, safety provided by family and ancestral origin. The ruler of this sign is the Moon, which is here both diurnal and nocturnal according to Ptolemy's Table of Essential Dignities. This is also the female sign, the element is the water and the colors are blue, silver and all pearly shades. Cancer is the cardinal sign and the Moon rules during Monday. Countries under this sign are USA, Holland, Madagascar, and Bahamas.

Organs under the Moon's or Cancer's rulership are stomach, breasts, and womb, but in the case when the baby is inside the mother. This is also the symbol for the egg in a woman or any animal. This is the flow of water inside of us and therefore, it's imperative for females. Any organ filled with water becomes the Moon's belonging in those moments of fullness.

This is the symbol for big, watery eyes, commonly blue, babies and nutrition. Any pregnant woman is under the rulership of the Moon. Moodiness is a frequent flow of emotions, extreme sensitivity, night time, lakes, greater water surface with the full Moon mirroring in it, mirrors, tears, pearls. Constant changes in incomes, schedules, feelings. Good for dairy production, taking care of children, babies, nursing, taking care of elderly people, running restaurants, hotels, hostels.

The Sun in Cancer or placed in the fourth house of the chart describes sensitive person attached to mother, family or ancestors in general. Patriotism is strong here, although the Sun doesn't show his powers openly. This represents the nation, national pride, and heritage. Everything which deals with ideas of helping others through genuine care will be shown through this Sun. Perhaps it's too soft, but this Sun is not weak in the sign of Crab, it just doesn't want to show off and parade as it does in other signs. Their place of residence looks humble from the outside, but marvelous inside.

This Moon in Cancer is in its own house. This Moon feels protected and there is a clear lineage of women ancestors from whom the native learns about life, care, and support. This is the symbol of fertility, but at the same time, it indicates the frequent moves of the entire family. The kitchen is the prominent place for family gathering and many meals are based on milk, cheese and especially butter. The native with this placement knows how to heal members of the family, specifically children, with warm milk with spices and honey, soups, and teas. Although attached to the home, this native will often move to new locations and he will tend to settle down beside a lake or a larger pond.

Mercury placed in this sign of the fourth house indicates that person is very attached to the home, gains "down to earth" every day's knowledge usually from the mother, many people are transiting through the home, neighbors, friends, house full of siblings. There is a lot of information exchanged through mother or home environment, good for people who are working remotely online. They want small apartments, but close to the center of cities, small kitchens, small chairs or rooms, small items.

Venus in Cancer or placed in the fourth house of horoscope usually portraits the woman with big eyes, round face, bigger breasts, prone to weight gains due to excess water in her body. She is sensitive, focused on family, nurturing, somewhat conservative. Loves romance, nice items, nice manners. This is the symbol for the hidden mother in any woman, a lot of female friends, love can be found in the home through a visitor. She values security above all and she will be faithful in any sense of the word, to any man who is protecting her. Her complete soul will belong to her family.

Mars in Cancer or specially placed in the fourth house is in its fall here. Generally speaking, this is the worst position for the warrior. Just imagine the situation of letting the soldier take care of a baby, or letting a heavily armed warrior in the kitchen. His nature is fiery and he will cause all sorts of disputes in the home. In personal relationships, this is the image of a couple in a constant fight, verbal or physical. The man can abuse his wife, but at the same time, his whole family. The same goes for an aggressive woman. Fiery weapons held in the home, the danger of shooting, the danger of something burning in the kitchen, constant danger of fires. In the best case scenario, this is the person who constantly does some repairs or improvements in the home, so the drilling and breaking of the walls are a never-ending annoying sound for the entire family. And because Mars is so weak here, the native can become the bravest one, because he/she had to learn how to fight with everyone from the earliest age. Hot foods, stomachache, and a metabolism so fast that it tends to burn out the body earlier in life.

Jupiter in Cancer and divinely placed in the fourth house is in the sign of its exaltation. It's the common belief that this Jupiter can bring the expansion of the family's properties and wealth in general, but the truth is somewhat different than just this one aspect. This is the sign of exaltation for the big celestial guru, because higher knowledge should be inherited from the mother and female lineage in the family. From an early age, the mother should be the one to teach her children about fine manners, ability to listen and to feel, to absorb positive information, good foods, and stable emotions. This is the excellent position to feel protected from the inside, because Mars and the Sun are in charge of the outer protection, fighting and winning in the male style. Jupiter placed here is all about refined education and the healthy educational and intellectual abilities derived from healthy food and having a healthy mother. This is also the sign that properties are huge, food is plentiful and the surrounding area of the home is reflecting nature, meaning that there are lots of parks there, areas for sporting activities and even a temple related to the religion of origin.

Saturn in Cancer is in the sign of his detriment, unfortunately. This indicates obstacles in relation to the mother, chronic diseases, usually derived from sensitive stomach, problems with digestion, allergies to dairy, allergies to everything which came from the female lineage. Problems with heating, a person is often cold and catches colds in the house, the cold and dry atmosphere among the members of the family, growing up with grandparents and in many cases, the grandmother takes the role of the mother. This is a good position for producing ice-creams, distilled drinks, creating an exclusive retreat out of the old property, vineries, houses made of stones.

Uranus in Cancer announces frequent changes regarding home, moving in a sudden manner, a lot of uncertainty, neurotic mother, problems with electricity, irregular digestion, irregular childhood, growing amongst "crazy" or at least unusual people, growing beside electricity plant, problems with electricity, electrical devices behave out of control, especially in the kitchen, someone experiments with all sorts of technical items in the home, inventors, disruptors.

Neptune in the sign of Crab or placed in the fourth house of the chart indicates very foggy problems at home. The mother could have some eyesight issues; there could be an alcoholic always present, if not at home, then one of the close neighbors is prone to addiction of some sort, words and emotions are not clear, floods coming from the bathroom, spilled milk, always something boiling with the danger of exploding. Someone practicing homeopathy or creating pharmaceutical drugs from home. Home factory of illegal drugs, tarot card readers, something chemical or alchemical always going on. Frequent problems with bacterial infection and food poisoning. Some good advice is to avoid mushrooms.

Pluto in Cancer or placed in the fourth house indicates that some sort of the criminal act was done regarding ancestors. There could be a body buried underneath the home or around the property. A sudden explosion, crime, murder. On the positive side of this aspect, the native can discover a hidden treasure or any sort hiding in his home or origin.

Leo

The Sun transits through the sign of Leo from the 22nd of July until the 23rd of August and during this period of time the Sun is about dignity, pride, and domination. This is the symbol for royalty, entertainment, and children.

The sign of Leo or the fifth house is all about ruling over others, being just and doing well. The ruler of this sign is the Sun, which is here both diurnal and nocturnal according to Ptolemy's Table of Essential Dignities. This is the male sign, the element is the fire and the colors are yellow, gold and all glittery shades. Leo is the fixed sign and the Sun rules during Sunday. Countries under this sign are France, Italy, Mongolia, Bolivia.

Organs under the Sun's or Leo's rulership are the heart, spine and bone marrow. This is also the symbol of the life itself because the Sun is the light or the fire within. Natives born in this sign almost never get cancer of any kind and they manage to eliminate diseases very fast. However, they are in the greater danger of having a heart attack.

Odd but true, Leo has two sides of his character. He is like a child, enthusiastic about everything, open-minded and always in a good mood – he shines like the Sun. On the other side, he is the great organizer, structured and orderly leader with the clear set of intentions and instructions. He loves tradition and national history, he exalts in luxury, but only when he is the one, the alpha. He is the big hearted and large-minded individual with the established sense of hierarchy.

This native resolves all disputes in gentleman's manner, there is no point for jealousy because he/she is the best one and if the love partner is not clear or doesn't understand this, native will just leave with pride to find someone else who will respect him/her more. Marriage usually happens in the middle age when he had already accomplished something grand in his own life and this marriage is usually with the "trophy partner".

Children of the Lion are courageous and they should spend their times together with others learning to treat everyone equally. With afflicted planets, these children tend to gain weight very early in life.

The Sun in Leo or placed in the fifth house of horoscope is the basic image of the king (or queen), good heritage, dignity, and honesty. This is the person with strong principles and ordered mind, someone who loves formalism, good manners and open and honest conversation. In the negative context, this can also point toward snobbism, vanity or arrogance. This person has bright, often light eyes, greyish, wide forehead, curly hair, and strong stature. Later in life, the native is prone to become stubby. She has a talent for acting, drama, entertainment, and humor in general. Childish, but with the pure heart and this is the image of a child wanting to rule the whole world. Coat of arms, lions, flags, parades, bees, baroque – they all belong to Leo and the mighty Sun.

The Moon in Leo or placed in the fifth house can be a bit dried out when it comes to emotions. Feelings are present, but they are covered with a sense of duty and common sense. The native feels great love toward children and enjoys the idea to have many of them, but this is also the sign of having just one child in most cases. However, this is the wonderful placement for entertainment industry or working as the teacher in elementary school. There is increased flow through the heart, but a mobile spine at the same time.

Mercury in the sign of Leo or placed in the fifth area of the chart is the gift of a great speaker, especially when it comes to motivation. This Mercury is capable to mobilize masses from their depressive state of mind into any adventures, to make them go to war, build the fortress or calm down. These are also all expensive vehicles and the children of the rich people, who are capable of expanding the industries of their parents or just to enjoy their fortune and without fail to record experiences of a luxury life through social media.

Venus in the sign of Leo is always dressed to impress. She is branded from head to toe, and even if she doesn't possess means to wear expensive items yet, she will find some appropriate clothes which will resemble her dream to be dominant. This is the symbol for gold, exquisite jewelry, high heeled shoes with red soles, and small handbags with golden or platinum credit cards inside. Usually, her hair is long and blond, and she tries to keep her body in the best shape as long as she can. A native with this position of Venus finds love in the places of celebration, theaters or receptions. This is someone who will appear just in quality or luxury places and search for the adequate partner. Reason is leading the feelings and even when the third party gets involved, the native resolves the unpleasant situation without jealousy by just leaving in dignity.

Mars in Leo or in the fifth house indicates the soldier who wants to show off. This is the leader on the military parade. The pompous king who lives for adoration coming from his people. This is the portrait of a person who needs to be on the top and who will do anything to get there. At the same time, this indicates troubles with heart, easy exhaustion, passion and rage for life which can easily turn into weakness or illness. Good for practicing sports though.

Jupiter in Leo or placed in the fifth house is a person with a big heart in the positive and negative sense of the word. This could be the marvelous teacher, magnificent actor, someone who loves children and is blessed with very educated and successful progeny. At the same time, in the case that Jupiter receives negative aspects coming from other planets, this can be the person who wants to act like he/she is rich, educated and successful, but in reality, all those attempts fail with public humiliation. This can also be the lottery winners in some cases and problems with fat deposits in the arteries too.

Saturn in Leo is all about longing for progeny because this is the sign of his detriment. Usually, people with this position of Saturn want very passionately to become parents, but their wish comes true later in life and they always tend to have fewer children than they wished for. In bad aspects, this signifies afflictions with children, problematic romances, and a sad love life. Saturn here is also the sign of the great leader or politician, but someone who will have to rise through oppression or he will fall in shame. Changes in politics, turnarounds, turmoil, fall of the royal house.

Uranus in Leo creates special situations. This is someone who comes from the lower social rank and through the ideas of anarchy, communism or social politics tends to ruin the established system only to position him/herself as the next ruler. This is the image for crimes in high society, for exclusive frauds and disruptors of tradition. Placed in the fifth house, Uranus indicates highly unstable love life, frequent relationships with psychologically immature partners and electrically disrupted heart.

Neptune in Leo is the clear sign of an unclear love life. Children might not belong to the native, they could be spurious, or the native could create children and then just disappear from their lives. This is the sign of love affairs; disrupted love life followed with all sorts of sexual disorders, love for illegal substances, especially in the liquid or gas states. This is also an indication of bacterial or viral infection of the heart or something unclear when it comes to heart or spinal function. On the positive side, these are talented musicians or poets.

Pluto placed in the fifth house or in the sign of Leo, if in the significant aspects with other celestial bodies, will create a sudden and great emperor in politics, in business, in entertainment. Everything around this person will be grandiose, destined and doomed. Also, this is the symbol for powerful children, exceptional life force coming straight from the heart, raw behavior, for avatars and gurus with supernatural powers, sudden death, unexplained murder.

VIRGO

The Sun transits through the sign of Virgo from the 23rd of August until the 23rd of September and during this period of time, the Sun is about collecting the fruits, healing, and serving. This is the symbol for the fullness of the autumn, hard workers, and natural healers.

The sign of Virgo or the sixth house is all about fixing, ordering or editing, being in service and doing the best for others. The ruler of this sign is the planet Mercury, which is here both nocturnal (during the night) according to a Ptolemy's Table of Essential Dignities. This is the female sign, the element is the earth and the colors are brown, golden brown, yellow, brown-red and all colors of the fall months.

Virgo is the mutable sign and Mercury rules during Wednesday. Countries under this sign are Greece, Turkey, Brazil, Mexico, Switzerland.

Organs under Virgo's or Mercury's rulership are small intestine, spleen, and pancreas. This is also the symbol for the complete health of the body because Virgo controls our metabolic processes.

Virgo is known as the excellent worker, someone who serves others, a person with tremendous analytical abilities, sometimes neat picky, but with good intentions. They tend to become excellent doctors, lawyers, writers, administrative workers, thriving in all these professions, which are demanding precise and timely data.

Virgos will have stable marriages, but only after they go through a crisis of adjusting to their partner, and they, above all other signs, can be too demanding in the terms of clean, scheduled and precise living conditions. Little Virgo children should be involved with education, especially natural sciences because their minds will very quickly awake and they will take control over their future if directed properly from an early age.

The Sun in Virgo or placed in the sixth house of the horoscope demonstrates a darker type or person, someone slim and not very tall. This position of the Sun shows the natural ability for serving others or generally being of service toward anyone or anything in life. Great doctors are born in this sign, as well as nurses, natural healers, and nutritionists. This is also auspicious for administrative works, extended writing, editing or checking and rechecking. What has been sowed in the springtime, time of Aries and Taurus, now is reaped. This is the period of the year where we take the look back at the agricultural results and make necessary calculations for the future.

The Moon in the sign of Virgo or placed in the sixth area of the chart describes the person with the sensitive stomach, many minor illnesses, bloating, but this placement also indicates working with women, in the female environment or frequent contacts with many people. This is an excellent position for taking care of babies or elderly people. Women or a motherly figure in the native's life can also behave like a small enemy. This is someone who is a good psychologist or a social worker.

Mercury in the sign of the Virgin shows an excellent writer, editor, someone who will very thoroughly control and correct other people's papers or words. This is also someone who is magnificently talented for the healing of any sort, but especially natural methods. This person uses the wide knowledge regarding herbs, light exercises like yoga or qigong, homeopathy, nutrition and those methodologies the native had tried on him/herself first, because of the earlier digestive disputes. Food heals everything, a person might often claim, with the same passion and fire as one Leo claims that the Sun cures everything. On the negative side of the Virgin, this Mercury is prone to exhausting verbal fights, talks too much in general and annoys children or children are annoying to this native.

Venus in Virgo or positioned in the sixth house of the chart is the worst place for this essence of pleasure. Venus is in the sign of its fall here in the astrological sense. Too much analyzing, too much realism, work is hard and people are looking at the soil, crops and fruit trees, not noticing how beautiful this Venus is. She also grows in poverty here and she has to find a way out, trough calculations related to the perfect choice for marriage, or through using her beauty, body or clever mind to secure her future, but those details will mainly depend upon other planetary aspects too.

Mars placed in the sixth house of the sign of the Virgin is the clear sign of digestive or serious inflammatory problems with the gut. And diabetes belongs to this category. A person is usually allergic to grains and from the grains, all other health problems arise. But at this place, Mars also indicates the elevated levels of stress, working in the aggressive kind of environment, meeting many furious younger men and dealing with them. The native also has a very analytical type of reasoning and this person is really diligent. This is a great position for scientific or medical research, planning and designing machinery or real-estate blueprints.

Jupiter is in the sign of his detriment in the sign of Virgo or generally speaking, this great teacher feels badly placed in the sixth house which deals with daily obligations and usually non-important matters when the sea of knowledge is waiting to be found somewhere far. This is the avatar that is standing on the edge of the farmer's market trying to sell eggs or vegetables. He will surely have some hard times to finish this task because in that particular place people are less interested in his insights about the perfect cosmic shapes of the egg or the structure of energy inside one apple. Jupiter feels here very restricted and misunderstood. This position also indicates gaining fats around the waist area. This is good for using the scientific agricultural method on the large properties.

Saturn placed in the sign of the Virgin and especially in the sixth house describes annoying chronic diseases and this might be the punishment for the native for not becoming a doctor because greatest diagnostics are born with their Saturn in Virgo. This is the case when the mind goes very deep searching and finding the real cause of any disease. This can also be the indication for gallbladder stones or very slow and sensitive digestion. This Saturn points to the poor ancestors who probably had to cope with the hunger and oppression to survive. On the positive side, this is the extremely good position if the native is in the industry of dried foods, like dried fruits and vegetables. Good for storing and selling grains, nuts, and seeds, also for the "dry" foods like biscuits.

Uranus in Virgo or placed in the sixth house can describe the sudden problems with pancreas, diabetes, strange sensitivity of the gut caused by electricity or any form of EMF waves, causing danger with some modern types of diagnostics, like the ultrasound. On the positive side, this is the image of the excellent radiologist or, generally, a doctor who deals with latest diagnostic machinery. This is also the symbol for the sudden destruction of crops caused by lighting and storms, and very serious viral infections going on in the guts.

Neptune in the sign of Virgin is the archaic symbol for the holy smoke. This is the clear inclination toward smoking tobacco or any other herb, especially those with hallucinogenic traits. This is a very dangerous placement for people who are prone to food poisoning, extremely toxic mushrooms, and all chemicals used for food preservation or for the purposes of the modern agriculture. This is the sign of unclear bacterial infection of the guts and of the crops in the field too. On the positive side, this Neptune placed in the sixth house can give talent for imagination and excellent storytelling if supported by other planets.

Pluto placed in the sign of Virgo or positioned in the sixth house if in major aspects with the other important celestial bodies, can point in the direction of discovering hidden or, most likely, buried treasure on the family's property. This can also be the sign that the native can suddenly realize that some ancestral heritage can be used in marvelous ways, while on the negative side this is a tumor or a bullet in the stomach, horrible or magnificent health depending on other aspects.

LIBRA

The Sun transits through the sign of Libra from the 23rd of September until the 23rd of October and during this period of time, the Sun is about relationships, justice, and balance. This is the symbol for the business or marital partnerships, always focused on harmony.

The sign of Libra or the seventh house is all about dealing with others, being just, accomplishing the balance and success of both or all parties. The ruler of this sign is the planet Venus, which is here diurnal (during the day) according to a Ptolemy's Table of Essential Dignities. This is the male sign, the element is the air and the colors are green, light blue, turquoise, all gentle colors. Libra is the cardinal sign and Venus rules during Friday. Countries under this sign are Austria, Argentina, Tibet, Canada, Saudi Arabia.

Organs under Libra's or Venus's rulership are: kidneys and they are in the direct relations with the head (sign of Aries) in regards to controlling the blood pressure. This is also the symbolic sign describing how we function in the outer world receiving and answering to outer conditions.

Libra is the most famous sign of the beauty ideals, harmony between people and ideas of justice. However, on the negative side, this sign is full of snobbism, shallow behavior and pretending. Natives can be nice on the surface, but deep down in their souls, they are full of insecurities and therefore need established sets of rules. Generally, Librans are afraid of loneliness and when desperate they will commit to anyone willing to be with them. If the marriage starts earlier in life, it will usually break, but the later or the second marriage will last forever. Children of this sign should be thought to be independent and with a strong will, capable of making and sticking to their own decisions.

The Sun in the sign of Libra is in its fall. In other words, this in the worst possible place for the Sun. This means that the will of the person is weak because it is directed toward others. In this time of the year, everything is preparing to die or to sleep, harvest season is ending, and the whole nature is calming down. In ancient religions, this time was considered as the true beginning of the year because "And there was evening and there was morning, the first day" Bible, Book of Genesis, 1:3-5, everything begins from the dark, even before its conception, while being just the idea. Doing for others and having in mind their needs first is the death of the ego, therefore death for the Sun.

The Moon in the sign of Libra or in the seventh house is not such a good position either. Not so bad, like this is the case with the Sun, but still not very useful because the mind of the person is driven by emotions and those emotions are often scattered all around trying to be everywhere in every moment being present for everyone. This is hardly possible and many of the natives with this position of the Moon are considered to be shallow in their emotions. On the other side, this is the image of someone who lives for and through the social admiration. All of those fantasy or fake lives shown on social media platforms are the mirror reflection of this Libra's Moon. Positively speaking, a person needs to be close to someone through committed love or a business partner to be able to feel full and useful. In some cases, this is the indication of volatility in marriage or multiple marriages in the life of this person.

Mercury in the seventh house or in the sign of Scales is the clear image of the great lawyer, public speaker, someone who loves to show his words, speech or ideas in public. This is also the indication for the talented actor capable of memorizing huge amounts of dialogs. Excellent entrepreneur, even better negotiator. On the negative side, this person can be tricky and if Mercury receives negative aspects, this will show grandeur liar or deceiver. In any case, the native's children will be well raised and with good manners.

Venus in the sign of Libra or positioned in the seventh house is in its own home. However, this Venus is focused on relationships, instead of just material possessions. These possessions, in fact, in the kingdom of Libra are in the realm of spiritual, being airy in nature. These are all about beauty, balance, harmony, proper measure, proper manners, and the ability for lovely social communication. Great for partnerships of any kind. This Venus has slim, fairy body, lighter eyes or hair with delicate and beautiful moves, which are not so erotic in their nature, but more prone to elegancy.

Mars in the sign of Libra or positioned in the seventh house is in his sign of detriment. This Mars doesn't feel so good in the circle of women, in the ceremonial type of situations or mannered conversation. Especially in the seventh house, it can indicate frequent marital disputes and even a divorce. A person usually knows what is right and what is wrong in the relationship, but their partner simply can't adjust to harmonious life together and this is the source of all troubles. On the positive side, this is one very strategically oriented Mars. Ancient martial arts are based on this position due to the fact that they all have a foundation in the idea of harmony. The game of chess also belongs to this category.

Jupiter in the sign of Libra or placed in the seventh house of the chart describes the person who has good abilities when it comes to aesthetics, someone who is loved and respected in society and, most likely, someone who is very popular and can easily spread ideas in certain social circles. This is also the respected actor or performer of any kind of art. The person with this position tends to rise in society after marriage, but it can be good for business partnerships too. If afflicted this planet gives some sort of religious disputes with the spouse or even troubles in society regarding personal religious or spiritual views.

Saturn in the sign of Scales exalts in that particular place, and this is also the case when it's in the seventh house. A person might wait a bit longer to get married, but once this marriage happens, it will be unbreakable. Saturn is all about duty and justice, and in the sign of Libra, this planet can show all of his power amongst other people surrounding the native with this position. It's pretty easy to be the best one and stand alone on the top of the mountain of success, which is the case with Saturn in Capricorn. However, it's far more demanding to be fair, focused and balanced when the baby is crying, the husband needs his dinner, while your mother is on the phone asking did you call her dentist, for instance. This is the excellent example of being in balance and with the stable mind when everything around you is crashing down. This is the real and the most powerful emanation of the planet Saturn. In relation to this is the story about the piece of coal, which had to go through extreme temperatures and pressures to become the diamond.

Uranus in Libra or placed in the seventh house is always about the partnership disruptions, divorces or marrying divorced person. These are fast and unstable partnerships, even in the business sense.

Neptune in Libra or especially when this planet is positioned in the seventh house indicates something unclear regarding marriage. In the best case scenario, a person will marry someone with eye problems or someone involved in film or TV acting. In all other cases, this could be the sign of lying or cheating in marriage and in business.

Pluto in the sign of Libra or when it's forming significant aspects with the other planets from the seventh house tends to behave in the brutal sense to the public. If the aspects Pluto makes are negative, this is someone who is hated by everyone, and popular due to this fact. It can also be related to a fated love stories or complete withdrawal from others.

Scorpio

The Sun transits through the sign of Libra from the 23rd of October until the 22nd of November and during this period of time the Sun is about death, depths, and resurrection. This is the symbol for the transformation, sexual energy, as well as unearned incomes.

The sign of Scorpio or the eighth house is all about transforming the ideas, body, diving deep into the world of the occult or unknown. The ruler of this sign is the planet Mars, which is here nocturnal (during the night) according to Ptolemy's Table of Essential Dignities. This is the female sign, the element is the water and the colors are black, of course, burgundy red and purple. Scorpio is the fixed sign and Mars rules during Tuesday. After its discovery, planet Pluto is generally considered to be the co-ruler of this sign together with Mars. Countries under this sign are Turkey, Panama, Lebanon, Cambodia, Angola.

Organs under Scorpio's rulership are: the genitals and all excretion organs. This is also the symbolic sign describing how the life is transformed in us through the energy of passion, creating a new being, and also what we need to let go of to become free.

This is the sign of the "other side". The person had to go through some harsh experience in life, perhaps even more of those experiences to become initiated into the real Scorpion. This is the special sign because its transformations are always going through three phases. First, the native is a Scorpio, low, furious and bad. Then it becomes the Eagle, above everyone else, but vengeful. And the third stage is when the native becomes the Phoenix or the Dragon, which depends on the astrological tradition of a certain area. In this phase, a person is higher than anyone else, but it can also transform lives and this time in a powerful and positive way.

The Sun in the sign of Scorpio or placed in the eighth house of the chart is all about very dramatic transformations throughout the whole life. This Sun already died in the sign of Libra, so now it's wandering through the underworld seeking for the purpose and the meaning, not just of life, but of death itself. The will is here focused, magnetic, dramatic and it searches for the way to make a breakthrough. This Sun doesn't fear responsibility or risk, it can't and it won't stop in its pursuits, no matter whether the native with this position of the Sun achieves something or just watches.

The Moon in the sign of Scorpio or in the eighth house is in the sign of its fall, the worst place for sensitive Moon, indeed. The soul is forced to dive deep into the unknown and usually, the native with this position is forced to go through some serious problems from an early age. This person was hurt in a very horrible way due to disputes with the mother or any motherly figure around. He/she was emotionally abandoned and ridiculed by the ones this person needed the most, or in some cases, the mother couldn't protect the child because she had to go through tremendous pain. The second phase this Moon has to go through is self-hatred and hatred toward members of the family, tribe or anyone involved with a challenging experience. The Moon like this is capable of thinking and conducting any type of revenge and even black magic rituals. And the third step toward transformation is forgiveness. This Moon understands and forgives for all the troubles it had to experience and in those moments, it gains supernatural powers to heal others. This is a great placement for energy healers, exquisite doctors, pharmacists or chemists.

Mercury positioned in the eighth house or in the sign of Scorpio is the clear indication for someone who is talented in occult sciences or with the gift of clairvoyance. This is great for astrologers, tarot card readers and similar professions. At the same time, this is the excellent position for diagnostics in medicine, but the native might have a dirty or simply rude way of speaking.

Venus in the sign of Scorpio or placed in the eighth house is in its sign of detriment. The queen of pleasure is lost in the darkness and here she has nowhere to turn but directly to the king of the underworld. She is prone to sexuality, her beauty can become cheap or aggressive depending on the other planetary positions and she thrives through challenging or lost romances. The person with this position of the planet Venus had his/her heart broken many times and love can even be found through some very tragic events. Although mainly considered as cheap, this Venus can be an exclusive type of a woman who went through all sorts of dramatic events in her life and now became excellent in the skills of war and strategic thinking. She is the type of a perfect female warrior which is used in the battle when all other options have failed. And consequently, she is the queen in the game of chess who will be sacrificed for victory. A woman with this mission is the highest symbol for this Venus.

Mars in Scorpio is in his own kingdom, but with some slight differences than in his other house – Aries. Here this planet is in his night mode, so we no longer deal with that naïve and open-minded type of Mars. This planet in Scorpio is known as the excellent strategist, he is something like the war advisor for the Sun and his opinion, targets, and goals are always hidden. Mars is the warrior who is skilled and extremely precise with weapons, but unlike the Aries Mars who loves to join forces with others, this one thrives when he works alone. This is the image of the hitman, the sniper or someone who waits in the dark corner of the street with a knife. In the medical sense, this is the perfect position for the best surgeons, but if this is not the case, then the native falls ill in a sudden manner and most of those illnesses are acute, hard, but short lasting. These are commonly inflammations of the sexual organs or bladder.

Jupiter placed in Scorpio or in the eighth house of the chart can lead a person toward such extensive and positive transformations that this person can become much more skilled, better or far in front of everyone else in life. If negatively aspected, in this case, Jupiter will direct such a person toward a leading position, but in a shameful business, like running a mafia or dangerous religious cult. This position also indicates great returns on investments or a marriage with a person who makes a significant income.

Saturn placed in the eighth house of the horoscope or in the sign of Scorpio describes a long life, but usually with long chronic illnesses too. The person might have problems with kidney stones or sand and something is always wrong with the sexual drive or large intestine. On the positive side, this is good for investing in precious metals and stones, and also properties, especially old and valuable ones.

Uranus in Scorpio or in the eighth house can be very dangerous because Uranus is considered to be the higher octave of the planet

Mercury. This Uranus can indicate sexual perversion, harsh character or sudden death caused by electricity. The energy created in this area of the chart is too strong, and it causes disruptions and eruptions.

Neptune in the sign of Scorpio or placed in the eighth house points to the danger of drowning. Besides this, a person is in the constant danger of infection through water, bathing or sexual contacts. This is also a love of drugs, legal or illegal and if other aspects are supportive in a negative or positive way, this person can become a drug dealer or a pharmacist

Pluto placed in Scorpio or in the eighth house can be very peaceful if it's not in aspect with the other planets or triggered by their transits. If this Pluto is active in the chart, then this can be the sign of a great healer, but it can also point to the direction of a murderer, deadly explosions, fires, military graveyards and all things related to the symbolism of joined Mars and Pluto, which means fear, terror, and trauma.

SAGITTARIUS

The Sun transits through the sign of Sagittarius from the 22nd of November until the 21st of December and during this period of time the Sun is about discoveries, higher learning, and expansion. This is the symbol of the spirituality, joy of newness trough intellectual and physical activity.

The sign of Sagittarius or the ninth house is all about reaching for the higher ground and exploring the depthless quality of the human or a godly soul. The ruler of this sign is the planet Jupiter, which is here diurnal (during the day) according to Ptolemy's Table of Essential Dignities. This is the male sign, the element is fire and the colors are golden yellow and saffron orange. Sagittarius is the mutable sign and Jupiter rules during Thursday. Countries under this sign are Australia, Spain, China, South Africa, Kenya.

Organs under Sagittarius' rulership are the liver, buttocks, and thighs. This is also the symbolic sign describing how freedom is achieved after the drama coming from Scorpio, where we keep out the inner fire and how to reach it.

The sign of the Archer values his freedom the most and therefore earlier marriages usually end through divorce. Second marriage might be with the person with the greater age or cultural difference when most of the Sagittarians search for novelty and liberty is already satisfied. Children of this sign should be thought to respect social norms, but to spend most of their time outside pursuing sports and pieces of evidence in the field of natural sciences. The broadness of the mind or the human soul are their highest aims, so don't limit them and they will show their best.

Sun in the sign of Sagittarius or placed in the ninth house of the horoscope clearly describes the person who is prone to becoming a great teacher, the real guru for younger generations. This is also someone who loves to travel to distant places and delights through the ideas of constant growth and research. A person like this is always talented for comedy and even in the midst of very hard or demanding events, this person finds the way to lighten everyone around them. Physically this is the portrait of someone with a big or at least tall body, but if afflicted this Sun will show someone who is short and fat.

The Moon in the sign of Sagittarius or positioned in the ninth house is someone who is restless when it comes to traveling. This person will change many places and his home will be on the road. Later on in life, the native can settle through marriage, but most likely with the person who originates from completely different religious or cultural background. On this place, the soul is seeking for better answers than the ones which were given just through the official process of education. The mother figure is prominent in the native's life as someone who is truly educated, but at the same time bighearted and open-minded.

Mercury in the sign of Sagittarius is not in its best position because this is the sign of its detriment. And the same applies for the Mercury in the ninth house. The mind of the person is down to earth here where it's supposed to fly higher. It's like someone let the supermarket cashier into the university laboratory to supervise experiments, or it can look like the gathering of the traders in the temple. The person with this position lacks a deeper understanding of life and therefore shows as inadequate for the situations he/she has to go through. On the positive side, this is the image of the person who works on the supportive and administrative types of jobs for universities or spiritual organizations.

Venus placed in the sign of Sagittarius or placed in the ninth house of the horoscope is an indication that this person, or a woman, or a female energy in a native, will just love to travel to exotic destinations. A woman like this doesn't seek luxury and comfort; she delights in oriental scents, customs, and patterns. Her clothes can be sloppy, but colorful and she just loves the hippy style. Her desires are broad and related to erotica, not so much real passion. And she will never forget to show her long legs or talk about her Ph.D. Giving her the freedom to speak her mind and to move wherever she wants will be the best way to attach her to yourself.

Mars positioned in the ninth house or in the sign of Sagittarius is known for his good mood in any situation. This is truly strong, but at the same time, this is a peaceful Mars which uses his strength for some higher purposes than just fighting. These are the people who love horse riding, hunting, tennis, car races, tennis, archery, all those sports or activities which will move the person further, but at the same time indicate the certain dose of nobility. This type of Mars won't get provoked so easily, he will rather think about the whole situation with humor and probably decide to walk away from an excessive situation. This is the great position for archaeologists, travel guides, sports instructors and also doing business related to spiritual or religious themes or working with foreigners.

Jupiter in the sign of Sagittarius or placed in the ninth house can ensure magnificent success in philosophy and any natural sciences. This is someone who is generous, righteous and good-hearted, but at the same time, this is a person who is internally free and besides this, also has significant social and financial successes. This success is ensured in his plans, speculations or any type of endeavor too. Good positions for this native are a lawyer, judge, priest, organizer of others, but mostly in the field of spirituality. In good aspects, this person is noble with high moral standards and influence on others, while with affected Jupiter, this shows like someone who exaggerates in everything and this can lead him to failure in life and completely ruin his reputation.

Saturn in the sign of Sagittarius or placed in the ninth house of the chart is the portrait of a serious deep thinker and someone successful regarding metaphysical issues. This can also be an indicator for a great astronomer if other aspects are supporting. In usual cases, this is the sign of someone who wants to pursue higher education in the form of the university diploma, but due to circumstances the person can't achieve this, mainly due to the necessity of daily working tasks needed for financial survival. This is also the symbol for refugees, walls, obstacles trying to reach better living conditions, problems with authorities and issues with legal matters.

Uranus placed in the ninth house or in the sign of Sagittarius can pull the person toward spiritual disruptions in some sense. A person usually seeks to run away from national or family religious traditions and in this search finds many new teachings which are not appropriate or leave this person disappointed. If positioned well through aspects with other celestial bodies in the chart, this is the portrait of someone who is talented for incorporating the latest technology into traditional ways of learning, and also someone talented for astronomy, astrology and maintaining frequent contacts with technologically savvy foreign people.

Neptune in the sign of Sagittarius or positioned in the ninth house of the chart is someone who dreams about distant exotic places and those dreams are filled with fantasies of peace, meditation, rest, relaxing. In a good position, this person visits temples, especially monasteries where spiritual knowledge is delivered through wise and often foreign persons. In negative aspects, this is someone who can suffer from asthma, there is also the possibility of breathing problems related to hiking or alpinism, or generally speaking, problems with religious beliefs covered with illusions or inhaling illegal or harmful substances.

Pluto in the ninth house or placed in the sign of Archer is all about phantasm, ideological movements, and turnarounds which ruin cultural monuments, irrational philosophical systems planned for the future, using force to reach freedom, using pray to heal, complete transformation through religion.

CAPRICORN

The Sun transits through the sign of Capricorn from the 21st of December until the 20th of January and during this period of time the Sun is about hierarchy, structure, and power. This is the symbol for the established position, hard work, and dedication.

The sign of Capricorn or the tenth house is all about reaching the top of the mountain, corporate ladder, or any other type of reputation we project into the outer world. The ruler of this sign is the planet Saturn, which is here nocturnal (during the night) according to Ptolemy's Table of Essential Dignities. This is the female sign, the element is the earth and the colors are black, coal shades of gray and sometimes brown. Capricorn is the cardinal sign and Saturn rules during Saturday. Countries under this sign are Great Britain, India, Mexico, Sudan, Bulgaria.

Organs under Capricorn's rulership are bones in general, knees and teeth. This is also the symbolic sign describing how the position and reputation are fought for, established and maintained through constant hard work and focused efforts.

This is the sign of the strong family or national tradition. Through struggle, oppression and hard environmental conditions, the native will sharpen his/her skills and become very powerful, seeking for the better or the best of life. Capricorn is the sign of the true material wealth and people born like Goats will ensure their lives with the best lands, real-estates, and piles of gold. They tend to get married a little later in life, but those marriages are stable as rocks and their partners know what is expected of them right from the start. Children are shy and they should be encouraged to enjoy life more and to try to be more empathetic toward others.

The Sun in the sign of Capricorn or placed in the tenth house of the chart indicates the person who is goal oriented, has respectful and highly established fatherly figure in his/her life and seeks to repeat his father's success or usually do better. This person might feel lonely and isolated in the earlier ages, but in the second part of life, the native suddenly awakens, focuses and achieves success through dedication. The Sun doesn't feel particularly good in this sign; however, this Sun is absolutely certain that it can't get a position or gain possessions solely through the ego, but through using all sorts of interactions with others, positive as well as negative. Strong, but controlled and guided will is fully operational.

The Moon in the sign of Capricorn or placed in the tenth house is in the sign of its detriment. The Moon simply doesn't feel good in the cold and rough environment. Perhaps it can be good for a father's type of energy, but it surely doesn't suit the soul of the mother. This can be the indication that relationship with the mother was rather cold or she was unavailable for the native during the phase of childhood in some sense. Feelings are frozen or very slow in expression. This doesn't mean that this person is senseless in any way, but he/she is closed, conservative and afraid because the outer world is oppressive and even brutal.

Mercury in the sign of the Goat or placed in the tenth house points to someone who is slow, but meticulous during childhood years, probably with speech problems, and this person can even seem to be not so bright for people surrounding him/her. However, in the more mature phases of life, this Mercury starts to catch the general rules of life, especially business and becomes a very shrewd businessman. This is the great entrepreneurial spirit, someone capable of running multiple businesses at once.

Venus in the sign of Capricorn or placed in the tenth house is the portrait of a lady, simply put. In the second part of life, this Venus starts to show her beauty and magnificent sense of elegance. These are usually wives of powerful business and political figures, neatly dressed and with the excellent manners. When her hair becomes gray, she reaches the peak of her power. If she gets acquainted with the business or corporate world, then success can be found through female types of industries, like fashion, accessories, and cosmetics. Love is found through the area of work and in many cases, there is the age difference greater than seven years between marriage partners.

Mars in the sign of Capricorn or placed in the tenth house of the chart is a phenomenally good place for this Mars because this is the sign of his exaltation. This planet becomes the strongest here, not just in the terms of his physical power, but this is included also. He is at his peak because he has the focused mind and his will is made of steel. In most cases, he came from a very poor environment and he had to fight for everything in life. He is accustomed to hunger and to lacking the basic means in life. So, he fights and learns along his path. In the physical sense, this is one very naturally strong Mars because he didn't build his muscles spending time in the gym, but through physical work, which made him capable of wrestling with a bear, any bear in life. In the terms of a career, this position is great for real-estate business, construction building, and engineering, dealing with metallurgy or any highly developed industry.

Jupiter placed in the sign of Capricorn or in the tenth house of the horoscope is someone who achieved success in the public life, but through a long process or proving his/her skills or expertise. This process most likely came with the help of foreigners or priests and it seemed to everyone else that it was accomplished with the godly peace or in a noble manner. This is also the portrait of the supreme judge in the state, the highest priest or the best public speaker or a guru. The native can climb very high regarding careers, which are dealing with education, especially related to the business kinds of education. However, Jupiter is in its fall here and he always feels limited by circumstances.

Saturn placed in his home sign, the sign of Capricorn or in the tenth house speaks volumes about the long and hard pursuit for security, expertise and recognition. This is someone who grew old trying to create his/her kingdom and now stands on the top of the world or on the top of the mountain. Saturn placed here is all about tradition, crypts, old castles with dungeons and dragons underneath. These are all servants, slaves and poor oppressed people. This is the sign of someone who loves to eat simple peasant food, goat's meat, burnt a bit, with dried foods also. If in positive aspects this is the indication for the rich and powerful person, not necessarily famous or loved by everyone. This is the symbol for properties, lands, wealth in the big sense of this world. Industries related to this position are mining, archeology, metallurgy, machinery and similar hard, but at the same time very profitable jobs.

Uranus in the sign of Capricorn or placed in the tenth house of the chart describes a very unusual career for the native. This can be the sign of someone who applies very advanced technologies and mixes them with traditional methods. Astronauts, IT engineers, inventors and many more fall into this category. In negative aspects, this is someone who changes careers frequently, doesn't get along with authorities and therefore pursues a unique type of career and recognition.

Neptune in the sign of the Goat or placed in the tenth house can indicate someone who is involved in the shady businesses or politics, but in very problematic ways which frequently include lies. If this planet is receiving positive aspects in the chart, then it indicates great success in the chemical, agro-chemical, pharmaceutical or oil industry and the person with this position can rise above everyone else if the planet Saturn is positioned well also.

Planet Pluto placed in the sign of Capricorn or in the tenth house can be the sign of the remarkable career in all areas which deal with engineering, machinery, real-estate, properties in general, excavations, mining and highest levels of banking. On the negative side, this is the aggressive oppression, military power, war criminal, dangerous magic and cults, production of weapons, dogs of wars, nuclear power plants and weapons.

AQUARIUS

The Sun transits through the sign of Aquarius from the 20th of January until the 18th of February and during this period of time, the Sun is about newness, equality, and diversity at the same time. This is the symbol for the technological and social advancement, as well as grouping of the people.

The sign of Aquarius or the eleventh house is all about being equal with others, uniting for the sake of the common cause and at the same time streaming for the higher ideal. The ruler of this sign is the planet Saturn, which is here diurnal (during the day) according to Ptolemy's Table of Essential Dignities. This is the male sign, the element is the air and the colors are light blue, silvery blue and washed out gray shades. Aquarius is the fixed sign and Saturn rules during Saturday. After its discovery, planet Uranus is considered to be the co-ruler together with Saturn. Countries under this sign are Russia, Iran, Syria, Sweden, Sri Lanka.

Organs under Aquarius' rulership are lower legs, complete neurology and lymphatic system. This is also the symbolic sign describing how our dreams can become the reality if we all unite, focus and work for mutual benefits.

Nothing is stable in this sign, especially marriages and relationships of any sort. People unite under one idea and then separate when conditions tend to change. Children are good hearted, but often without any manners and they should be thought to respect order a little bit more, and also they should be kept away from technological gadgets. But this is a lost battle in advance.

The Sun in the sign of Aquarius or placed in the eleventh house of the horoscope is its sign of fall here. This is the time of exhausting winter on the northern hemisphere and the Sun shows its face for a very short time during the day. At the same time, astrological interpretation points toward the sign of Leo where the Sun is in its home. Leo is the symbol for the ruler, the king, while Aquarius is the symbol for the people. And the Sun naturally doesn't feel supreme surrounded with those plain, raw and often rude souls. On the other side, the Sun placed here is all about the change and creating plans for the better future.

The Moon placed in the sign of Aquarius or in the eleventh area of the chart is describing someone who is prone to change and those emotional changes are highly dependent upon the changes going on the social circles of the native. A person with this position is interested and open toward anyone and any idea, but at the same time, the native lacks the deeper understanding how the life operates.

Yes, it's not fair, the native often thinks and more often speaks, *why don't all rich people/corporations/countries just give up all money/properties/wealth to the poor and we will all be equal and happy*. At the same time, this person forgets about the hierarchy of power and the laws of evolution. There is not such a thing as being equal in this Universe and that is out of the reach or understanding of this Moon. On the positive side, it's easy to cheer up this person and the mother or the motherly figure was creative and joyous through this person's childhood.

Mercury placed in the sign of Aquarius or in the eleventh house could be, and in some rare cases is, the talent of the magnificent writer, if this person could manage to organize his/her mind and escape from shallow or daily disruptions. In all other cases, this is the real messenger and this person thrives in the careers related to IT technology, content writing, social media influence, journalism, trending and similar types of jobs which don't require deep understanding or proven and double checked information. If positioned negatively relative to other celestial bodies, this Mercury is capable to ruin its own reputation with rumors and gossips and hardly able to plan or to envision the future. The native just loves technological gadgets.

Venus placed in the eleventh house or in the sign of Aquarius is more about showing off in society than feeling the real pleasure inside. Love can be found in the places of mass gathering, like fairs, national celebrations, clubs, parties and of course, social media. In this particular horoscope house, love shouldn't be deep or dramatic; it's more about the leisure type and "look at me, look at us" representation. Erotica is present but without any real or lasting sexual passion. This Venus also thrives on sex exchanging games; she can be he, or even it, whatever that means in her/his/ its head. She loves to look different than the norm, but at the same time, she needs to be protected by the social circle which dresses or behaves in the same or similar manner.

Mars in the sign of Aquarius or placed in the eleventh house of the chart describes the person who is inclined generally in technology and engineering. These are all those guys who are prone to mechanical repairs related to cars, electricity, plumbing, construction building. This Mars is not the strongest and he is completely aware of this fact, but at the same time, he knows he can become unbeatable if he unites with others. If Mars receives negative aspects, then this can be the indication of a street gang membership, grouping for destruction causes. In positive aspects, this Mars unites with others to be able to make a breakthrough in technology, daily working tasks or exploring the unknown territories. Poor and oppressed groups of people who are seeking for their happiness elsewhere traveling long distances are the symbol for joined efforts of this type of masculine energy.

Jupiter in the sign of Aquarius or placed in the eleventh house is not in such perfect condition here, but this is far from being bad for the native's life. This person surrounds herself with a great number of other people and most of them are educated or at least influential in society. Networks of friends, business associates, valuable mentors, good social position, great plans for the future, these things are all covered and protected by the planet Jupiter in Aquarius. If in a positive aspect with Uranus, this can also indicate lottery winning or a sudden windfall of money. Also, Jupiter placed here can be the wonderful teacher for the masses and an excellent social worker. In negative aspects, the native has a distorted sense of spirituality and bad social position.

Saturn in the sign of Aquarius or placed in the eleventh house of horoscope is in his own house here, where this planet delights in the ideals of uniting the poor and turning against the established government or king or whoever is in charge. This is the symbol for washed out working uniforms, great movements of pioneers or refuges, hunger, but with the burning desire for a better future. At the same time, this points in the direction that person is surrounded with older or poor people, bounded by the same principles, beliefs, and prejudices.

Uranus in the sign of Aquarius or placed in the eleventh house of the horoscope speaks volumes about instability related to relationships or career. This is also someone who takes risky investments and in negative aspects, this is the person who is the blind follower of trends, easily changes his/her mind and the shallow thinker. In the positive aspects, this is the image of a great inventor, someone who stands out from all due to his/her unique way of thinking and living.

Neptune in the eleventh house or placed in the sign of Aquarius indicates someone who enjoys very foggy company. Something is not clear here when the friends are involved. They might be prone to illegal substances, actions or ideas. Good for electronic types of music or modern arts related to technology, bad for investments and planning.

Pluto in the eleventh house or placed in the sign of Aquarius, and if affected significantly by other planets, has the ability to turn friends into enemies. This could also be the member or the leader of the very dangerous closed type of organization, or this can be someone with clairvoyant or visionary ideas.

PISCES

The Sun transits through the sign of Aquarius from the 18th of February until the 20th of March and during this period of time the Sun is about diving deep into the unknown cosmic sea, mysteries and hidden issues of creation. This is the symbol for spirituality, but in the personal and internal sense, isolation and seeking wisdom through silence.

The sign of Pisces or the twelfth house is all about being equal with the higher power, being alone in the sea of changes, diving into the self and at the same time diving into the divine. The ruler of this sign is the planet Jupiter, which is here nocturnal (during the night) according to Ptolemy's Table of Essential Dignities. This is the female sign, the element is the water and the colors are dark blue, silver, and all pearly shades. Pisces is the mutable sign and Jupiter rules during Thursday. After its discovery, planet Neptune is considered to be the co-ruler here together with Jupiter. Countries under this sign are Portugal, North Africa, Scandinavia, Namibia, Samoa.

Organs under Pisces' rulership are feet, blood, and complete circulatory system. This is also the symbolic sign describing our inner desires, fears, and readiness to explore the inner types of truths.

Pisceans are known as the best pharmacists, musicians, and spiritual leaders, although many of them can be perceived as confused and lost in this world. They usually tend to wait longer for the proper marital partner and the children born in this sign should be thought to be more social and realistic.

The Sun in the sign of Pisces or placed in the twelfth house of horoscope describes the person who is shy, patient and kind. This Sun doesn't use any of his entitled credits or special treatments. The native seems to have a very hard first third of life and finds success in reclusive types of professions. Basically, he seeks to help others and achieves this goal through the hospital or religious types of job, and often he can be seen as the lonely artist. In positive aspects, this native gets help or achieves success traveling and living overseas and in certain cases, he gets valuable help from highly educated foreigners.

The Moon in the sign of Pisces or placed in the twelfth house is the image of a person with very unclear feelings, lost in the sea of deep revelations and always changing. This person is highly sensitive, and there is something unusual in native's relationship with the mother. The mother could be absent, seriously ill or even dead if this position is negatively affected by other natal planets and person seeks to build his/her own ideal of motherly energy around this fact. The soul feels a deep loss and it always desires to come back home, wherever this spiritual and safe place is. If the mother is present, then she takes the role of a teacher, a real guru in the native's life and this education takes unusual forms, which can have extreme quality or be disastrous, depending on other aspects.

Mercury in the sign of Pisces or placed in the twelfth house is in his sign of fall and detriment here also. This planet is all about the transmission of information and especially verbal expression, and at this place, this can't be done. Words scatter, they lose their meaning and information is distorted. This is the place where a person shouldn't speak or write at all, where the mind and logic are drowned in the sea of wider knowledge than this Mercury will ever be able to understand. However, you can't prove this to the mercurial type of person. He/she will try in spite any advice to keep silent and make many mistakes along the way. This is also the sign of the danger of being robbed by a pickpocket, of being gossiped about and having some small, but very determined enemy.

Venus in the sign of Pisces or placed in the twelfth house of the horoscope is in her position of exaltation here. But don't get so excited too soon because this place is all about isolation and Venus can have the purest feelings and the best looks in Pisces and still stand alone. This is the greatest position for artistic pursuits, especially singing and poetry, not so good for marriage, because Venus is still in the sign which is the symbol of loneliness. She is lovely, romantic and delicate in her communication. Love can be found in all closed places, like hospitals, islands or distant foreign lands.

Mars in the sign of Pisces or in the twelfth house describes the introverted type of character. He is far from being weak in this weird place, but he is turned toward inner, deeper or higher breakthroughs, and he is simply not interested in the outer world. Good professions for this position are sailors, scientific researchers, all people who have to explore something away from the crowd and usual noise. If affected negatively, this native will have very powerful enemies, sudden and dangerous diseases and he could be even physically attacked in the dark. In positive aspects, this can be the military doctor or even a silent hero.

Jupiter placed in the sign of Pisces or in the twelfth house is in his own house here. This might mean some emotional or psychological instability, especially in the childhood, because native with this position simply feels that there is much more in life than just passing fancy and shining, but truly shallow objects, events or people. Later on, this person develops broader knowledge and starts to understand the magic of all realms of existence. This is a very auspicious position for people who aim for the highest types of university education, as well as people who are prone to become monks or priests. At the same time, this points in the direction of valuable help coming from the educated person or moving permanently very far, in most cases over the ocean. If affected, this Jupiter will describe a person who is lost in this world and ends up in the hospital or in the monastery.

Saturn in the sign of Fish or placed in the twelfth house is someone very emotionally close, prone to deep thinking and also prone to prolonged, chronic diseases. The person will surely have to deal with some hidden enemies and in most of the cases, those will be elderly and very powerful people. Many times this person will suffer from some serious trauma related to the people representing a religion of origin. If affected negatively by other aspects, this position could lead a native right to jail. In some cases, this might be working there as the guardian, manager or a doctor, but in extreme situations, this will mean imprisonment. Health is overall weak and the danger of blood clots is always present.

Uranus in the sign of Pisces or in the twelfth house portraits the person who delights around the ideas of how close is the end of the world, conspiracy theories and of course, extraterrestrial visitors. This is someone who is full of extraordinary and even fascinating ideas, but the real problem here is that this person lacks the focus or stable energy to make those ideas true. At the same time, this position can represent the danger of sudden and very challenging viral infections or attacks coming from a psychologically unstable person.

Neptune positioned in the twelfth house or in the sign of Pisces simply loves to reside here, because this is its home. Based on this place's inspiration, music, poetry or craziness can go sky high. In the sign of Aquarius Neptune loves pharmaceutical supplement, but here, this planet will go deep into natural types of healing, like herbalism or homeopathy. The person with this position feels the strong desire to run away from reality and in negative aspects, this could mean the danger of drowning or choking. Great for pharmacists, though.

Pluto in the sign of Pisces or in the twelfth house is the symbol for hard internal battle, guilt complex, ecstasy and powerful healings through the process of praying.

Tarot Cards:
Chapter One: Getting Started

What is Tarot?

The tarot is a deck of seventy-eight cards, which are used for divination, for gaining insight and guidance on your current situation and your path in life. All of human life, perhaps even all of life, is contained within the images of the tarot. By learning to read the cards, you will gain knowledge of yourself, of your relationships with others, and of the bigger picture, the pattern of your life. Deep symbolism and many layers of knowledge are encoded in the images of the tarot, and by learning to read the cards, you learn to delve into these layers and the many ways they reflect our human experience.

As well as giving you the individual meanings of the cards, this book will show you the ways they fit together and the stories they tell. The tarot is a picture book, illustrating human life, our responses to the world and ways of acting in it, and this book will show you how to read it. The book of the tarot works on both an outer level, showing us the events and circumstances around us, and an inner level, reflecting back to us our emotions, hopes and fears and the way they affect our actions. Tarot is a language, told in images, universal symbolism and motifs, and this book will help you to become fluent in it.

The seventy-eight cards of the tarot deck are divided into two main sections, the Major Arcana or Greater Trumps and the Minor Arcana or Lesser Trumps. The Major Arcana can be seen as a psychological or spiritual journey towards greater understanding and fulfilment, of ourselves and of the world around us. There are twenty-two 'greater trumps", taking us on a journey through the great archetypes and energies which inform our lives, from the Fool with his leap into the unknown to the completion and success of the World. The Major Arcana cards show universal forces and life experiences which we may not be able to control, but which have a profound effect on us and the way we live our lives. They include figures such as the Empress and Emperor, representing the archetypal mother and the archetypal father, and heavenly bodies such as the Sun and the Moon

The fifty-six cards of the Minor Arcana are divided into four suits, usually known as Wands, Swords, Cups and Pentacles. They are similar to the spades, hearts, diamonds and clubs of a standard deck of playing cards. Each suit is related to a particular element, symbolising, in turn, a particular area of life. Wands are the suit of fire, symbolising creativity, passion and action, and Swords are linked to the element of Air, to logic, reason and communication. Cups are the suit of water, representing our feelings and imagination, and finally, the Pentacles bring it all into manifestation in the realm of earth, symbolising the material world, our work, home and resources.

Each suit contains fourteen cards, beginning with the Ace and going up to Ten. The number cards combine symbolism from numerology with the elemental attributions of the suits to describe the realities of our journey through life, our experiences of relationships and connections with other people, the work that we do and the place that we live, all of the choices that we make on a day to day basis.

The Court cards are the Page, Knight, Queen and King, and they represent personalities and ways that we use the elemental powers in our lives. They are a kind of tarot "family" showing our progression from youth to maturity and the different ways that we experience and act in the world as we grow.

WHY DO WE READ THE CARDS, AND HOW DO THEY WORK?

Most people think of tarot cards as a way of telling the future, and that is one of the ways of using the cards. But it's important to remember that we all have free will. The cards do not determine our future, our decisions and choices do that. What the tarot cards can do is help us to make those decisions, to look at possible outcomes of choices we may make, and in this way guide us on our path. The cards reflect our inner as well as our outer experience, so that they may show you your feelings around a situation, or your hopes and dreams, just as clearly as they show the situation itself.

There are many misconceptions and superstitions surrounding the tarot, and many people are put off using the cards, or even going for a reading because they fear being told that something bad will happen to them. Whilst its true that the tarot sometimes doesn't pull any punches, and may tell you what you don't want to hear, it will also tell you what you can do about it. Nothing is set in stone and even if a situation is beyond our control, we usually have some degree of choice in how we react to it. Whilst the tarot is most well known as a tool for prediction, it is actually more often used as a tool for contemplation and reflection, for connecting to our inner selves. You will find that often, you already know what the tarot cards tell you, you just didn't know that you knew!

When people say that they are scared of the tarot or of what it might tell them, their fear is more likely a fear of being exposed, of having their inner feelings and experiences brought into the open. Not only does this make many people uncomfortable, but the fact that a deck of cards, mere images printed on paper, may do so, makes them even more uncomfortable. But we might say that this discomfort also shows us tarot's greatest strength, as an objective viewpoint on our lives. The cards seemingly fall at random, and yet their meanings connect deeply to our experience and show us the "truth" of our lives, as we are experiencing it at that moment. Some believe that there is some unseen force at work around us, ensuring that the cards we pull are exactly the ones we need to see right now, others that some hidden part of our mind influences us as we shuffle and lay out the cards. There are many ideas and explanations about why the tarot works, but most come back to the idea of synchronicity, or correspondences. Most of occult (the word "occult" simply means hidden knowledge) thought is based on the idea that there is a correspondence or link between something outside of ourselves, such as the tarot cards or the planets in astrology, and something within our psyche. They do not cause or affect each other, rather they are at work in parallel, so that by looking at the external manifestation of the force, for example in the image on a tarot card, we become aware of the corresponding energy at work within us. Occultists refer to this idea using the phrase "As above, so below" - as the energies play out above us in the universe, so they also play out within us. You may have already experienced "synchronicities" when events around you seem to reflect your emotions or what is happening within you. Using the tarot is a way of consciously inviting these synchronicities, understanding them and using them to live our best lives.

The History and Evolution of the Tarot

The tarot cards have their origins in fifteenth-century Italy, where they developed partly as a game (giving rise also to modern day playing cards) and partly as a kind of teaching aid showing medieval religious and social images, such as Strength, Temperance and Judgement. For years they were mainly used for the game of Tarocchi and for gambling, although they were sometimes also used for fortune telling. In the eighteenth century and nineteenth centuries, occultists (those who study hidden and esoteric knowledge) became aware of the tarot cards and their powerful images, and decided that there was more to these cards than met the eye. They linked them to the hidden knowledge of ancient Egypt, to the Jewish mystical tradition of the Kabbalah, and even to traditions of ceremonial magic. Nineteenth-century occultists, especially the members of the Order of the Golden Dawn in the late nineteenth century, worked with the cards and developed them into the images that we know today. Whilst they added extra layers of meaning and correspondences to other spiritual systems such as astrology, the basic structure of the deck has changed little since the artist Bonifacio Bembo painted the first deck for a wealthy Italian family, the Viscontis, in the middle of the fifteenth century.

Many of the decks most easily available today are based on the so-called Waite-Smith deck, developed by Arthur Waite (one of those Victorian occultists mentioned above) and illustrated by Pamela Colman Smith. It was first published in 1910 and has become the basis for most tarot decks published today.

The Waite-Smith deck was the first to use images on the Minor Arcana cards. The earlier Marseilles or European tradition (still popular and widely used today) has images on the Major Arcana cards and "pips" for the Minor Arcana – seven pentacles for the seven of pentacles, three swords for the Three of Swords, and so on. Many people find that having scenes painted on all the cards, including the Minor Arcana, makes them easier to read and remember, and this is especially useful when you are first learning the cards. However the Waite Smith version of the tarot is not as definitive as some would believe, and the earlier European tradition still has much to teach us.

Over time, as you become more familiar with the cards, you will find the images and tradition which work best for you. This book uses mainly the Waite Smith images, simply because they are most commonly found and referred to in the world of tarot, whilst also drawing on other traditions and versions of the tarot images.

CHOOSING A TAROT DECK

When we begin to work with tarot cards, we are making a choice to work on a symbolic level, which goes deeper than using our mind and intellect. From the many hundreds of different decks available today, the right deck for you is the one whose symbolism resonates deeply for you, the one which gives you a flash of recognition as soon as you see the cards. This may not be something you can articulate or communicate with others, but as you'll soon learn, there is much about the tarot that defies easy explanation, and herein lies its power.

A wide variety of decks are available, from the traditional to the modern, with themes drawing on different belief systems and traditions and on many aspects of popular culture. Whether your interest is fairies, tattoos or Buddhism, there's a tarot deck out there to suit you. When choosing a deck, listen to your intuition and choose the one with images you are drawn to, as you will get the most profound results that way. Working with the tarot means working with symbolic energies and images, so choosing a deck with images which reflect your worldview, or maybe even challenge your worldview, is likely to bring you the best results. There's no right or wrong way to choose a deck, as long as it speaks to you on some level, and has images that resonate with your life experience and the way you see the world.

You may also want to take into account practical considerations such as the shape and size of the cards, and how easy you find shuffling them. Even something as simple as the colour palette can evoke an emotional response, and an emotional response is what you want when choosing "your" deck.

Decks can be bought online as well as in "new age" shops and bookshops. New age shops often have a folder or file with sample cards from the different decks they have available so that you can look at the cards without having to open a sealed deck. Online, there are websites such as aeclectic.net and tarotgarden.com have lists and reviews of hundreds of decks, so you can do some research before you buy to be sure of getting the deck that's right for you. Some people believe that you must be gifted a tarot deck, but there is no reliable origin for this so-called tradition, which probably dates back to when tarot decks were difficult to find and knowing somebody who had one was really the only way to obtain one. Now they are widely available, we have more opportunities to find "our" deck and make that all-important personal connection with it.

Many tarot readers end up acquiring more than one tarot deck, and some have large collections. You may find that you work regularly with one or two decks, and have others simply because you like the images. Some decks work better for quick readings, others for deep personal explorations, still others for meditation and spiritual practice.

LOOKING AFTER YOUR CARDS

So you've got your cards, now what? The first thing to note is some easy ways to look after them, as they tend to come in a cardboard box which can get worn very quickly when you are constantly taking the cards in and out of it. Again, there are many traditions, usually of quite a modern origin, about how you should look after your cards, and again, you shouldn't worry too much about them, but follow what feels right to you. Many people believe that tarot cards should be wrapped in silk because silk is a natural fibre and is seen as a good insulator against psychic energies. So silk protects your cards on both a physical and a spiritual level. Other natural fibres such as cotton are also good, and keeping your cards in a wooden box is also a popular way to protect them. Your cards are a sacred tool and should be treated as such – look after them and they will look after you!

Many people prefer not to let others touch their tarot deck, as it can muddy the psychic energies the cards carry. Again, this is a personal preference, and of course, there is a difference between letting your nearest and dearest occasionally look through your cards, and complete strangers rifling through them.

When reading for others, many readers ask the querent (the person receiving the reading) to shuffle the decks, to add their own energy to the reading. This is also optional of course, and there are other ways for your querent to add their energy to the reading, without actually touching the cards, For example, they could tell you when to stop shuffling, or indicate the cards they want to choose from the pile.

Whilst to an outsider the cards may simply be pieces of cardboard, you will soon begin to feel a connection to them and see them as something more than mere objects. They do pick up and carry psychic energies. This is nothing to be afraid of and simply the way the cards work, but cleansing them every once in a while, or after doing lots of readings, is useful and some even consider it necessary.

There are many ways to cleanse your cards, and most make use of natural energies to do so. You can leave them out overnight in the light of the full moon, or the bright light of the sun. Be aware if you're doing the latter that some cards can bend a little in heat or humidity, so don't leave them for too long. Some people use crystals such as clear quartz or amethyst laid on top of the deck. If you do this, cleanse the crystal afterwards by passing it through running water. Smudging, or passing through the smoke from incense or even a fire, is a popular way to cleanse tarot cards, and is very effective. Many people use sage, although this is a Native American tradition and has been so widely appropriated that white sage is now an endangered species. Try to use a herb from your own cultural tradition, or look up the magical correspondences of the herbs you have in your kitchen. Rosemary or lavender are good, as are sandalwood or frankincense. Its fine to try a few different methods of cleansing your cards, and see what works best for you, and for your deck.

HOW TO READ THE TAROT CARDS

Studying and reading the tarot can be a life's work, but all you really need to get started is a deck of cards, your intuition (a kind of inner knowing everybody has which goes beyond the intellectual) and some basic card meanings, which this book will give you. To do a tarot reading, we shuffle the cards and lay them out in a particular order, known as a spread. Each position in a spread has a meaning. A popular and simple three card spread, for example, includes cards representing the past, present and future. We then interpret the cards according to their position, using meanings developed over centuries as well as our own intuition. Becoming a good tarot reader means learning to synthesise these three elements – the meaning of the individual card, its position in the spread and in relation to the other cards in the spread, and the intuitive meanings which may seem to come out of the blue as you gaze at the cards.

Anyone can read the tarot cards, you don't have to have psychic skills or lots of book learning. All you need is the ability to still and open your mind and respond to the images you see before you. This book will guide you through the basics of tarot card meanings and how to combine them in a reading. Whilst learning the meanings off by heart using a book such as this one is useful, ultimately the best way to learn to use tarot cards is simply that, to use them. Do readings for yourself, for your friends and family.

The first thing to do before doing a reading, or using your cards at all, is to shuffle them. This comes naturally to some people, but others find it challenging. If you are not confident of your shuffling skills, there are other methods of making sure the cards are properly mixed up. For example, you could simply lay them face down on the table in front of you, and push them gently with a circling motion, so that they spread out into a "pool". Once you have moved them sufficiently, you can gather them back up into a stack, or simply choose the cards from the pool.

Some readers turn some of the cards upside down when shuffling so that in a reading they are "reversed". This can change the way they are interpreted, as reversals are seen as the shadow side of the energy of the card. Reversed cards may ask you to pay extra attention to that message, or show where energy is blocked and not quite ready to come into conscious awareness. This can be helpful, but some people find it confusing and see the full range of meanings in the card when it is upright. Reversed cards are often seen as the "negative" version of the card meaning, and so some people see them as alarming. However, the reversed meaning of a challenging card, such as the Tower or some of the Swords cards, can actually lighten the energy and make it less challenging. Once again, its a personal choice to include reversals in your readings, and there is no right or wrong answer. However its best to be consistent, so decide whether or not you want to work with reversals and then stick to it.

GETTING TO KNOW YOUR TAROT DECK – SOME

SIMPLE EXERCISES

Whilst you will want to start doing readings as soon as you can, it's a good idea to spend some time getting to know your cards and trying out different ways of using them. This allows you to build up a personal connection to the cards, and gain a knowledge of the tarot that goes deeper than simple book learning.

An excellent way to begin learning is to pull a single card when you get up each morning and keep the image in mind as you go through your day. At the end of the day, look in the book to review the standard meaning of the card, and see if how it relates to your day. You will find that patterns emerge – lots of Swords cards when you are studying for an exam, or lots of Major Arcana cards when you are going through a big change in life.

Another good technique is close observation. Choose a card, at random or one that you'd like to know better, and simply spend several minutes looking at it closely. Note as many details as you can – colours, clothing, posture, facial expressions. Look at the layout of the picture, where everything is in relation to everything else. Look at the background, there are often details there that are easy to miss. When you have observed the picture for a while, you can take a metaphorical step back and consider the mood, the attitude of any people in the image, and what meaning these imply.

If you read lots of books on the tarot or talk to lots of tarot readers, you may find that there are sometimes apparently contradictory meanings for the same card. This is because there are so many layers of interpretation to each card, and a meaning that resonates for one reader may leave another cold. When you are starting out, there are several places you'll want to look to get a sense of the possible interpretations for a particular card. The "LWB" or Little White Book, which comes with the deck, usually gives brief meanings for that specific deck, and some tarot cards come with a full book covering the particular meanings used by the creators of that deck. Other books, such as this one, give an overview of the traditional meanings for a card, and you can use these with any deck. As you gain experience with the cards, you will also find that you intuitively "sense" meanings for specific cards, during readings or meditations, and these can come across quite strongly. Personal intuitive meanings are by their nature subjective, but some see them as more meaningful than traditional interpretations for exactly this reason. They may work in a specific situation, for example when reading for a querent who has a specific reaction to a particular card.

All of these layers of meaning can be confusing, and you may find yourself wondering which is the "right" meaning. The answer is all of them, or maybe none. Every interpretation is equally valid, and the ones which resonate with you will be the ones which are right for you. The only answer is to practice reading, for yourself and others, and you will begin to get a sense of which method of interpretation works best for you. Some people prefer to memorise traditional meanings and use them as a jumping off point, others rely purely on the images and symbolism on the cards, and what their intuition is telling them that day. As you gain experience with the cards, you will naturally find yourself working in a particular way and responding to the meanings which ring true for you and your querent. Even the most experienced tarot readers are constantly discovering something new in the cards. The meanings are not fixed, and that is another of the great gifts of tarot. You may even find that the way you interpret particular cards changes and evolves over time, and that's fine too.

CHAPTER TWO: THE MAJOR ARCANA

THE JOURNEY OF THE MAJOR ARCANA

The twenty-two cards of the Major Arcana tell a story, describing the journey of the Fool as he moves from innocence to experience, from youth to maturity, from ignorance to enlightenment. This is a psychological and spiritual journey, giving us not only a deeper awareness and understanding of our worldly concerns but also a connection to universal energies. This is not a journey which takes place on a uniquely linear plane - life goes in spirals, and we travel around the path many times in our lifetime. The spiritual wholeness of the final card, The World, leads straight back to the innocence of The Fool, which is generally seen as the beginning of the sequence, but also fits in at the end. The journey of the tarot works on both a macro and a micro level - it is the journey of a whole lifetime, from birth through youth, middle and old age to death, and also the multitudinous smaller journeys, spirals within an individual life.

The first Septenary, from the Magician to the Chariot, describes the journey to maturity. The Fool encounters the masculine and feminine energies of the archetypal Mother (the Empress) and Father (the Emperor) as well as the Magician and the High Priestess, who represent the spiritual aspects of the masculine and feminine. The

Fool becomes aware that he is part of a cultural or religious tradition, meeting the Hierophant, who can help him to decide where s/he belongs. As he grows to maturity, he becomes aware of others and may fall in love, learning to relate to others and make choices for himself. Finally, the Chariot represents worldly ambition, as the Fool gains the power to achieve his goals.

However, achieving our goals doesn't always feel as satisfying as we might have hoped. Sometimes we get all that we ever wanted and wonder why we are not happy. Sometimes we don't get anything we wanted and simply wonder why. We begin to question our assumptions and social conditioning, why we think the way we do, whether there is more to life than we've been led to believe. This is the journey of the Second Septenary, as the Fool begins to question his path in life and to seek a deeper level of meaning. He discovers their inner Strength and develops a sense of right and wrong (Justice). He begins to look inwards, as the Hermit, and to seek his own wisdom and path in life, as he gains in maturity and experience. He begins to understand that life's ups and downs are not always of our making, encountering the Wheel of Fortune, and at the same time meeting the paradox that we may have more control over life than we assume. He may retreat for a while, shift his perspective and even find his world turned upside down, becoming the Hanged Man. This change in worldview may lead to a time of endings, of letting go of past ways of acting and being, as in the Death card. We have to let go of the old, to make way for the more meaningful life that we seek. This new freedom is reflected in the following card, Temperance, which represents the renewed balance between consciousness and unconscious, and is one of the calmest and most harmonious cards in the major Arcana.

In the final Septenary the Fool looks beyond his individual growth, and begins to wrestle with universal energies, coming to a deeper level of awareness and therefore a more profound ability to create change. Encountering the Devil, he becomes aware of the ways that we give away our power, to other people or to our own expectations, and the Fool is challenged to take back that power. The Tower follows, a breaking down of inner and outer structures which may feel painful (especially if we resist it), but which clears the way for a greater understanding. The Star brings a time of calm - coming through the disruption of the Tower brings a sense of relief and a renewed sense of trust and faith in the universe. The worst may have happened, but we have not only survived but thrived. The Fool meets the dreamy energies of the Moon and may get sucked into that shadowy and uncertain realm, but the clarity of the Sun helps him to connect to his inner truth, and find ways to express it. The Judgement card symbolises this rebirth and ability to follow our highest calling, leading finally to the fulfilment and integration of the World. Of course, nothing in life is static, and the completion of the World card opens the way for the next chapter, bringing us back to the Fool at the beginning of his journey.

We may not encounter the cards in this linear sequence when we do readings (although sometimes we do, and is always a sign that your path is unfolding as it should). However knowing the story and the journey we take means that when Major Arcana comes up in readings, we have a sense of where we are on our journey, and what the next lessons might be. We can keep the journey in mind as we consider each of the Major Arcana cards individually.

INDIVIDUAL CARD MEANINGS FOR THE MAJOR ARCANA CARDS

0 THE FOOL

Keywords: Free spirit, a leap into the unknown, a new beginning, the unexpected

The Fool card shows a young person, standing on the edge of a cliff. He carries little baggage and ignores the dog, symbolising conscious awareness, who barks at his feet. The Fool is spontaneous and lives fully in the moment. His actions may seem like folly to others, but he has faith and trusts that all will comes right in the end. He is open to whatever gifts come his way and has no expectations, either good or bad. Indeed he is acting from his impulses, which may or may not prove to be right. The Fool moves towards change without knowing what kind of change it is or where he will end up, and this doesn't worry him. In fact, he welcomes the unknown, the excitement of a new journey with no particular destination in mine. The Fool is playful and open, not minding that this can also make him vulnerable or even foolhardy. The archetype of the Fool appears in many mythologies, as a trickster, reminding kings and heroes of their truth and not letting them get caught up in their own hubris. Sometimes, the apparently foolish are the only ones able to speak truth to the established powers. We also see the importance of the Fool when we note that he is the only one of the Trumps to have survived the transition to the modern deck of playing cards. Just like the Joker, the tarot Fool travels where he will through the pack of cards and doesn't follow any rules.

Reversed or shadow aspects of the Fool include a tendency to rush ahead without any awareness of the possible consequences. On the other hand, it may mean remaining in your comfort zone and refusing to try anything new or simply taking life too seriously, being cynical or pessimistic.

When the Fool comes up in a reading, a new adventure is about to begin. It's time to take a risk, to leap off the cliff often depicted in this card and trust that the path will be there to catch you. This is the card of following your bliss, of ignoring the expectations of others and doing what feels right for you. Listen to the cosmic messages of the universe and also to your own inner voice, then take a deep breath, and jump!

1 THE MAGICIAN

Keywords: Inner power, creativity, focus, attention, putting ideas into action

The Magician is a powerful figure, with the forces of the universe at his command, shown by the position of his arms. His right arm is held high to receive the energies of spirit, and his left hand points downwards, indicating that he brings those energies into everyday reality, and makes something tangible with them. His magic wand symbolises authority and confidence, the masculine or active energies we use to do our work in the world. On his table are the tools of the four suits of the Minor Arcana, showing his inner resources and talents. The Magician is single-minded and pure in his intentions and represents our ability to establish our priorities, focus on our goals and then take action to make them a reality. The Magician is both potential and experience and reminds us that when we act from a higher purpose, we connect to our highest self. He represents knowledge, learning and initiative, all bringing the potential for growth. Like the Fool, the Magician can be a trickster, and in early tarot decks, he was often shown as a conjurer or even a juggler. He is the archetype of the wizard, the wise magician who can change the world with his powers. In some decks, he is depicted as a shaman, who walks in the otherworld and brings its wisdom back to the mundane world.

Reversed or shadow aspects of the Magician can be trickery or deceit, acting from self-interest or for personal gain, and not respecting the needs of others. Using his power to dominate others or for selfish reasons results in the Magician losing his connection to the higher power which guides him. The shadow side of the trickster is the conman who cheats others for his own personal gain.

In a reading, the Magician tells you that you have what you need to make your dreams a reality. It's time to take action to realise your potential, to tap into your willpower and inner vitality. Have confidence in yourself and your abilities, and use the power of your conscious mind to achieve your goal. Concentrating on the project at hand, whilst also listening to the wisdom of your higher self, is the best way forwards.

2 THE HIGH PRIESTESS

Keywords: intuition, secret knowledge, deeper meaning, hidden self

The High Priestess is a mysterious figure, connected with dreams, intuition and the messages of the unconscious. She is the Magician's opposite, the power of the unconscious mind, the shadowy inner self and the power of receptivity and stillness. As the keeper of ancient and eternal wisdom, she represents knowledge and awareness of the mystery of life, as well as collective and personal memory. The black and white pillars often shown on either side of her throne symbolise light and dark, inner and outer, thought and feeling, all the dualities which we experience in our lives. Behind the curtain, she guards the mystery which brings them into balance. Her connection to the moon, shown in her headdress and also in the crescent moon at her feet, reminds us that life moves in cycles, the ebb and flow and that the quiet dark is just as important as the times of light and action. She is the archetype of deep feminine understanding, connected to wisdom goddesses such as Sophia and Isis, and she understands the deep power of the unconscious and of the underworld. A historical or legendary source for this card is the story of the woman who was once elected Pope (strictly against the rules of the Catholic Church), only being revealed as a woman when she gave birth during an Easter celebration, and until the eighteenth century, this card was called the Papess. The persistence of this story reflects the importance of the feminine archetype even in the male-dominated medieval Christian church and also reflects the meaning of the High Priestess as a mysterious figure whose full self must remain hidden.

Reversed or shadow aspects of the High Priestess can be an inability to connect to our dreams or listen to our intuition, thinking literally or superficially, and assuming that we already know everything. The reversed High Priestess might also indicate that we have been passive for too long, and need to take action to change our situation.

When she comes up in a reading, the High Priestess says that now is not the time for action. This is a time to go inwards, to listen to your intuition which is likely to be strong right now. There may be hidden potential or a new possibility about to come to light. This is a time when you can connect to the inner mysteries, to a sense of something greater than yourself.

3 THE EMPRESS

Keywords: fertility, creativity, generating new life, abundance, fruition, feminine energy

The Empress is the energy of the archetypal Mother, bringing new life to birth and embodying the fertility and abundance of nature. She is often shown as a pregnant or surrounded by the fruits of the harvest, showing the luxuriant energy of life and all its bounty. She speaks of creative abundance, of the fulfilment of our heart's desires, of the pleasures of the senses. Her sceptre of power is topped by a globe, reminding us that we create, literally bring into being, our own world. The Empress symbolises the passionate, even sensual approach to life, the power to give and take experience and emotions without limit or restriction. The stream often depicted at her feet symbolises both the unconscious, connecting her back to the High Priestess, and the waters of life, which ensure that everything grows and flourishes. She shows us how we can use our imagination and creativity to generate ideas and to birth them in reality. She also reminds us of the need to balance patience and action, to allow the harvest to develop in its own time so that it can grow to its full potential. The Empress represents synthesis and harmony, the unity which is born from the dualities of light and dark, action and receptivity. She is firmly rooted in our present experience and our connection to the world around us but also holds an awareness of our potential and what we are able to create.

Reversed or shadow aspects of the Empress may be struggling to connect with our emotions or ability to nurture ourselves and others, not giving others the space they need to be themselves, and sometimes destroying instead of creating. Reversed, the Empress might also suggest an over-abundance rather than a lack of emotions.

In a reading, she indicates a time of abundance, creativity and growth. You may be bringing a new project into being, nourishing and nurturing it into reality. It's a time to connect to nature and to the powers of your senses. She reminds us that abundance is not just about the material, but about gratitude for the many gifts life gives us each day. Take time to nourish whatever is most important to you, focusing your energy and attention on it.

4 THE EMPEROR

Keywords: authority, power, control, boundaries, masculine energy

The Emperor is the archetypal energy of the father, an authority figure who seeks to control and organise. He may represent social conformity, rules and regulations and the need to maintain order. He is confident in his right to rule and expects others to follow his lead. He is the master builder and the force of civilisation, bringing order to chaos and setting the rules which ensure that society functions successfully. He sets standards and social expectations and expects them to be met. The Emperor is a man of reason and logic, as well as action. He protects all those within his care, bringing security and comfort to his people. He has served his time on the battlefield and still wears his armour under his robes, ready to defend his people if he needs to. Now he represents the establishment and the social order, the father as guide, protector and provider. He is often seen as a very traditional, perhaps even old-fashioned, version of the father archetype as somebody rather remote and distant, who makes the rules and enforces discipline. A more positive approach is to see the Emperor as the creator of boundaries, helping us to know who we are as an individual and what our place is in the world. Most of us need to interact with mainstream society, to a greater or lesser extent, in order to live our daily lives, and we need to conform to certain behaviours to be accepted into that society, such as not harming others.

Reversed or shadow aspects of the Emperor include a tendency to control others, getting angry or defensive if our authority is challenged, becoming aggressive or dominating. On the other hand, the Emperor reversed can mean an inability to make decisions or take control of the situation.

In a reading, the Emperor asks you to look at your boundaries, and to your sense of inner authority. Are you in control of your life or are you trying to control those around you? It might be time to take on a leadership role, or to get clear about your direction and purpose in life. The Emperor indicates a need to take responsibility for yourself, to become the ruler of your own life. Getting organised and focused are also indicated by this card.

5 THE HIEROPHANT

Keywords: tradition, spiritual knowledge, teaching, education, group awareness

The Hierophant is a priest-like figure, usually shown with one or two acolytes or students who receive the knowledge and traditions he passes down. He symbolises established knowledge, the cultural and religious beliefs which inform our view of the world. His beliefs and ideas have been proven over time, which gives them authority and power but may also make them feel restrictive or rigid. The original name for this card was the Pope, linking it to the inner wisdom of the Papess or High Priestess, and this card can be seen as the outer manifestations of that wisdom, the church or belief systems which guide our society. However many people are now rejecting the established churches and choosing to follow their own spiritual path and ideally, the Hierophant is an inner teacher, the part of ourselves which seeks to understand the mysteries of the universe and the powers that guide us. He guides us through rituals and celebrations, the events which mark the rhythms of our lives and give them meaning. The Hierophant also represents groups and structures in society, the desire to conform and feel part of a group. This sense of belonging can bring security or restriction, and again as our inner guide, the Hierophant asks us to question our beliefs, not to mindlessly follow the ideas of others. We can draw on the wisdom of our traditions whilst also adapting it to work better in our own lives. Sometimes this card can refer to a giving away of responsibility, sticking to the rules in order to avoid thinking for ourselves about what is right and wrong.

Reversed or shadow aspects of the Hierophant may be intolerance of the beliefs of others, or blindly accepting other people's ideas, group or personal dogma. The Hierophant reversed can also suggest rebelling for the sake of it, rejecting the traditional or conventional but not replacing it with anything meaningful, or developing our own original ideas.

When the Hierophant comes up in a reading, you may be feeling drawn to a spiritual or religious tradition, or feeling the need to rebel against it and seek your own wisdom. You may be considering your group identity and wondering where you belong, or considering your beliefs and worldview, and how they inform your choices in life.

6 THE LOVERS

Keywords: relationship, love, inner and outer union, bringing together of opposites, choice

In the Lovers, we meet the "other" for the first time and must learn how to relate to others. The Lovers represent union, both with another person and within ourselves, and the coming together of opposites. This card is about forming bonds and connections, in romantic relationships and also more generally. Relationships with others, whether close and lasting or fleeting, offer us opportunities for growth, for getting to know ourselves better and also for learning to focus on something beyond ourselves. Whilst it's tempting always to interpret this card in that context, it's important to remember that we also have a relationship with ourselves, and this card also symbolises integrating the masculine and feminine (we all have both, although we do not always express them equally) within ourselves. The angel shown in many of the more modern versions of the Lovers represents a mediating force, helping us to balance our inner and outer dualities. When we feel complete and accepting of ourselves, we can meet others as a more honest version of ourselves, avoiding the projections which can influence our relationships. Our active or masculine side is often directed by our feminine or unconscious side, and this card symbolises this dynamic and the way it guides our actions.

The shadow or reversed aspects of the Lovers might be difficulty trusting or opening up to others, refusing to accept conflicting aspects of ourselves, and also expecting another person to complete or heal us rather than taking responsibility for our own emotional wellbeing. It may suggest being in a relationship for the "wrong" reasons, such as a fear of being alone, or love as a destructive rather than a unifying force.

In a reading, this card can be easy to interpret – it indicates a relationship, the strengthening of a bond with a loved one, perhaps a commitment or even marriage. However, it can also indicate the need to make a choice, often between staying in your comfort zone or moving towards a new level of maturity. Sometimes it represents the need to bring the masculine and feminine, the active and receptive, sides of ourselves into balance.

7 The Chariot

Keywords: action, momentum, power, focus, determination, achievement, purpose

The Chariot is the card of victory, of being in control and achieving your goals. It can mean bringing the opposing energies sometimes indicated by the Lovers under control, by force or otherwise, and using this energy to move forward in pursuit of your ambitions. The two animals pulling the vehicle depicted in the card are often different colours or trying to go in different directions. As the driver of the Chariot, you need to keep them in balance, for both are necessary to move forward. Driving such a vehicle at speed requires total control over the animals, and so this card symbolises strong willpower. The charioteer is the victorious hero, who conquers all that he sets out to conquer. This card indicates worldly success achieved through sustained effort. Its a card of determination and enthusiasm, and often indicates the potential for leadership and accomplishment. There is always movement with the Chariot, a constant moving forwards in a dynamic balance. The sphinxes or horses once again represent the dualities within us, thinking and feeling, and acting and reacting. The Chariot can symbolise our "persona", the mask we create as we grow up which allows us to deal with the outside world and hide the parts of ourselves we are not so comfortable with.

The reverse or shadow side of the Chariot may be controlling yourself or others too much, or not enough, and having little sense of purpose or direction. It may also mean trying too hard to achieve a goal which is not right for you at this time. You may need to change your perspective or path, rather than following a course simply because it's the one you are already on.

When the Chariot comes up in a reading, you are likely to be in pursuit of a goal, probably with single-minded focus and a sense of purpose. Success is secure as long as you keep the momentum going, and keep your inner and outer selves, your thoughts and emotions, in balance. This is the card of the ego, which organises and controls our persona and allows us to act in the world but can become rigid and fearful if we are not careful.

8 STRENGTH

Keywords: inner strength, compassion, gentle control, patience

Like the Chariot, the Strength card symbolises willpower and our ability to control the circumstances around us and use them to our advantage. However the strength represented here is not forceful control or power over others, but rather power from within, a kind of gentle control which is patient and tolerant of the needs and desires of others. This card usually shows a woman who has tamed a lion or other wild beast, which allow her to touch it. The animal symbolises our inner "wild side", our animal instincts. Our strength and power come from those instincts and this card symbolises the power to use them wisely, rather than allowing them to take over, so that we act without conscious consideration. In some ways this card can be seen as balancing our conscious minds with our unconscious instincts, to make the best use of both of them. This is a strength of "allowing" rather than forcing, of using our inner rather than our physical powers. We can follow and fulfil our desires without allowing them to take us over or to hurt others, by transforming the devouring energies of our inner wildness into something in harmony with our higher self. The strength shown here is the strength to face life, especially when we are faced with challenges or change, with hope, able to see the opportunities or growth rather than becoming overwhelmed or giving up.

The reverse or shadow aspects of this card can be a lack of self-control, courage or integrity, being forceful or aggressive, and also losing focus and scattering your energy. It can also mean a lack of self-belief or loss of confidence in yourself.

In a reading, this card shows that you have this strength, and do not need to force others to bend to your will. Instead, you can inspire others with your tolerance and compassion. You can be guided by your instincts without being overtaken by them. This is a time to balance action and the urge to move forwards with intuition and the need for patience. You may be becoming aware of the power of your emotions and the need to use it consciously.

9 THE HERMIT

Keywords: solitude, inner wisdom, truth, patience, experience

The Hermit card shows a mature figure, carrying a lamp which symbolises inner wisdom, the knowledge we have built up with our life experience, which we can now use to light our way. The Hermit is a contemplative figure, who looks inwards and reflects on his knowledge in order to find the way forward. He is not in a rush and knows that true wisdom takes time. In fact the Hermit also symbolises the past, and old age, the power of time to bring change and growth. After the worldly cards of the first stages of the Fool's journey, now the Hermit asks us to draw on our inner strength and look within, to explore our own unconscious minds, to figure out what is most meaningful to us and use that awareness to guide our choices. He holds his lamp in his right hand, symbolising this conscious awareness of our inner wisdom. The Hermit symbolises humility before a higher power, and he knows that the more he learns, the more he realises he doesn't know. The Hermit is another powerful and deep-rooted archetype, and throughout history, people have withdrawn from society in order to contemplate the greater mysteries, like the medieval hermit living in a cave or the woods. On a symbolic level, the Hermit represents the idea that by withdrawing from the demands and concerns of the outer world, we can connect more deeply to our inner world. The Hermit asks us to consider where we are focusing our attention and energy, and whether it is truly worth our time.

The shadow or reversed aspects of the Hermit can be a feeling of isolation or loneliness, feeling uncomfortable with your inner self and unwilling to look within. You may find yourself taking refuge in meaningless activities or spending time with others to avoid the unsettling call of your higher wisdom.

When the Hermit appears in a reading, he indicates a time of quiet, calm introspection, even solitude. You are likely to be seeking something, perhaps a greater understanding of your life so far or your future path, or simply a deeper awareness of your place in the universe. It may be time to reevaluate your priorities, values and goals, especially if they are not allowing you to grow.

10 THE WHEEL OF FORTUNE

Keywords: cycles, change, ebb and flow, ups and downs

The Wheel of Fortune is a traditional image showing the ups and downs of life – sometimes the circumstances around us are positive and things seem to go our way, and at others times we may struggle or feel that we are unable to make progress. Often we do not have any control over these changes, and so the meaning of this card is also acceptance, as well as fate or destiny. This card can symbolise the natural rhythm of life, the season of growth and the season of fallow energy, and the awareness that both are necessary to keep us in balance. The Wheel teaches us when to go with the flow, when to endure, and how to understand out situation deeply enough that we know which of these approaches will serve us best. We are part of something bigger than ourselves, and an awareness of the Wheel of Fortune can give us a glimpse of this greater pattern. In history and mythology, the Wheel of Fortune can symbolise both the natural and mysterious laws of the universe, the seemingly random events of life, and also our attempts to influence those laws and change our apparent fate. As the halfway point of the Major Arcana sequence, the Wheel shows us how our lives are balanced between elements that we can control and a kind of fate or destiny which is more mysterious.

The reversed or shadow aspects of the Wheel of Fortune can be procrastination and passivity, assuming that our fate is out of our hands and there is nothing we can do to change it. Fighting or resisting necessary change can also be a negative manifestation of this card.

In a reading, the Wheel can indicate a time of change, a period when things seem to be happening beyond your control and you have no choice but to go with them. On the other hand, it can indicate a time when you feel stuck and don't seem to be able to move forward. Either way, the message of this card is often that whilst we may not be able to choose the circumstances around us, we can choose how we react to them and use the energy available to us.

11 JUSTICE

Keywords: balance, integrity, harmony, right action, equilibrium

As you might expect, Justice is the card of right and wrong, or right action and the repercussions of our actions. It can symbolise the structures around this in our society, such as the law, but on a deeper level, it speaks of our ethics and morality, the need to act with integrity and honesty. It symbolises impartiality, fairness, balance and objectivity, the need to act from our head, not from our heart. The principles of social or legal justice are more correctly ruled by the Emperor, whereas the Justice card represents a kind of cosmic equilibrium, the forces which keep the universe in balance as well as our individual lives. This can be a card of karma, of accepting that all of our choices and actions have consequences and that even if they are unintended, they are still our responsibility. This can be a liberating process, as it frees us from constantly repeating the same life patterns until we have learned the lessons of that past behaviour, and Justice brings us an awareness that our apparent free will is shaped by our past actions. Justice doesn't simply ask that we balance all the dualities and contradictions within us, but accept that each has something to teach us. We need to listen to and accept all viewpoints, to acknowledge them all as equally valid. The objectivity of Justice helps us to understand the ups and downs of the Wheel of Fortune and to bring those extremes into harmony.

The reversed or shadow aspects of Justice can be refusing to take responsibility for our actions or to accept the consequences of our decisions, and also leaping ahead to make a decision without considering all the facts. Acting from our heart rather than using our head is also relevant here.

In a reading, the appearance of the Justice card may indicate the need to make a decision, or perhaps to consider the causes and effects of your actions. It indicates a need to take responsibility and to act with integrity, doing what we know to be right rather than what is easy. When we see the Justice card, we need to consider how to honour our contradictions and bring ourselves into harmony.

12 THE HANGED MAN

Keywords: release, surrender, shift in perspective, sacrifice, suspension

The Hanged Man is a mysterious figure, unsettling to some as he appears to be in an uncomfortable position. However, in most of the images of this card, he looks peaceful and even happy. The Hanged Man is a paradox, for he teaches us that sometimes, the best way to succeed is to stop trying. After the turning inward of the last few cards and the uncomfortable truths we may be discovering about ourselves, the Hanged Man brings a period of peace. We need to suspend our actions for a while, reverse our perspective and surrender to what comes. This is a card of knowing when the time is right, and not doing anything until that time. The power of the Hanged Man lies in his stillness, his openness to a new way of being, and his ability simply to wait for the right time. He teaches us to reframe our experience, to seek the positive in a challenging situation or the reality of an illusion. He can also show us our place in the bigger picture, allowing us to see beyond our individual concerns and connect to something greater than ourselves. This new perspective can allow us to sacrifice some of those individual concerns, especially those which are proving to be meaningless and make space for a clearer sense of who we really are. The Hanged Man can bring a kind of independence of thinking, an ability to release our social conditioning and follow the path of our hearts.

Reversed or shadow aspects of this card include holding on to a way of being which no longer serves us or refusing to consider change. We may not be willing to make the necessary sacrifices which will allow us to move forward, or we may sacrifice too much of ourselves or take on a victim mentality.

When he comes up in a reading, the Hanged Man tends to indicate a time when trying or taking conscious action to change our situation will not help. We need to release, to let go of our urge to control and allow events to unfold as they will. This is a card of patience and stillness, of allowing ourselves simply to be.

13 DEATH

Keywords: release, endings, transformation, change

Many fear this card, and perhaps with good reason, for it carries a powerful energy. It rarely indicates a literal death, but it does mean a change, a process of release and transformation which we must allow to happen if we are to move forward. Endings inevitably bring sadness, but almost every image of this card shows a new dawn beyond the skeleton, a new beginning on the horizon. In most cases, the changes heralded by the Death card are natural changes, for ultimately death is simply a part of life, one of life's few inevitablilities. The cycle of life, death and rebirth is the foundation of all things, and it must be acknowledged as such. The Hanged Man brings us to an awareness of what we need to release, and the Death card describes that process of release. It may be messy and painful, it may be a relief and a source of joy, but either way it is powerful and brings about deep transformation. We live in a world that often encourages us to ignore what is difficult, but it is there that the greatest power and potential lies. Death is usually seen as something to be feared, but it is actually the unknown that we fear, for who can really know what happens after we die? Symbolically, our ego resists change because of this same fear of the unknown. The image of dawn in the background of the card shows the positive potential of the unknown, the chance to experience life in all its glory.

The shadow or reversed aspects of the Death card can be resistance to change, stagnation and inertia, and holding on to worldly power or possessions to avoid the challenge of transformation and growth.

In a reading, the Death card indicates a process of inevitable change, and the need to acknowledge it rather than resisting or fighting against it. Whether it's an outdated emotional pattern or a job we no longer enjoy, saying goodbye to the past is the only way to move into our future. Sometimes we may be held back by unresolved feelings from our past, and acknowledging and releasing these clears the space for a new beginning.

14 TEMPERANCE

Keywords: balance, harmony, union of opposites, health

Temperance brings a calm energy after the powerful transformation of Death, a sense of inner union which comes from having faced our fears. Often shown as an angel pouring water between two containers, Temperance brings a sense of equilibrium and flow. She represents the principle of guiding and blending the dualities we have confronted in the last few cards, combining them to produce a sense of harmony. We are able to combine spontaneity with the knowledge we have gained so far and move beyond the restrictive masks of the ego self. The word "Temperance" comes from the Latin "temperare" which means "to mix" or "to combine properly". We do not just throw everything in together, we allow the process of combining to flow in its natural sequence. Like so many others in the second Septenary, this a card of allowing energies to flow rather than trying too hard or forcing them. Change comes when the time is right when all the pieces are in the right place and can come together in the most productive way. This card is often linked to rainbows, for example through the iris flowers shown in the image below and the resemblance of the angel to the Greek goddess Iris, goddess of the rainbow. The rainbow is a symbol of new life, of something magical seemingly created from nothing. It shows the energy of life which comes after the process of Death, our new awareness of our connection to the greater universe.

Reversed or shadow meanings of this card include being self-centred or going to extremes, mood swings or unstable actions, chaos or lack of self-control. Temperance reversed can indicate that you keep the various parts of your life too separate and risk becoming fragmented or losing a sense of who you are as a whole person.

When it appears in a reading, the Temperance card can mean a need for moderation or balance, for not going to extremes. It can indicate a time when we are in our "flow", able to connect to a deeper sense of self and act from that, bringing creative energy and a sense of being in touch with our true self. This card can also relate to health and a sense of wellbeing.

15 THE DEVIL

Keywords: power, bondage, freedom, materialism

The Devil is another card which many find challenging, with its often unsettling images of a horned figure presiding over two figures in chains. However look closer and you'll see that the chains are loose, and that the figures could remove them if they chose. Whilst this card can indicate feeling trapped or controlled, it also shows us that we have the ability to break our bonds. Often the Devil symbolises our shadow side, the parts of ourselves that we prefer to deny or ignore. We may be overly concerned with appearances or social status, with things that are not really meaningful and which take our power away from our spiritual growth. The Devil symbolises not only a focus on the material and meaningless, but also the illusion that nothing exists beyond that, a denial of the gifts and mysteries of spirit. The illusions of the material realm limit and restrict us, and can become addictions, in extreme cases. They do not bring true satisfaction, and so we keep going, thinking that the next shiny new thing will be the one that finally makes us happy. Once we acknowledge these feelings and the futility of this quest, we are released and can use the energy we reclaim for something genuinely meaningful. Like the Death card, facing our fears and challenges here is a powerful experience, one that can transform us deeply. The Devil card signifies the life force which we lock away in our shadow side or unconscious mind, and the ability to unlock it.

The shadow or reversed meaning of the Devil tends to mean giving in to our shadow side, focusing only on the shallow or superficial and ignoring the pull of anything deeper. On the other hand, it can mean the process of releasing our chains and taking back our power, acknowledging the shadow self.

In a reading, the Devil asks us to look to our power, and where we give it away. It may indicate that we are too caught up in the material and are neglecting our deeper self, or that we are ignoring our true self in an attempt to conform to the expectations of others. Either way, we are called to break our bonds and release our power.

16 THE TOWER

Keywords: breaking down, release, revelation, structures

Another unsettling card, the Tower shows figures being struck by lightning and falling from a high tower. It can indicate unexpected and even unwelcome change and upheaval or crisis over which we have no control. It often reflects the truism that bad luck seems to come in phases so that everything happens at once and we are left floundering as we try to deal with it all. On a deeper level though, it symbolises the need to break out of the structures we have built for ourselves, to change outdated patterns which no longer serve us. Having faced our shadow in the Devil, the structure of our ego may have taken a blow, as we are forced the confront the walls we have built around ourselves. As these walls shatter, we may feel that we are left stranded, our sense of security and safety gone. However, when we open our eyes and look around, we realise that we can see further than we have ever seen before and that new possibilities, things we might not have even imagined, are opening up before us. The Tower symbolises an awakening, a time when illusions are shattered and seemingly permanent structures are proved to be flimsy or false. Whilst this can be distressing, now you have the opportunity to build something stronger, and also more flexible, in accordance with your own values instead of the expectations or needs of others. This card can also symbolise a flash of insight or even enlightenment, a breaking open of awareness which gives us a much broader view of life.

The reversed or shadow meanings of the Tower include avoidance of change, refusal to understand or allow your awareness to grow, and holding on to rigid attitudes and entrenched ideas. It can also suggest a milder version of the upright meaning, a less dramatic version of necessary changes.

When the Tower comes up in a reading, it inevitably indicates a time of change. Whilst this can be unsettling or even painful, it also usually brings revelation. We are broken out of our comfort zone, and possibilities open up around us. It's time to let go of what no longer works and build something more fulfilling.

17 THE STAR

Keywords: hope, optimism, trust, faith

A time of calm follows a time of upheaval. The Star brings a sense of relief and a renewed sense of trust and faith in the universe. The pool often shown in this card represents our connection to something greater than ourselves, and we can tap into this when we are in need of reassurance or inspiration. The Star symbolises hope and optimism, a sense that we are on the right path. The light of the Star is the light of understanding, awareness, and truth, stimulating our imagination and our sense of connection to something greater than ourselves. The universe, spirit, the divine – however we think of it or define it, we are offered a continuous supply of wisdom, of energy for growth and understanding. The Star shines above us to guide our way, showing us a deeper sense of meaning and direction in our lives. The pool often shown in the Star card symbolises our connection to the unconscious mind, on both a personal and a collective level, and we can connect to the waters of the pool by tuning in to our still inner voice. The Star inspires us to bring the gifts of the unconscious into tangible reality, through our creative talents. Our inner transformation and newfound connection to the source of life (visualized by the pool in the image) brings the potential to the way we work and act in the world. This is a card of inner calm and serenity, bringing healing and a holistic awareness. All the masks have fallen away (which is why the figure in this card is almost always nude), we know our place in the universe and our true self.

The shadow or reversed meanings of the Star include denying our talents and inner truths, losing ourselves in idealism without bringing our ideals into reality. It may mean insecurity, losing hope or taking a pessimistic attitude.

The appearance of the Star in a reading suggests an ability to connect to our deeper self and to trust that all will be well. Love and energy flow freely and are available to us as we need them, for ourselves or to share with others. This is a time to align ourselves with a higher consciousness, to grow in our connection to spirit, and to honour our creative imagination.

18 THE MOON

Keywords: cycles, imagination, shadow, illusion

The Moon can be a shadowy figure, indicating shadows and illusions as well as imagination and dreams. This card symbolises the unconscious mind and the darkness, which we often see as frightening. We fear the unknown, but it also brings great gifts of imagination and inspiration. The Moon symbolises the knowledge we hold deep in our cells, the embodied wisdom which goes beyond our intellect and connects us to our instincts and intuition. Intimately connected with our feeling self, the Moon asks us to listen to the wisdom of our emotions and to acknowledge their power. Delving deep into ourselves, we may encounter fears and delusions, perhaps old emotional patterns which no longer serve us and we can bring them into the Moon's gentle light and let them go. The Moon is connected with the cycles of growth and decay and asks us to pay attention to those cycles in our lives, learning when to let our energies build and when to release them. The darkness is just as important as the light, allowing us to nurture the seeds of new growth and also to rest and retreat when we need to. The Moon card always indicates the activity of the unconscious. This may be our personal unconscious minds, speaking to us through dreams, fears, and feelings, but may also be the collective unconscious. The Moon shows our connection to this more universal shadow, the aspects of it we connect to most deeply and how that connection affects us.

The shadow or reversed side of the Moon can be failing to acknowledge our feelings, imagination and sensitivity, ignoring the shadow, or paying too much attention to illusions and allowing them to rule us. Ignoring the pull of the unconscious means that it will simply try harder to get your attention, which can lead to distorted emotions and fears.

In a reading, the Moon suggests that this is a time when linear thinking will not work. Instead, you need to go with the flow, to follow your intuition and to let your inner voice guide you. It may be a time of psychic or intuitive awakening when you are learning to listen to new forms of knowledge. You may need to be careful not to be overwhelmed with fears or anxieties. Your instincts can guide you to know what is real and what is an illusion.

19 THE SUN

Keywords: creativity, enlightenment, confidence, optimism, joy

The light of the Sun can literally bring enlightenment, a sense of clarity and vitality which revitalises and energises us. This is a card of confidence and creativity, of letting yourself shine and of having your achievements recognised. It can be a card of understanding, enthusiasm and positive energy, and of getting to the heart of the matter. The Sun gives us vital and constant energy, a micro-regeneration each day which allows us to work in, and on, the warmth and light of our conscious growth. This is another card of good health (along with Temperance), of feeling invigorated, charged up and full of enthusiasm. There's a reason that so many cultures honour the Sun as a god or goddess, for it brings life to the earth, and on a symbolic level, consciousness to the self. Rather than a card of the controlling ego, the Sun symbolises our true, authentic self, without the masks or personas we sometimes rely on, hence the nudity of the child often shown in the card. The child is our inner child, the pureness of our being and the horse often ridden by the child symbolises power and vital force, the ability to move forward with confidence along our life's journey. In the Sun we are aware of the beauty of life, understanding the power of the life force in all its manifestations, experiencing life as pure energy. We feel joy, optimism and a sense of wonder, and radiate these feelings to those around us.

The reversed or shadow aspects of the Sun can be ignoring our inner child, a fear of trust or lack of confidence in ourselves. The Sun reversed suggest surviving rather than thriving, and a need for more illumination in our lives. The positive energy of the Sun is not lost but may become confused and less clear.

The Sun showing up in a reading is generally seen as a very positive omen, indicating a time when you are clear in your purpose, understanding and ability to shine. Masks have been set aside and you are able to let your true self shine through. You may find yourself the centre of attention, encouraging and inspiring others. It may also indicate a time of strong vital and physical energy.

20 JUDGEMENT

Keywords: inner calling, rebirth, awakening, forgiveness

Judgement is a card of awakening, of becoming aware of a higher purpose or calling which inspires you. There is an inner conviction, a sense of something you have to do, even – especially – if it is difficult or challenging in your current circumstances. The angel blowing the trumpet which features in many depictions of this card is the summons which calls us to a higher consciousness, a new level of awareness. This call is within us, a kind of yearning which bubbles up and demands attention, and also experience it as something outside us, coming from a force much greater and more mysterious than ourselves. The Judgement card symbolises rising up out of the restrictions of self-doubt and the expectations of others, bringing a kind of rebirth, the opening up of a new sense of self. Judgement can show you your true vocation or purpose in life, asking you to listen for what makes your soul sing and then find a way to follow that path. It can be challenging, but the potential rewards are great. This card can also indicate a more literal kind of judgement, perhaps a time of evaluating your life and making some necessary changes or releasing and guilt or sorrow we carry from the past so that we can move forward. Often we judge ourselves much more harshly than we judge others so this card is as much about forgiving ourselves as it is about forgiving others.

The reversed or shadow meanings of the Judgement card include being critical or judgemental of ourselves or others, and feeling disconnected from our spiritual awareness and stuck in the material, refusing to hear the call or trying to ignore it. It may also mean that you want to answer the call, but don't know what to do or where to begin.

In a reading, the Judgement card can indicate a time of rebirth, of answering the inner call, following the yearning of your heart to find fulfilment and a sense of purpose. Sometimes it indicates a literal judgement to be made, a truth to be found or a decision to be made. There is an energy of regeneration inherent in this card, which brings hope and the opening up of new possibilities.

21 THE WORLD

Keywords: completion, integration, accomplishment, fulfilment

The World is a card of completion, of everything coming together to achieve something that is greater than the sum of its parts. As the final card of the Major Arcana, it brings together the energies of all the previous cards, synthesising and integrating them. It symbolises wholeness, happiness and a deep sense of connection. This is not a static energy, but a dynamic balance. We are connected to the dance of life, free of the fears and doubts which may have held us back in the past and able to see both ourselves and the world around us more clearly. The World is the last numbered card of the Major Arcana, and as the end of the cycle, implies the beginning of the new one. This is why the Fool is sometimes referred to as card number twenty-two, as once we have reached the unity of the World, we step once more into our clearest, most spontaneous self, and begin again the spiral of growth. Like the universe, we are in constant movement, always part of the cycles of our inner self as well as the great cycles of the universe around us. The figure in the World card is the cosmic dancer, often seen as androgynous, having finally united all the dualities within. S/he moves with the cycles, endlessly flowing, transforming and renewing. The World and the Fool are the only two cards in the Major Arcana which show moving figures, connected to the great spiral of being which is part of us all, and of which we all form a part.

The shadow or reversed meanings of the World can be a refusal to acknowledge that a cycle has come to an end, stagnation and a refusal to move on, or keeping yourself isolated and cut off from the rest of the world.

When it appears in a reading, the World indicates the end of a cycle, the fulfilment of a goal, a dream realised. This is a time of satisfaction and contentment, of gratitude for what you have and the results of your efforts. When the World card comes up, it reminds us that we are part of something much bigger than our daily concerns and individual lives, and connects us to planetary and even cosmic consciousness.

Chapter Three: The Minor Arcana

The Structure of the Minor Arcana

The Minor Arcana consists of four suits, each containing fourteen cards, numbered Ace through to Ten and then Page, Knight, Queen and King. Each suit connects to one of the four elements, fire, air, water and earth. According to traditional occult symbolism, each element represents a different area of life. Through the elemental energies, the cards of the Minor Arcana show the energies which play out in our everyday lives.

The suit of Wands connects to the element of fire. It symbolises action, passion, vision and creativity. Cards in the suit of Wands often relate to our work or other projects we put energy into.

The suit of Swords connects to the element of air. It describes the realm of the mind, our thoughts and ideas, and the way we communicate them with others. Traditionally the suit of Swords has symbolised conflict, and so some of the images can be unsettling, but conflict is only one of the meanings of the Swords cards.

The suit of Cups is linked to the element of water, the element of feelings, emotions and the imagination. The Cups cards show us the realm of dreams and the unconscious as well as the way we feel about and relate to others.

Finally, the suit of Pentacles brings it all into the realm of the material, the element of earth. The Pentacles cards deal with money, home and work, but also with our resources, values and sense of abundance.

THE JOURNEY THROUGH THE NUMBER CARDS

Each of the numbers carries its own symbolism, and in combination with the element of the suit decides the meaning of the card. In general, the even numbers are harmonious whilst the odd numbers bring challenges. The basic numerological meanings are as follows:

- The Aces are the spark, the new beginning. They introduce the basic energy and message of the suit and are often seen as a divine gift.

- The Twos are a decision or a balance to be found, a need to integrate the dualities in our lives.

- Threes are the creation of something new, the opportunity to manifest the energy sparked by the Ace.

- Fours are the building of a solid structure and represent the natural order.

- Fives bring change and chaos and may bring tests and challenges.

- The Sixes bring balance and equilibrium, a sense of wholeness or completion.

- The Sevens bring a yearning for deeper connection, a process of initiation or transformation.

- The Eights connect us to rhythm and harmony, but also demand that we choose our priorities.

- Nines are the peak of their suit and can represent success and completion.
- The Tens are the end of the cycle, containing within them the seeds of the next cycle.

The Court Card Families

The Court card families, based on a rather medieval hierarchy of Page, Knight, Queen and King, are the "personality" cards of the tarot. The Page embodies the childlike, innocent experience of the elemental energy, and is often a messenger or student. They are learning about their element and are often absorbed in it. The Knight is on a quest to understand the energy of the element and to take it out into the world. They are seekers and explorers, always hoping for an adventure. The Queens hold the energy of their element, transforming it from within and inspiring others to do the same. The Kings are the masters of their element, wielding it in the world with authority and using their experience to help others. In a reading, Court cards can represent an actual person who is part of the querent's life, somebody influential who may affect the querent's experience or choices. They can also symbolise an aspect of the querent themselves, or a role they are playing or an energy they are embodying at the time of the reading.

The Suit of Wands

Ace of Wands
The Ace of Wands is the creative spark, an exciting new possibility opening up for you. The lightning rod of the Ace of Wands channels and focuses the energy of fire, making it available for the querent to follow their passion, create something new, or find a new and inspiring vision to carry them forwards. The divine gift of the Ace is

a sense of optimism and purpose, and also a sense of meaning, of why we do what we do. We open up to new experiences and find meaning as well as pleasure in them, and perhaps a new sense of direction. This card can indicate listening to your intuition and becoming aware of a more spiritual side of life and to your self. It may mean the beginning of a process of spiritual development or a new level of creative experience.

TWO OF WANDS

This can be a card of making a decision, of moving forwards towards a new goal. However it begins with preparation and evaluation, and so this card may indicate a need to consider your options, to look at all of your possible futures and choose your direction. The Two of Wands indicates that you are moving into your personal power, able to move forward with courage and originality and that the potential of the Ace is beginning to take form. This may mean moving out of your comfort zone, and the decision demanded by this card may be simply that, to move away from the familiar and onto a new path. When the Two of Wands comes up, it suggests that you are feeling restless, and there is a need to honour that restlessness, to prepare for movement even if you are not actually ready to move yet.

THREE OF WANDS

The Three of Wands is a card of expanding your vision and exploring the unknown. It can indicate that you have achieved quite a lot already and that now is the time to evaluate those achievements and decide which of them to build on. You have stepped onto the path and maybe even travelled some way down it and now is the time to decide where it will lead you next. The Three is always a number of integration and the Three of Wands asks for the integration of what has gone before with what will come next. This means looking at the bigger picture and perhaps considering what is still unknown to you, calling on all of your knowledge and experience to see as clearly as you can. The Three of Wands is a card of foresight and also leadership, for in making your own choices you can inspire others to do the same.

Four of Wands

The structure of the Four is seen as positive in the suit of Wands, as it contains the fire safely whilst also allowing it to burn consistently, for as long as it is fed. This card represents celebrations, home and a sense of security which brings contentment and excitement. These things fuel your inner fire, helping you to feel safe and confident enough to explore our creative self and to reach for your goals. This card can also indicate a time of rest, of gathering in the harvest of work done so far and enjoying the results before moving into the next phase. Four of Wands energy is productive and constructive, the energy of plans put into action and carried out successfully. Good results bring confidence and a sense of inner strength, a solid foundation which helps us to move forward.

Five of Wands

The combination of the chaotic Five and the difficult to control energies of fire bring competition, minor annoyances which can cause stress or disruption, and a lack of focus. Your confidence and self-belief may be challenged and competition with others may cause confusion. There may be conflicting values or competing demands, leading to stalled progress and frustration. However, the chaos can also be helpful, allowing you to brainstorm creative strategies and solutions, finding a way to bring them together harmoniously and usefully. There may be tension or disorder, but these can be stimulants for growth and for a new way of thinking, as long as all parties involved are willing to be open and honest. The important thing is to accept that change is needed and work towards making the necessary changes. Denying the issue at hand will only compound it and lead to bigger problems.

SIX OF WANDS

The Six restores harmony, and in the Six of Wands your achievements are finally recognised and the struggles of the previous card are resolved. It's a time when you can feel proud and enjoy the acclaim of others and the traditional meanings for this card include victory, conquest and success. It is a card of leadership, accomplishment and ambitions fulfilled, and also of the need to acknowledge the support of others in achieving your goals. Your victory is the result of your efforts and the efforts of those around you, a success that is earned and is all the sweeter for that. It symbolises the confidence that comes from using your abilities and talents not only for your own good but for the good of others, and the sense of satisfaction which follows. This brings a sense of ease and an ability to move forward into the future with confidence.

SEVEN OF WANDS

The Seven of Wands symbolises courage in the face of opposition, the need to stand your ground and

have the courage of your convictions. Following the success of the Six, new challenges appear. In most versions of this card, the figure holds the higher ground, symbolising the solid and positive position brought by past efforts and successes. However, the figure is usually also beset from all sides and may be outnumbered. When this card comes up, you may need to look at where you are on the defensive and where you have the strength to stand and fight. There may be a change you are resisting and sometimes letting go of the resistance is all that's needed to remove the obstacles to your progress. You may be called on to act with the courage of your convictions, and also to evaluate your priorities.

EIGHT OF WANDS

The Eight of Wands signifies movement or rapid change, events which bring growth but which may feel rushed or as if your feet don't have time to touch the ground. In most versions of this image, the eight Wands are flying high in the air, carrying you into an exciting new future. The key is to use this energy to achieve your goals, without speeding ahead and losing sight of your priorities or focus. To others, it may seem as if you are moving for the sake of it, perhaps without necessary planning or thought, but to you, it most likely feels like you are "on a roll", and need to make the most of the momentum that is being generated for you. As well as action and movement, this card may mean receiving news which changes your situation, and lots of changes happening at once.

NINE OF WANDS

This is a card of sustained effort and willpower, of not just finding your own path but creating each step as you go along. The work may feel challenging but also has the potential to bring great reward, as you are able to break old habits of excessive fear or caution. The energy of the Nines is quite self-contained, and this card can also mean the courage and energy to create your own destiny, rather than following convention or the expectations of others. This is not always an easy road, and there may be times when you are on the defensive, feeling frustrated at having to fight your corner over and over again. The key is taking responsibility for resolving any past issues which still affect you, and making space for healing rather than retreating into your comfort zone.

Ten of Wands

The Ten of Wands is a card of commitment and dedication, having the determination to achieve your goals. It can mean giving service to something greater than yourself, such as family or the wider community, and accepting that the hard work and responsibility are worth it. It may mean that you have chosen your direction, and are happy to do whatever it takes to get there. However, it can also symbolise feeling burdened, as if you've taken on too much and can no longer see the way forward clearly. It may be time to let some commitments go, or at least to re-evaluate your priorities. The most important tasks are those which allow you to be true to yourself and to your higher purpose. Anything which doesn't serve those may need to be released or delegated, especially if you are only taking responsibility for it out of habit.

Page of Wands

When the Page of Wands appears he brings opportunities to feed your passion and creativity. He encourages you to try something new, just for the fun of it. He is playful, curious, and always makes the choice which seems like the most fun. The Page is restless and may be easily distracted, because he is exploring, learning, seeking his path, and doesn't want to miss out on anything. All of these traits are part of a process of learning who he is and what his purpose is in life, and he is still at the beginning of this journey. The Page of Wands may need to acknowledge that he may not yet have the knowledge or experience he needs to define his goal more clearly. The key is to enjoy the process of gaining this knowledge and make the most of all the opportunities that come his way.

Knight of Wands

The Knight of Wands is an adventurer, setting off on a quest purely for the joy of taking action. He may enjoy taking risks and tends not to think before he acts. This is not because of a lack of intelligence, more that he is so inspired and enthusiastic about the task at hand that he cannot wait to get started, and so optimistic that he cannot see what might go wrong. He may come across as insensitive or intolerant because he is so focused on his quest that he is not aware of the needs or desires of others. He may also come across as somewhat erratic, as his energies burn fiercely whilst he is inspired by a task, but quickly dissipate when he loses interest until the next exciting quest comes along. He is likely to be very good at starting things, getting all fired up and passionate, but then losing interest when the initial excitement dissipates.

QUEEN OF WANDS

A confident and passionate woman, the Queen of Wands is someone who encourages and inspires others with her creativity and enthusiasm. She has learned to hold the fiery energies within and release them when the time is right so that enthusiasm is sustained and the goal can be reached. She is independent and sure of herself, full of confidence but not arrogance, with enough self-awareness to encourage others without feeling threatened by them. Like all of the fiery Courts, at times she may seem domineering or even forceful, and she is likely to have little patience with those who are unwilling to take a risk. She takes a positive and optimistic approach and may get frustrated with those who she sees as unnecessarily negative or too fearful, perhaps not realising that not everyone can be as strong-willed as she is.

KING OF WANDS

The King of Wands is an assertive and charismatic Leader, willing to take chances and inspire action in others. He clearly expresses his creative imagination and is good at bringing his vision into reality. Unlike the Queen, he is not keen on working behind the scenes or in pursuit of someone else's vision, preferring to inspire others to help him bring his own vision into reality. He is good at influencing others and may become domineering, refusing to compromise his vision. He has little patience with those who do not share his confidence and determination, and his clear sense of focus. He will always take charge and shape the situation in the way that he wants or which advances his own plans. Sometimes he may struggle to understand that there are quieter forms of strength which are just as powerful as he is.

THE SUIT OF SWORDS

ACE OF SWORDS

The Ace of Swords brings a burst of mental energy, new ideas and a sense of clarity. The divine gifts of this Ace include reason, logic, intellectual thinking and mental discipline. The single sword cuts through mental and psychic clutter and brings a clearer vision, an ability to perceive the truth and to understand it. It brings a well of mental energy which can be focused on developing ideas and communicating them, and the growth of conscious awareness. This is a card of rational analysis and objectivity, the need to step back from emotions and view a situation dispassionately. It can also symbolise a sense of space, mental or otherwise, which allows new ideas to reach up into our conscious minds, bringing also the ability to understand them and decide what to do with them. The Ace of Swords connects us with the source of our ideas and also of our ability to communicate them with others.

TWO OF SWORDS

When the Two of Swords appears, it may mean that you are feeling stuck or in a stalemate, not knowing how to move forwards or perhaps unable to make a decision. This card symbolises our inability or reluctance to see the truth or to deal with it, and possibly a refusal to change our opinion, blindfolding ourselves as the image often shows. Being closed off from others in this way can leave us isolated and lonely, or can give us the mental space we need to resolve the issues we are facing. Sometimes the message of this card is simply to make a decision. There is no right and wrong here, simply different choices, and we need to choose one of them and move on. Uncrossing the swords means reawakening the heart, and this card can be about the need to balance your thoughts with your feelings, the pull of logic with your emotions.

THREE OF SWORDS

The Three of Swords is one of those cards that many see as difficult, as most of the images of it show a heart pierced by three swords. It's true that this card can mean painful feelings or a struggle with difficult emotions, but it can also mean releasing old emotional patterns and using our mind and intellect to understand our feelings. Sometimes we allow ourselves to be dominated by feelings which have actually moved on, or by fears which are no longer relevant. Applying the creative thinking of the Three of Swords allows us to see more clearly, and to realise that our feelings are simply that, our feelings, a part of us but not the whole of us. When this card appears, it's time to acknowledge our feelings, and then let them go. This card can also symbolise bringing thoughts and feelings into creative harmony.

FOUR OF SWORDS

The regularity and structure of the Four mean bringing your thoughts into harmony, clearing your mind of clutter and finding some mental space. You may need some time to process your emotions after the shifts of the Three, to practise not taking things personally and finding some objectivity. Taking time out allows us to get a sense of perspective, perhaps to reassess our priorities and make sense of our situation. This is a card of rest, retreat, taking time for reflection and contemplation, of letting go of our striving for a while. Every now and then we all need a little introspection, a time to step back from the demands of daily life and check in with ourselves. We do not always need to be "doing" and being productive, sometimes it's important just to be, with no goal or effort in mind.

FIVE OF SWORDS

The image of the Five of Swords usually shows a man walking away from a battlefield, perhaps carrying several swords and with the others lying on the ground. The airy clarity of the Swords is lacking and the energy is turbulent and confused. This card can symbolise defeat, a battle lost, or won through deception. It asks you to check your motivation and state of mind. Are you focusing on your own needs at the expense of others, or seeking a balance between the two? When the Five of Swords appears, it can indicate a time of communication breakdown or a lack of clarity. There can be a need to choose your battles, to reassess your priorities and put your energy only into that which is most important. Otherwise, you may find yourself with scattered energy and scattered thoughts, lacking the focus to move forward and carry out your plans.

SIX OF SWORDS

Once again the harmonious Six restores harmony after the chaos of the Five, and the image for the Six of Swords usually shows one or more people in a boat being ferried across calm waters. This card symbolises transition or evolution, the truism that change may not be dramatic and exciting but may come gradually, as we work on our inner and outer growth. The six Swords are carried in the ferry boat, and they may depict the inner truths or burdens you carry forwards with you or the established ideas which help you to make sense of life. They may also be interpreted as treasured possessions, past pain being held on to, or valuable resources with which to pay the ferryman. Either way, they are in some way necessary to the voyage and the transition into the next stage of life.

SEVEN OF SWORDS

The traditional meanings for this card include secrecy and cunning, possible deception or not being able to see the whole picture. It can indicate taking a subtle or even hidden approach rather than acting openly, perhaps keeping your plans to yourself. Sometimes there is an element of mistrust and when this card comes up, it's important to check in with your own motivations and those of the people around you. It may simply mean that the time is not yet right to share your ideas. Whatever level this card is working on, it implies a time of solitude and relying on your own inner resources, acting independently rather than relying on the support of others. The Sevens always symbolise a process, an energy which grows over time, rather than a single event, and the Seven of Swords suggests a process of getting clear about your ideas and how you are putting them into action.

EIGHT OF SWORDS

In contrast to the movement of the Seven, the Eight of Swords usually shows a figure who is standing still, often trapped and surrounded by swords. This card suggests that you are feeling powerless, restricted, or simply confused. There may be a sense of insecurity or self-doubt, perhaps a reluctance to make a choice due to lack of confidence or overthinking all the options. All of these things can restrict your thinking, leading to indecisiveness and an inability to break out of these habitual patterns of thought. However, we may be less trapped than we think. In most of the images of this card, the figure is only loosely tied around the arms and there are gaps between the swords. Sometimes all you need to do is make the choice to break out, and you will find its easier than you expect so that the Eight of Swords is also a card of liberation.

Nine of Swords

The Nine of Swords shows us the challenges of this process of liberating your mind from the thoughts that hold you back. It indicates a time when you may be allowing your worries or anxieties to take over, imagining the worst and struggling to clear your mind. Like the previous card, it shows the power of the mind and the effect it can have on you, holding back growth due to imagined doubts and often unfounded fears. When the Nine of Swords comes up, there is a need to clear the mind, perhaps doing something physical which allows you to bypass the busy thinking brain. Rather than giving equal energy to worries or concerns which may not even happen, its time to sort through them and work out which are genuine and which are simply old habitual patterns of feeling and thinking.

Ten of Swords

The Ten of Swords shows the end of the cycle, often illustrated by a figure lying on the ground, with all ten swords in their back. One of the meanings for this card can be having a victim mentality, believing that everything is against you in a rather dramatic way. However, the regeneration of the Tens is also shown, with the lightening sky of a new dawn often shown beyond the figure. There is a need to accept and release the past, to let go of the patterns of thinking which keep you pinned down, clearing the way for a new beginning. The Ten of Swords can show a time of gathering and replenishing your energies, of recommitting to your path. It can also mean taking your ideas out into the world, teaching or sharing them with others, which is of course also a kind of release.

Page of Swords

The Page of Swords is setting out on his journey to gain knowledge of himself and the world around him, to understand the world and his place in it. He is determined, self-willed and perhaps somewhat detached, not quite ready to form close relationships with others yet. Instead, he is keen to make his own way, to be allowed to make his own mistakes if necessary. He is exploring his ideas, concepts and seeking his own truth, using his intellect and the powers of his mind in quite an abstract way, as he doesn't yet have the life experience to do otherwise. When the Page of Swords appears, you are likely to be practising using your mental energy and ability to communicate with others. This card can symbolise messages and new ideas which bring a new level of awareness, perhaps studying or learning something new which expands your horizons.

Knight of Swords

This Knight is on a quest to fight for the truth and welcomes conflict as an opportunity to get closer to that truth. He is courageous and clever, always ready to defend his ideas and his honour, and always on the move. He has strong powers of logic and reason, often seeing the world as black and white and acting accordingly. Quick thinking and even impulsive, he has the courage of his convictions, to the point that he may struggle to let go of an idea even when it is proved wrong. He thinks quickly but not necessarily deeply, and may choose action based on a half-developed idea over a carefully planned strategy. His insistence on logic and objectivity may mean that he lacks tact and empathy with others, sometimes riding roughshod over individuals and their needs in order to achieve his goal.

Queen of Swords

Honest and astute, the Queen of Swords tells it like it is and doesn't flinch from the truth. Ideally, she transforms sorrow into wisdom by applying her powerful intellect to her emotional experiences, finding a sense of perspective and an ability to see the bigger picture. Her experience meeting the ups and downs of life has brought resilience and courage, as well as empathy for others and a heart connection which is not always present in the Swords cards. She is able to use logic and reason to quash any self-doubts or confused thinking and to help others to do the same. She is quick-witted and has a love of ideas, along with the maturity to develop them fully and share her understanding and wisdom with others. The Queen of Swords makes decisions quickly and with compassion, and lives by her ideals.

KING OF SWORDS

Articulate and intellectual, the King of Swords sees straight to the truth of the matter and has excellent analytical skills. He is an intellectual leader and keen strategist, always acting from high ideals, high standards and a deep level of experience and understanding. At times this may mean that he seems to lack compassion or tolerance, and he may consider the greater good to be more important than the needs of the individual. He is a trusted adviser, forthright and reliable, who is able to be realistic as well as idealistic. He stands for law, order, discipline and sound judgement, and as such may come across as a strong authority figure who does not like to be opposed. When the King of Swords appears, it's time to use your judgement and find some clarity about your situation, and then take decisive action.

THE SUIT OF CUPS

ACE OF CUPS

The Ace of Cups brings a rush of emotional energy or an opening up of the imagination. It can symbolise a return to the source of yourself, getting in touch with your unconscious mind through your dreams and intuition. There may be a new attraction or bond with another, an overflowing of feeling which feels exciting and full of promise. A new chapter is beginning in which relationships and connections with others, as well as connection to your own feelings and imagination, bring personal growth and a deeper connection to the spiritual side of life. This is a time to be open to new opportunities, to focus on and express your gratitude for what you have. You may be feeling a little vulnerable and sensitive, especially if there are strong emotional energies around you, so it's important to practise self-care and love yourself as well.

TWO OF CUPS

When the Two of Cups appears, you may be making a soul connection with another, a union which allows you to grow on an inner level as well as an outer. This card can symbolise the beginning or deepening of a relationship, and also building and enjoying partnerships in a more general sense. You are likely to be feeling compassionate and empathetic towards others, able to appreciate their uniqueness and the gifts they bring to your life. The Two of Cups symbolises positive and helpful unions, the connections you make with others, especially one to one, which helps you to get to know yourself better. Meeting the other person as they really are, rather than as we want them to be, is really important with this card, otherwise you risk building relationships based on your own projections rather than a genuine connection.

Three of Cups

The Three of Cups traditionally symbolises friendships and social connections, feeling positive and enjoying life. It's a card of abundant emotions, celebrating with loved ones, and feeling content and happy. The gifts of joy and laughter bring just a much inner growth and change for us as do suffering and painful emotions, so this card asks you to make space in your life to feel and enjoy those positive emotions, and to take a light-hearted approach. On a deeper level, this card symbolises the emotional security which comes from knowing where you belong and feeling comfortable and able to be yourself. It's about finding your soul friends, the people who are family whether you are related to them by blood or not. The Three of Cups is a card of building and celebrating those connections and enjoying the deep emotional bond they bring.

Four of Cups

When the Four of Cups appears, it indicates that you might be feeling stuck in a rut, perhaps somewhat self-absorbed or apathetic, unable to see the gifts life offers you. You may have a sense of dissatisfaction, perhaps feeling that something isn't quite right but not really knowing what to do about it. You may feel trapped in old emotional patterns, unable or unwilling to move out of them. The Four of Cups can indicate a necessary period of introspection, a time to get in touch with your feelings and process any past emotions which you no longer need and which may be holding you back. Past hurts can blind you to new opportunities, meaning that you hold yourself back in fear and remain in your comfort zone. Whilst it's understandable that you fear being hurt again, you also risk missing out on positive new connections.

Five of Cups

The shifts and changes of the Fives, in the feeling realm of the Cups, can mean feeling loss or regret and needing to acknowledge painful emotions in order to begin the healing process. The Fives of Cups can indicate a time of grief or disappointment, of feeling let down or hurt by someone that we cared about, and needing to take the time to process the experience. It's important not to repress or ignore difficult feelings, or they have a tendency to reappear in a much more destructive form. On the other hand, this card also counsels against spending too much time wallowing in self-pity or blaming others for what has happened to you. Only you can make the choice to move on, and this card affirms that the time will come and that negative feelings do not define you.

Six of Cups

The traditional meanings for the Six of Cups include nostalgia, childhood, and innocence. You may find yourself thinking about the past, about the influence it had on your growth and the choices you made in life. This can be helpful, if you use your memories creatively, but can also lead to viewing life through rose-tinted spectacles. Sometimes the past is idealised and it's important to appreciate all the experiences, good and bad, which made you the person you are today. Attending to unfinished business is useful, as long as it doesn't hold back your current growth. On a deeper level, this card can symbolise getting in touch with our inner child, perhaps rediscovering y creativity or ability to play and finding new ways to express your true self. The Six of Cups invokes positive feelings of kindness and generosity, empathy and compassion for others.

Seven of Cups

The seven of Cups is traditionally seen as a card of daydreaming and wishful thinking, of having so many options that you are unable to settle on any of them. The seven Cups in the image are often shown full of various items which may tempt us, such as jewels, fruits, the snake which symbolises regeneration or the laurel wreath which symbolises victory. When the Seven of Cups appears, you may be feeling that you want it all, or that you have no idea what you want. The Seven of Cups can symbolise illusions and an excess of imagination. This is a card of abundance, but it also indicates a need for discernment, for looking closely at each option and deciding whether it is superficial or meaningful, something that we truly want or something that is imposed on us by others. This discernment is necessary to bring the products of your imagination into tangible reality.

Eight of Cups

As with all of the Eights, the Eight of Cups brings an urge to reestablish harmony, a need to get back in touch whatever is most meaningful in your life. This may mean taking some time for introspection, to decide what that is and how to change your life to accommodate it. This card is often the beginning of a journey of inner discovery, moving on from what you have built so far to seek higher wisdom and deeper understanding. This may mean giving up parts of your life to which you have become attached, to give up on goals or plans which are no longer fulfilling or inspiring. This may not be popular with those around you and may mean going against the expectations of friends, family or mainstream society. The Eight of Cups is therefore also a card of being true to yourself, even if it means making some painful decisions.

Nine of Cups

The Nine of Cups is often known as the "wish card", as it symbolises emotional and physical satisfaction, of having your wishes and dreams fulfilled, and enjoying the results of your hard work. It's a card of enjoying the pleasures of the senses, which may mean connecting more meaningfully to your emotions, or may mean ignoring them, especially the challenging ones. There is a sense of complacency about this card, a smugness and self-satisfaction which suggests a disconnection from others. Most versions of this card show a solitary figure, suggesting someone who is unable or unwilling to share their success. Whilst is good to enjoy the results of your hard work and the happiness you have earned for yourself, enjoying it alone may not be satisfying for long. This card symbolises the rewards of generosity and shared abundance, the realisation that holding your happiness for yourself limits it, whereas sharing it with others increases it.

TEN OF CUPS

The Ten of Cups brings a deep sense of emotional fulfilment and emotional security, an awareness of the abundance and blessings of life. Most of the images for this card show a happy family or couple, secure in their deep connection and love for each other. This card indicates a sense of belonging to family or tribe, an appreciation of the support of others and the willingness to support others yourself. The Ten of Cups is a card of inspiration, love and harmony, of dreams coming true through your own sustained efforts. It carries a sense of "coming home" in an emotional sense, of discovering where you belong and the people you belong with. Whereas the Nine of Cups suggests outer satisfaction, the Ten of Cups brings inner satisfaction, not just material abundance but emotional abundance too. You are able to see beyond yourself and appreciate all the gifts life has brought you.

PAGE OF CUPS

The Page of Cups is beginning a journey of acknowledging and reveling in his feelings, of understanding them and also simply feeling them, even allowing them to overwhelm him at times. He has a strong sense of imagination and a deep ability to love, although he may be quite naïve and innocent. He can be sensitive, but is loyal and trustworthy, and not afraid to be vulnerable. When this Page appears, you may need to open up and take an emotional risk, to let others see and understand the real you. It may be time to recognise and begin the work of understanding hidden emotions and intense feelings. Whilst this is easy for positive feelings such as joy and love, it's also important not to ignore the challenging feelings. The journey for this Page is the quest to feel all of our emotions,

however difficult and to appreciate their gifts.

KNIGHT OF CUPS

The Knight of Cups is a romantic daydreamer, sensitive and fond of poetry and flights of fancy. In some ways he is the Knight closest to the chivalry and divine inspiration of medieval knights, risking all for love or for an idealistic dream. He feels intensely and may come across a quite dramatic at times, unable to see beyond his overwhelming feelings and his need to express them. He is charismatic, the kind of person others are drawn to, but may also be given to illusion or even deception, of himself as well as others. Unlike the Wand and Sword Knights, his horse is usually shown standing still, as for him the action and movement take place on an inner level. His quest is one of the heart, the quest for true love or devotion and service to a higher being or ideal.

QUEEN OF CUPS

Kind and tenderhearted towards others, this Queen is empathetic and strongly in touch with her psychic side and her powerful imagination. She is sensitive and feels intensely, but has the power to hold these feelings and also to share them with others to inspire or reassure them. As well as being good at connecting to her own feelings, she can encourage others to acknowledge and express their own feelings and is likely to be seen as a caring and compassionate figure. She is closely connected with her dreams and intuition and is often shown with at least one foot in the waters of the unconscious. She symbolises emotional integrity, nurturing others with her love and care. She is often artistic and creative, seeking ways of expressing her emotions tangibly and in ways others can understand. She may also have a deep connection to the spiritual side of life.

KING OF CUPS

A wise guide and counsellor, the King of Cups has a deep understanding of the emotional self and a strong sense of empathy. He has worked hard to gain mastery of the emotional realm and may put his skills to use as a counsellor or adviser for others. As with all the Kings, he carries the authority of the suit and takes responsibility for the realm of feelings and imagination. He understands and accepts that emotions are complicated, and this can make him detached, by choice or otherwise. Unlike his Queen, he is generally depicted standing or sitting completely on land, by the side of the water rather than in it. He chooses to stay disconnected in order to be able to heal, teach and help others, without getting drawn in or personally involved. He is creative but may be more focused on creating frameworks for helping others than on expressing his personal creativity.

THE SUIT OF PENTACLES

ACE OF PENTACLES

The Ace of Pentacles brings a divine gift of abundance which increases your possibilities for material security. It represents a surge of personal power and energy which you can use to increase your material abundance and build a more solid foundation for your endeavors. It may indicate a new awareness of a growing skill or talent, or new opportunities to practice those skills and talents. When the Ace of Pentacles appears, it brings favorable conditions for manifesting ideas, for starting a business or a new professional or artistic project. Everything may seem to fall into place so that suddenly you have all the resources you need, or a burst of inspiration may remind of resources that are already available to you. This Ace brings the potential for building a greater sense of self-worth and a feeling of inner as well as outer security.

Two of Pentacles

The Two of Pentacles symbolises the ability to be flexible and to find ways to balance all the demands that life makes of you. Most of the images for this card show a figure holding a pentacle in each hand, juggling or balancing them. Whether it's your job and your personal life, your family and your work or simply two different, equally demanding, projects, you may be finding that you are struggling to balance these different areas of your life. In the first place, the Two of Pentacles often simply affirms that you are able to do this, that you are learning to be flexible and how best to use your energies. This card asks you to enjoy the process and to appreciate the gifts and challenges of all of the different demands on your time and energy. Each is there for a reason and has something to teach you.

Three of Pentacles

When the Three of Pentacles appears, you may find yourself working with others in a team or group, making your contribution and enjoying the support of others. This is a card of shared effort, of coming together to build something that is greater than the sum of its parts. It can also symbolise the need and ability to ground your creative visions in physical work, to take the steps you need to bring your dream into reality. The Three of Pentacles indicates our skills, our mastery of them and our ability to use them to achieve our own and shared goals. It asks us to use them well, planning our work and working to our highest ability. This is a card of integrity, dedication and commitment. The Three of Pentacles also depicts taking satisfaction and pleasure in our work, our ability to create something from nothing.

Four of Pentacles

The fixed structure of the Four, in combination with the earthy energy of the Pentacles, creates something lasting and solid, and the ability to structure and organise your life. However taken too far, this can mean getting stuck in a rut, and sticking to the familiar, staying in your comfort zone and avoiding growth. It can also symbolise possessiveness, the urge to hold on to what we have, to cling to material possessions as the only means of security. This can mean that you close yourself off from a more meaningful life or a sense of something outside of yourself, leading to a limited vision or a perceived lack of possibilities. The Four of Pentacles can symbolise shelter and protection, which everybody needs, but can also indicate hiding in that shelter as a way of avoiding life. This card asks you to open up, to share what you have and to re-connect with the world.

Five of Pentacles

The Five of Pentacles traditionally indicates a time of feeling insecure or lacking in support, a time when you are more aware of what you lack than what you have. Most of the images for it are of isolation or being left out in the cold, lacking in shelter or resources. Like all of the Fives, the Five of Pentacles indicates a time of transition, changes which may initially be prompted by outer circumstances but which lead to inner growth. The Five of Pentacles can be said to illustrate the dangers of relying too much on the material for your security. This can leave you spiritually bereft and lacking a sense of meaning so that the motivation to move forward and do something productive is lost. When the Five of Pentacles appears, it's time to learn the lessons of the dark night of the soul and accept the support that is offered.

SIX OF PENTACLES

The Six of Pentacles symbolises the process of giving and receiving, the exchange of energy which sustains us and those around us. This is a card of inner and outer resources, and of giving and taking, of learning to share what we have. You may be the wealthy merchant who is able to be generous or the poorer relation who needs to accept help. Many people actually find the latter more difficult, preferring to stay in the cold isolation of the Five rather than accept the extra support that may be offered. Whichever position you are in, this card asks you to take a look at your attitudes and habits around giving and receiving. Do you give out of genuine concern for others, or to make yourself feel better? Perhaps you are concerned that any help you accept might come with conditions or expectations. The Six of Pentacles brings a chance to gain awareness of these dynamics.

SEVEN OF PENTACLES

The Seven of Pentacles often indicates a process of shifting the balance of your life away from material concerns and towards something more meaningful, for example moving from a job which pays the bills to a vocation which is more fulfilling and allows you to be true to yourself. It can also indicate a time to pause and allow your harvest to develop, reassessing or evaluating your situation. This card suggests an enjoyment of the work for its own sake, rather than a focus on the end goal or what you have achieved so far. Looking at what you have achieved so far brings its own rewards though, and this card indicates that you are beginning to see the results of your hard work and to make a genuine difference in the world. The Seven of Pentacles indicates that patience and determination are the recipe for success.

Eight of Pentacles

The Eight of Pentacles symbolises sustained effort, the repeated practising of a skill or honing of a talent. When this card appears, you are more likely to be working for the joy of it rather than in expectation of reward, working to gain mastery of your craft for your own personal satisfaction. On one level, this card is simply about focusing on the task before you and doing your best, taking your time to do a good job. On a deeper level, it can be about finding your passion, the work or vocation which brings you the greatest fulfilment and which will become your life's work. Like the Seven, this card carries energies of patience, determination and persistence. The rewards take time, but that is part of what makes them worth having. This is a card of giving service, to your higher self as well as the greater good.

Nine of Pentacles

The Nine of Pentacles brings the rewards of your own efforts and the sense of security which comes from having achieved your goals. This is a card of discipline, self-control and self-reliance, and of reaping the rewards of long application of those qualities. The images for this card usually show a solitary figure standing in a garden, which symbolises fruition and fulfilment. The Nine of Pentacles indicates a time when you can enjoy a sense of material security and the knowledge that you have achieved that for yourself, through your own hard work. This card symbolises wealth and abundance, success and satisfaction, all coming from a sense of dedication to purpose and a strong and clear focus. It can mean taking the time to enjoy what you have, feeling secure in your values and the comfort you have built for yourself.

Ten of Pentacles

The Ten of Pentacles brings a sense of affluence and abundance, on a material but also at a deeper level. Rather than a solitary figure, most versions of this card show an extended family, perhaps several generations, indicating that this card can mean a legacy, the urge to pass on not just material security but also the wisdom and learning of a life well lived. As with the other Tens, this card indicates sharing the lessons of the suit with the community and passing on the lessons learned, in readiness for closing this cycle of growth and beginning a new one. The Ten of Pentacles symbolises the security of family and inheritance, and also the sense of belonging to something greater than ourselves. This card can indicate where your roots are, or where you choose to put them down, and also a connection to your ancestors and an awareness of how they have influenced your life, directly or indirectly.

Page of Pentacles

The Page of Pentacles epitomizes lifelong learning, the idea that all of life has something to teach us, and also that learning is not just about the intellect. He is beginning a journey of learning from experience, through study but also through observation, experimentation and simply doing the work. When the Page of Pentacles appears, it's time to start putting your ideas into practice, beginning with small steps and building your momentum. This Page is patient and determined, but also always busy, believing that it's important for both mind and body to be well occupied. He seeks ways to make a tangible difference in the world and sees his learning as something to apply in a practical situation, rather than an abstract understanding. His work is to change outward experiences to inner understanding, and so sometimes he may appear self-absorbed.

Knight of Pentacles

The Knight of Pentacles embodies diligence and hard work, a reliable figure who is trustworthy and loyal. He symbolises structure and organisation, and also dedication and commitment. He takes responsibility and accepts his obligations without complaint, and is more likely to focus on fulfilling his duty than on a personal quest or individual project. Sometimes this Knight is seen as dull, staid or even rigid, as he represents the need for steady hard work, drawing on the traditions of the past rather than seeking innovation. However, he always gets the job done, fulfilling all of his goals and commitments. He takes a methodical approach and is always productive, preferring to work towards a specific purpose rather than for the sake of it. Sometimes he is seen as a farmer, working with nature and the seasons to ensure that all grows in its due time.

Queen of Pentacles

This Queen is an earth mother figure who nourishes and nurtures, providing practical help and advice as well as emotional support. She is resourceful and trustworthy and inspires others to make the best use of their talents by making the best use of her own. She embodies the abundance of nature and the gifts of the earth, and in some ways can be seen as a more down to earth version of the Empress. Like the other Queens, she holds and transforms the energy of her suit, and then radiates it outwards, encouraging others to live by their values and in harmony with their environment. She embodies the truth that by living and working with integrity, we can find satisfaction in our work and that work in the material realm can be an important path to spiritual growth and personal integration.

King of Pentacles

The King of Pentacles is an enterprising person who has a natural head for business and is able to make the most of an opportunity. He is shrewd, good at planning and taking a long-term view, willing to work hard to maximise his growth over time. As the master of the earthly realm, this King symbolises the rewards of sustained effort and our achievements in the material world. He has material abundance and likes to enjoy it, but he doesn't lose sight of what is really important, valuing people and connections over possessions. He is a good Leader, although he may tend towards a more traditional rather than an innovative approach, valuing the past and the lessons it can teach us. He has high standards and good judgement and expects others to maintain those just as well as he does.

Chapter Four : How to do a tarot reading

Tarot Spreads and how they work

A tarot spread is a map, or layout, in which you place cards in specific positions. A spread can contain anything from one or two cards to the whole deck, but most spreads contain between three and twelve cards. The spread you choose will depend on the question you want to ask, and how detailed you would like the answer to be. A spread might be one or two cards first thing in the morning to give an overview of the energies of the day or a reading for a full year with one or more cards for each month.

When doing a tarot reading, whether for yourself or someone else, taking your time to set up your space is important, as it helps to shift your mood and open up your intuition. You may like to light some candles or incense, and lay the cards out on a nice cloth which is only used for tarot readings. All of these actions create a "ritual" around the cards, reminding us that doing a tarot reading as a meaningful and important experience. The little rituals we use as we begin a reading help to align our inner and outer realities and open us up to messages from the universe and from our higher self.

Most tarot readings start with a question, even if it's only a vague desire to know what is happening around you at the moment. Asking the right question can be key to a good tarot reading, and it's worth taking some time before you start the reading to word your question carefully. The tarot doesn't tend to answer closed questions or those with seeking yes / no answers very well. What do I need to know about my relationship with X? works better than Does X love me? or Is X the one for me? It's always best to focus the question, and therefore the reading, on the querent themselves, rather than a third party. If they are nor present, or even aware that the reading is happening, their energies do not come through so clearly. There is also a question of ethics here, as asking about a third party invades their privacy. Many tarot readers also prefer to avoid emotive questions regarding pregnancy, health or the law, and if a querent asks you about such matters it is perfectly acceptable and even advisable, to refer them to the relevant professional.

Once you have decided on your question, and the spread you want to use, the next step is to shuffle the cards. Everyone has their own way of doing this, and you'll discover yours as you gain experience. Many people like to "cut" the deck by splitting it into three piles and then re-stacking them in a different order. When you are satisfied that you have shuffled the deck sufficiently (as with so much of tarot reading, this is a matter for your intuition, and over time you'll come to know when its "enough"), lay the cards down one at a time in the order and positions given in the layout diagram.

When doing a reading, we consider the story the cards tell. Each card is interpreted individually, but also in the context of both its position in the reading and also the cards around it. Once you have laid out the cards, look at them all together. Are there any similarities or cards which link together? For example, there may be lots of Cups cards, several Major Arcana cards or no Major Arcana cards, or more than one card with the same number. By looking at the overview of the spread, we can get a sense of the general energies of the reading. Lots of Cups cards might mean a time of emotional changes or when the querent is ruled by their feelings. Lots of Major Arcana cards implies that this is an important question, even if it doesn't seem so on the surface, whereas no Major Arcana cards would suggest that this is an everyday concern, with a relatively straightforward solution or result. Looking at the colours in the cards can also give us valuable information. Are they all bright, all dark, or is there a contrast? If there are people in the cards, which direction are they looking in? Do they face each other or have their backs to each other? All of these visual clues awaken our intuition and help us to decide the meaning of the cards in the specific context of this reading and this question.

THE THREE CARD SPREAD, WITH EXAMPLES

The three card spread is one of the most popular and has many variations. Three cards is a good balance between not overloading yourself or your querent with information, whilst still gaining enough insight to show you a way forward. Some of the most popular include:

- Past, present, future,
- Issue, action, outcome,
- Body, mind, spirit,
- Situation, opportunity, challenge.

The cards are usually laid out in a straight line, as shown above, but they may also be laid out in a triangular shape. Examples of two three card readings are given below.

This is a past, present, future reading, for the simple question "What do I need to know right now?"

The Tower is in the past position, the Ace of Cups in the present, and the Fool in the future. Two Major Arcana cards in a three card reading is a high percentage, so immediately we can see that although the querent is asking a very general question, she seems to be going through some important changes, and may be struggling to get a grasp on them. The Tower in the past position confirms this, suggesting that there may have been some drama for the querent in the last few months and that it may not have been something that she chose or was able to control. However, the Ace of Cups in the present position shows that even if those changes felt difficult at the time, the way has been cleared for a new beginning. It may not be clear yet what that will look like, but there is a flow of emotional energy and a connection to the powers of the imagination which brings a sense of possibility and potential. Again, this is confirmed by the Fool as the future card. This shows the querent embracing those new possibilities and moving out of her comfort zone to a brand new chapter of life. The structures of the Tower have broken down, bringing the querent the freedom to follow her bliss, perhaps to do something she has dreamed of or imagined (the Ace of Cups) but has never had the courage to do before. We can see this process by looking at the colours of the cards. The dark greys of the Tower can feel oppressive, but the Ace of Cups and the Fool are much lighter and clearer, reflecting the calmer energies around the querent as she moves away from the experience of the Tower.

The querent for this reading asked, "What do I need to know about my relationship?" The first card, the Two of Cups, shows the current Situation, the second, the Lovers, shows the Opportunity available to the querent, and the final card, the Empress, shows a potential Challenge the querent may face. Again, there are two Major Arcana cards, so this is likely to be an influential relationship for the querent, which brings growth and possibly some life changes. The Two of Cups in the Situation position shows that this may be quite a new relationship and that both parties are feeling a strong sense of a soul connection, an attraction with the potential to develop into something more. They are likely to be getting on well and discovering that they have lots in common. The positive potential of this card is reflected in the Lovers as the Opportunity card, showing that this relationship has the potential to develop into something more meaningful. Both of these cards together show that the relationship is likely to bring opportunities to grow and find fulfilment for both individuals. The Empress in the position of Challenge shows what may cause problems in the relationship, or at least what will need to be faced in order for the relationship to thrive. On a literal level, the Empress may imply that having children could become an issue for the couple, perhaps with one partner more positive about the idea than the other. On a deeper level, it may suggest that one partner will find themselves "mothering" the other, with that partner putting more emotional energy into the relationship than the other. It could also mean that the couple will become so engrossed in their passion and pleasure in being together, that they neglect their duties or responsibilities. If you are reading for yourself, you will have a sense of which of these layers of meaning is most relevant. If you are reading for someone else, asking them some gentle questions, without prying, can help you both to figure out the energies going on. With a spread like this which flags up a potential challenge, the querent then has some concrete information to take away. In this case, they may decide to get clear on their own feelings about having children before talking to their partner. They may decide to draw some boundaries around how much emotional energy they are investing in "looking after" their partner, or they may realise that they are the one being looked after and resolve to do the same for their partner. The important thing is that they have a sense of how they can use the information the tarot has given them.

The Celtic Cross

The Celtic Cross is perhaps the most well-known of all tarot spreads. It contains ten cards, set out in a cross shape consisting of the first six cards, with the remaining four in a column at the side.

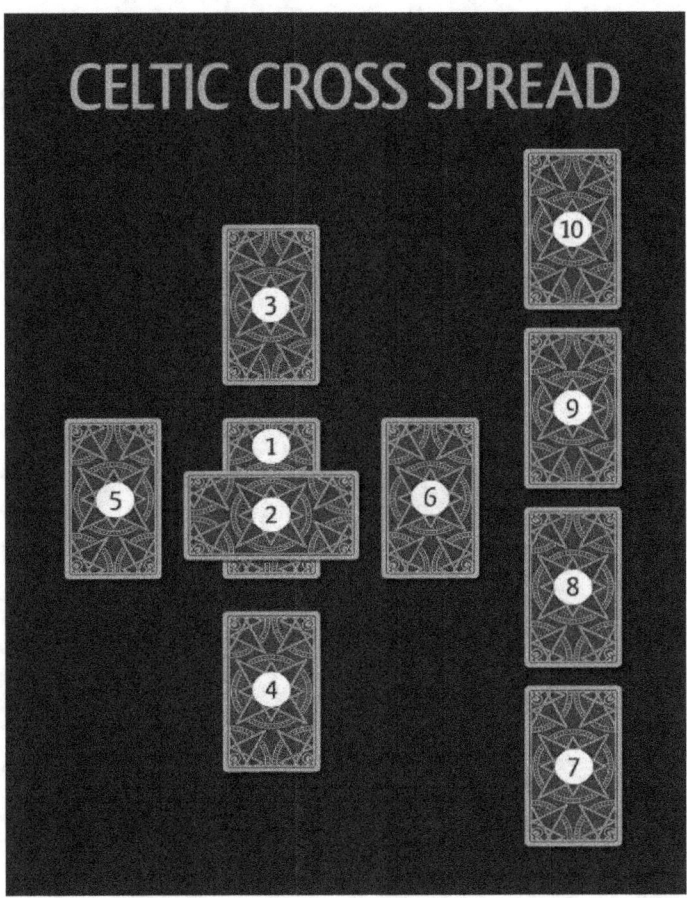

1. Your current situation

2. What is challenging or opposing you at present

These two cards together represent the current energies around the querent, summing up the situation. The second card is usually an opposing energy to the first. This doesn't necessarily mean that the first card is positive and the second more challenging. If the querent is currently going through a challenging time, the second card may offer a more positive input.

3. Conscious mind / higher self

4. Hidden or unconscious influences

The cards above and below the central cross show the querent's state of mind. The bottom card reflects what is hidden, but may unconsciously be the driver for the current situation. The top card can show what is on the querent's mind, what she is most conscious of at this time. It also gives a sense of the highest potential available.

5. Past

6. Immediate future

The two cards to the right and left of the central cross are the timeline so that the central line of the reading is past, present and future. The Future card here shows the immediate future, perhaps if no action is taken or changes are made.

7.   Your inner self

The first card of the outside column shows how the querent is feeling, how they see the situation and also see themselves, and how these affect the situation in question.

8.   External influences

This card reflects the environment or circumstances around the querent, and how these factors might affect the question.

9.   Hopes and fears

This card shows how the querent's attitudes or assumptions might affect the course of events.

10.   Final outcome

The final outcome brings all the other cards together, combining the influences of the whole reading to give a possible or likely outcome. As with any tarot reading, this outcome is not fixed, and if it causes concern to the querent its common to pull one or two more cards to seek clarity on why such an outcome may happen, or how to avoid it.

A Sample Reading using the Celtic Cross

The reading illustrated, using the Tarot of Marseilles, is for a querent asking what she needs to know about her career at this time. There are only two Major Arcana cards, and neither of them is in the central cross, showing that any changes are likely to feel more like an evolution than a revolution. There are quite a few cards which fall late in the number sequence, such as Tens and Eights, and also two which come at the beginning, an Ace and a Two. This suggests that there may be a phase ending and a new chapter beginning for the querent.

1.   King of Wands

The King of Wands as her current situation shows that she is already well established in her career, confident in her knowledge and able to take the lead both to direct others and to keep her own focus.

2. Two of Wands

The Two of Wands in the opposing position shows that she may be seeking something new, making the decision to step away from what she has been doing so far and seek a new challenge.

3. Ten of Cups

The Ten of Cups is a card of emotional abundance, and in the position of Conscious mind / higher self is suggests that she is currently very aware of her emotions and how they are affecting her. It may be that she loves her job, or possibly that she finds it overwhelming in some way. On the other hand, this card could be an indication that what is on her mind is more focused on family and feelings, and she is ready to leave the high flying career behind.

4. Eight of Cups

As the unconscious influence, the Eight of Cups reinforces the possibility that the querent is ready to move on in some way. When this card appears in a reading, it usually means that the querent is seeking something more meaningful, a move out of their comfort zone towards a more fulfilling path.

5. Ten of Pentacles

The Ten is the end of the number cycle and generally indicates that we have reached a culmination point. It may suggest that the querent needs to be careful not to focus so much on the material that she neglects her Ten of Cups feelings. In this position, the Ten of Pentacles suggests that she has built up a good level of material security, and now she is ready for a new, perhaps more meaningful challenge.

6.   Ace of Swords

In the Future position, the Ace of Swords brings in a brand new energy and is the only Swords card in the reading. This might suggest that the querent has not focused too much on her intellect in her career so far, but that now she is ready for study or some new ideas.

7.   The Chariot

In the position of Self, the Chariot indicates that the querent knows what she wants, and what she needs to do to get it. It suggests that she is a person with lots of control and focus, who doesn't hold back when she has set her mind to something.

8.   Seven of Cups

In contrast to the Self position, the Seven of Cups as outside influences may suggest that other people see the querent as lacking in focus or following an unrealistic dream. It might also suggest that those around her are making suggestions about what she should do, whereas she already knows, as indicated by the Chariot in the previous position. The Seven of Cups here might also suggest that people keep trying to "tempt" the querent off her intended course by giving her other options.

9.   The Emperor

As her card of hopes and fears, the Emperor may suggest that the querent wants to take a more responsible role in her career, perhaps moving into management or leadership. This is backed up by the King of Wands in the centre position. On the other hand, she may feel blocked by somebody who is already in such a position, or perhaps be fearful of losing control.

10. Page of Pentacles

The Page of Pentacles is in the position of the final outcome, and like the Ace of Swords in the Future position suggests studying, or at least following a new path. The Pages bring a sense of curiosity and fascination to whatever they do, and this card suggests that taking such an approach is what the querent needs to revitalise her career.

NEXT STEPS IN YOUR TAROT JOURNEY

As well as doing tarot readings, there are many other ways to use the cards which you can explore as you get to know them. There are many books and online resources giving spreads for just about every question under the sun, and in time you may also want to start inventing your own spreads. Keeping a tarot journal is a very useful exercise. In it, you can note down your daily cards, and keep a record of readings done for yourself and others. Over time your journal can become a valuable resource. You will be able to see the patterns in the cards that appear for you, how their meaning applies to your life and how that may change over time.

A powerful way to work with the cards and build a strong personal connection with them is to meditate on them or use them for visualisation. If you've never done this before, it may take a little practice, but its definitely worth persevering. The easiest way to begin is simply to journey in your imagination into the image on the card. To do this, find a time and place when you won't be disturbed, and somewhere you can sit or lie down comfortably. You may like to light a candle to indicate to your higher self that this is a meaningful process. Take a few minutes to relax your body and your breathing, and then hold the card in front of you and gaze lightly at the image. After a few minutes, close your eyes and hold the image in your mind. Once you have it there clearly, you can step into the image, moving from a two-dimensional version to a three-dimensional version. Using your active imagination, travel around inside the image, perhaps talking to the figures there or simply exploring.

When you have finished, step back out of the image and into your body, and note your experiences in your journal.

Getting to know the tarot cards can be the journey of a lifetime, and there will always be something new to learn. As with all the best things in life, the most important thing is to enjoy the journey!

BIBLIOGRAPHY

Aelfric. (2017). *Odin's Runes: The Ancient Germanic Rune Poems.* Halldream Recordings.

Frazer, J. G. (1890). *The Golden Bough.* United Kingdom: Macmillan Publishers.

Gardner, G. B. (2009). *The Gardnerian Book of Shadows.* United States: BiblioLife.

Givens, E. (2008). *Original King James Bible.* United Kingdom: Xulon Press.

Graves, R. (2013). *The White Goddess.* New York: Farrar, Straus and Giroux.

Leland, C. G. (2018). *Aradia, or the Gospel of the Witches.* United Kingdom: Wilder Publications.

Levi, E. (1999). *The History of Magic.* United States: Weiser Books.

Mead, H. T. (2017). *The Corpus Hermeticum.* United States: Createspace Independent Publishing Platform.

Roper, L. (n.d.). *Witch Craze.* Yale University Press, New Edition (October 31, 2006).

Yurkon, G. L. (n.d.). *Gerald Brosseau Gardner.*

Bryant, Tamera (2005). The Life & Times of Hammurabi. Bear: Mitchell Lane Publishers.

Cameron, Alan G. (2011). The Last Pagans of Rome. New York: Oxford University Press.

Crowley, Aleister. The Equinox of the Gods. New Falcon Publications, 1991.

Cunningham, Scott, (1987), Cunningham's Encyclopedia of Crystal, Gem, and Metal Magic.

Cunningham, Scott, (1985) Cunningham's Encyclopedia of Magical Herbs.

Dixson, Alan F., and Barnaby Dixson. 2011. "Venus Figurines of the European Paleolithic: Symbols of Fertility or Attractiveness?" Journal of Anthropology 2011.

Doyle White, Ethan (2016). "Old Stones, New Rites: Contemporary Pagan Interactions with the Medway Megaliths". Material Religion: The Journal of Objects, Art and Belief.

Friberg, Eino; Landström, Björn; Schoolfield, George C., eds. (1988), The Kalevala: Epic of the Finnish People.

Gardner, Gerald (1954). Witchcraft Today. London: Rider.

Goscinny, René & Uderzo, Albert, (1963) Astérix et Cléopâtre, Pilote magazine.

Gaiman, Neil, (2017) Norse Mythology, Bloomsbury Publishing PLC.

Kazantzakis, Nikos. At the Palaces of Knossos. London: Owen, 1988.

Kramer, Heinrich & Sprenger, Jacob, (1486) Malleus Maleficarum, translated by Montague Summers, 2011, Martino Fine Books.

Leland, Charles Godfrey (1899). Aradia, or the Gospel of the Witches. David Nutt.

Medhurst, W. H. Ancient China. The Shoo King or the Historical Classic. Shanghai: The Mission Press.

Mitchell, Mandy, (2014) Hedgewitch Book of Days: Spells, Rituals, and Recipes for the Magical Year, Weiser Books.

Murray, Margaret A. (1921). The Witch-Cult in Western Europe. Oxford: Clarendon Press.

Murray, Margaret A. (1931). The God of the Witches. London: Faber and Faber.

Old Testament: The Book of Genesis.

Ruickbie, Leo, Witchcraft Out of the Shadows: A Complete History, Robert Hale; New edition (April 1, 2012).

Runyon, Carroll (1997). Secrets of the Golden Dawn Cipher Manuscripts. C.H.S.

Valiente, Doreen (1989). The Rebirth of Witchcraft. London: Robert Hale.

Walsh, William, (1970) The Story of Santa Klaus, Gale Research Company.

Yates, Frances A., Giordano Bruno and the Hermetic Tradition. University of Chicago Press, 1964.

The Complete I Ching - 10th Anniversary Edition : The Definitive Translation by Taoist Master Alfred Huang, Inner Traditions Bear and Company.

WEBSITES:

"The Wiccan Rede" (Full Version) as depicted in The Celtic Connection website, https://wicca.com/celtic/wicca/rede.htm

www.ingramcontent.com/pod-product-compliance
Lightning Source LLC
Chambersburg PA
CBHW071723080526
44588CB00013B/1878